CRITICAL

RECONSTRUCTIONS

The Relationship of
Fiction and Life

EDITED BY ROBERT M. POLHEMUS

AND ROGER B. HENKLE

STANFORD UNIVERSITY PRESS

Stanford, California   1994

In grateful memory of Roger B. Henkle

1935–1991

Stanford University Press, Stanford, California
© 1994 by the Board of Trustees of the
Leland Stanford Junior University
Printed in the United States of America

Published with the assistance of
the English Department, Stanford University

CIP data appear at the end of the book

Stanford University Press publications
are distributed exclusively by Stanford
University Press within the United
States, Canada, and Mexico; they are
distributed exclusively by Cambridge
University Press throughout the rest
of the world.

For Ian Watt,

with the contributors' gratitude, esteem, and affection

Acknowledgments

I WISH TO ACKNOWLEDGE WITH SPECIAL THANKS James Baer of Palo Alto, graduate of Stanford University in English, whose generous contribution and dedication to letters, learning, and—in his own work as well as in that of others—aesthetic excellence have helped to make possible the publication of this book.

Roger Henkle conceived the idea for this volume, but, after his sudden and untimely death, the book could not have been completed without the encouragement, cooperation, grace, and good will of his wife, Carol Henkle. I wish also to thank the contributors for their patience and understanding.

I want especially to thank Helen Tartar of Stanford University Press for both her support for this project and her indispensable wisdom and practical suggestions along the way. I thank Robert Newsom for his wise, useful, and generous criticism of the whole manuscript, and I want to express gratitude to, among others, John Bender, George Dekker, Regenia Gagnier, Murray Baumgarten, John Jordan, Fred Kaplan, Norris Pope, and Hilary Schor for their specific suggestions and expertise. I thank Keith Todd for his care, industriousness, scholarly sense, and good humor in helping ready the manuscript for submission. The good sense, kindness, and judiciousness of Ellen F. Smith aided greatly in readying the book for publication, as did the fine copyediting of Ann Klefstad. I am grateful to Victoria Olsen for her help and patience in arranging for the illustrations and for her fine work in preparing the index.

This project has received important institutional aid from Stanford. I owe much to the English Department chairs, J. Martin Evans and Ronald

Rebholz, and to the department administrative assistant, Carolyn Fetler, whose unstinting help has made this volume possible. I wish to thank also the School of Humanities and Sciences, and deans Ewart Thomas and Susan Stephens specifically, for support.

Finally, I want to acknowledge the great generosity of Mary Jean Corbett, Nancy H. Packer, Ruth Watt, and, most of all, Patricia Brandt Polhemus, whose faith and friendship made possible the completion of this long-meditated volume.

R. M. P.

Contents

Contributors

JOHN BENDER is Professor of English and Comparative Literature at Stanford University. He is the author of *Spenser and Literary Pictorialism* and *Imagining the Penitentiary: Fiction and the Architecture of Mind in Eighteenth-Century England*. He recently coedited *The Ends of Rhetoric: History, Theory, Practice* and *Chronotypes: The Construction of Time*. A longer version of his essay "Impersonal Violence" will appear in *Vision and Textuality*, edited by Stephen Melville and Bill Readings, to be published by Macmillan, England.

WILLIAM M. CHACE is president of Wesleyan University in Connecticut. From 1968 to 1988 he was Professor of English at Stanford University. He is the author of, among other works, *The Political Identities of Ezra Pound and T. S. Eliot* and *Lionel Trilling: Criticism and Politics*.

GEORGE DEKKER is the Joseph S. Atha Professor in Humanities at Stanford University. His books include *The American Historical Romance*; *James Fenimore Cooper: The Novelist*; *Coleridge and the Literature of Sensibility*; and *Sailing After Knowledge: The Cantos of Ezra Pound*. He is currently working on a book on Henry James and the romance tradition.

JOSEPH FRANK is the author of many books, among them *The Widening Gyre* and the multivolumed *Dostoevsky*, a biography of the novelist, the fourth volume of which he has recently completed. He is Professor Emeritus of Comparative Literature and Slavic Literature at Princeton and Stanford universities.

ROGER B. HENKLE was Professor of English and Chair of the English Department at Brown University. He is the author of *Comedy and Culture* and numerous essays, articles, and reviews.

MICHAEL H. LEVENSON, Professor of English at the University of Virginia, is the author of *A Genealogy of Modernism* and *The Fate of Individuality*, both published by Cambridge University Press. With coauthor Karen Chase, he is currently at work on a new study called *The Domestic Imagination in the Age of Dickens*.

JULIET McMASTER is the author of *Thackeray: The Major Novels*; *Jane Austen on Love*; *Trollope's Palliser Novels*; and *Dickens the Designer*. She is also editor of *Jane Austen's Achievement*, and coauthor (with R. D. McMaster) of *The Novel from Sterne to James*. A University Professor of English at the University of Alberta, she is currently working on a book on body and character in the eighteenth-century novel.

THOMAS C. MOSER has written *Joseph Conrad: Achievement and Decline* and *The Life in the Fiction of Ford Madox Ford*; he has also done the first scholarly editions of *Lord Jim* (Norton) and *The Good Soldier* (World's Classics). Currently he is working on a psychobiographical study of William Faulkner's creativity. Moser has taught at Stanford University since 1956 and, as English Department head, hired Ian Watt in 1964.

ROBERT M. POLHEMUS is Howard H. and Jessie T. Watkins University Professor of English at Stanford University. He is the author of *Erotic Faith: Being in Love from Jane Austen to D. H. Lawrence*; *Comic Faith: The Great Tradition from Austen to Joyce*; and *The Changing World of Anthony Trollope*. He is currently at work on a book about faith in the child and the representation of children in literature and art.

JOHN HENRY RALEIGH is Professor Emeritus of English at the University of California at Berkeley. His books include *The Plays of Eugene O'Neill*; *Matthew Arnold and American Culture*; *Time, Place, and Idea*; and *The Chronicle of Leopold and Molly Bloom*. He is presently engaged in writing on historical novels.

EDWARD W. SAID is Old Dominion Foundation Professor in the Humanities at Columbia University. Among his books are *Joseph Conrad and the Fiction of Autobiography*; *Orientalism*; *The Question of Palestine*; and *The World, the Text, and the Critic*.

TZVETAN TODOROV works at the Centre Nationale de la Recherche Scientifique in Paris. His recent work concentrates on moral and political issues: studies in the history of French thought (*Nous et les autres*) and case studies in modern history (*Conquest of America* and *Face à l'extrême* [on the lessons of the concentration camp]).

CRITICAL RECONSTRUCTIONS

The Relationship of Fiction and Life

Introduction

ROBERT M. POLHEMUS AND

ROGER B. HENKLE

FOR THOSE WHO READ WIDELY AND SERIOUSLY, living inevitably means reflections on literature and literature means reflections on life. The sweeping, overall subject of this book, suggested by the writings of Ian Watt, is the relationship of fiction and life—the subject Henry James alludes to when he celebrates the novel's "large, free character of immense and exquisite correspondence with life." That relationship set down in writing, however, can only continue to exist when reconstructed by acts of critical reading. Informed by the deconstructive moves in recent criticism, we now can better see the referential power of literature—the power of fiction to refer to, affect, represent, form, and reform reality—and we need to affirm it in fresh ways. The essays of this volume concern themselves, in their own distinctive fashions, with reestablishing—reconstructing—bases for asserting the centrality of literary fiction in life.

I

Reconstruction means broadly for us reformulating and refocusing on ties between particular practices and theories of prose fiction and the facts of life, that is, historical, biographical, and textual facts about authors, readers, critics, and their works and worlds. Critical reconstruction can even show how previous fictions have helped to call into being subsequent realities and subjectivities. But the project of reconstruction must be plural and textually specific, if it is not to be reductive and, from our late-twentieth-century roller-coaster perspective on history, to turn quickly into old-hat totalizing. There are myriad ways for critics to reconstruct a relationship between a text and some aspect of reality. Let a hundred blooms flower.

This book, as a whole and in its parts, features the interplay of fictions with "the real world," but it explores and expands ideas of what fiction and reality might be. In discussions of particular texts, it raises and addresses such questions, both timely and perennial, as these: How does fiction work to represent and communicate truth about the world? What is the connection between perceived historical reality and the form of language in which a novel is narrated? How does writing mediate the tensions between public and private life, and what has fiction to do with formulating the very concept of such a split? What is it exactly that people of a given time want and get from a particular novel? How does a novelist's life give form to a novel? How are reality, the novel, knowledge, and the practice and form of fiction known as *realism* related, and what might *realism* mean now as modern critics reconstruct ideas about it? How does a critical theorist of literature move to political theory? How do the effects of writing "travel," both geographically and in time? And, most significantly for us, what continues to matter about some particular work or works? All these are questions Ian Watt's work has floated for us and helped bring into focus.

It needs to be stressed how important Watt's classic *The Rise of the Novel* (1957) has been—and continues to be—in generating, directly or indirectly, modern critical study of the novel and of the problematic relationship of fiction to life. The book has lasted in a way that is remarkable in literary criticism, and the most interesting and widely regarded recent studies of the development of the novel in English still explicitly reckon with it. More successfully than any other writer, Ian Watt made the historical and material circumstances of the novel's "rise" an unavoidable topic. The words and stance of Michael McKeon, in the introduction to his own challenging and influential account of that "rise," *The Origins of the English Novel, 1600–1740* (1987), are both typical and revealing: "The most successful attempt to explain the origins of the English novel has been, for many years now, the work of Ian Watt. Any effort to extend this work—to engage the difficult problems that *The Rise of the Novel* either failed to resolve or, through its very brilliance, has thrown into high relief—would do well to recall first the grounds of Watt's achievement" (1).

Watt integrated the skills and virtues of New Criticism's close readings with a concern for such historical factors as economic change, class and gender determinants, the dynamic nature of a reading public, cultural and philosophic influences, social psychology, shifts in signifying practices, and theories of narrative that had been missing, lost, or slighted in much influential postwar literary criticism. His boldness in taking the study of literature initially beyond pure textual analysis into realms of sociology, ideology, and cultural relations, and then back into individual novels for richer and more complex readings was a brilliant accomplishment that broadened the range of literary scholarship. He opened up fields for scholars of all bents—fields consisting, to be sure, of turf to fight about. His interdisciplinary method was instrumental in helping to bring about the interaction of many critical practices and positions—structuralist, psychoanalytic, and feminist interpretation, reader-response theory, neo-Marxism, and the "new historicism," for instance—that continues to preoccupy critics.

He has spoken of the assumption (which he shares) that all good critics bring to their discussion of literature and their understanding of life an underlying set of notions about the interrelatedness of different bodies of knowledge and about ways of approaching problems of representation and interpretation in literature and society. He has insisted strongly, however, that one's critical position not obscure literature's truth about the time and conditions it inevitably represents. He has urged critics not to forget that it is a condition of literature's wider truth to life that it is not exclusively cognitive; that it covers the whole range of human actions and feelings, memories, and imaginings; and that to treat literature as cognitive both in subject and meaning is not only to misrepresent it, but to prevent it from fulfilling its capacity to enlarge our imaginative sympathies. The contributors, therefore, have been confronted by Watt with a major issue: literature's relation to the cognitive, and beyond that to what we may call the reading libido (readers' desires) and to "truth to life." They all deal with that complex issue in their different ways.

The critical protocol that Watt charted for us moves from examining the author's and the text's relation to life to analyzing the exercises of the imagination and its transformation of authorial fantasies, social ideas, and ethical concerns into a novelistic fiction. It is more than an example of critical practice. It becomes, as the studies in this volume show, a model for the workings of literary power in realism and the novel. These essays have been arranged to illustrate, through their frequent dialectical interaction, the development of the social imagination into novelistic representation and the movement from the private apprehension of life to a public expression of it. Each essay examines in detail, and in a range of differing texts, the phases of the generative process by which apprehensions of "the real"—the epistemological and psychological bases for realism—are reworked through the imagination into a representation that carries cultural implications. By "reconstruction," then, we mean the long complex critical act; the essays in this book define the imaginative process of realistic fiction, set it in a finite historical framework, and provide elements of a model for a collective critical enterprise that takes into account the complexities of that process.

II

Let us quickly review some of Ian Watt's specific contributions to literary study that offer a context for this volume. "[M]y main effort," he says in *The Rise of the Novel*, "has been to elucidate in a fairly systematic fashion the enduring connection between the distinctive literary qualities of the novel and those of the society in which it began and flourished" (7). His title plays on the old historical cliché "the rise of the middle classes," and that linking of a set of people growing in numbers and power with a developing literary art form inevitably historicizes ideas about literature and art. In his first chapter, he attempts to define what characterizes "the novel" as it appeared in eighteenth-century England, discusses the changing philosophical concepts of realism, and inductively identifies the novel's distinctive narrative method as a circumstantial view of life that he famously names "formal realism"—"formal because the term realism does not here refer to any special literary doctrine or purpose, but only to a set of narrative procedures" (32).

His work on "formal realism," "the realism of presentation," and "the realism of assessment" (288) refigured notions of realism—particularly realism as an ethos—as did no other text save Eric Auerbach's *Mimesis*. Most students and critics of the novel have had—and still have, in one way or another, as the essays in this volume all variously show, to come to terms with Watt's opening speculations on the nature of fiction and with the following statement and its implications: "Formal realism, in fact, is the narrative embodiment of a premise that Defoe and Richardson accepted very literally, but which is implicit in the novel form in general: the premise, or primary convention, that the novel is a full and authentic report of human experience, and is therefore under an obligation to satisfy its readers with such details of the story as the individuality of the actors concerned, the particulars of the times and places of their actions, details which are presented through a more largely referential use of language than is common in other literary forms. Formal realism is, of course, like the rules of evidence, only a convention" (32). This famous assertion has been irresistible food for speculation, amplification, debate, and discussion—a tempting dialectical hot potato, in fact—and the vast number of studies the concept of formal realism has generated, for instance, about "realism," about the nature and history of what is called the novel, and about what the referential language of fiction might mean or whether it even exists, shows how crucial these words have been to literary critics and cultural historians.

Broadly speaking, our contributors have all grappled, at one time or another, with the issue that Watt first adumbrated and to which he here alludes; the problematic definition and analysis of realism itself. A concept such as "the realism of assessment" means that the evaluation by author and critic of their "real" worlds will inform their textual presentation: notions of empiricism, of ethical and religious values, of politics, of the centering (or decentering) of the individual subject (either in psychology or in theories of the construction of the individual subject), and of the potentialities for representing "truth," will all determine the very nature of the realism of a work. By the same token, "realism of presentation" does not connote a straightforward, reflective naturalism, but rather a *representation* of the character of representation itself, of the novel's structure and governing patterns and practices. The composition of the work can become the object of realistic presentation, and a criticism that unearths and examines that composition can provide a text with a new dimension.

In his chapter "The Reading Public and the Rise of the Novel," Watt goes on to analyze the composition of the audience and the potential desires of readers in eighteenth-century Britain. That original analysis helped critics in turn to see and study in new ways the role of readers in literary transactions and the historical purposes of a specific popular art. In the rest of his book, he relates particular works of Richardson, Defoe, and Fielding to their times, moving, as Michael Levenson puts it, from intellectual history to sociological detail to literary interpretation. He also assesses critically the novels and novelists he discusses, and his critical practice is very much in tune with what he calls "the realism of assessment," that is, "a responsible wisdom about human affairs" and a "wise assessment of life" which he sees as necessary in shaping literary value. Literary value depends very much on the realism of assessment, which, as he sees it, must be the property of both writers and readers.

Conrad in the Nineteenth Century (1979), Watt's comprehensive account of the novelist's early literary career, centers that critical dynamic by fusing biographical, historical, and interpretive materials and methods in studying one figure. It is his full and radiant answer to the fundamental question "What is an author?" The "main emphasis" is "exegetic"—that is, trying to explain what this particular author and his particular novels are and mean—but for Watt there is no text without context. Sources in Conrad's personal experience, different international strands of nineteenth-century literary and social history, and the intertwining of various traditions and traumas make meaningful interpretation of his novels possible. In his preface, Watt puts forth his problematic and influential concept of "the literal imagination": "This attempt," he writes of his work, "imposes a special kind of critical approach: there must be enough quotation to enable the reader to see the evidence in the text for the interpretation given; and the primary commitment must be to what may be called the literal imagination—the analytic commentary restricts itself to what the imagination can discover through a literal reading of the work" (x). This might at first blush seem simple enough, but it actually signifies a challenging and complex critical program. For Watt the terms "literal imagination" and "literal reading" become the heart of an elaborate, impressive process of multiple reconstruction: reconstruction of biographical and historical materials as they may have influenced and been used by the writer; precise reconstruction of the intellectual, artistic, and political milieu in which Conrad and his contemporary audience lived; reconstruction of the meaning of passages in light of the knowledge that contextualization makes possible; and reconstruction of the way the language and rhetoric of fiction might shape the perceptions and feelings of later readers and critics. Watt tries to reconstruct a context in which one might judge the correspondence of novels to external reality and determine and evaluate the truth of a work.

Close reading and historicism meet in "the literal imagination." Here, the term "literal" gives a focus to criticism by fixing it on a written and read text, and "imagination" points to the potential breadth and free force of criticism by implying that interpreters can and must range far and wide intellectually in order to see into a text with the full powers of the mind's eye. Many have been committed in practice to "the literal imagination" who would not subscribe to it in theory, including some contributors.

What matters most is that the literal imagination uses whatever it can find out about the making of a writer's text and its radiating significance.

In *Conrad*, as in all his work, Watt champions the concept of literary value and the evaluation of writing in its possible relationship to readers' lives: "[T]he presumption is that the essence of a good novel should be a view of reality which is somehow transferable; only the carry-over of social criticism or moral insight into the reader's understanding can justify the fictional vehicle" (47). He insists on the moral and utilitarian force of "great" writers and their literary work, "privileging"—to use current jargon—its emotional power and its potentially volatile, deconstructive, and illuminating insights on personal psychology, culture, and ideology: "[T]he greatest authors are rarely representative of the ideology of their period; they tend rather to expose its internal contradictions or the very partial nature of its capacity for dealing with the facts of experience" (147). In those deceptively modest words lurks a proud claim for the power of the writer and writing to transcend the spirit of an age and provide for the critical reconstruction of reality. That various reconstruction is the subject of this book.

III

Critical Reconstructions presents a number of skilled hands reconceiving a range of critical approaches—looking at the composition of a text, at literary disputes, at fictional structure, at social context, at psychological patternings, at authorial intentions, at both distinctions and the blurring of distinctions between history and fiction—in ways that reformulate the term "realism" and show the power of imaginative literature and language to be ineluctably a part of what people believe to be real. The essays for the most part concern themselves with novels and novelists—with aspects, examples, and problems of the risen novel in its ascendence as the principal form of fiction. We frame our collection, however, with complementary pieces by Tzvetan Todorov and Edward Said that treat the issues of the credibility and effects of writings which precede and antedate the rise and predominance of the novel. In Todorov, at the start, we find wildly imaginative accounts of exploration from the edges of the world flowing into and feeding growing social appetites for fictional "truth" and novel knowledge; and in Said, at the end, we see the power and credibility of fiction and literary criticism turning into political theory that reaches and touches the alienated wretched of the earth. After the defamiliarizing opening by Todorov that returns us to a time before fictional realism, we move to three examples of the critical imagination focusing on one novelist, as Watt focuses on Conrad. Here, the writer is Charles Dickens. These essays, by Michael Levenson, Robert Polhemus, and Roger Henkle, on different Dickens fictions, emphasize the role of cultural psychology in the writing and the reception of this most popular of nineteenth-century novelists and stress the novel's historical function in mediating between "inner" and "outer" life. They show the means by which private fantasy evolves into an art that speaks, in a public manner, to the contradictory demands of reality. Next come three studies of realism, one by John Bender on the political and epistemological implications of power and violence that in-here in techniques of narration typical of realist prose fiction—specifically, in Godwin's *Caleb Williams*; one by George Dekker on the dialectical in-terplay of conceptions of fiction and realism by Henry James and Robert Louis Stevenson; and one by William Chace on Joyce's realism in *Ulysses*. Just as the first set of essays maps the process by which the imagination reworks private materials into the "reality" of a time and culture, this group moves to explore how that creative, transformative process calls at-tention to its act of representation: the reality and structure of fictions themselves, as their own objects of representation, become subjects of the realistic text.

At this point Joseph Frank and Thomas Moser follow with biographi-cal studies of Dostoevsky and Faulkner that take us deep into the active processes by which these novelists bring their subjective visions to the structuring of their fictions and relate certain key experiences in their lives to the making of two of their finest novels. Then we present two essays in practical criticism that insist that the value and interest of fiction lie in its ability to represent and define reality. Juliet McMaster, using Jane Austen's *The Watsons*, illustrates the ways in which criticism can go about recon-structing an unfinished work; John Henry Raleigh shows how the reality of a fictional text might be validated against other testimonies and come to have striking evidential power and effect. Both writers are interested in the relationship of novels and historical authenticity, and both try to re-vivify novels through the use of "the literal imagination," one reconstruct-ing the meaning of an Austen text from a fragment, the other salvaging an important novel of war and violent struggle from obscurity and claiming it as valid historical evidence. The final piece by Said, analyzing the impli-cations of critical theory as it "travels" and acquires new potency in other historical and political contexts, returns to, and leaves us with, the relationship of fiction to political discourse and action, life on the margin, and literature's fluid status.

Fantasies, particularly those that are transformed into a culture's collective fantasies, are part of "reality" and engender not only art but history. Tzvetan Todorov, looking at two "discoverers" of novel worlds before the novel, explores among other things the fictional basis of the real and the historical road to realism (and specifically, if implicitly, to both *Robinson Crusoe* and *The Rise of the Novel*). Taking as his subject two texts of exploration, George Psalmanazar's eighteenth-century *Description of the Island of Formosa in Asia* and Amerigo Vespucci's accounts of his "discovery" of America, he discusses the relationship of truth and fiction, of fiction and history, and of two sorts of truths that he calls "truth as correspondence to reality and truth as revelation." The Psalmanazar opus illustrates problems about the principles of historical truth and cultural rhetoric that have lately provoked controversy and challenge. Concocted by an impostor, this "history" of Formosa briefly flourished because it offered tactical support in political battles within scientific and (most significantly) religious circles, but sensational and wickedly inventive as it was, it survives only as a great hoax. Its woeful lack of correspondence to reality was soon made clear, and, since it presented itself as history and not fiction, it did not offer Todorov's "truth of revelation," the revelation of fictional hypothesis. It lacked literary skill and realized no latent, lasting historical desires for the culture.

Amerigo Vespucci's two accounts of his "discovery" of America, *Mundus Novus* and *Quatuor Navigationes*, on the other hand, converted fabrication into a form of cultural truth and won him a hemisphere in his name. He sought to delight an audience, getting it to feel and imagine the power of the new, of *news* (explorations of what is novel to people would become one of the great attractions of the novel). Todorov's examination of the texts of Vespucci, as against those of Christopher Columbus and Peter Martyr, who had equal claims to the first arrival on the new continent, show how writing skills and imagination can win the day and shape reality. Amerigo's version, the rhetoric of his fiction, was better able to get at and articulate truths of the European imagination than that of his competitors. Todorov moves beyond the premise that the historian seeks truth as verified by facts and the fiction writer seeks a truth of revelation. The literary act of interpretation and reconstruction takes history from one realm to the other. Literary qualities of narration, voice, imagination, and building a relation to readers come into play at key moments for a culture and help to determine and define its reality. His reconstruction of the pleasures of Amerigo's text and his rhetorical victory could be entitled "The Rise of Subjectivity that Made the Novel Possible."

How does the novel mediate between psychology and sociology, between private and collective fantasies? That is the subject of Michael Levenson's meditation on the relationship of inner, private fantasies to narrative art and the public form of the novel, an impressive critical application of psychoanalytic thought to fiction. Drawing on observations by both Watt and Todorov on psychological needs and the fantastic, respectively, Levenson analyzes Freudian notions of "phantasy," Freud's brief study "A Child Is Being Beaten," and one of Freud's favorite novels, *David Copperfield*, as he tracks the path from fantasy to the art of the novel. The essay construes the link between private experience and the novel in terms of Freud's reflections on fantasy. Levenson's argument turns on reinterpreting distinctions between fantasy and the imagination and using literature and art to allude to the social, public materials that inhere in fantasy. He uses Freud's essay recounting the phases of dream-work and meaning in his patients' recurrent dream of a child being beaten to speculate on the progression of these phases into the construction of the subjectivity of the fantasist and dreams, of repression, and then of subjectivity displaced and made public. The process Levenson describes tells us a great deal about the transformation of personal fantasy material into the art of fiction.

The final movement of this essay offers a characterization of a particular form of public fantasy that would seem to lie at the core of novelistic imagination. Two issues come together in *David Copperfield*: Dickens's recasting of an autobiographical fragment within the conventions of the novel, and David's erotic passage from Dora to Agnes. Levenson sees both of these events through the key concept he calls the *aging* of fantasy, a concept he has found in Freud's beating fantasies. Fantasy, Levenson shows, has a life history, an inner pattern of rise and fall; it moves by its own imaginative logic into the social world. Desire is not only reworked by the individual imagination into artistic expression, but reconstructed into a public discourse, so that it fulfills a hegemonic dream: one shall desire what one morally ought to desire. "Indeed," he says, "in one of its many aspects, the novel appears as that form which has taught us how to dream the real and to hallucinate the moral."

Also reading Dickens, Robert Polhemus shows how well that statement fits *The Old Curiosity Shop*. The desire that shapes that novel reflects more than fantasy, though Dickens's intense idealization of and desire for his dead sister-in-law Mary Hogarth do inspire his text. His imagination gets at a broad set of cultural as well as personal contradictions through which desire is displaced from love, but through which, nonetheless, tabooed incestuous desires provide the force for familial cohesion. Polhemus's noted terms "comic faith" and "erotic faith" combine dynamically in *The Old Curiosity Shop*, which he characterizes as a kind of secular, popular, literary cathedral—an accretive Gothic literary structure with chapels that illustrate different kinds of faith. In the novel's nineteenth-century English domesticated Gothic, the holy appeal of the Virgin has been transposed to a child. The child, little Nell, functions as a Protestant Holy Virgin of the Novel—fiction as secular Scripture. She embodies a religious role as a victim and sacrificial figure reconstructing and purging male guilt over lustful, acquisitive, and incestuous desires. As with the Virgin Mary, the idealized child displaces religious faith and love from sexuality. Polhemus reaches back into Christian exegesis and turn-of-the-nineteenth-century Gothic fiction, and he moves forward to Ruskin, late Dickens, Freud, and Joyce to show how crucial this set of transpositions has been to Western cultural expression. Like Levenson, Polhemus shows how one can use fiction to psychoanalyze, as it were, the culture itself.

Roger Henkle finds in the crisis of faith that haunts Dickens and in the social and psychological urgencies of his imagination a crisis of representation in the nineteenth-century realist novel. Reading *Dombey and Son*, he argues that it is a pivotal novel of the new post-industrial-revolution order and a problematic, troubling working-through of important ideological tensions and contradictions in terms of familial and sexual relations. Little Paul Dombey dies relatively early in the novel, and his sacrifice does not redeem his world, as Nell's does hers: the view of life expressed through him is at odds with the social reality of the novel. Dickens discards the fantasy vision of childhood innocence because it furnishes no site of subjectivity from which to evaluate the modern world and act within it. The alternative sensibility of the modern tycoon Dombey, however, proves to be just as empty. There exists no core of subjectivity in which to situate evaluation of the modern world of social and economic change, especially since the other conventional site of subjectivity, the selflessly maternal (embodied in one of Dickens's child-mothers, Florence Dombey), is marginalized.

Although Dombey would seem to be the Victorian incorporation of the *homo economicus* that Ian Watt describes in Defoe's *Robinson Crusoe*, the

difference between the two configurations is revealing. Dickens depicts a
new era of pure capital, commercial and legal fictions, and economic for-
mulations: an alienated world removed from the experiential world of personal, sensual immediacy. Such a world carries disquieting implications
about the nature of representation itself, and Henkle suggests that *Dombey
and Son* speaks to that crisis as eloquently as it does to the state of society.
In an argument of broad implication, he shows how Dickens invests passion, sexual energy, and—most tellingly—the powers of the subjective artist in the figures of immorality in the novel. Because Carker and Edith
embody the commodifying and consuming aspects of the developing
economy, Henkle makes clear that the artist—here, the *novelist*—is implicated in spreading the rapacious desires, messages, and casts of mind of
the new empire of capital: the writer, like the greedy financier, is involved
in the despoliation of the mythic harmony and beauty of preindustrial
England.

In the Dickens of this and the other two essays, we are well on the
way to authorial and novelistic self-consciousness, contradictions, and dynamic tensions about the relationship of fantasy, the imagination, and fiction to one another and to "real life." Contradiction, according to John
Bender, is inherent in the assumptions and practices of realism as it developed out of the Enlightenment. Using an eclectic critical approach featuring deconstructive, neo-Marxian, and feminist insights, he reconstructs a
vision of realism out of the impersonal violence he finds in the narrative
field of William Godwin's *Caleb Williams*. He claims that narrative modes
are forms of knowledge. Describing the conjunction of forms of authority
in the world and forms of narrative discourse, he shows how the power of
narrative form can skew conscious authorial intention and disrupt conventional attitudes toward the representations of fiction. In his provocative,
subtle, but radical study of Enlightenment epistemology and "realistic"
narrative modes—specifically "free indirect discourse"—in *Caleb Williams*, with its tellingly disjointed nature, he stresses the impersonal assault
that lies in the apparently "sympathetic" literary act of representing the
inner and outer life of characters. He finds in realism's attention and penetration to the inner self—ostensibly an act of empathy—a violation and
an assumption of authority of immense consequence, both for narrative
fiction and society. Desires that Bender sees lurking in the practice and
rhetorical effects of free indirect discourse have much in common with the
erotics of fantasy in fiction that Levenson discusses.

For Bender, the gaze we have heard so much about lately that objectifies the flesh and violates and defines the "other" finds an important focus in the form of realism developing in the late eighteenth century. He brings together brilliantly his sense of the implicit violence, power, and erotic drive in eighteenth-century benevolent moral thought (e.g., Adam Smith and Rousseau), in free indirect discourse, and in the sympathetic, "sympathizing" hero of the novel, Caleb, with contemporary theories of the gaze from the history of science, art, and film. In analyzing Godwin, he locates a tendency of indirect discourse to dissect and feminize its subject, and he makes clear the relation of fictive modes to developing ideas of gender, cultural structures of authority, and social values and morality. Paying tribute to *The Rise of the Novel*, Bender insists we must understand the interaction of political thought and narrative technique.

In a different context, George Dekker revealingly focuses on the subject of novelists' implication in reality, retracing the late-nineteenth-century course of Henry James's theories about the art of fiction and the relationship of realism and romance in the critical interchange between James and his friend Robert Louis Stevenson about what fiction should be and do. This study resonates dialogically with the questions hovering around the transformation of fantasy into art that Levenson raises and the different kinds of truth that interest Todorov. As Dekker tells us and we have remarked, James, in his famous 1884 piece on the art of fiction, asserts that such art lies in the novel's "correspondence with life," its realism broadly conceived as the mature imagination in harmony with a reality that it illuminates, but does not discard. Stevenson insists, however, on fiction as play, free play—even, literally, child's play, with its roots in fantasy and the need to dream roles and make up stories that Levenson discusses.

Dekker records and reconstructs the movement of the Jamesian sensibility as it both disapproves of and delights in the imaginative freedom and play of fictional romance, praising it for sustaining some of "the finest feelings—suspense, daring, decision, passion, curiosity, gallantry, eloquence, friendship" (all personal qualities he found and loved in R.L.S.). Yet by the time he wrote his famous prefaces to the New York Edition of his novels, James had nostalgically, even regretfully, relegated romance to the phases of his own artistic youth, to a moment when free play, with a kind of glory, seemed to reign above social duty and the rigors of self-criticism. The preface to *The American* is itself a high romantic utterance, and Dekker gracefully shows the interplay of life with the theorizing of fiction, the emotional blending with (as Watt would have it) "the cognitive." The life of Stevenson and James's love for it deeply influenced James's sense of the romantic possibilities of fiction and the art of the novel. Dekker makes us see that this famous critical debate about fiction and the Jamesian critical reconciliation of forms had as much to do with psychological needs and drives as abstract generic categories. Even the theory of fiction bespeaks a narrative of the emotions.

William Chace's article on "Joycean Realism" continues to probe the relationship of the artist's imagination to the demands of realism, and it significantly expands the category of realistic representation. James Joyce, like his character Stephen Dedalus in *Ulysses*, undertook the Odyssean task of navigating "between the dangers of a theory defending solipsism (the artist need not pay his respects to the world or even grant it a real existence) and a theory stating that the artist can create something only by reassembling the given pieces of the world as he finds them." We again meet issues raised by Todorov's two kinds of truth (i.e., of correspondence and revelation) and by the James-Stevenson dialogue; we have the apparent dilemma of choosing between imaginative self-indulgence and the rigors (and potential banalities) of empiricism. Such a dilemma, Chace argues, poses false choices: He shows clearly how Joyce, with his rapture over language as reality itself and his bold linguistic and formal experiments, expanded the definition of the realist enterprise so that the novel's modes of representation figured centrally in fiction's claim to be realistic. In *Ulysses*, as Joyce composed it, another dimension of realism comes sharply into view: the reality of the book, not simply as a medium of representation, but as its own subject and project.

What forms a novel—its composition, its styles and techniques of prose, its narrative, figures, events, subjects, and subjectivities—is the result of the actual experience, the choices, and the imagination of a real person: a life. Biography, though out of fashion with some, can sharpen our reading of novels, and novels help us to read lives. A novel can make people eager to know the life of an author, and the most interesting thing about seeing the life of a writer in light of a finished novel may be that it is evidence in itself of how fiction can form both our curiosity and our perception of "real" life: we not only see novelists' lives through their works, we see life generally through them, if they are powerful. Joseph Frank and Thomas Moser use different kinds of biographical material to reconstruct the course of creation and the emergent form of two famous works, *Crime and Punishment* and *The Sound and the Fury*, respectively, but both point to the dialectical relationship between fiction and biography that can lead to more richly focused readings and the discovery of new resonances in novels.

Frank unveils, through careful attention to the first draft of *Crime and Punishment* and to the accounts of its long composition in Dostoevsky's notebooks, a gathering complexity in Raskolnikov's feelings and thoughts about the murder he commits. In the early stages of composition, Raskolnikov's reaction is primarily anguish over his isolation from humanity because of his guilt. Nothing, however, in that emotional state would seem sufficient to prompt him to turn himself in to the police, as was projected in the original plans for the novel. The motives for his confession emerge in Dostoevsky's notes for revision. Frank analyzes the matter: "Here is an entirely different character from the one previously portrayed, and Dostoevsky may have stopped writing at this point because his figure had evolved beyond his initial conception." Here, Frank argues, the author was compelled to make a breakthrough. First he turns to his own fragmentary sketch for a novel, *The Drunkards*, for the Marmeladov family, who, through the figure of Sonya, can provide the element of pity that will ultimately bring Raskolnikov to confess, thereby infusing the novel with its strongest emotional theme. Dostoevsky also reaches out for a cognitive element, the ideology of a radical intellectual who believes he is an "extraordinary" human being, not needing constraint by the rules that govern ordinary people.

The interweaving of these new conceptual and emotive matters into his hero makes Dostoevsky's initial plan for a first-person narration impossible. Frank ingeniously analyzes the process through which the novelist moves from a detached third-person narrator (who could sardonically comment on the "superman" idea) to a narrative persona who can come closer to expressing the original dramatic intent of a self-confession. Joseph Frank's story is one of complex interplay among emotive, intellectual, and rhetorical imperatives: of "truths of life" pushing the compositional process in specific directions.

Thomas Moser's daringly speculative essay takes as a given the lately contested idea that a writer's psychobiography and experience can have valuable explanatory functions in understanding and evaluating texts. Of course biographical criticism can be misleading and tautological (what you find in the novel you single-mindedly go about finding in the life, and what you find in the life you crudely read into the novel), but the best of this scholarship can set up reverberations that sharply highlight what is at stake in a given work, the role of individuality and personal responsibility in the creative process, and the flow of early experience into fantasy and then back to experience through the formal structuring of perceptions through art (see Michael Levenson). That is what Moser does. His essay could be subtitled, "A Child Is Being Beaten into Formal Language to Shape a Novel." He reconstructs the love of William Faulkner for Estelle Oldham, which began in childhood, and explores the relationship of their bumpy erotic history to Faulkner's early work and, finally, to his triumphant creation of the figure Caddy in *The Sound and the Fury*. As in much of his work, Moser aims to show how personal loss and its compensatory strategies govern creative impulse. He, like many of our contributors, looks to life to find specifically how desire shapes fiction.

From biographical reconstruction, we move to an experiment in criticism reconstructing the meaning of a work that does not fully exist; using her "literal imagination," Juliet McMaster interprets Jane Austen's unfinished novel *The Watsons*. McMaster calls herself an empirical critic, but her empiricism turns out to be imaginative and to embrace the hypothetical. It is more than the care she brings to individual passages and scenes, to the precise phrasing of a character's speech, or to the turns of narrative that allow her to map out the crucial factors of social and ethical refinement that were to form the theme of Austen's fragment. A textual fragment, as recent scholarship has been stressing, offers the critic great challenges—especially a critic bound to a tough code of empirical inquiry; the full circle of the whole (to use McMaster's own figure of speech) cannot be plotted from an arc with purely mathematical precision. Her reconstruction of the presumed totality depends upon her imaginative knowledge of Jane Austen's disposition, of the way she has organized her other texts, of her use of secondary characters to show variations on central moral concerns, and of the complex and various nature of her other heroines. McMaster demonstrates that even the most perspicacious of critics, working with the most rigorous of realistic novelists, must elaborate and take risks as part of the critical process; the result of interpretation must, as in this compelling reading of *The Watsons*, *seem* to be right.

For John Henry Raleigh a virtue of fiction is that it *seems* to be right about history. In analyzing a novel of war, Frederic Manning's *Her Privates We*, and in reconstructing the rhetorical and emotional power of this novel's "realism of assessment," Raleigh's discussion reads almost like a test case for asserting the centrality of (1) fiction as human record, (2) the literal imagination in comprehending public life, and (3) the novel as a truthfinder for determining both inner and outer realities. Comparing the novel to a number of post-"Great War" texts—memoirs, battle accounts, political and personal commentaries, and the like—he argues for the historical authenticity of *Her Privates We* as a representation of life on the front in World War I. At the end of the twentieth century, we can see both that the historical experience of world war was crucial and that its rendering in fiction from the point of view of individualism has high significance. The novel provides an accurate distillation of what huge numbers of other texts report and what hundreds of witnesses not only thought but felt to be the realities of war. Moreover, the novelist and his autobiographical protagonist, Bourne, bring to the war and the life it engenders their own intellectual history of literature and philosophy, so that the representation of the novel is intertextual (in our jargon) as well as highly sensuous and emotional. Raleigh speculates on the way Manning shows how men under stress fall back on self-definition by assuming characters almost as novelists assume the identity of *their* characters and set them acting accordingly. The challenge of this essay is its claim that there is no better way to know both the meaning and the feeling of World War I than through a fiction—Manning's novel: the creative imagination makes history, and the novel, during the time of its risen status, gives best evidence of what is historically real.

Raleigh's study, like Todorov's and Said's in far different contexts, points to the whole problematic relationship of art and history and—beyond that—to the emerging subject of the force of aesthetics on epistemology. One basic premise of the piece, which might have been considered old-fashioned a few years ago, now appears to us fresh and sure to be a topic of focus and conflict in the next decade—namely, the idea that fiction can and does constitute history. Deconstruction of literature has led to the deconstruction of the rest of written and spoken utterance, a phenomenon that paradoxically shows the comparative truth-power and historical responsibility of fiction. The subject of the "reality" of fiction and what such a reality might mean has moved again to the center of literary criticism and debate.

Edward Said's subtle, suggestive essay, "Travelling Theory Reconsidered," might seem at first to have little to do with fiction or the novel per se, though it has everything to do with historical consciousness. Its subtext, however, shows the continual intertwining and merging of theory and fiction, and its larger implications make clear the historical importance of the novel, its representations of reality, and the critical speculation about it. We infer here that modern habits of thought and discourse on the relationships of theory and practice, of writing and social reality, of art and society, of the subject-object split in both particular and general life, would be inconceivable without the rise of the novel.

In his study, Said revises his earlier views on how political theory loses its original power and subversive force as it travels and moves away from the immediate human conditions and political desires out of which it grew. He reconstructs a probable history of Georg Lukács's theory in *History and Class Consciousness* as it "travelled" and "totally influenced" Theodor Adorno and Frantz Fanon, and, far from being domesticated or losing force, had "its fiery core . . . reignited" by them at different sites. Said reminds us that before Lukács wrote this insurrectionary Marxist *History* embracing the reconciliation of subject-object relationship and the overcoming of capitalism's alienation in "the viewpoint of the proletariat," he had written his *Theory of the Novel*, "premised on the notion that in a world abandoned by God, the novel embodies the trajectory of an epic whose hero is either demonic or mad, whose constitutive element is a temporality basically disappointing and demystifying, and whose representative status as the art form of modernity is based on its tremendous constitutive ironies, the irony of 'errant souls [adventuring] in an inessential, empty reality,' or . . .'the irony [which] has to seek the only world that is adequate to it along the *via dolorosa* of interiority but is doomed never to find it there.'" In other words, the "travelling theory" has roots in fiction. For our purposes, it is essential to see in this essay that the novel and its meaning—novels and their plethora of meanings—may be reconstructed as theory.

Said amends his earlier idea on the the loss of force of theory by focusing on two works that both modify and revivify the fierceness of Lukács: one, Adorno's *Philosophy of Modern Music* and his discussion of the proper, implicitly inherent refusal of any compromise or synthesis with existing social order in Schoenberg's atonal music; the other, Frantz Fanon's *Wretched of the Earth*, which in its rejection of postcolonial nationalism for formerly colonized peoples likewise does not accept the reconciliatory denouement of Lukács's theory. Writing travels and becomes novel. What is striking here in the argument is Said's representation of theory as a malleable fiction read and interpreted imaginatively. He finds an unstable fusion and continuing flow in the trio of theory, fiction, and social reality (for example, he describes the raging political fervor of Lukács with his sense of the novel as a historical phenomenon turning to class-consciousness theory, and he later shows the alienation of Adorno and his theorizing on Schoenberg turning into Thomas Mann's novel *Dr. Faustus*). Said's conclusion, as he describes Fanon's wrestling with the problems of imperialism and postcolonialism and his creative, imaginative transformation of Lukács, could only have been written by someone strongly engaged and familiar with the history of the novel and its vital, if problematic, relationship with social and psychological realities: "This movement suggests the possibility of actively different locales, sites, situations for theory, without facile universalism or over-general totalizing."

As Said and the rest of the contributors show, no serious critical reconstruction on any political, social, aesthetic, or psychological subject can escape the influence of the relationship between fiction and life—the news of the novel. That common perception we share means that the fundamental dynamic of Ian Watt's work, the desire to expose and know the play between the novel's text and reality outside that text, has traveled with a passion and a vengeance.

Fictions and Truths

TZVETAN TODOROV

VALÉRY OBSERVED THAT, WHEN WE ADMIRE the portrait of a historical figure, we tend to pronounce it *true*—even if we have no means of *verifying* such a judgment. He extended this remark to books as well: for those that describe a somewhat distant past, if we take into account only the reader's reaction, "there is no basis for distinguishing," he writes, between writers of history and writers of fiction, between books by "true witnesses and those by imaginary witnesses. . . . One may choose to consider all of them as *inventors*, or else all of them as *reporters*."[1] It is not that we spontaneously judge them all to be equally true; but the reasons that lead us to declare some truer than others have nothing to do with the actual truthfulness of the accounts, for we know nothing of this. What we evaluate, one might say (even if Valéry does not use these terms), is their verisimilitude, not their truth; their *truth effect*, their *effet de réel*, rather than their actual reality or truth.

Here Valéry articulates, in his own way, a feeling that is quite widespread among modern authors (since, let us say, the middle of the nineteenth century); he does not, however, express it in extreme terms, since he does not fail to specify that this impossibility of distinguishing between true texts and fictional texts is observed only "in their immediate effects upon the reader," thereby allowing for the possibility of later verification, and thus for that of a distinction established by experts. Many of our contemporaries are not hampered by such caution; believing that there are no facts, but only interpretations (the formula is Nietzsche's, but innumerable other authors have restated it on their own account, in one form or another), they extend the effects of this immediate impossibility—no *textual* sign can guarantee the truth of the text for us—to the nature of knowledge itself, as well as to the nature of the world. Indeed, the complete formula would be as follows: there are no facts, but only discourses on facts; as a result, there is no such thing in this world as truth, but only interpretations of truth, of the world.

In any case, this discovery is hardly unique to the Moderns; what is new, perhaps, is only the euphoric sentiment accompanying the affirmation. Plato, on the other hand, asserts quite bitterly that the judges sitting on a tribunal have to deal with discourses and never, or almost never, with facts (they did not witness the crimes they are investigating); as a result, the pleading counsel, in the hopes of persuading the judges, depend on verisimilitude, on what is convincing, rather than on the truth, the effects of which are uncertain. Before a tribunal, eloquence, or the ability to produce the effect of truth, is more highly valued than truth itself; whence the success of the Sophists, masters of eloquence. From this assertion, therefore, Plato draws conclusions opposed to those of most modern authors: rather than sing the praises of the poets, those "imaginary witnesses," he recommends their exclusion from the city.

Alongside this first interpretation of the relationship between fiction and truth, our modernity is familiar with another, still more radical interpretation, which consists in saying not that the two are indistinguishable, but that fiction is truer than history: the distinction is maintained, but the hierarchy is inverted. In his recent book *La traversée du Luxembourg*, which itself partakes of several genres—novel, sociology, autobiography, essay—Marc Augé cites a publisher's blurb that touts a work of ethnology for being "as virulently true as a novel by Balzac."[2] Discussing this surprising claim (the novelist stands surety for the historian's truth), Augé concludes that it is a legitimate one: the historian and the ethnologist, according to the stubborn rules of their professions, are expected to report only what has taken place, what they can establish as fact; whereas the novelist, who "does not have this superstition about the true word,"[3] can accede to a superior truth, beyond the truth of details. Historians and ethnologists, then, would do well to learn from novelists.

Here again, the notion is not an original one. To cite only one other example from the more or less recent past, here is Stendhal, writing in his journal on May 24, 1834: "Madame de Tracy said to me: 'It has become impossible to achieve *truth* except in the novel.' Every day, more and more, I see that everywhere else this claim is an imposture."[4] The context of this entry shows that Stendhal considers the novel to be superior, on one hand, to history books (biographies, etc., such as his *Vie de Rossini*, for example), because it permits us to move beyond the factual; and on the other hand, to philosophy books, to abstract treatises (we may think of his *De l'amour*) because it does not abandon the particular, because it is able to remain anchored in detail. For Stendhal, the novel is both a middle and a royal road: more philosophical than history, more concrete than philosophy; it is probably for the same reason that, some time earlier, Rousseau described *Emile*, his most ambitious and most misunderstood book, as "the novel of human nature."[5] However, the term Stendhal chooses to describe this property is neither "effectiveness" nor "eloquence," but "truth." In this "middle" virtue is an echo of Aristotle, Plato's heterodox disciple who, over twenty centuries before Stendhal, had already declared poetry nobler and more philosophical than history, for reasons similar to those offered by Stendhal and Augé (because poetry is more general, because it escapes the contingent); poets, rescued from the banishment to which Plato had condemned them, were reinstated to a far more worthy function, within the city limits. It should be noted that Aristotle did not declare poets *truer* than historians; only (only?) nobler and more philosophical.

Here then are two opinions, equally ancient and equally convincing, that have in common a refusal to valorize history over fiction. However, if we turn from such great thinkers toward the humble reality of everyday life, we have some difficulty accepting this conclusion. Picture yourself as a defendant in court, charged with a crime that you have not committed: would you accept as a foregone conclusion that fiction and truth are of equal value, or that fiction is truer than history? Imagine that someone denies the reality of the genocide carried out by the Nazis: would you answer that, whatever is said by those on either side of the question, the debate is unimportant because in any case we never deal with anything other than interpretations? Imagine that you read the following statement spray-painted on the walls of a building, as I did the other day on my way to the Bibliothèque Nationale: "Immigrants are Nazi forces in civilian dress"; would you be content to analyze the structure of the metaphor, or even to make a moral judgment as to the values suggested by this slogan? Would you not ask yourself whether the affirmation is true or false? And if you opt to maintain the distinction in real life, why would you deny its place in theory?

Fine, you will tell me. But then what status do we assign to the "truth" of fictions? Were they mistaken, all these authors of times past, who believed that poetry could speak the truth? Are we mistaken when, hearing

Baudelaire's poetry, reading Balzac's novels, we feel ourselves closer to a human truth? And are we to banish poets, on the grounds that they do not speak the truth?

Perhaps we could answer these new questions by first of all agreeing to a closer scrutiny of the notion of "truth," which seems to be problematic here. We must distinguish between two meanings of the word, at least: truth as correspondence to reality and truth as unveiling, the first measured only in terms of all or nothing, the second in terms of more or less. That X committed a crime is either true or false, whatever the extenuating circumstances; and the same applies to whether or not, yes or no, the Jews were incinerated in the ovens of Auschwitz. However, if the question has to do with the causes of Nazism or with the identity of the average French person in 1987, no such answer is conceivable; the answers can contain truth only to a greater or lesser degree, because they aim to reveal the identity of a phenomenon, not to establish facts. Novelists aspire only to this second type of truth; and they have nothing to teach historians as to the first.

But if this distinction is a necessary point of departure, it is not for all that sufficient. First, if it is true that novelists aspire only to the truth of revelation, historians, for their part (or ethnologists, or sociologists) cannot be content simply to establish unquestionable facts. Historians, in sum, face a dilemma: either they may restrict themselves to the facts, indisputable but in themselves rather uninstructive; or they may seek to interpret them, but then they leave themselves open to criticism; and very few indeed are those who have chosen the first route (nobody is satisfied with knowing the color of Henry IV's horse). But then, how does one pass from the first to the second conception of truth? And if it is a question of two very distinct things, does it make sense to retain the single term "truth," bound to create confusion? If we say that Balzac is *truer* than the historians and the ethnologists, or that he is nobler and more philosophical, are we not bringing into play criteria other than those of truth as correspondence to reality—other and necessarily superior? Criteria that, all things considered, can originate only in a moral position (since knowledge is not what tells me that a given conception of humanity is nobler than another). But if truth is subordinated to morality, if the only truths are pragmatic ones, who will decide what is truer and more philosophical than truth? The philosopher-king? A majority of the citizens? There are obvious drawbacks to these solutions, even if we sometimes tend to forget them. But if we avoid subordinating one type of truth to another, or even connecting them, how do we contain them within a single frame?

Having reached this point in my exploration, I am tempted to change methods. After these indispensable but general preliminaries, I feel the need for a detailed examination of some particular cases, both to test my conclusions and to refine them. I will tell two stories, which will lead us, respectively, toward the East and toward the West; but both, each in its own way, bring alive the interferences between truth and fiction. I will thus have followed one of Stendahl's injunctions, stating his preference for "the somewhat detailed truth" over all the rest.

I

In April of 1704, in London, a work appears (it will be translated into French as soon as August of the same year, published in Amsterdam) under the title *An Historical and Geographical Description of Formosa*.[6] This rather large tome, liberally illustrated with engravings, develops two themes. The first is the one indicated by the title. Formosa (or Taiwan) is at this time but little known, and the author takes the opportunity to acquaint us with its geography, history, and inhabitants. We learn that the island, separated only by a strait from Japan, is politically dominated by the latter: the Japanese took over following a war whose decisive battle was won by means of a portable wooden house, transported by two elephants, and welcomed by the unsuspecting Formosans; it turned out to be full of fierce Japanese warriors. The author also introduces us to the Formosans' language and their (phonetic) system of writing, and shows us pictures of their palaces and houses as well as of the costumes worn by the nobles and the common people (Figures 1 through 3).

But the most sensational details in this description of the customs of the Formosans concern their religious life. Indeed, it so happens that they practice cruel human sacrifices. Two prophets, or pseudo-prophets, converted the country to this barbarous religion, which requires 18,000 children under nine years of age to be sacrificed each year. The accomplishment of these rites does not lack for macabre elements: the sacrificial priests tear out the children's hearts and offer them to the sun; thereupon follows a cannibalistic meal. "The priests pray for the sanctification of the victims. Then their throats are cut, and the blood is poured into a cauldron near the altar; the flesh is divided into small pieces, and boiled in the blood. . . . As soon as the meat is cooked, the men, women, and children over nine years old in turn approach the altar, where after receiving from the priest's hands a piece of this flesh boiled in blood, they kneel on one knee and eat

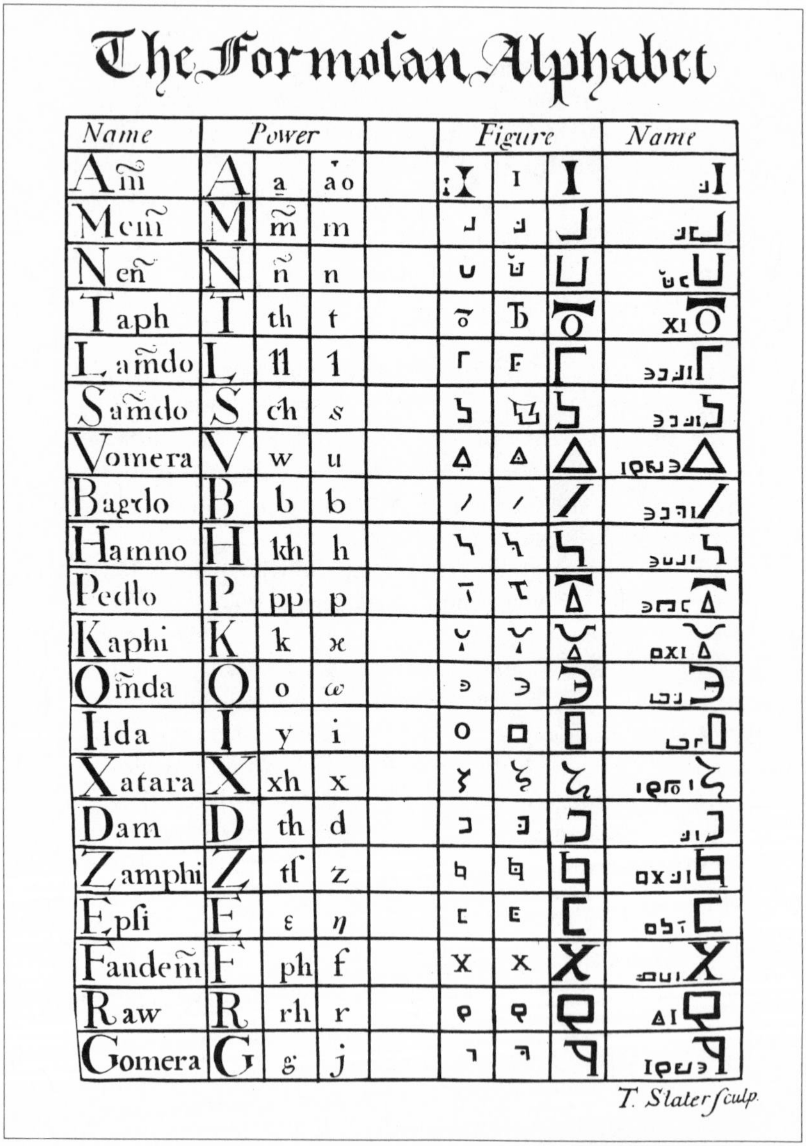

The Formosan Alphabet

Name	Power				Figure			Name
Am̃	A	a	ao		ːχ	I	I	I˩
Mem̃	M	m̃	m		˩	˩	⌐	⌐˩
Nen̆	N	n̆	n		ʋ	ŭ	⊔	⊔̆
Taph	T	th	t		ƌ	Ƌ	⌐	xı̅
Lam̃do	L	11	1		˥	F	˥	˥⅃⌐Ɛ
Sam̃do	S	ch	s		˥	˥	˥	˥⅃ɛƐ
Vomera	V	w	u		△	△	△	ıƠ⋉Ɛ△
Bagdo	B	b	b		⁄	⁄	⁄	Ɛ⅃⌐⁄
Hamno	H	kh	h		˥	˥	˥	Ɛ⊔⅃ı˥
Pedlo	P	pp	p		˥	˥	△	ƆƆ⊏△
Kaphi	K	k	x		˅̇	Ÿ	˅	Ɒxı△
Om̃da	O	o	ω		Ɔ	Ɛ	Ɛ	⌐Ɔ˩
Ilda	I	y	i		o	▢	▯	⌐⌐Ɛ▯
Xatara	X	xh	x		˥	˥	˥	ıƠ៑ı˥
Dam	D	th	d		⊐	Ɉ	⌐	⅃ı⌐
Zamphi	Z	tſ	z		Ꮷ	Ꮷ	⌐	⌐xⅉı⌐
Epſi	E	ε	η		⊏	Ɛ	⌐	Ɒ˥ı⌐
Fandem̃	F	ph	f		x	x	X	⊓Ɒ⌐ıX
Raw	R	rh	r		ϼ	Ϙ	Ϙ	▵ıϘ
Gomera	G	g	j		˥	˥	Ꮆ	ıƠ⋉ƐᎶ

T. Slater ſculp.

Figure 1. The English version of the Formosan alphabet. From George Psalmanazar, *An Historical and Geographical Description of Formosa* (London, 1704), p. 1; reprinted in Frederic J. Foley, *The Great Formosan Impostor* (St. Louis, Mo., 1968), pp. 16–17.

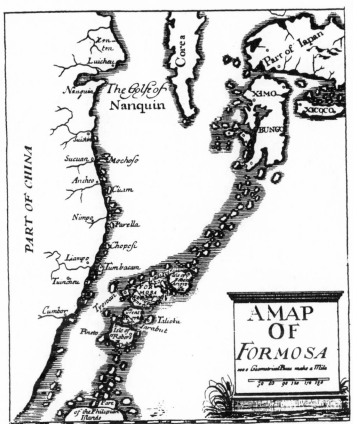

Figure 2. A map of Formosa. From Psalmanazar, *Historical and Geographical Description of Formosa*, p. 1; Foley, *Great Formosan Impostor*, pp. 36–37.

it." The author specifies in a note: "There are two or three priests, each of whom holds a small gold or silver spit, very sharp-tipped and approximately two feet long, on which are skewered a number of these pieces of cooked meat, taken from the cauldron as others are pulled off the spit one after another and distributed to the people."[7]

The second theme, seemingly related to the first only by contiguity, tells the story of the author of the book, George Psalmanazar (some of the *a*'s in his name are doubled in several editions), a native of this island who lived there until the age of nineteen and received instruction from a European tutor. One day the latter decides to return to Europe, and he takes

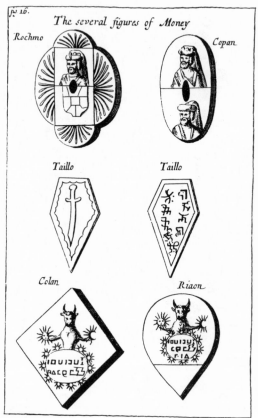

Figure 3. Formosan coins. From Psalmanazar,
Historical and Geographical Description of Formosa,
p. 278; Foley, *Great Formosan Impostor,* pp. 36–37.

his disciple with him; after a long voyage, the two disembark on the southern coast of France, and from there make their way to Avignon. They enter a convent, where the tutor is greeted respectfully by all: the young Psalmanazar discovers that he is among the Jesuits, and that his tutor is one of them. The youth is forced to convert to Catholicism. While he does not scorn Christianity, he hesitates to submit to individuals whose virtue appears so dubious to him; however, he is threatened with the Inquisition. Then one night he manages to escape, and heads north. Once in the Netherlands, he meets the English army and a Scottish chaplain who, to Psalmanazar's great satisfaction, welcomes him into the bosom of the

Reformed Church. From there Psalmanazar goes to London, where the bishop himself receives him and grants him protection; and this is where his book will be written.

The Psalmanazar book elicits a lively response. Translated the very same year into French (with the translation reprinted in 1708, 1712, and 1739), it will be published in Dutch in 1705, and in German in 1716. In London itself, a second edition appears in 1705, and, within the space of one season (but what more can one ask of *la mode?*) he is the talk of the town, the toast of all of London. Everyone wants to hear Psalmanazar recite his incredible story in person; his youth and his eloquence win him universal sympathy.

Not quite universal, to tell the truth. Even before the publication of the book, Psalmanazar's story is known all over London and elicits curiosity in various circles. The Royal Society itself decides to hear him and, in the course of its meeting of February 2, 1704, in the presence of other experts, Psalmanazar is asked to furnish additional details. It is a perfectly ordinary meeting: first the report of Mr. Collins is heard on a person who is able to live without food; another member displays the penis of an opossum and cysts removed from an ovary; a third presents a new type of air pump. Then comes Psalmanazar's turn. His story has already been heard during an earlier meeting, but now his answers to more precise questions are sought, doubt having arisen in the minds of some. One of the questioners is Dr. Halley, famous for his comet, who asks Psalmanazar how long the twilight lasts in Formosa. Hearing the answer, which contradicts astronomical data available elsewhere, he declares Psalmanazar an imposter. Next comes the turn of the French Jesuit Jean de Fontenay, who had traveled to China by order of Louis XIV; he claims that Formosa belongs to China, not to Japan; he cannot understand a word of the Formosan language reported by Psalmanazar, and he has never heard of the human sacrifices.

Psalmanazar, aware of these doubts, decides to tackle them in the preface to his work (at the same time, however, giving them increased notoriety). His counterarguments are of several types. Accounts of other travelers are used against him; but reading these others reveals that they report facts that are even less believable. For example, Candidius, a prominent authority on the subject, maintains that when a woman under the age of 37 becomes pregnant, the priestesses lay her on the ground and jump on her belly, until she has aborted: is it possible to believe such nonsense, and is an author who reports it to be trusted? Besides, as to unbelievable facts, these can be true, anyway. People protest that with 18,000 children sacrificed every year, the population of the island would have trouble replenishing itself; Psalmanazar explains that polygamy exists to compensate for the losses. In any case, we might add, considerations of verisimilitude do not touch the truth: even if Psalmanazar had eliminated or modified the most improbable details of his story, this would not have made it possible to affirm with certainty that he was a native of the island and that the rest of his narrative was truthful.

Another counterargument has an even greater effect. It consists in asking the opponent the question that, not so long ago, saw its hour of glory in France: "From where are you speaking?" Faced with an affirmation, people avoid the question of its truth, or its meaning, in favor of this one: what is the *interest* of the person speaking? To return to the modern parallel: it is known that certain contemporary authors have denied the reality of the Jewish genocide; when their theses have been challenged, they have replied: but those who contradict us are all Jews (or lackeys of imperialism). This argument might have been persuasive if we knew as little about Auschwitz as the English of that time did about Formosa. In the case of Psalmanazar, this party shields him from two adversaries. On the one hand, the free thinkers of Halley's type were attacking, as was well known, the institution of Christianity; that they took Psalmanazar to task was, in the eyes of the faithful majority, proof that his story was *true*: if my enemies attack something, that means it is good. The case of the Jesuits is even more clear-cut, since Psalmanazar's account casts an unfavorable light upon them: their "tolerance" with regard to foreign religions (here the Formosan religion, with all its horrors) borders on indifference to Christianity; their cruelty to the poor Psalmanazar is no less blameworthy. The word of such a biased witness can only be doubted. How could they not wish to destroy the author's credibility, by showing that his description of Formosa was inaccurate? The Jesuits were trying to discredit the anti-Jesuit portion of the work by showing that the Formosan part was false; Psalmanazar, on the other hand, appeals to the anti-Jesuit sentiments of his readers in order to authenticate his exotic descriptions.

The newspapers of the time make hay of the matter. Opinions are divided. On one side, unlikelihoods are pointed out, and the challengers Halley and Fontenay are cited; on the other, support for Psalmanazar from the bishop of London (is he someone who commits himself without cause?) and other respectable figures is recalled. The work corresponds to a familiar genre, the account of distant travels, with its juxtaposition of narrative and description, and at the time such literature is eagerly devoured. The *Histoire des Ouvrages des Savans* reports, in its November 1704 issue, that the author is subjected to extraordinary trials: "In London, someone took it into his head to test Psalmanazar, and to force him to prove what he said of the Formosans by making him eat the flesh of someone who had been hanged [Psalmanazar reports that this is common practice in Formosa, and that the flesh of young women who have undergone prolonged suffering before execution is particularly desirable]. He did so without repugnance; but far from being convinced, his doubters were so horrified that they beat him."[8] Here again, as with Halley, the result is the opposite of what was counted on (unforeseen by effect of the proof). Overall, the doubters are more numerous than the believers, but people do not go so far as to reject the account as a whole, by virtue of the principle at work in slander and rumors: where there's smoke there's fire, as they say; even if this accusation is false, it cannot be totally unfounded.

Then several years pass, and people begin to forget Psalmanazar and his adventures. But the man himself is still alive, and naturally he forgets nothing. The problem is that with age Psalmanazar, who leads a modest life and earns his living as a hack writer, becomes increasingly religious, and the episode of his youth begins to weigh upon him. In 1747 (Psalmanazar was born in 1679: he is therefore 68 years old), he decides to lay bare the facts in an article on Formosa, written (anonymously) for a geographical encyclopedia. The author of the article affirms that Psalmanazar, whom he knew, has authorized him to announce that his account was, for the most part, "fabulous." It will be observed that this destruction of the fiction requires the construction of a new fiction, namely that of the difference between Psalmanazar and the author of the article. The rest of the story will be saved for his *Memoirs*,[9] which Psalmanazar is to finish in 1758, and which will be published in 1764, one year after his death; later historians will also add a number of details.

In his *Memoirs*, Psalmanazar comes clean on many topics, but he continues to conceal others (this despite his increased religious faith); thus he tells us neither his real name nor where he was born. Some people think he comes from Gascony (because he lies?), others that he is a Jew (because of his wandering?); apparently, he bears no resemblance to the Japanese. He speaks all the European languages (not to mention "Formosan") without an accent; his *Description* was originally written in Latin. It appears that during his youth he lived with his mother in the south of France, and that he attended a school run by Jesuits. Later on, his mother sent him to his father, somewhere in Germany; but the father wants nothing to do with him, and the son takes off for the Netherlands. On the way, the future Psalmanazar, penniless, has to eat somehow, so he begs in Latin from clergymen he meets. Then one day, to attract more attention, he decides to present himself as a Japanese convert to Christianity. As he gets a kick out of the role-playing, he invents a grammar, a calendar, and a religion, and takes the name Psalmanazar, which he finds (without the P) in the Bible.

But by the time he arrives in Holland, he is playing another game: he introduces himself as a pagan who worships the sun and the moon, and who might be converted to Christianity in exchange for protection. It is then that he meets the Scottish chaplain who, first of all, sees through the hoax and second, far from denouncing it, decides to exploit it for his own gain. He describes the case to the bishop of London, then "baptizes" Psalmanazar. Straightaway the chaplain is promoted, and the bishop summons Psalmanazar to London. Now he needs only write the book to confirm his story. He then remembers the story of the Jesuit Alexander of Rhodes who, leaving Macao in 1645, brought with him a young Chinese boy, who later became a Jesuit himself. Psalmanazar gives the same name to his imaginary "tutor" and decides to take part in the battle then being waged by the Reformed Church against Catholicism in general and the Jesuits in particular. After all, isn't communion, as practiced by Catholics, a form of cannibalism? Other particulars are culled from his past readings (Ulysses' Trojan horse, human sacrifice among the Aztecs, details borrowed from Candidius).

Today, therefore, we know with certainty that the *Description of Formosa* is a hoax, that Psalmanazar never went to China, and moreover that his name was not Psalmanazar. It is rare for a case to be so clear-cut. Without wishing to insinuate anything in the least, I wonder whether all the descriptions of phonological systems brought back by linguists from their fieldwork, all the rites observed and reported by ethnologists, can be situated with as much certainty on one side or another of the line separating "true witnesses" from "imaginary witnesses." Or, to take another example even closer to home: I wonder whether many of my readers have already heard of Psalmanazar, or whether the present article will send them to the above-mentioned Bibliothèque Nationale, to verify whether Psalmanazar really existed, or whether he was a fictive (*fabulous*) character, like those to whom Borges sometimes likes to refer.

What does the story of Psalmanazar, as I have just told it, teach us about the frontier separating truth and fiction? The description of Formosa possesses neither the truth of correspondence to reality nor the truth of unveiling. And, because it is not *presented* as fiction but as truth, it *is not* fiction, but rather lies and deception. What Edmund Halley and Jean de Fontenay do, with recourse, respectively, to astronomy and to history, is not to produce an "interpretation," a "discourse," to put alongside Psalmanazar's "interpretation" or "discourse"; rather, they speak the truth where he speaks falsehood. It is absolutely essential, if we wish to know Formosa and its inhabitants, to make the distinction between the two. The description of the Jesuits has no truth or correspondence to reality, either, even if it does have relatively more in the way of truth of unveiling: the details making up the portrait of the Jesuits in this story are not cut out of whole cloth. But this truth owes nothing to Psalmanazar: his writing is pure falsehood. He is like Colonel Henry in the Dreyfus affair: in order to prove the latter's guilt, in order to serve what seems to him to be a just cause, the Colonel decides to invent a forgery. Psalmanazar's slander is simply more innocent, since instead of targeting any one person in particular (when he wrote, the real Alexander of Rhodes was long since dead), he attacks an order and an ideology—which we must not rush to defend as good simply because it was the victim of unfair treatment.

As historical writing, Psalmanazar's *Description* does not deserve our respect, because it is false. Nor does it command our admiration as fiction, because it does not present itself as such, and because its author is not exceptionally eloquent. But what if he had been?

II

Today every schoolchild knows that "Columbus discovered America," and yet the proposition is rife with "untruths." Let us first set aside the most obvious of these, contained in the word "discovered": this is legitimate only if it has been decided at the outset that the history of humanity is to be identified with the history of Europe, and therefore that the history of other continents begins when they are visited by Europeans. It would not occur to anyone to celebrate the "discovery" of England by the French, or that of France by the English, for the simple reason that neither of these peoples is considered to be more central than the other. If we abandon the Eurocentric perspective, we can no longer speak of the "discovery" but rather (as does Francis Jennings in his book of this title) of the "invasion of America."[10]

Next, we call to mind that Columbus was not the first navigator to have crossed the Atlantic. Others had preceded him in the north, and perhaps in the south; but their voyages clearly did not have the same consequences: in this respect Columbus's role was exceptional. "Columbus," therefore, is no more justified than "discovery." Finally, and this is the paradox on which I would like to expand, it is after all peculiar that, having chosen Columbus as "discoverer," we have given to the land "discovered" by him the name of *America*, which is that of another navigator who came after Columbus: Amerigo Vespucci. Why America and not Columbia?

There is a simple historical answer to this question: the authors of an influential geographical treatise, the *Cosmographiae Introductio*, published in 1507 in Saint-Dié in the Vosges mountains, deemed that Amerigo's merits warranted giving his name to the newly "discovered" lands.[11] This proposition was gradually adopted, first for what we now call South America, and then (some twenty years later) for "North America"; moreover, Spain and Portugal, at the time the countries with the greatest interest in these lands, did not accept this name until the eighteenth century, preferring up to that time the "West Indies." But this "answer" merely displaces the problem a notch or so: why did the group of learned men in Saint-Dié who put out the *Cosmographiae Introductio* consider Amerigo's contribution more important than that of any other navigator—than that of Columbus in particular?

A first reply to this new question could be that Amerigo was the first to touch *terra firma*. Indeed, we know that in the course of his first two voyages, in 1492–93 and 1493–96, Columbus reaches only the islands of the Gulf of Mexico. He lands on the continent in the course of his third voyage, in 1498. Now, Amerigo is supposed to have reached these same continental lands during his own first voyage, in 1497. But this argument does not hold water, for a number of reasons. First, it is not even certain that Amerigo made the voyage in question: it happens that his own account, which is moreover confined to a single letter, is the only source affirming that he did. We cannot prove that the voyage did not take place, but neither are we able to assert that it did with any certainty. Second, even if the account is true, Amerigo was not the captain, and credit is traditionally given to the leader of the expedition. Third, if we suppose that Amerigo did sail in 1497, he would not have been the first to reach the continent: before Columbus, before Vespucci, there was John Cabot (Giovanni Caboto), a Venetian navigator in the service of England, who arrives there (close to Newfoundland) also in 1497. Fourth, we must keep in mind what the navigators thought they had done, not just what we know today that they did. Now, nothing proves that in 1497 either Cabot or Vespucci thought he had been on the continent; as for Columbus, he thought he had been there as of 1494, since he would not accept that Cuba could be only an island! Fifth, and last—and this is clearly the most important reason—precedence of voyage is not what motivated the decision of the group in Saint-Dié. For the same reason, considerations based on the analysis of maps are not pertinent. A map of 1500, prepared by Juan de la Cosa, shows Cuba as separate from America; it is thought that this map was drawn on the basis of information furnished by Amerigo and acquired in the course of the voyage of 1497. But the authors of Saint-Dié refer to Amerigo's writings, not to maps.

Thus a second answer urges itself upon us, and it is the one given by all recent historians of the question (the latest being Edmundo O'Gorman).[12] Amerigo's merit lies in having been the first, not to tread upon American soil, but to realize he had done so: the discovery is an intellectual rather than a physical one. Amerigo's discovery must be dated not 1497, the year of an unconfirmed voyage, but rather 1503, the year his letter, with the deeply significant title *Mundus Novus*, was published,[13] and 1506–7, marking the publication of Italian and Latin versions (the latter in the *Cosmographiae Introductio*) of his other famous letter, called *Quatuor Navigationes*.[14] Indeed, the first affirms and the second confirms Amerigo's *awareness* of having reached an unknown continent—whereas Columbus believed he had touched Asia by the "western route." It matters little, in the end, from this perspective, whether or not Amerigo made the voyage; the main thing is that he *understood*; this he could have done while remaining in his study (assuming he had one). This intellectual discovery, then, is what was celebrated by the intellectuals gathered in the *Gymnasium* at Saint-Dié.

This answer is certainly much closer to the truth than the first one. And yet it sparks some objections of its own; on the question of the intellectual discovery, again, Amerigo is faced with some serious competition. The first is precisely a man who, having never traveled, was content merely to write: he was Peter Martyr, a Spanish courtier who writes "open" letters to important foreign figures in which he summarizes the news of expeditions as fast as such news reaches him in Madrid. In a letter dated November 13, 1493, and addressed to Cardinal Sforza, he presents Columbus's voyage in a manner that differs perceptibly from what we find in the latter's own accounts: Peter Martyr says that Colum-

bus "discovered this unknown land" and that he "found all the signs of a
previously unknown continent." [15] One year later, in his letter of October
20, 1494, to Borromeo, he even uses the expression *orbe novo*, "new
world," which was to serve as the title for the published collection of his
letters (1530), and which we also encounter in Amerigo. These letters of
Peter Martyr are not private letters; they even constitute the principal
source from which educated Europeans of the time derive their information on the extraordinary voyages undertaken by the Spanish and the
Portuguese.

Amerigo's second rival, again in the intellectual sphere, is none other
than Columbus himself. The 1498 voyage, in the course of which Columbus reaches the American coast, results in a report, addressed by him to
the King and Queen of Spain, in which Columbus clearly states his belief
that he has touched *terra firma* which, this time, is not Asia (he knows
that Asia is in the northern hemisphere, whereas he is heading south): it
is, he writes, "a land stretching infinitely toward the south, one that was
formerly completely unknown." [16] Amerigo will say the same.

But if Peter Martyr and Columbus had written these lines (the scholars of Saint-Dié must have known of the former and may have heard of
the latter), why did these men nevertheless choose to honor Amerigo
rather than one or another of his rivals? Since we are unable to enter into
the minds of these figures of the past and we have to go on extant texts,
we can find only one answer to this question: it is because the accounts in
which Amerigo is the principal character are *better written* than the letters
of Columbus (and, in another way, than those of Peter Martyr). What the
new christening of the continent celebrates is not the intellectual discovery, but—whether its godfathers knew it or not—a superior literary
achievement. Amerigo's glory is due to the forty-odd little pages making
up the two letters published in his lifetime.

In order to establish this literary quality, it would be useful to compare
two letters of approximately the same length: the one written by Columbus to Santangelo in 1493, and the one sent by Amerigo to Lorenzo de
Medici (not the same as Lorenzo the Magnificent) in 1503, known by the
title *Mundus Novus*; these are in fact the two most popular works of the
period, those that were the most frequently reprinted (Amerigo's more
than Columbus's); their comparison, implicit or explicit, is what motivated the decision of the learned men of Saint-Dié.

Let us first observe the general composition of the letters. Columbus's
gives no evidence of a concerted plan. He describes his voyage, then the
natural history of the islands (Haiti and Cuba), next sketching a portrait

of the inhabitants. He then returns to geography, adding additional re-marks upon the "Indians." He goes on to discuss "monsters," and con-cludes first by assuring the King and Queen that these lands are without a doubt very rich, and then by thanking God for having enabled him to make these discoveries.

Amerigo's letter, in contrast, reveals someone who has received a fair amount of rhetorical instruction. It begins and ends with several para-graphs summarizing the main points; here, and we will return to this, is where we find the staggering assertion that this is a new world. Within this frame, the text is clearly divided into two parts: the first one describes the voyage (with a digression on Amerigo's excellent skills as a pilot); the second part describes the new lands, with three subsections—announced in advance, at the end of the first part—concerning the people, the land, and the sky. Amerigo's letter has a quasi-geometrical *form* that is absent from Columbus's and which cannot but seduce the reader.

The reader, in fact, holds the place of honor with Amerigo. Colum-bus's letter shows no such concern for the reader. It must be said that the positions of the two narrator-navigators differ radically. Whether he is writing to Santangelo, a high official and shipowner, or to other public figures, Columbus is in fact always, first and foremost, addressing the King and Queen of Spain, Ferdinand and Isabella, whom he wishes to convince of the wealth of the discovered lands and of the necessity of underwriting new expeditions (first toward America and later toward Jerusalem); these then are utilitarian missives, bread-and-butter letters. Nothing of the kind may be said of Amerigo's letters. Voyaging in search of glory, not of money, he writes for the same reason ("the glory of God" and "the honor of my old age" [307]). Amerigo's letters aim, above all, to dazzle his friends in Florence, to distract them and enchant them: he has *Mundus Novus* translated into Latin so that the educated public of all Europe "may know how many wonderful things are daily being discovered" (307). In *Quatuor Navigationes*, written in the guise of a letter to Soderini, another Floren-tine notable, Amerigo again emphasizes the point: he is certain that his addressee will take pleasure in reading what he has to say, and he con-cludes his preamble with a formula that, however conventional, is none-theless significant: "although Your Magnificence is constantly busied with affairs of state, you must occasionally . . . devote a little time to pleasant and agreeable things, and just as it is customary to give fennel after deli-cious viands to fit them for . . . digestion, so may you by way of relief from your numerous occupations order [this my letter] to be read" (308). Co-lumbus writes documents; Amerigo writes literature.

Not only is Amerigo writing to a man whom he hopes to amuse, rather than to push to finance new expeditions; additionally, he thinks he will have other readers, and within his letter he pays heed to them as well. Whence, from the outset, the clarity of his plan and the summaries at beginning and end: this concern for clarity and preoccupation with the comprehension of these other readers are essential. Thus, when he embarks upon matters of cosmography in which his reader may not be versed, he redoubles his explanations with the justification "that you may the more clearly understand" (306), and he even adds a little diagram (Figure 4). Columbus does no such thing. In *Quatuor Navigationes*, Amerigo, as an experienced narrator, attends to the reader's interest, and not only to his comprehension, by enticing him with promises of what is to follow: "Your Magnificence . . . on each of my voyages I have noted down the most marvellous things" (319). He had already done likewise in *Mundus Novus*: "these things I shall relate in order" (302).

The future reader is also flattered in another way: Amerigo allows a certain distance to come between the narrator that he is and the character that he was; he invites the reader to slip into the space thus created, even

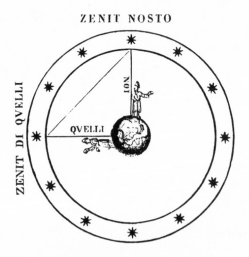

Figure 4. Explanatory diagram drawn by Amerigo Vespucci; reprinted in Amerigo Vespucci, *El Nuevo Mundo*, ed. Roberto Levillier (Buenos Aires: Nova, 1951), p. 192.

offering him the possibility of feeling somewhat superior to the explorers. Rather than describe the sufferings they endured during the crossing, he suggests them by paraleipsis, with this justification: "this I leave to the judgment of those who out of rich experience have well learned what it is to seek the uncertain and to attempt discoveries even though ignorant" (300). Likewise, in *Quatuor Navigationes*, when he must explain his own decisions he appeals to experiences the reader may have in common with him: "So when I had come to know the constant toil which man expends in gaining . . . , subjecting himself to so many discomforts and perils, I resolved to give up trade" (309). Columbus, in contrast, produces only one image: that of himself.

In the choice of subjects treated Amerigo again manifests considerable concern for the reader. The observed (or imaginary) facts, however, do not differ much from Columbus to Amerigo. Columbus describes the Indians as naked, fearful, generous, lacking in religion, and sometimes cannibalistic. Amerigo, starting with the same raw materials, will deploy them in three different directions. Combining the elements of nakedness, lack of religion, nonaggressiveness, and indifference to property, and associating them with classical representations of the Golden Age, he will produce the modern image of the noble savage.

The second direction is that of cannibalism. Columbus, although understanding nothing of the Indian languages, reported cannibalism as hearsay; Amerigo, in contrast, expands upon it in lengthy discussions: the Indians take prisoners of war in order to consume them later on; the male willingly eats his wife and children; he, Amerigo, spoke to a man who admitted he had eaten more than three hundred of his neighbors; and in the course of a walk among the Indians, he saw salted human flesh, hanging from the beams, just like our salt pork. Amerigo thus recounts these juicy (if I may say so) details, before he reveals to us the Indians' point of view: they do not understand the Europeans' disgust before such succulent victuals. There is no question but that this theme was judiciously chosen: we need only see how frequently it occurs in the illustrations of the period or in later accounts (through Psalmanazar and beyond).

Finally, the third direction is that of sexuality. Columbus limited himself to the following observation on this subject: "Throughout these islands, it seems that the men have only one wife" (185). Amerigo's approach goes to the other extreme: on this topic his imagination runs wild. The Indian women are extremely lustful, he repeats, and he entertains his readers (European males) with the following details: the women make poisonous animals bite their partners' penises; the penis swells to incredible proportions, so that it finally explodes and the men become eunuchs (one can imagine the shock and the relief experienced by the reader). In the most recent French translation of *Mundus Novus*, dating from 1855, this passage was omitted and, in its place, we read this note: "Here follow ten or twelve lines on the behavior of the women. This passage, which we have no choice but to omit, is perhaps not among those least responsible for the popularity of the name of Amerigo Vespucci."[17] A new bonus for the European reader comes to light shortly afterwards: he learns how well European voyagers were received by Indian women—not, one would think, by submitting to the same risky treatment. "When they had the opportunity of copulating with Christians, urged by excessive lust, they defiled and prostituted themselves" (303). And again Amerigo asserts that he is not telling all: "of which in the interest of modesty, I make no mention" (303); or in *Quatuor Navigationes*: "I refrain out of decency from telling you the trick which they play to satisfy their immoderate lust" (312). This is a familiar procedure for enlisting the reader's imagination.

These parts of the *Mundus Novus* appeal to a general readership (all of whom, to reiterate, were male and European). Other parts must flatter the pride of the most cultured among them, the most learned, and at the same time allow all the rest to feel as if they belonged to the cultural elite. In *Quatuor Navigationes*, Amerigo cites classical and modern authors, Pliny, Dante, Petrarch; in *Mundus Novus*, after describing the noble savages, he concludes casually: "They . . . may be called Epicureans rather than Stoics" (303); elsewhere, he does not fail to allude to writings of the philosophers. Another passage, in the first part of the letter, is quite significant: Amerigo complains that the pilot of the ship was incompetent and that without Amerigo, no one would have known what distance had been covered; he is the only one on board who knows how to read the stars, and to use the quadrant and the astrolabe. And Amerigo adds: "For this reason they subsequently made me the object of great honor; although a man without practical experience, yet through the teaching of the marine chart for navigators, I was more skilled than all the shipmasters of the world. For these have no knowledge except of those waters to which they often sail" (301). How could this boastful description of the superiority of intellectuals and theoreticians over practicing sailors not go straight to the heart of the cartographer Martin Waldseemüller, or of the poet Mathias Ringmann, who had never ventured far from their home in Saint-Dié? How could these two not conceive a feeling of gratitude toward Amerigo, or not seek to thank him? In return, they offered him a continent. It is no accident that engravings of the time have transmitted an image of Amerigo as a scholar himself (Figures 5 and 6).

Lastly, apart from all the pains Amerigo took on behalf of his reader, the latter found himself, in these writings, immediately situated in a universe that was close to him. As we have seen, the allusions are to Italian poets, classical philosophers—but very seldom to Christian sources. Columbus, on the other hand, has in mind only Christian texts and the marvelous tales of Marco Polo or of Cardinal Pierre d'Ailly. Columbus is a man of the Middle Ages, while Amerigo belongs to the Renaissance. Another clue is to be found in certain rudiments of cultural relativism that are present in Amerigo: he transcribes what he knows of the Indians' perceptions of Europeans (and not only his own perception of the others). Avid readers of these bulletins were also participants in the modern world. We have seen that Amerigo's world was prosaically divided into men, land, and sky (stars). Columbus's world, however, while it contains the rubrics "men" and "nature," also contains another: monsters. Columbus clearly

Figure 5. Portrait of Amerigo Vespucci from Martin Waldseemüller's map (1507); reprinted in Ernst Lehner and Johanna Lehner, *How They Saw the New World* (New York, 1966), p. 15.

Figure 6. Allegorical representation of Amerigo Vespucci encountering America, engraved by Jean Van Stracten (Florence, late 16th c.); reprinted in Lehner and Lehner, *How They Saw the New World*, p. 158.

has a list of monsters in his head, and mentally checks off their presence or absence: Amazons, yes; two-headed men, no; men with tails, yes; with dog's heads, no; and so forth. Compared to this, Amerigo's world is strictly human. If he too is given to mentioning the monstrous, it is as a curiosity: the word appears, for example, when he describes the ornamental wear of the Indians, who pierce their cheeks or lips and set stones in the holes. The only improbabilities, in Amerigo, are exaggerations; they point to the bad faith of the carnival barker rather than to the believer's naiveté: the Indians live to the age of one hundred and fifty, he says here, and in *Quatuor Navigationes* he reports a tribe whose women are as tall as European men, with the men taller still. A look at the ways in which Columbus and Amerigo mention the earthly paradise is enough to measure the distance between them: Columbus believed in it literally, and thinks he has discovered it (in South America); Amerigo merely uses it as a hyperbole (enlivened, perhaps, by Columbus's ecstatic descriptions), and uses it to crown a perfectly conventional description of nature over there: "And surely if the terrestrial paradise be in any part of this world, I esteem that it is not distant from these parts" (304).

Quatuor Navigationes confirms the literary qualities exemplified in *Mundus Novus*. Here again, the general plan is dictated solely by a concern for the reader. To each of his four voyages, Amerigo devotes a decreasing number of pages: not because each voyage is shorter than the preceding one (such is not the case), but because the reader has fewer and fewer things to learn. The description of the Indians, rather similar to the one in *Mundus Novus* (which related the third voyage), now appears in the first: this place is dictated not by the chronology of the voyage, but by that of the reading experience. The adventure episodes alternate regularly with peaceful descriptions. Here, moreover, Amerigo develops the art of the narrative vignette, absent from the *Mundus Novus*: a brief episode containing bizarre revelations or unexpected reversals. Thus, on the one hand, suggestive descriptions of the iguana (a wingless dragon!), of hammocks (nets hung in the air), of pearls growing, of vegetative Indians who do without water; and on the other hand, episodes all built on an identical scheme: the Europeans think themselves stronger, particularly with respect to women, but to their great humiliation they suffer defeat. Thus the episode of the giants during the second voyage: Amerigo and his companions are preparing to capture 3 tall girls, when 36 fearsome brawny types enter the hut; the Europeans prudently beat a retreat. Or again, in the course of the third voyage: seeing only women on the shore, the Europeans send a handsome boy to seduce and subdue them. But while some of them make doe eyes at him, another comes up behind with a heavy club, and knocks him out. The women then seize the body and fix it on a large spit to cook it to perfection. The Christians, terrified, take in the scene from afar.

We can now better understand the reason for Amerigo's extraordinary success, which was evident not only in numerous reprintings and the honor granted by the scholars of Saint-Dié, but also in the fact that these are the most liberally illustrated texts of the period. Columbus's letter is accompanied by purely conventional engravings, showing castles and people similar to those in Europe. The first images that attempt to capture what is specifically American are those illustrating Amerigo's narratives, for the latter lend themselves well to vivid renderings of local color. Hence the roasted Christian (on the Kunstmann II map); the same, just prior to being stunned; the Indians urinating in front of each other (another detail revealed—or invented?—by Amerigo) shown in Figures 7 and 8. One of the oldest and most interesting engravings, which dates from 1505, condenses, in its image and the accompanying legend, the whole of *Mundus*

Figure 7. Cannibal preparing one of Amerigo Vespucci's men for a meal, from the Kunstmann II map (1502) in the Bayerische Staatsbibliothek, Munich; reprinted in Fred Chiapelli, ed., *First Images of America: The Impact of the New World on the Old* (Berkeley: 1976), vol. 2, p. 644.

Figure 8. Woodcuts illustrating an early German edition of Amerigo Vespucci's *Quatuor Navigationes* (Strasburg: Johannes Gruninger, 1509); reprinted in J. H. Parry, *The Discovery of South America* (New York, 1979), p. 10.

Figure 9. The "Munich" woodcut from Amerigo Vespucci's *Mundus Novus* (Munich, 1505 or 1506) in the Bayerische Staatsbibliothek, Munich; reprinted in Chiapelli, *First Images of America*, vol. 2, p. 655.

Novus, showing plainly what struck readers' imaginations most of all: the Indians are naked, wearing only feathers; they are practicing sexual freedom and incest, and eating each other; they have no sense of private property, live to the age of one hundred and fifty, and have no laws (Figure 9).

These are the elements that explain Amerigo's success and the sympathy he elicits from the learned men of Saint-Dié. We do not know exactly who is the author of the lines proposing that the new lands be named "America": Waldseemüller is the cartographer, but the text could well have been written by Ringmann. This Ringmann, then 25 years old, is precisely a "humanist" and a poet; how could he not have sensed in Amerigo a kindred spirit, whose glory he would be only too happy to sing! Especially since Amerigo can hardly be said to suffer from an excess of modesty: "as my last voyage showed," "I have found a continent" (299)—these are his own expressions. He justifies his conclusions thus: "We knew that land to be a continent and not an island both because it stretches forth in the form of a very long and unbending coast, and because it is replete with infinite inhabitants" (300). Above all, Amerigo knows how to exploit one thing as neither Peter Martyr nor Columbus could do: the entire first page of his letter is devoted to proclaiming the newness of his discovery (with respect, it is true, not to Columbus, but to the classical authors); the continent in question is comparable to Europe, Asia, and Africa. The title of the letter is itself a stroke of genius. What a contrast to Columbus, whose previously cited sentence about the new continent was noticeable only to the most attentive eye, lost as it was in a dogmatic discourse on the Earthly Paradise, a hypothesis that is much closer to Columbus's heart than is the existence of "America." The latter, to be sure, is formulated only as a backup, should the first one prove a failure. "If this river does not flow out of the Earthly Paradise," writes Columbus, but he hastens to add: "However, I firmly believe, in my heart of hearts, that the place of which I speak is the Earthly Paradise" (237).

If we consider as established that the decision made by Waldseemüller and Ringmann is motivated, perhaps unconsciously, by the literary qualities of Amerigo's writings, a new question arises: Is this aesthetic justice actually supported by a historical justice? In other words: Does Amerigo's role, such as it emerges out of his own writings, correspond to the role really played by the character? Does the name of the continent glorify fiction or truth? All the arguments I have just enumerated in Amerigo's favor could indeed apply equally well to a completely false text, like Psalmanazar's—if the latter had lived at another time, and if he had had Amerigo's literary talent.

This leads us to the controversial issue of the authenticity of the letters. This term may be interpreted in two senses: who is the true author of the letters, and do these letters tell the truth? The two senses are autonomous, although interdependent: the letters may be the work of Amerigo, and yet be purely fictional; conversely, they may be improperly attributed to Amerigo, and nevertheless tell the truth; or they may be neither one nor the other, or else both at once. Experts on Vespucci have paid the most attention to the first question. *Mundus Novus* and *Quatuor Navigationes* were the only letters published during the author's lifetime, but since then others have been found, two of which are particularly interesting, since they relate to the American voyages: the first, dated July 18, 1500, to the same Lorenzo de Medici, concerns the second voyage; the other, from 1502, again to the same addressee, relates to the third voyage (these letters were published in 1745 and 1789, respectively).[18] Now, until fairly recently, these other letters were considered to be apocryphal, and the published letters were thought to be the only authentic ones. One of the reasons put forth to justify this decision was the difference in style between the published letters and those that remained in manuscript form. Another reason stems from the internal contradictions of the manuscript letters, or the implausibilities that they contain.

Then in 1926 an Italian scholar, Alberto Magnaghi, reversed the situation dramatically.[19] The evidence of discrepancies between the manuscript letters and the published letters led him to draw the opposite conclusion: namely, that only the manuscript letters are authentic, whereas *Mundus Novus* and *Quatuor Navigationes* are forgeries. The latter two in any case contain as many internal contradictions and improbable elements as the manuscript letters. Moreover, the falsification of the published letters is easily explained as the work of Florentine men of letters who used Amerigo's real missives, whether preserved or lost, to produce amusing and instructive literature. (It is much more plausible that a publication was falsified than that a letter was forged only to be buried in archives and not found until 250 years later!) The true authors of the letters, according to this hypothesis, would be professional writers who might never have left their city. Thus these letters would have been written not only *for* readers, but also *by* readers.

Magnaghi's conclusions were vehemently contested by a strong new partisan of Vespucci, Roberto Levillier, who lost no time in declaring that all the letters attributed to the explorer are authentic.[20] In truth, we need not get bogged down in the details of these issues, as they have mostly to do with the question of the true author, whereas what most concerns us is the truthfulness of the letters; nevertheless, some of the arguments remain pertinent to both controversies. But let us return to the matter at hand, and ask ourselves: what can our reading of the letters tell us about their truthfulness?

We have already seen that *Mundus Novus* and *Quatuor Navigationes* recount a certain number of impossibilities (longevity, giants); these will not lead us to conclude that the letters are inauthentic if we recall that Columbus's letters, which are indisputably authentic, contain as many and more such elements. The explorers observe the unfamiliar world, naturally, but they also project their own prejudices and fantasies. It is equally true that *Mundus Novus* contains internal contradictions; but these can be attributed to the Latin translator, or even to the copyists (since the original Italian text was lost, and no manuscript of it survives).

But a comparison of the letters leads to more disturbing conclusions. *Quatuor Navigationes* contains the accounts of four voyages; *Mundus Novus*, that of the third; we may thus compare two versions of the same voyage. The differences turn out to be significant. If we are to believe

Quatuor Navigationes, it was during the third voyage that Amerigo's companion was bludgeoned and consumed, before the horrified eyes of other Christians. But *Mundus Novus*, written earlier and thus closer to the time of the voyage itself, expounds at length on cannibalism, but reports no such episode. This silence is difficult to explain. More generally, this third voyage is, according to *Quatuor Navigationes*, particularly lacking in contacts (apart from those necessary to obtain food), whereas in *Mundus Novus* the explorers' relations with the Indians are described as "brotherly" (301), and Amerigo states that he stayed among the cannibals for 27 days. If we follow *Quatuor Navigationes*, it is difficult to see when this stay could have taken place. The whole richly drawn portrait of the Indians in *Mundus Novus* appears impossible to conceive on the basis of the third voyage as this voyage is reported in the *Quatuor Navigationes*. However, the latter does situate a long "ethnographic" stay during the first voyage, the account of which contains a description of the Indians that parallels the description in *Mundus Novus*.

We often get the impression that certain details "drift" easily from one voyage to another. For example, according to *Quatuor Navigationes*, the Indians expressed astonishment to Amerigo during the first voyage: "they wondered when they heard us say that we did not eat our enemies" (315); but according to *Mundus Novus*, the Indians spoke these words in the course of the third voyage: "They themselves wonder why we do not eat our enemies" (303). The realization that the newly found land was a continent is placed by *Mundus Novus* at the time of the third voyage; *Quatuor Navigationes* situates it during the first. According to *Quatuor Navigationes*, only the first voyage ends with the capture of slaves: 250, to be precise, of whom 222 survived the crossing to Spain; while the letter of 1500, describing the second voyage, reports that this one ends with slaves being taken: 232 at the outset, with 200 surviving. The figures are strikingly close.

The comparison of *Mundus Novus* with the letter of 1502—both of them relating the third voyage—is equally troubling. First, both are addressed to one and the same Lorenzo de Medici; as they are close both in content and in date of composition, it is difficult to see why the second letter was deemed necessary (especially as Lorenzo had died in the meantime—although Amerigo might not have been aware of this). In many respects, *Mundus Novus* resembles not a new letter to the same figure but a new version of the same *work*, correcting and rearranging the previous version. In 1502, Amerigo reports that an Indian he knew had eaten "over two hundred" human beings (292); in 1503, the figure has become "more than three hundred" (303). In 1502, the aged Indian man is 132 years old; in 1503, 150 years has become the average age of the Indians. In 1502, the human meat hung from the beams was smoked (292); in 1503, it is salted (303).

The literary analysis of *Mundus Novus* does not argue in favor of its veracity. Here the description of nature is purely conventional: "there are there many sorts of wild animals, and especially lions and bears and innumerable serpents and other horrid and ugly beasts. . . . The land in those parts is very fertile and pleasing, abounding in numerous hills and mountains, boundless valleys and mighty rivers, and filled with broad, dense and wellnigh impenetrable forests full of every sort of wild animal" (304). One can write such a description at leisure without even leaving one's library in Florence (the same could not be said of Columbus's descriptions of nature). The cosmographic section of *Mundus Novus* is meager and functions rather as a message from the narrator: See how knowledgeable I am (and at the same time: I presume that you, my reader, are as well). The descriptions of the people add nothing essential to the elements contained in Columbus's letter, ten years earlier, even if they are more felicitously phrased in the later text. The narrative of the voyage itself includes no memorable episodes (with the slight exception of the floundering pilots—simple technicians that they are). Not a single proper name is to be found in it. Nothing, in *Mundus Novus*, serves to indicate that it reports the truth; everything, including the harmonious form of the whole, pleads in favor of fiction (which Amerigo himself might or might not have authored).

Such is not the case with *Quatuor Navigationes*, where the abundance of particular anecdotes can be interpreted as the index of a real experience; but it is, one senses, a highly retouched account. How many voyages were there really—two or four? One supposition is that Vespucci (or his "editors") doubled each of the voyages, so he would receive credit for four—as many as Columbus. Just when did he become aware of the newness of his discovery? Moreover, aren't the episodes also rearranged in this order to produce the best response in the reader, rather than because events really took place that way? Only one thing is certain: we cannot consider this narrative to be either pure fiction or a document absolutely worthy of our trust; it is a patchwork of true and false.

What conclusions are to be drawn from this admission? Is Amerigo's glory undeserved? Are we to rejoice in or to mourn this triumph of fiction? We know that posterity has rendered varying judgments. The superlative opinion of the scholars of Saint-Dié was for a large part shared in the sixteenth century. But as early as the middle of that same century, Las Casas, in his *Historia de las Indias* (unpublished until 1875), opens fire on Vespucci, at the same time praising the merits of Columbus.[21] Las Casas will be followed, at the beginning of the seventeenth century, by the influential Herrera, then, in the nineteenth, by scholars such as Navarrete and Markham, or by Washington Irving.[22] No doubt the most severe pronouncement belongs to Emerson: "Strange, that the new world should have no better luck—that broad America must wear the name of a thief. Amerigo Vespucci, the pickle dealer at Seville, who went out, in 1499, a subaltern with Hojeda, and whose highest naval rank was boatswain's mate in an expedition that never sailed, managed in this lying world to supplant Columbus, and baptize half the earth with his own dishonest name."[23] But, in the middle of the nineteenth century, the opposite opinion begins to gain ground, from Alexander von Humboldt and Varnhagen, through Harrisse and Vignaud, to Levillier and O'Gorman, all of whom recognize Vespucci's eminent role in the discovery and identification of America.[24]

My own judgment on the matter may well leave both sides disappointed (if it is permissible to picture them all living simultaneously and hearing my arguments). Amerigo's voyages seem rather shaky to me, and his description of them hardly reliable. Certainly it contains some true elements; but we will never know which ones. Amerigo is, for me, on the side of fiction, not of truth; the historian must prefer true witnesses to imaginary witnesses. But, on the other hand, I find Amerigo's writings incontrovertibly superior to those of his contemporaries; the insufficient correspondence to reality is balanced by the greater truth of unveiling: not of the American reality, it is true, but of the European imagination. His merit is great—but not where it is usually sought. Far from bemoaning, as does Emerson, the fact that Amerigo was only a tale-spinner, I rejoice to see that half the world bears a writer's name rather than that of some mundane *conquistador*, or adventurer, or slave trader (even if this one exception doesn't change the rule). Certainly, the truth of poets is not identical to that of historians; but it does not therefore follow that poets are liars and must be banished from the city—quite the contrary.

We are not certain that Amerigo was the author of his letters, nor that he wrote them as we can read them today; but there is no doubt that he is their narrator-persona, and it is as such that he must be honored. He reminds me not so much of Columbus or of Cabot but rather of Sinbad and

Ulysses, two other protagonists of marvelous adventures—better ones than his, perhaps; and it must not be mere coincidence that what was chosen for the name of a continent was not his family name (Vespucci) but his first name (Amerigo), not like Columbus but like Sinbad: for a character, a first name is enough. In this Amerigo presents a contrast to Peter Martyr, an author and nothing more. Like Sinbad too, Amerigo vows in the course of each odyssey never to undertake such sufferings again; but hardly has he returned home when he again throws himself into new discoveries: "resting from the numerous hardships that I had suffered in my two voyages and desirous of returning to the land of pearls, it was then that fortune, not content with my sufferings, brought it about . . ." (329). Like Odysseus, whose fabrications were invariably preceded by a formula such as "I am going to answer truthfully," Amerigo declares, at the beginning of his narrative (to Soderini), that what leads him to take up his pen is "the confidence in the truth of my writing" (308). Far from wishing to debaptize America, I would propose rather that Southern Asia be called Sinbadia, and the Mediterranean, Odyssea. If I have any regrets, it is that Amerigo was not satisfied with this role of half-imaginary persona, but wanted to pass himself off as an author altogether of the real: outside the confines of the book, fabrications become lies.

Translated by Jennifer Curtiss Gage

The Private Life of a Public Form:
Freud, Fantasy, and the Novel

MICHAEL H. LEVENSON

LET ME BEGIN BY PLACING IAN WATT in his position of sociological dignity, and let me place myself at an oblique psychoanalytic remove. Then let me define the large goal of this essay as an effort to traverse the ground between these distant points. That the intimacy of private imagining has its own social logic; that the most secret desires discover a path to public expression; that fantasy can inadvertently convert itself to art: these perceptions may begin to secure the link between a sociological and a psychoanalytic construal of the rising novel. *David Copperfield* will stand here as a specimen of the novel risen, risen in history, risen in fantasy, standing almost precisely between *Robinson Crusoe* and us, representing a way to understand certain psychoanalytic claims and a way to reformulate them.

The chapter on "Private Experience and the Novel" in *The Rise of the Novel* epitomizes the graceful movement from intellectual history to sociological detail to literary interpretation that has been Watt's signature. The burden of the chapter is to establish the historical conditions of private experience and their formal manifestation in the emerging novel, with the result that the changing physical contours of London, the rise of the sub-urb, the fragmentation of social roles, the rise of familiar letter-writing, meet in a broad explanatory account of Richardson's new novelistic psychology. The inner life appears in effect as a space opened when organic community loses its coherence, as a dark hole created when the old urban forms collapse, letting us see that the Richardsonian novel, revolutionary though it undoubtedly was, also appears as a deep crevice discovered amid ruins.

Another pattern of emphasis in the argument, however, leads to questions not about the causes of privacy but about its imaginative effects, in particular the opportunities for psychic investment offered to author and readers. Watt connects Richardson's dislike of the city to his fondness for the familiar letter, and then remarks, "The pen alone offered him the possibility of satisfying his deepest psychological needs, needs which were otherwise mutually exclusive: withdrawal from society, and emotional release."[1] As for his readers, they "found in his novels the same complete engrossment of their inner feelings, and the same welcome withdrawal into an imaginary world."[2] The anonymity of print releases the intimate fantasies of author and audience; the fact that we are generally alone when we read novels becomes an invitation to the idleness of daydream; and thus the moral reach of the new form is shadowed by the opportunities for imaginative regression.

Although Freud makes no appearance in this chapter, the opening to psychoanalysis is plain. Watt does not choose to walk through it—and why should he, when the father of psychoanalysis so often refused to walk in the other direction? Of the life of the imagination, Freud wrote in *Civilization and Its Discontents* that

at the time when the development of the sense of reality took place, this region was expressly exempted from the demands of reality-testing and was set apart for the purpose of fulfilling wishes which were difficult to carry out. At the head of these satisfactions through phantasy stands the enjoyment of works of art. Nevertheless, the mild narcosis induced in us by art can do no more than bring about a transient withdrawal from the pressure of real needs, and it is not strong enough to make us forget real misery.[3]

In this and similar passages Freud not only refuses to let art participate in the struggle to test reality; he segregates the imagination in a self-enclosed region where the wish need never meet the obdurate stuff of the world. But what Freud thought he believed about art, imagination, and fantasy is one thing, and what his theories suggest is another and better thing. The movement of the present essay is to recover a coherent line of inquiry which underlies the official psychoanalytic position, and which shows fantasy stumbling, in spite of itself, into the heart of the real.

I

Through the long course of the essay "The Uncanny" Freud accumulates diverse examples of the phenomenon—such as the thought of losing one's eyes or seeing one's double or witnessing the reanimation of the dead—only to bring these under a psychological principle of great

generality: "the 'uncanny' is that class of the frightening which leads back
to what is known of old and long familiar."[4] In generating his instances,
Freud draws indiscriminately on personal reminiscence, folk psychology,
myth, and literature, and not until the last stage of his argument does he
avail himself of any distinction between life and art. He does so by way of
acknowledging an apparent difficulty for his thesis: If it is true that the
source of the uncanny is the resurgence of long-forgotten sensations, why
is it that many experiences that fit this description fail to generate any
feeling of uncanniness?

Here Freud points out that nearly all the examples that seem to contradict his hypothesis come from the realm of fiction and remarks, "This
suggests that we should differentiate between the uncanny that we actually
experience, and the uncanny that we merely picture or read about."[5] He
goes on to make some rudimentary observations about literary mode, arguing in effect that whereas realist literature increases our susceptibility to
the uncanny (because the author can resort to manipulations unavailable
in ordinary life), literature in the romance mode changes our expectations
so that we can accept the most ghostly images without a shudder.

At one point in the fragment of autobiography that Dickens offered
to his future biographer John Forster he recalls the coffee shops he knew
during his wretched days in the blacking warehouse, recollecting one with
a door in which "there was an oval glass plate, with COFFEE-ROOM
painted on it, addressed towards the street." He then adds, "If I ever find
myself in a very different kind of coffee-room now, but where there is such
an inscription on the glass, and read it backwards on the wrong side
MOOЯ-ƎƎƆƆ (as I often used to do then, in a dismal reverie), a shock
goes through my blood."[6]

This image stands as a powerful instance of the Freudian uncanny, but
in the context of Dickens's autobiographical fragment it has its own further importance. The return of the distant but familiar past creates in
Dickens the terror that the intervening years will drop away and that he
will find himself back where the uncanny began. In a telling passage he
writes of the society of boys in the warehouse:

No words can express the secret agony of my soul as I sunk into this companionship; compared these everyday associates with those of my happier childhood; and
felt my early hopes of growing up to be a learned and distinguished man crushed
in my breast. The deep remembrance of the sense I had of being utterly neglected
and hopeless; of the shame I felt in my position; of the misery it was to my young
heart to believe that, day by day, what I had learned, and thought, and delighted
in, and raised my fancy and my emulation by, was passing away from me, never to

be brought back any more, cannot be written. My whole nature was so penetrated with the grief and humiliation of such considerations, that even now, famous and caressed and happy, I often forget in my dreams that I have a dear wife and children; even that I am a man; and wander desolately back to that time of my life.[7]

It is important to what will follow here that fantasy stands in two places in this complicated mental picture. The uncanny resurgence of the past creates the spectre that often haunts Dickens's fiction, the spectre of a former phase of one's existence returning to imply that everything since has been mere fantasy and that one is doomed to return to the old scene of misery. At the same time the passage suggests that Dickens's present, "famous and caressed and happy," is the successful completion of his early fantasies—his word is typically "fancy"—of personal distinction. Here is the looming ambiguity of the present tense: it appears as merely a fantasy vulnerable to instant annihilation, or it appears not as a "mere" fantasy, but as a fantasy gloriously achieved, the realization of an ancient image. The question for Dickens, and it is the question that animates the present paper, is how fantasy in the first sense can be transformed into fantasy in the second, how an illusion can be transformed into an imaginative project guiding a life's labor.

When Freud draws the opposition referred to above, "the uncanny that we actually experience, and the uncanny that we merely picture or read about," he writes as though he is distinguishing two things when he is clearly distinguishing three. Between what we directly encounter and what we read, there is what "we merely picture," that is, what we imagine, and though Freud himself is unconcerned to separate these latter two experiences, the structure of his sentence suggests another perception that lies, as it were, in the unconscious of psychoanalysis. The suggestion is that fantasy stands as a third term between experience and art, that it is indeed a mediating term between the actual and the aesthetic. The point toward which this essay aims is not merely that this is a better way to conceive of fantasy but that it is faithful to a suppressed logic within psychoanalysis itself.

In an essay called "Fantasy, Imagination and the Screen," Roger Scruton offers a line of argument that is initially productive and finally stunted. From Coleridge's distinction between imagination and fancy Scruton derives his own distinction between imagination and fantasy, but in fact his version has little to do with Coleridge and everything to do with Freud. The aim of the imagination, as Scruton puts it, "is to grasp, in the circuitous ways exemplified by art, the nature of reality. Fantasy, on the other

hand, constitutes a flight from reality, and art which serves as the object
of fantasy is diverted or corrupted from its proper purpose."[8] Consistent
with a psychoanalytic understanding, Scruton identifies fantasy as the satisfaction of a desire through the pursuit of a substitute object, a form of
evasion that amounts to a renunciation of the reality principle. As Freud
put it in an elaborate metaphor found in the *Introductory Lectures on
Psychoanalysis*:

The creation of the mental realm of phantasy finds a perfect parallel in the establishment of "reservations" or "nature reserves" in places where the requirements of
agriculture, communications and industry threaten to bring about changes in the
original face of the earth which will quickly make it unrecognizable. A nature
reserve preserves its original state which everywhere else has to our regret been
sacrificed to necessity. Everything, including what is useless and even what is nox-
ious, can grow and proliferate there as it pleases. The mental realm of phantasy is
just such a reservation withdrawn from the reality principle.[9]

Where Scruton persuasively extends the Freudian reflection is in his recognition that it is part of the inner history of fantasy not to content itself
with private imaginings in the seclusion of one's own mental theater, but
to seek its realization in the world beyond the self. It is not, to take Scruton's own example, that the pathologically morbid man will seek real
scenes of human suffering and agony. It is more likely that he will seek out
images of suffering; the man "wants something, but he wants it *in the form
of a substitute*." This perception leads to Scruton's definition of fantasy as
"a real desire which, through prohibition, seeks an unreal, but realized
object";[10] it also leads to warnings against the psychic and moral decay
encouraged by an active fantasy life.

[T]he fantasy-ridden soul will tend to have a diminished sense of the objectivity of
his world, and a diminished sense of his own agency within it. The habit of pursuing the "realized unreal" seems to conflict with the habit, which we all, I believe,
have reason to acquire, of pursuing what is real. There is no expenditure of effort
involved in the gratification of fantasy, and hence the fantasist is engaged in no
transformation of his world. On the contrary his desires invade and permeate his
world, which ceases to have any independent meaning. The nature of the fantasy
object is *dictated* by the passion which seeks to realize it; and the world therefore
has no power either to control or to resist the passion.[11]

As opposed to the corruptions of a fantasy that continually appropriates
the promptings of the world to its scene of desire, imagination, according
to Scruton, follows a principle of objectivity. In viewing a performance of
Othello, at least in viewing it correctly, we acknowledge the drama as

imaginary and thus must abandon any attempt to realize our desires through the events of the play. To say this is not to deny that we experience emotion, but to insist that the emotions "are *responses* to a given situation, and neither pre-exist nor determine it. They arise out of the attempt to *understand* what is pictured. In this they are wholly unlike fantasy emotions." [12]

Wholly unlike? This is where Scruton's argument huffs and puffs, in this insistence that fantasy and imagination are fundamentally distinct modes of engagement. Can it really be that in responding to the death of Desdemona, the emotions we feel do not "pre-exist" the drama but come into being for the first time? Is it not better to say that the emotions that enter into the experience of art have an earlier life, even an earlier life in the realm of corrupt fantasy, but that in the encounter with art, they may be challenged and modified?

The difference between desires that appropriate art to their own ends and desires that accommodate themselves to the independent reality of the work seems a real distinction, but not a distinction between two radically separate faculties or two opposed paths for human desire. What Scruton calls "fantasy" and "imagination" appear rather as points on a single continuum of desire and emotion, the critical task then being to account for the movement from one to the other. The question Scruton ignores, but which is decisive to my rapprochement with Ian Watt, is how one passes from fantasy to imagination, from the imperialism of desire to its negotiations with an autonomous world.

A passage from Coleridge (cited by Watt) attacks the fiction provided by the circulating libraries as "a sort of beggarly day-dreaming, during which the mind of the dreamer furnishes for itself nothing but laziness and a little mawkish sensibility." Such novels transmit "the moving phantasms of one man's delirium, so as to people the barrenness of a hundred other brains afflicted with the same trance or suspension of all common sense and all definite purpose." [13] This piece of bitterness has the advantage of securing the connection between the novel and daydream, and the added advantage of linking the fantasy of the author to the fantasies of the audience. Having quoted this passage, Watt goes on to argue that the "unwholesome ends" occasionally pursued by Richardson must be set against the "remarkable opening up of the new domain of private experience for literary exploration." [14] But now are *these* possibilities clearly distinct? Is the unwholesome character of daydream clearly separable from the worthy formal advance? Watt bluntly acknowledges the moral ambiguity in the new genre, "the peculiar triumphs and degradations of the novel form in general," noting that the capacity to plumb the intimacy of the psyche and the subtlety of human relationship "is the same power over the consciousness which, far from extending psychological and moral awareness, makes possible the novel's role as a popular purveyor of vicarious sexual experience and adolescent wish-fulfillment."[15] The question we are then led to ask is not how a triumphant form can come to degrade itself, but rather how it is that triumph can grow out of the heart of degradation.

II

The great thematic labor of *David Copperfield* is the overcoming of fantasy. The provocation within that labor is the passage from Dora to Agnes, the transfer of love from a first to a second wife; and a manifest struggle for the novel is to moralize what, on the plane of narrative invention, amounts to the murder of one woman for the sake of another. The phrase that becomes the keynote of this moralizing is taken from Annie Strong's description of her childish infatuation with the scamp Jack Maldon, an infatuation named as the "first mistaken impulse of an undisciplined heart."[16] But it is one thing to identify the moral task as the correcting of a mistake, the tutoring of an impulse and the disciplining of a heart; and it is another to render that process in such a way as to relieve the cruelty of the change.

In this connection, it is a signal feature of David's romance with Dora that, short though it is, it comes to seem interminable. This is in part because the marriage appears so static when set against the drama surrounding it, in part because the history of the marriage is so often told in narrative summary, and in part because almost as soon as he is married, David begins to grow moodily retrospective. "All this time," begins chapter 33, "I had gone on loving Dora, harder than ever," and the effect, here as throughout, is to throw emphasis on the length of the romance. When Dora begins to fail and her toy dog Jip begins to fail with her, she remarks that Jip is growing "slow and lazy"—to which Aunt Betsey responds that "he has a worse disorder than that. Age, Dora" (ch. 48). Dora's own illness is so vague that we might as well say that she dies of aging fantasy— David's aging fantasy, which can no longer protect itself against imaginative fatigue.

The notion that fantasies can age is central to the argument I want to follow in these pages. Certainly a tendency in casual reflection on the life of fantasy is to focus upon its persistence, its resistance to the lessons of experience, its endurance in the face of its own failure. But the more attentively one thinks about fantasy, and the more one combines the insights of psychoanalysis with the insights of literature, the clearer it becomes that fantasy has a life history of its own, and accordingly a mortality of its own. Nothing, after all, is more characteristic of the pornographic imagination than the exhaustion of once quickening imagery and the need to find new pictures to stimulate the fastidious glands.

The privacy of novel reading, about which Watt has had many useful things to say, needs to be associated with another feature, namely, its duration. We typically read novels alone, and they typically take a long time. They take longer, one might note, than your standard daydream. Without putting a clock to the daydreamer's labor, we can say with confidence that it is part of the logic of fantasy, as indeed part of the logic of dream, that it unfolds in a relatively compressed period of time, more on the order of a lyric poem, say, than the order of an epic. And yet it is evident that dream and daydream have a distinctly narrative character, a miniature plot straining toward expansion.

That the novel stirs and then *prolongs* wishes creates a doubleness in its imaginative condition. Desires are excited but then deprived of rapid consummation; time passes; and the fulfillment of a wish is extended through the long duration of a plot and the interruptions of our reading. On the margins of the novelistic tradition the contortions of Sadean fantasy—new paraphernalia, new pyramids—offer vivid testimony to the self-transcending character of imaginary wish-fulfillment prolonged through time. A more central and more profound example occurs in *Wuthering Heights* where Heathcliff's desire for Cathy persists for years until, without ever changing its object, it has passed from open, boyish yearning into something ancient, close, and cruel. The difficult suggestion in the portrait of Heathcliff is that quite apart from the influence of external circumstance, the passions can grow old, and in aging, change their aspect. Because our engagement with novels is long as well as private, the rhythm of reading follows the same pattern of excitement deferred and desire modified; and because the premise of formal realism, as Watt puts it, is that "the novel is a full and authentic report of human experience,"[17] it will always tend to exceed the life span of particular fantasies.

It is a small but significant point that when David Copperfield finds that the enchantment of Dora has worn away, the word "fancy" takes on a new meaning in the novel. It had been used in the sense of idle romantic imaginings—"I am sure my fancy [for Emily] raised up something round that blue-eyed mite of a child, which etherealized and made a very angel of her" (ch. 3)—but as David begins to succeed as a writer, it appears as the name for creative vision. So Dora implies, when she explains to David why she wants to sit near him while he writes: "You'll not forget me then, while you are full of silent fancies" (ch. 64). The mind of a writer thus succeeds the mind of a lover, and the use of the common term suggests the mobility of Dickensian fancy which can move quickly between those two poles that Scruton austerely separates into fantasy and imagination.

III

"Mr. Murdstone! Sir!" I cried to him. "Don't! Pray don't beat me! I have tried to learn, sir, but I can't learn while you and Miss Murdstone are by. I can't indeed!"
  "Can't you, indeed, David?" he said. "We'll try that."
  He had my head as in a vice, but I twined round him somehow, and stopped him for a moment, entreating him not to beat me. It was only a moment that I stopped him, for he cut me heavily an instant afterwards, and in the same instant I caught the hand with which he held me in my mouth, between my teeth, and bit it through. It sets my teeth on edge to think of it.
  He beat me then, as if he would have beaten me to death. (ch. 4)

Freud's essay entitled "A Child Is Being Beaten" makes no attempt to say anything about art, and perhaps this is why it is so suggestive for aesthetic reflection. Freud takes his title from a recurrent fantasy reported to him by his patients, a fantasy which resolves into a single pattern of imagery, the beating of a child, an unknown child, usually a boy, usually beaten on its bare bottom. The substance of the paper, whose subtitle is "A Contribution to the Study of the Origin of Sexual Perversions," lies in the recovery of early fantasies that are said to precede and explain the patients' obsessive return to the scene of anonymous violence. Freud, who distinguishes the responses of male and female patients and concentrates his attentions on the latter, poses the problem of how the young girl gradually comes under the influence of this imaginative habit. To put it in Freud's own terms: "By what path has the phantasy of strange and unknown boys being beaten (a phantasy which has by this time become sadistic) found its way into the permanent possession of the little girl's libidinal trends?"[18] Although this question certainly seems remote from the aesthetics of the novel, it nevertheless suggests, in its forbiddingly technical tones, a way to think about the origins of the narrative imagination.

In pursuing the source of the beating fantasy his patients bring into therapy, Freud traces it back to a distant image of the patient's father beating another child, a child who is identified as a rival for parental affection. The Ur-image can then be written in propositional form:

My father is beating the child [whom I hate].

In this first imaginative phase, according to Freud, the violence satisfies the child's jealousy of the rival, usually a younger sibling; the unconscious meaning of the image is "My father does not love this other child, *he loves only me.*"[19] But this thought, at once sexual and sadistic, suffers the fate of all incestuous desires; it attracts guilt to itself; and ultimately it undergoes repression. Furthermore, as Freud puts it, "the sense of guilt can discover no punishment more severe" than the reversal of the original triumph.[20] The result is that the initial image is redrawn as the fantasy enters a second stage in its complex history. Instead of the picture of the father beating a rival, one finds an image captured in the next proposition:

I am being beaten by my father.

Freud calls this the "most important and most momentous" phase in the sequence of fantasies, noting that it has remained unconscious for the patient, only to be recovered through the work of analysis.[21] In accounting for the intensity of the repression, he notes that the second image is not only a guilty reversal of the first, masochism substituted for sadism, but it is also a "regressive substitute" for the very incestuous desire it punishes. Being beaten is at once a disguised form of sexual satisfaction, and a guilty retribution for that action.

Quite apart from the account of its unconscious mechanism, the form of this image bears on the distinctions in imaginative life proposed by Scruton. The ascendancy of subjectivity that he sees as the essential mark of fantasy—where the desires of the fantasist "invade and permeate [the] world, which ceases to have any independent meaning"—appears in a kind of psycho/syntactic extreme in the verbal formula Freud identifies. "I am being beaten by my father" might be taken as a grotesque paradigm of the triumph of subjectivity, the self placed at the center of the world, passively enduring the violent proof of its centrality.

Even here, though, in the extreme simplicity of the fantastic, a principle of objectivity quietly leaves its mark. For it is the peculiar force of Freud's essay to show how fantasy arises not only in response to the world without, but in response to its own past history. "I am being beaten by my father" exists as a transformation of "My father is beating the child," a revision of the ur-gesture that initiated the distorted movement of mind. Freud's hypothesis is that the incestuous character of the second image prevents it from becoming conscious and that only when a further transformation has occurred, obliterating the taint of incest, does the patient consciously entertain the fantasy that gives Freud's paper its title:

A child is being beaten.

What is most significant about this phase is that the participants in the scene no longer retain their earlier identities. As Freud puts it,

The person beating is never the father, but is either left undetermined just as in the first phase, or turns in a characteristic way into a representative of the father, such as a teacher. The figure of the child who is producing the beating-phantasy no longer itself appears in it. In reply to pressing enquiries the patients only declare: "I am probably looking on." Instead of the one child that is being beaten, there are now a number of children present as a rule.[22]

Freud is uncharacteristically tentative in accounting for the movement to this final phase of the sequence, which in any case concerns him less than the earlier unconscious phases identified as the motive forces of the obsession. But if we leave aside the pursuit of origins and worry less about the relative contributions of sadism, masochism, guilt, and regression, then it is possible to see the sequence as an emblematic history of the growth of the imagination, and an enactment of the groping movement of fantasy toward art.

In this connection two features of the imaginative history are notable. First is the change in dramatis personae. That a father may give way to a teacher is for Freud only another and fairly tedious instance of the subterfuges of the psyche. Still, a sociologist should be interested in the fact the psychoanalyst casually records: namely, that the satisfactions of fantasy can be so readily transferred from a private to a public context. School, says Freud in another place, merely reanimates the earlier and fundamental pattern of desire, but it is a telling aspect of his account that as fantasy conceals its tracks it moves naturally from a domestic to a social setting. Even if it is only to preserve the secrets of its intimacy, the primal imagination makes social, indeed institutional, life an essential resource.

The second striking aspect of the sequence is the movement toward and then beyond the subjectivity of the fantasist. In the first transformation, the "I" converts the universe as its own emanation, but then in a decisive next step it releases the world to become a spectacle free from the marks of the self. Of this last phase Freud writes that "the child who produces the phantasy appears almost as a spectator"—a change that again arouses only mild curiosity in Freud but may stir deeper interest in us.[23] It suggests how even the most personal and secret desires can lead to forms of impersonality rarely associated with the workings of fantasy. Much as the family yields to the institution, so the imagining subject recedes, leaving the image to enjoy the independence and objectivity we associate with art.

Art itself receives just two passing mentions in "A Child Is Being Beaten." We are told that as the patients left childhood, the effects of reading give new stimulus to the beating fantasies, especially the effect of reading such works as the "Bibliothèque rose" or *Uncle Tom's Cabin.* At this point, "the child began to compete with these works of fiction by producing his own phantasies and by constructing a wealth of situations and institutions, in which children were beaten."[24] This remark confirms a link between fantasy and narrative art, specifically novelistic art, but it implies the familiar equivalence of art and fantasy that constrains so much of Freud's aesthetic speculation.

The other reference to art, however, though equally incidental, opens to a line of thought challenging the official psychoanalytic aesthetic. Freud had observed that the beating fantasy was habitually in the service of masturbatory satisfaction, but when one recalls that he is basing his judgments on extensive acquaintance with only *four* female patients, then it is startling to find him remarking that in *two* of the cases the obsession led to an "elaborate superstructure of day-dreams," extended stories that carried great meaning for the patients, creating in them a state of "satisfied excitation" but without masturbatory arousal.[25] Soon thereafter Freud comments, again in passing, that in one of the cases the daydreams "almost rose to the level of a work of art."[26]

No criterion is offered for the distinction between art and the daydreams with which Freud so persistently linked it. But it is surely noteworthy that when this erotic fantasy is aggressively pursued it would come to offer narrative satisfactions no longer in the service of the body. What we may extract from the argument is a complex view according to which fantasy endures its own historical evolution, disguising its private secrets by creating public dramas, concealing the role of the imaginative agent who withdraws from the narrative, and compounding the intricacy of its plot until the attending doctor finds it almost a work of art. At what point would the "almost" disappear? Clearly the question does not apply. But what may be evident is that one cannot sustain a firm distinction between a corrupt fantasy and a healthy imagination, and that fantasy in pursuing its vulgar ends may become so transformed that it begins to produce images drained of immediate personal reference, and thus creates that "satisfied excitation" so characteristic of aesthetic response. Elsewhere Freud had written that daydreams "are either, each one of them, dropped after a short time and replaced by a fresh one, or they are retained, spun out into long stories."[27] This is enough to make us suspect that in setting out to excavate the origins of the perversions, Freud uncovered the origins of the novelistic imagination.

IV

In a bit of comic business at the center of *David Copperfield*, David hosts a dinner, hoists a bottle, and finds his mind floating to the ceiling while his body sinks to the floor:

Somebody was smoking. We were all smoking. *I* was smoking, and trying to suppress a rising tendency to shudder . . . Somebody was leaning out of my bedroom window, refreshing his forehead against the cool stone of the parapet, and feeling the air upon his face. It was myself. I was addressing myself as "Copperfield," and saying, "Why did you try to smoke? You might have known you couldn't do it." Now, somebody was contemplating his features in the looking-glass. That was I too. (ch. 24)

This is as instructive as it is irresistible. The idea of the self as some/body, somebody vulgar or somebody weak or somebody intoxicated or loveless or fearful or tainted, is a common one in Dickens. It receives a kind of consummation in David's remark that "I positively began to have a dread of myself as a kind of wild boy who did bite." (This is in reference to the placard "Take care of him. He bites." fixed to David's back when he enters Creakle's school in ch. 5). What is notable is that when he remembers the incident, he stands, as it were, behind himself, reading the placard as others must have read it then. He is a spectator regarding himself.

In the essay "Screen Memories" Freud takes up the question of how we know whether an image really belongs to memory or whether it is a construction of later psychic history, suggesting that if we imagine a past scene as "an observer from outside" would see it, then this indicates that "the original impression has been worked over" and that the memory is doubtful.[28] In the essay on writers and daydreaming he notoriously dismisses aesthetic form as merely a bribe, a "fore-pleasure," but it is striking how concerned he is with the problem of point of view in his technical papers.[29] Stages in the development of an illness are cast in terms of the relationship of the self to its own images—or as David Copperfield might put it, the transformation of myself into Somebody.

Where do we stand inside our imaginings? This is how we might put Freud's question about memory, a question Richard Wollheim has addressed explicitly and inventively. Whenever we imagine a scene, argues Wollheim, we can either place ourselves inside the perspective of someone participating in it, or we can hover above the imaginary landscape, adopting no particular standpoint, limited to no particular angle. If, to take Wollheim's example, we imagine the entrance of the Sultan Mahomet II into Constantinople, we might project for ourselves "the sights and sounds and smells and internal sensations as they would have reached the eyes and ears and nose and the proprioperceptive system of the triumphant Sultan."[30] On the other hand we might occupy no position within the imagined historical event; we might stand entirely apart from the scene we visualize, with no individual preeminent within the mental image but with every individual and every site equally available to the inner eye.

The first of these possibilities Wollheim calls "centrally imagining" and the second "acentrally imagining."[31] He insists that the difference is not that between picturing oneself within a scene and picturing some other. Just as it is possible to imagine Sultan Mahomet II "from the inside," so it is possible to imagine oneself acentrally, to picture oneself not from within but from some outer view. The fantasy that "a child is being beaten," that the child is not oneself, that the beating hand is no longer the hand of one's father, and that as one produces the fantasy one does not appear within it but can only say "I am probably looking on"—this might serve as a paradigm of an acentral image. So might David Copperfield's vision of his fuming drunken self as somebody else.

A more complicated and less paradigmatic example is suggested by the late preface to the novel, where Dickens writes that "like many fond parents, I have in my heart of hearts a favourite child. And his name is David Copperfield."[32] Knowing what we know (and cannot unlearn) of Dickens's deep entanglement with his character, who remembers for him, imagines for him, suffers and succeeds for him, we may reasonably find ourselves obliged to read the sentence as reporting that in his heart of hearts Dickens is his own favorite child. The paradox of the image is the paradox contained in the evolution of fantasy, an evolution leading from the image as autobiography to the image as biography, but where the biographic image is just as much a rendering of the authorial self. To love oneself in the person of one's own favorite child is to achieve a union of self-delight and self-estrangement which may mark that ambiguous region where daydream turns into art.

I have argued that we neither need nor can sustain a formal distinction between a dangerously subjective fantasy and a reassuringly objective imagination. But Scruton's forcing of the issue does show us that we want a better understanding of the transitions in imaginative life. When Freud writes, "Every desire takes before long the form of picturing its own ful-fillment,"[33] he tersely and profoundly suggests a birth for the imagination; and when Wollheim separates acentral from central imagining, he suggests a next and decisive stage in development. To picture the satisfaction of desires is surely to stir the production of imagery, but to picture *some one* (the self or another) yearning, pursuing, imagining is for the imagination to take up a standpoint outside the desires that called it into being. The achievement of acentrality need not stand as some stern norm of aesthetic distance, but the capacity to see the self as Somebody—a condition that has nothing to do with a movement from first to third person—is a no-table passage in the career of the imagination.

That the novel permits an aging of fantasy, that it both encourages the indulgence of wishes and obliges those wishes to grow old during the act of reading, makes it a form well suited to marking this transition in imagi-native life. At a telling point in his memoir Thackeray's Henry Esmond returns to his early home at Castlewood and finds himself "looking back, as all men will, that revisit their home of childhood, over the great gulf of time, and surveying himself on the distant bank yonder, a sad little mel-ancholy boy."[34] Thackeray here only heightens a mood of retrospection perpetually tempting to the novel, where the pursuit of a "full and authen-tic report of human experience" invites nostalgia for an ever-receding ori-gin. A form that commits itself to rendering the curve of a life depends on memory of the past, and the convergence of intimacy and duration on which I have insisted makes the typical reader as nostalgic as Thackeray's Esmond.

When Leopold Bloom allows his mind to wander back to a happier time and concludes his memory with the unadorned thought "Me. And me now." he gives laconic expression to the temporalizing of identity that is such a marked feature of novelistic form. Indeed, we might come to speak of a "sociology of fantasy" where this implies no external view of the inner life, no quantification of mental imagery, no demographics of daydream; where it suggests first of all the tendency of the imagination to digest the objects of the social world, kings and queens, teachers and nurses; and where it suggests next the tendency of the imagination to react to its own past, to take up attitudes toward its history, and in so doing, to constitute its own community of fantasists. In this latter sense the primitive sociology of the imagination is the sociology of I, of Me and Me Now, the self dispersed through time, constituting its own small village.

The origins of *David Copperfield* are in this respect exemplary. In the autobiographical fragment we have the relentless presence of the Dickensian "I," moving throughout its span of life, now back to the days of early hope, now forward to the dashing of those hopes, now to the success of the present. When these pieces of autobiography enter the novel, the community of I's remain, but now they belong to the much larger community of the densely populated Dickensian universe. It is a commonplace to see Dickens's condition not only rethought through David but expanded through the avatars of Steerforth and Uriah Heep; it is another commonplace to recognize Dickens's parents diffused into Copperfields, Murdstones, and Micawbers. To move from the autobiography to the fiction is evidently and tediously to see how a life is converted into fiction; but at the same time it is more profoundly to see how a life, by concentrating upon itself, generates other lives, which may begin in the recesses of the self but end far from there. In Dickens, autobiographical fiction always becomes a form of fictional sociology, because in imagining himself he always imagines many versions in many contexts; for every self-serious Pip there is an anarchic Trabb's boy; and the result is that meditation on the self tends quickly to become a rendering of public life.

This growth of the fictional population, this socializing of autobiography stands in notable parallel to the grim mental work of Freud's patients as they achieve the final phase of their fantasies: "Instead of the one child that is being beaten, there are now a number of children present as a rule." Freud offers no explanation for this shift, but a telling feature of his account is the movement from the terrible privacy of the central fantasy to the cool publicity of the last, where in place of one victim, the patient herself, crouching inside the family, there are many indeterminate boys parading forward to the paddle.

For Freud the difference is of little note, since "[a]ll of the many unspecified children who are being beaten by the teacher are, after all, nothing more than substitutes for the child itself." The "after all" is a sign of psychoanalytic complacency, and the "nothing more" is a measure of Freud's reluctance to heed the suggestion of his own argument: that the vicissitudes of fantasy might come to achieve the force of art. It is one thing to trace the eruptions of imagery back to an ur-image, to collect multiplicity within a unifying origin; it is quite another to move from origins to ends and to let oneself be startled at the way a single psychic difficulty keeps expanding its imaginary range, at the way the self disappears from its own mental landscape and idiosyncratic life histories merge into public narrative conventions.

V

When Dora obligingly dies, and when a chastened David makes his way back to Agnes, the novel optimistically suggests that the "first mistaken impulse of an undisciplined heart" can be corrected, that there can be a second impulse, a disciplined impulse, resisting the temptations of fantasy in favor of a stern moral maturity. Dora was the self-confessed "child-wife"; Agnes is "modest," "orderly," and "placid"; and the metaphoric gesture that identifies Agnes and gives the book its concluding phrase, "pointing upwards," is also a description of the narrative geometry the novel seeks for itself. A strong upward curve, beyond pleasure and toward morality, is the shape drawn by plotting a movement from Dora to Agnes, and in this respect *David Copperfield* seeks a congruity between the conventions of the *Bildungsroman* and the conventions of the marriage plot.

One of the complexities of Dickensian narrative, however, is that the movement Upward is so often also a movement Backward. After David has resigned himself to the failure of his first marriage, he thinks back "to the better state preceding manhood that I had outgrown; and then the contented days with Agnes, in the dear old house, arose before me, like spectres of the dead, that might have some renewal in another world, but never more could be reanimated here" (ch. 48). As long as David has no hope of romance with Agnes, this appears merely as warm nostalgia. But when the plot takes its last turn, bringing the two together, it is impossible to avoid the thought that David has indeed recovered happiness by reanimating childhood. Throughout the work David calls Agnes his sister; she precedes his erotic swoon; and when he returns to visit her after his time abroad, he rejoices to find that "everything was as it used to be, in the happy time" (ch. 60). In effect, between Dora, the child-wife, and Agnes, the wife-sister, there is a competition of regressions. And although the official narrative stubbornly points upward, emphasizing the giddiness of the former and the earnestness of the latter, there are unmistakable and unsettling signs pointing in another direction, one leading back from the follies of sexual infatuation to the consolations of a child's trust. It is indeed a curious foundation for marriage, this "better state preceding manhood."

In discussing the ambiguity in the appeal of *Pamela*, Watt shows us how realism may enter the service of romance, how Richardson's "narrative skill was actually being used to re-create the pseudo-realism of the daydream, to give an air of authenticity to a triumph against all obstacles and contrary to every expectation, a triumph which was in the last analysis as improbable as any in romance."[35] The turn to romance is common through the long novelistic tradition, and certainly one way to understand the final movement of *David Copperfield* is to see all the anguish, all the mourning, all the heart's discipline as preparations for a romance dressed in the tones of Victorian sobriety. But as *The Rise of the Novel* notes of *Pamela*, if this is romance, "it is romance with a difference: the fairy godmother, the prince and the pumpkin are replaced by morality, a substantial squire and a real coach-and-six."[36]

It is the place of morality within novelistic romance that is most pertinent to the present argument, and most pertinent to the fate of David Copperfield. In the midst of David's despondency over his life with Dora, he lets himself entertain the thought of never having met her and then immediately realizes that this is the "idlest of all fancies": the thought of a wife who might be a "partner" sharing the burdens of life was "a dream of my youthful fancy"(ch. 48). In this improbable reversal of the novel's own conventions, life with Dora takes on the aspect of the reality principle, deflating airy dreams, while life with Agnes, earnest, sober, and wise, becomes a "fancy." But this improbability is the hard-won result of Dickens's imaginative labor, which has achieved a coincidence between the yearnings of fantasy and the demands of morality. By the end of the novel David only fancies doing what he ought.

Rather than see this as so much the worse for morality, I suggest that we recognize it as so much the better for fantasy. It is not a feature of our mental life we should take lightly, that our most persistent images can keep changing their terms and, as Freud puts it in relation to his beating fantasies, can change "as regards their relation to the author of the phantasy, and as regards their object, their content and their significance." Freud is concerned with the conditions that precede and underlie the changes, but one may be forgiven for having been impressed more by the outcome than by the source.

The drive of fantasy to enlarge its domain, to pass beyond the family and then beyond the self, to replace a father with a teacher, to multiply protagonists, to change their gender, to concatenate into an ongoing narrative, to compete with works of fiction, and thus to end at the greatest distance from its source—this is the power that brings the social world within the realm of greatest personal intimacy. It is also the power the novel has taken to itself. The exciting of fantasy, the exhaustion of fantasy, the transformation of fantasy, the moralizing of fantasy: these activities have been central to the form. Indeed, in one of its many aspects, the novel appears as that form which has taught us how to dream the real and to hallucinate the moral.

Comic and Erotic Faith Meet Faith in the Child:
Charles Dickens's *The Old Curiosity Shop*
("The Old Cupiosity Shape")

ROBERT M. POLHEMUS

LIKE IAN WATT, I AM INTERESTED IN THE WAY the novel represents, particularizes, and even forms large-scale social patterns and desires. Especially, I see and care about the nineteenth-century novel as a popular institutionalized means for seeking, imagining, and defining some kind of faith, and see literature and art as means for forming and exploring modes of faith and propagating them: that is my critical perspective and, broadly speaking, throwing light on that subject is my critical project.

The motives for the production and appreciation of art are many, but the religious impulse—the drive, whether personal, social, or both, to express and embody faith in striking form—has surely been one of the strongest.[1] A significant work of art, such as *The Birth of Venus, Pride and Prejudice*, or *Ulysses*, has a multiple existence. It may be a means to pleasure; it may stand in an artistic tradition as a form of aesthetic value by which a culture reifies its worth; it may be an instrument of control for people in power or of political subversion for outsiders; it may be seen as a representation of some form of reality, as an economic product, or as a privileged specimen preserving and focusing a moment of history; it may be a moral force, an expression of gender relationship, or a way of understanding the world and shaping the forms of the future. But whatever its rhetorical function or status and however it is regarded, art nearly always has to do with the need to put faith somehow in something. Focusing on Dickens's *The Old Curiosity Shop* (1841), I want to develop further my theme in *Comic Faith* (1980) and *Erotic Faith* (1990) that the Victorian novel was a means for imagining forms of faith that would augment, replace, or play off orthodox religious visions.

I

Let me begin with definitions.

Comic faith: a belief that the world is both funny and potentially good; a pattern of expressing or finding religious impulse, motive, and meaning in the forms of comedy; an implicit assumption that a basis for believing in the value of life can be found in the fact of comic expression itself.[2] A novelist's comic vision is the particular insight that allows him or her to find or excite mirth, to justify life, and to imagine the means of its regeneration. Dickens's comic vision is based on seeing the world as both funny and potentially good, on the comedy of expression, on the imaginative force of language and fantasy, on satisfying legitimate and natural appetite, and on the drive for liberty of mind, exuberance of spirit, pleasure, and imaginative regeneration. (In *The Old Curiosity Shop* we see these kinds of comedy at times in the Dick Swiveller–Marchioness plot; the Kit Nubbles–Garland sections; the image, fantastic language, and behavior of Daniel Quilp; and the amazing expressions of Swiveller, Brass, Mrs. Jarley, and many other characters.)

Erotic faith: an emotional conviction, ultimately religious in nature, that meaning, value, hope, and even transcendence can be found through love—erotically focused love, the kind of love we mean when we say that people are in love. (I use the term "erotic" not in its narrow sexual connotation but to indicate broadly libidinous desire and a passionate, sometimes romantic relationship with, affection for, or attachment to another person.)[3] Men and women in the hold of erotic faith feel that love can redeem personal life and offer a reason for being. In *The Old Curiosity Shop* this faith eventually shows in the Swiveller-Marchioness story, but it plays perversely about the whole saga of Little Nell too. In both these areas of the narrative it fuses with Dickens's faith in the child.

The Old Curiosity Shop is, among other things, a frantic attempt to find and show faith in a fallen world, the real nineteenth-century world of cash-nexus relations, the upheavals of the industrial revolution, and the shifts and ebbings of credence in traditional religion. With this novel, hugely popular in its time, Dickens would desperately try to shore up and sustain a broad Christian faith that could give solace in the face of life's misery and unfairness, and specifically for the death of his beloved sister-in-law, Mary Hogarth, upon whom he came to project his ideals of purity, innocence, goodness, and femininity. He is trying, in the novel, to keep viable and useful a nominal Christianity for his readers against all those historical forces that threatened it, even though his fiction shows little faith in formal religious institutions. He and the Victorians needed badly some sort of credible religious feeling to sustain hope and charity—to forgive both life and death. But there are other kinds of faith that this novel sets forth imaginatively, other ways of justifying life and trying to overcome death besides the broad Christian supernaturalism and moral structure in the text. The novel is a curiosity shop of strategies for survival and having faith in life despite its beastliness, its definition by the fact of death, and its uncontrollable nature.

Dickens was a key figure in the development and imaginative rendering of comic faith, erotic faith, and faith in the child in British fiction, and all three meet and play off the Christian moral sentiment in the story of Nell and her associates. The novel is full of contradictions, disjunctions, and many alternative kinds of being. I want to concentrate on the working and the interplay of Victorian religious sentimentalism, Dickens's reverence for the virgin girl-child, his comedy, and their inseparability from the strange eroticism in the novel.

This novel, with its focus on Nell, constitutes Dickens's rhetorical plea for acts of faith from his audience. Master Humphrey says of Nell, "She seemed to exist in a kind of allegory."[4] *The Old Curiosity Shop is* an allegory, but an open-ended, many-faceted allegory. The allegory is loose, it works metaphorically—especially through Nell, "the child"—to focus overlapping but various desires of the author and his many and diverse readers. If Nell is an allegorical figure, one of the most significant of her allegorical functions is becoming the symbol for her grandfather's rationalization of the obsessive desire for wealth. He lives a degraded, miserable existence scrambling and gambling for money—money he thinks of as not for himself, but for Nell's good. The purpose of his speculation, he says, is solely for her, but his "her" is an ideal, and the real "her" of the text he is willing to ignore and further degrade—even steal from, victimize, and put in the worst danger. Dickens is getting at, among other things, a common Victorian equation of love and money and the rationale for the money-mad, dog-eat-dog commercial world and the men who compete in it, wanting to believe that the whole money hustle is for the sake of their families—innocent children and women who need security and deserve the best. "The little woman," the child's well-being, the daughter's purity—money-grubbing and greed have often, in the Age of the Novel, found their excuse in such ideals.

I want to put forward the idea of *The Old Curiosity Shop* as a kind of secular, popular, literary cathedral, an accretive Gothic textual structure with chapels that emphasize different kinds of faith and include all kinds of beliefs in the crazy architecture of its fiction. The novel is a big-top circus kind of cathedral that features a literary version of the Gothic as defined a few years later in "The Nature of the Gothic" by John Ruskin, who stresses the religious impulse of the Gothic style.[5] His categories are savageness (rudeness), changefulness or variety, naturalism, grotesqueness (delight in the fantastic and ludicrous), rigidity, and redundancy (generosity). Keeping in mind Ruskin's terms and the influential Gothic tradition in the English novel of the late eighteenth and early nineteenth century, let us look at an important example of the Gothic mode that bears on the relationship of erotics, faith, and the novel, and specifically on Dickens's concerns in *The Old Curiosity Shop* about what might be the demands and possibilities for emotional and spiritual payoff in fiction.

II

In Matthew Lewis's lurid *The Monk* (1796), which appeared sensationally on the eve of a new century, Ambrosio, a handsome, charismatic young abbot, alone in his cell, stares at a portrait of the Madonna. Over time, he has come to adore a beautiful image of the Virgin, and he longs for her to come alive, wanting to fondle her golden ringlets and kiss her breasts. He wonders if he would abandon his vocation for such a being, but decides his faith and his dedication to the Virgin are proof against the seductive skill of the artist and any threat to his vows and his calling. But Spain is a place without "true devotion,"[6] where "superstition reigns" (I, 1: 7) and horrible crimes are perpetrated in the name of Christianity.

A novice interrupts the monk's reverie and reveals that "he" is in fact "she," Matilda, a woman in disguise who idolizes him. She would give up her life to be near him, but all she asks is that when they die, their bodies shall rest in the same grave (as Dickens wanted his remains to mingle with those of Mary Hogarth). He at first spurns her, but his vanity is flattered. Later he finds that she exactly resembles the beloved Virgin hanging opposite his bed. She tells him that she had her portrait done as the Madonna and then conspired to get it to Ambrosio, who prays to it. The alluring Virgin Mother of God and Matilda are fused: the painting not only mirrors the monk's desire, it is the means through which he can imagine it.

Soon, she begs for the "enjoyment" (I, 2: 89) of his body, and, overwhelmed by libido, he obliges. The moment is ecstatic, the passionate climax of desire, but he quickly comes to despise her, feeling that he has betrayed his faith and his life. The surge of sexual power, however, leads him to delight in the sensual "blessings of Love and Woman" (II, 2: 227). He wants and preys on other virgins, but he wants the esteem of men and the power of the Church too; he abandons the reality but not the appearance of celibacy. The priest can never think of marrying a woman. Eventually Matilda turns out to be an agent of the devil who leads Ambrosio on to commit every sort of moral atrocity, including necrophilia, matricide, incest-rape, murder of his sister, and betrayal of God and the Christian faith before his damnation. What is crucial in this novel is the displacement of orthodox religious faith by erotic desire and the degradation of organized religion, even while the form of religion, the need for faith, and the longing to believe in a holy virgin define the world of the text.[7]

The portrait that so fascinates the monk offers a paradigm. Lewis's picture, with its eroticized Virgin, shows how an art of love could metamorphose into the English novel; beyond that, it can stand symbolically for the whole body of nineteenth-century fiction that conflates sexual and religious desire. This Madonna turning into the love-provoking image of a female character explicitly shows art becoming narrative, religion becoming erotics, and all turning faithless and corrupt.

Within the novel, the work of art is evil and idolatrous. Ambrosio adores the icon, and that leads to his damnation. Behind the garish melodrama lies history. The puritan strain in English culture was highly suspicious of the religious heritage of the visual arts, related as it was to the papist tradition. The use of visual images by continental Roman Catholicism to reinforce its power and to interpose its clergy between Scripture and the laity had led to a Protestant backlash in Britain that glorified the word and denigrated the image. That in turn would lead for many reasons to the special moral burdens and expectations of the English novel. The picture in *The Monk* turns into the antipapal word, and the written word of fiction would come to have the moral function of architecture, painting, and sculpture in Catholic countries.

The image of a priest lusting after the Virgin turns the Catholic vision into a moral nightmare. In Christian theology and imagery conflicting emotions and tensions cluster around human sexuality and familial identity. Christianity from its first days could not do without both a Father and Son, and in its second millennium it also had to emphasize the sacred place of woman, gender, and generation by playing up the importance of Christ's Virgin Mother. This concept of a virgin mother indicates a religion somehow fixated on sex in its very obsession with separating faith and love from sexuality. Religion has often tried to be free of the mortal body by spiritualizing creation, and has also tried to revere the generative force by making it divine. Sacralization of the child in Dickens, and in the modern era, is one result of these tendencies.

III

Now consider *The Old Curiosity Shop*: What the Virgin Mary is to Chartres, little Nell, the girl-child, is to the novel. As the cathedral is dedicated to the Virgin Mary, so the book is dedicated to the Virgin Nell and behind her the Virgin Mary Hogarth and a mysterious religious ideal inhering in the image of a young and doomed virgin. The idea of holy virginity suffuses both building and book, but in Dickens's structure *Notre Dame* has become *Notre Jeune Fille*. Nell is a Protestant, Victorian version of immaculate conception and its symbolic importance to the nineteenth-century world.

Certain illustrations from the book graphically show Dickens's conception of Nell's role as Virgin. One is Samuel Williams's famous picture in the first chapter of innocent Nell on her bed in the curiosity shop surrounded by grotesque figures and menacing paraphernalia (Figure 1; 1: 57); another is the drawing of her on her deathbed by George Cattermole (Figure 2; 71: 652), which pointedly features the Bible in her hand and an image of the Virgin and Christ Child carved on her bedstead. Both settings are in the Gothic mode. In the last stages of her narrative, Nell actually haunts and usurps the church, allegorically taking it over. Dickens has her being and memory literally merged into the physical site of faith, the religious structure. The penultimate illustration (Figure 3; 72: 662) shows an old man looking down at the gravestone in the church, Nell's place of burial, and the word he stares at in the stone of the church is "Here." Nell and the religious institution—the church or cathedral—are now unified: the character is one with the church, and the church is the novel. By the end, in the very last picture, Nell is experiencing an assumption into heaven, surrounded by angels (Figure 4; Chapter the Last: 672), and is thus explicitly identified with the Virgin Mary. Dickens's novel has become a place of worship, and his central figure, as many have said, a literary icon.

In other words, rhetorically the child, Dickens's virgin, becomes in intention if not effect the same sort of spiritual center of faith in his world that the Virgin was for the society that made the cathedrals. Moreover,

Figure 1. The child Nell abed in the curiosity shop. Drawing by Samuel Williams from Charles Dickens's *The Old Curiosity Shop* (1841), ch. 1. Reprinted in *The Works of Charles Dickens in Thirty-four Volumes, with Introductions, General Essay, and Notes by Andrew Lang* (London: Chapman and Hall; New York: Scribner's, n.d.; "Gadshill Edition"), vol. 10, *The Old Curiosity Shop*, vol. 1, ch. 1.

she combines the purity of the Virgin with the fresh, sacrificial quality of the Christ Child; and, with the Scripture in her hand and her central role in the novel, she is the sacrificial virgin redeemer of the book—not "Our Lady," but "Our Child." As Dickens translates wild Gothic architecture to the novel, his quest to imagine and honor the virgin and her significance for faith energizes him, as it did the medieval makers of religious art. The Gothic, however, is domesticated through the attempt to transfer the Virgin's holy appeal for people to a child.

Dickens has made a new, prose Gothic edifice in his *Notre Jeune Fille*, but he gives even more prominence than the builders of the old *Notre Dames* to the gargoyle: Quilp has a voice and impact almost as great as Nell's. Dickens's energetic faith, to repeat, is accretive, like Hinduism or indeed any religion, but it is chaotic and full of conflicts—a text of competing urges. In understanding *The Old Curiosity Shop* and its odd, diverse effects, we might do well to recall what are probably the two most famous

Figure 2. Nell on her deathbed. Drawing by George Cattermole from Charles Dickens's *The Old Curiosity Shop* (1841), ch. 71. Reprinted in *The Works of Charles Dickens*, "Gadshill Edition," vol. II, *The Old Curiosity Shop*, vol. 2, ch. 71.

statements made about it: One is Dickens's description from the 1848 Preface: "in writing the book, I had it always in my fancy to surround the lonely figure of the child with grotesque and wild, but not impossible companions, and to gather about her pure and innocent intentions, associates as strange and uncongenial as the grim objects that are about her bed when her history is first foreshadowed" (Preface to the First Cheap Edition, 1848: 42). The second is Oscar Wilde's reputed *bon mot*, "One must have a heart of stone not to read the death of little Nell without laughing." (That sentiment—outrageously cutting through stock response, reversing things, breaking free of repression, defying and making light of pain and death—could be straight out of Quilp's dialogue.) Taken together, Dickens's and Wilde's words get at much of the contradictory desires of the text and show the bizarre implications of competing faiths.

His imagery surrounding Nell at the end and the illustration (Figure 3) allow us to take Wilde's statement with a literalness he never meant.

Figure 3. The old man in church looking at the spot under which Nell is buried. Drawing by George Cattermole from Charles Dickens's *The Old Curiosity Shop* (1841), ch. 72. Reprinted in *The Works of Charles Dickens*, "Gadshill Edition," vol. ii, *The Old Curiosity Shop*, vol. 2, ch. 72.

The religious, holy stone of the Gothic church in Dickens becomes little Nell, the new holy child of religious feeling: "They carried her to one old nook, where she had many and many a time sat musing, and laid their burden softly on the pavement" (72: 658). "Under that porch . . . she passed again and the old church received her in its quiet shade," under "the pavement-stone" where she had been wont to sit (72: 658). Nell and the old stone undergo a kind of transubstantiation, and the heart of Nell and the stone of the church and what they stand for become transmutable. If readers could believe in that metamorphosis of sacred substances—a virgin's heart and Christian rock—then the death of Little Nell would not be ridiculous.

Dickens puts forth the faith that the death of Nell represents explicitly:

Figure 4. Nell goes to heaven. Drawing by
George Cattermole from Charles Dickens's
The Old Curiosity Shop (1841), Chapter the
Last. Reprinted in *The Works of Charles
Dickens*, "Gadshill Edition," vol. 11, *The Old
Curiosity Shop*, vol. 2, Chapter the Last.

Oh! it is hard to take to heart the lesson that such deaths will teach, but let no man
reject it, for it is one that all must learn, and it is a mighty, universal Truth. When
Death strikes down the innocent and young, for every fragile form from which he
lets the panting spirit free, a hundred virtues rise, in shapes of mercy, charity, and
love, to walk the world, and bless it. Of every tear that sorrowing mortals shed on
such green graves, some good is born, some gentler nature comes. In the Destroy-
er's steps there spring up bright creations that defy his power, and his dark path
becomes a way of light to Heaven" (72: 659).

That is thanatology, rationalization for death and also for social and personal guilt and exploitation.

IV

I want to stress the strange, complex eroticism that exists in the figure
of Nell and to argue the importance of her virgin status: she is a Protestant
literary virgin who concentrates, as did the traditional Virgin of Roman

Catholicism, religious feeling and faith in nurturing idealism. She captures, so it seemed to many, the religious sentiment in the Massacre of the Innocents—the role, so prevalent and seemingly necessary in religion, of the sacrificial victim—along with the spirit of "Suffer the little children to come unto me." By making Nell about thirteen years old and denominating her again and again a "child," Dickens gives plausibility to her virgin status. Credence, of course, is everything in matters of faith. Though no Victorian would be as publicly cynical as the twentieth-century wit W. C. Fields, who defined a virgin as "a little girl, about three years old—very ugly," nevertheless the contemporary icon for virginity had to be a child to command credibility in modern times.

It seems crucial that Nell die a virgin, unpolluted by sexuality, but sexual vulnerability and peril are very much a part of her story and destiny. In the earlier part of the book until she finds her final home, she is definitely threatened by what was known as the "fate worse than death": Her virginity is ripe for exploitation, and her virgin status is very much a subject of suspense. "She's like a red, red rose that's newly sprung in June," says Dick Swiveller (8: 110). Dick, picked by her scheming brother to marry her eventually, remarks, "a young and lovely girl is growing into a woman expressly on my account and is now saving up for me" (8: 118), ironically true words, it turns out, though not about Nell. That language, in the way of this fallen world, does equate virginity, commodity, and potential sexual exploitation. The most serious threat to the virgin comes from lascivious Quilp who, wanting to occupy her bed, chortles over her, "Such a fresh, blooming, modest little bud . . . such a chubby, rosy, cosy little Nell," he insists on a kiss from her, "just on the rosy part" (9: 125), and coaxes her lecherously "to be my number two . . . to be my wife, my little cherry-cheeked, red-lipped wife . . . be a good girl Nelly . . . and see if . . . you don't come to be Mrs. Quilp of Tower Hill" (5: 93).

Unlike similar feminine figures of faith and goodness in English literature, such as Richardson's Clarissa, Fielding's Amelia, or Shakespeare's Cordelia and even the teenage Juliet, Nell is deemed a child, stays a virgin, and dies before the love of men can touch or tempt her. She has an even more overtly sacrificial quality about her, and anthropology might well compare her image to that of virgin girls sacrificed in far-flung religious rites. From late in the twentieth century, Nell looks to be a figure who could focus and purge cultural, collective, and personal guilt—particularly conscious and unconscious male guilt toward girls and women. Dickens's evocation of feeling around Nell in effect announces: "We adore this fe-

male child, sympathize with all she stands for, and feel dedicated to innocent, virtuous girlhood. Our society seeks not to brutalize but to protect
women and children."

The historical context for Nell and her counterpart, the "small servant" (51: 473) of the Brasses whom Swiveller denominates "the Marchioness" (57: 528), is that a poor, unprotected girl in the company of money-
hungry and morally irresponsible people is likely to be treated as an object
to be priced, bartered, used, seduced, degraded, and practically enslaved.
All over the world virgin girls throughout history have been sold. The
menace hovering about Nell would have been obvious to any informed
person of any class in the nineteenth century. That great eighteenth-
century optimist, progressive, and praiser of childhood Jean-Jacques Rousseau tells in his *Confessions* of an experience with his friend Cario in Venice
that expresses a whole climate of social and sexual attitudes. (It also suggests something of the equivocal nature of Swiveller's first reaction to the
plot to match him with Nell and his later benevolent relationship to the
Marchioness):

Cario . . . grew weary of always going to women who belonged to others and took
it into his head to have one of his own; and as we were inseparable he suggested
to me an arrangement which is not rare in Venice, that we should keep one between us. I agreed. The next question was to find a safe one. He made such thorough investigations that he unearthed a little girl of eleven or twelve, whom her
wretched mother wanted to sell. We went to see her together. My pity was stirred
at the sight of this child. She was fair and as gentle as a lamb. . . . We gave the
mother some money, and made arrangements for the daughter's keep. All this cost
us barely two *sequins* a month, and saved us more in other expenses, but as we had
to wait till she was mature, we had to sow a great deal before we could reap.
However, we were content to go and spend our evenings with the child, and
perhaps we got more agreeable amusement than if we had possessed her. . . .
Insensibly my heart grew fond of little Anzoletta, but with a paternal affection in
which my senses played so little part that as it increased the possibility of sensuality
entering into my feelings for her steadily diminished; I felt that I should be as
horrified at approaching this child, once she was old enough, as committing the
crime of incest. I saw the good Cario's feelings . . . taking a similar form. We were
procuring for ourselves, unthinkingly, pleasures no less charming but quite different from those we had first contemplated, and I am certain that however beautiful
that poor child might have become, far from being the corrupters of her innocence
we should have been its guardians.[8]

The importance of this passage and its relationship to Nell's virginity,
the male threat to her, male bonding and child abuse as subjects, the potential effects of a child-virgin on nineteenth-century sensibilities, and the

erotic twists of market economics stand out and need little emphasis. The passage, however, is not simple. The incident in Rousseau's words adds up to more than just an anecdote of corrupt sexism in the long history of the male piggishness that we love to squeal at nowadays (though it *is* worth a squeak). It points out in a matter-of-fact way the redemptive powers of the female virgin child and of incest taboos. It suggests reasons for the familial, incestuous bias of Victorian erotics as a way of defusing sexual exploitation. Familiarity with children breeds not contempt but potential sympathy, empathy, taboo, and sublimation.

From one point of view, the historical function and effects of Nell can be seen as an allegory—and not a very pretty one at all. The beautiful virgin-child at her death, *a sacrificial death*, is surrounded by a bunch of old men in the ecclesiastical grounds. Males famously made up a prominent, deeply affected audience for her picturesque demise—Dickens himself, for instance, and Thomas Carlyle, John Forster, New York stevedores, Colorado miners, as well as those grizzled veterans of misery around her bed.[9] A biblical passage from King David's last days, when the old, fading ruler is cold and lifeless, seems especially relevant here: "Wherefore his servants said unto him, Let there be sought for my lord the king a young virgin: and let her stand before the king and let her cherish him, and let her lie in thy bosom, that my lord the king may get heat" (1 Kings 1:1–4, 15). Nell, with her warmth and the promise of redemption and new hope for the world and the future—those utilitarian effects of her virgin's virtue—is brought in to revive the spiritual potency of the old dying patriarchal faith, now impotent to command the belief and authority it once could in the new world.

Virginity means untapped potential; that's one possible reading of Dickens's loose allegory. Sympathy for the innocent, sexually untouched child and her virgin goodness could become the basis of faith. But other, more cynical readings, like Wilde's, would become more likely. In James Joyce's *Finnegans Wake*, one of the funniest chapters in that "book of the dark" features a sermon by a Don Juan archetype masquerading as a priest and mock-Christ figure and preaching ostensibly moral advice to a group of schoolgirls.[10] The sermon he gives, however, keeps betraying desire; his righteousness is a cover for lecherous libido: Joyce is parodying the eroticism lurking beneath the moral rigidity of the previous century and the desire that hides behind the thin screens of prurience and repression.

The titles of Dickens novels in punning form creep into the lecher's admonitions to the girls about their modesty (e.g., "Doveyed Covetfilles"

[434.28] for *David Copperfield*). Joyce's sermonizer, letting a Victorian puss out of Dickens's bag, makes an outrageous pun by referring to feminine genital anatomy as "the old cupiosity shape" (434.30), a term that combines Cupid, concupiscence, and the figure of desire. Dickens's "cathedral" in Joyce has taken the shape of cupiosity. A Freudian, however, might well say that the Gothic cathedral, with its vaults, its crypts, its thrusting spires, its rounded apse and chapels, its flying buttresses, its built-in homage to virginity—like Dickens's literary version—has always been a structure made out of curious old cupiosity shapes and has always expressed a desire for regeneration (or regenerative desire) ultimately grounded in sacrificial eroticism.

V

Freud's brief, highly speculative inquiry into the nature of modern eroticism, "On the Universal Tendency to Debasement in the Sphere of Love,"[11] reflects, directly or indirectly, large patterns in the work of nineteenth-century novelists such as Dickens.[12] In it Freud notes how typical is the failure of men to unite affectionate feelings with the libido, and he states famously, "Where they love they do not desire and where they desire they cannot love."[13] He attributes in part the gap between love and desire to "the influences of strong childhood fixations and of later frustration in reality through the intervention of the barrier against incest."[14] Interestingly, in *The Old Curiosity Shop* Dickens genderizes this split between affection and desire in the figures of Nell and Quilp. This conflict is something like the classic nineteenth-century instance of the sex versus moral love, "whore versus virgin" syndrome in *Carmen*. (In Mérimée and Bizet both, Carmen opposes Micaela: Carmen is adult sex, while Micaela, the good girl, carries the letter and seal of the mother.)

Freud generalizes provocatively on the subject of love's dichotomies: "It sounds not only disagreeable but also paradoxical, yet it must nevertheless be said that anyone who is to be really free and happy in love must have surmounted his respect for women and have come to terms with the idea of incest with his mother or sister."[15] The very cultural situation to which Freud reacts is one that Dickens, a half-century earlier, for quite plausible reasons, morally favors and imaginatively projects: namely, a strong Oedipal and incestuous fixation, but with severe sexual taboos. As usual, the solution for one age becomes the problem for the next.

Dickens displaces and personifies the libidinous impulse. The lack of union between tenderness and sensuality shows up in bestial male figures who plague and torment girls they desire—figures such as Quilp and, in *Great Expectations*, Orlick and Bently Drummle, phallic blobs of id. There is no denying or minimizing the crisis of integrity in the erotic life that Dickens portrays. Schisms appear everywhere. Affection separates from desire; morality and love divide; sexuality is sundered from love. He touched those—and their name is legion—who wanted to believe in the redemptive force of love between male and female, but who felt that sexual desire was the disruptive enemy of kindness, fidelity, and religious idealism.

Civilization progresses, or at least survives, by the virginal wedding of one generation with the next in forbearance, chastity, and sympathetic concern for mutual suffering. Dickens's imagination sheds light on another observation by Freud in the "Debasement" essay: "Thus we may perhaps be forced to become reconciled to the idea that it is quite impossible to adjust the claims of the sexual instinct to the demands of civilization; that in consequence of its cultural development renunciation and suffering . . . cannot be avoided by the human race. . . . The very incapacity of the sexual instinct . . . becomes the source, however, of the noblest cultural achievements which are brought into being by ever more extensive sublimation."[16] The notion of a holy virgin would be one way of figuring that large concept.

Oedipus-Jocasta, Oedipus-Antigone, Electra-Agamemnon, Jocasta-Oedipus: I am groping awkwardly, as have many, for terms that loosely represent son-for-mother, father-for-daughter, daughter-for-father, and mother-for-son figures of erotic desire and constellations of libidinous flow. Such Victorian cross-generational erotic complexes were strategies and fixations of the nineteenth-century imagination evolving in particular historical conditions, destined by the growth of religiosity and the simultaneous undermining of supernaturalism; the transmission of reverence to women and children (in a time when the death rate for infants, children, and childbearing females remained high); the growing popularity of romantic love; new social awareness of the destabilizing nature of sexual desire; the cults of kindness, benevolent sentimentalism, and childhood innocence; the elevation of marketplace and biological competition into ideology; and the faster pace of change in all fields. Above all, as Mark Spilka puts it, there occurred the strengthening of "intensely insulated affections for members of the family, especially those of the opposite sex, and severe censure for sexual expression of any kind."[17]

In the age that glorified and popularized the close family as a moral, stabilizing institution, the Victorian ban on writing sex directly is linked to the symbolic eruptions of incestuous desire in novels and the fascination with the incest taboo in late-nineteenth-century anthropology and psychology. Sexual repression might flow into and shape images and fantasies that betray incestuous fixations, and they in turn might influence sexual impulse and behavior.

The Victorians, in an age of mutability, longed for emotional continuity. They wanted steady safe love lasting through life and, as conviction in otherworldly salvation waned, secure ties to the material past and future of this world.[18] The best way to achieve these things, many middle-class moralists thought, was to embrace the kind of attitude and action they found in affectionate filial responsibility and in loving parental concern—in short, "familialism." If such drives toward familial benevolence could include potential mates, if an erotic desire to want to marry someone who would be a good mother or father or an obedient, responsible child or a good big or little sister or brother could be inculcated, if people's libidos could be moralized, domesticated, and rhetorically shaped, they might desire responsibly. If incestuous drives could be desexed but preserved, if people would project and transfer them onto fitting partners or goals, then deflected libidinous energy from those various House-of-Atreus complexes might be safely gathered, refined, and used. Incestuous feeling controlled and transferred could become the friend of marriage, love, and family—not to mention literature.

William Thackeray's novel *Henry Esmond* (1853) revealingly broadcasts a nineteenth-century bent for idealized incestuous feeling. In it a poor eighteenth-century orphan gives up his passion for his wildly erotic foster-sister and marries his modest, insistently ethical foster-mother. By marrying the woman who mothered him, Esmond rejects sexual compulsion and chooses for his love filial and reverent emotion. In essence, he weds the supposedly libido-curbing socially responsible values of Victorian morality. Esmond's solution to his life's riddle was simply to follow and domesticate Oedipus.

Art, we know, often grows out of great tensions that, for various reasons, are difficult to express conceptually and explicitly. We can see why a society, a nation, and particular authors living with the traditional taboos surrounding incest and child exploitation—especially the use and abuse of girls—but also in circumstances that promote close, cloying family feeling and sexual temptation, would produce a literature permeated with incestuous conflicts and affect that nevertheless idealized virgin girls. Control the sexual impulse, sublimate incestuous energy, and you might release a potent force sustaining social coherence and ethical loyalties. Thus we get Dickens's paragon, self-sacrificing daughters, his child-mothers, his child-wives, his angel sisters, his loving and beloved orphans, and his rendering of passion across generations.

Thus also we find Quilp, the negative to the positive image of nineteenth-century sublimated incestuous bias. One reason Quilp carries such an emotional charge is that he breaks down the categories and barriers between child and adult. He is elderly, the putative father of the Marchioness, and in his sexual erotic prime, too, as testified to by his wife; but he is also like a child—small, juvenile in his behavior and many of his emotions. And he is like a walking, speaking, metaphorical and allegorical compendium of Freud's theories and examples of infantile sexuality. This literary gargoyle is to the *The Old Curiosity Shop*'s novelized cathedral of faiths what the id is to popularized, meliorative psychology. Quilp is polymorphously perverse, sadistic, a biter, who seems for all the world to be living out the oral, anal, and genital stages of infantile sexuality all at once. He is a violent, outrageous, narcissistic fantasy of infantile longing and adult exploitation of children, and his function is to drain away and make into a figure of play the vicious side of parent-child erotics.

VI

Plato's famous myth of love in his *Symposium* tells us that humans were originally one-sexed, but then these whole creatures were cut in half into two sexes, and all people now search compulsively for the missing other that would make them complete; love, in other words, is a search for complementary being. Dickens puts a slightly different slant on that erotic myth by showing that the sundering that begins and shapes the human quest for love is temporal and generational: One interpretation of the puzzling coming together of Pip and Miss Havisham in the fire scene of *Great Expectations*, or of the old man's feeling for Nell in *The Old Curiosity Shop*, would insist that people seek in love not only physical wholeness and unity of the sexes, but generational completeness and synchronicity of the human flesh, an imaginary bonding of oneness with the progenitors and progeny of the self in order—impossibly—to cancel out or reverse the process that makes human beings into lonely, desirous selves and alienated mental wanderers in private time. That incestuous desire itself must be accepted, figured, forgiven, fixed, mocked, inscribed, and purged in and by the fantastic imagination. Hence the deaths of Little Nell and Quilp, and the redemption of Swiveller and the child-servant in his fostering of her, and in their final union.

If Dickens's society is Oedipal, then its wishful dream is that it should be guided by a daughter, as Oedipus finally desires to be, to peace, harmony, and redemption. Ironically, Andrew Lang, in his faintly disparaging, late nineteenth-century introduction to *The Old Curiosity Shop*, questions the book's importance in these words: "Nobody has killed his father and married his mother, like Oedipous. To stir us greatly, as Sophocles does, by the situation of Oedipous, is to make a more daring and dangerous appeal, than is the attempt to stir us by a protracted description of the declining health and death of an interesting and sorely tried little girl."[19] But it is the Oedipus at Colonus, the blind old being led by the female progeny, that Dickens tried to make come alive for his world—and did for thousands of readers.

And there is a real New Oedipus—a pre-Oedipal Oedipus—in Dick Swiveller, the figure at the crossroads of Christian, comic, and erotic faith, and faith in a child, the improbable hero of a comic denouement. Dick can be seen to provide a novel solution to the erotic riddle that his era had posed. He reverses matters: Worldly love, so the philosophers had always hoped, would lead to a love of the good and higher things. Dick's answer to the plague of life, including the plague of love-life, is literally to create the Sphinx, Sophronia Sphinx, the name he later applies to the battered and abused little bastard servant-girl he first dubs the Marchioness. At the crossroads of his life, he meets a nameless, ageless child ("What's your name?" "Nothing." [51: 474] "How old are you?" "I don't know." [57: 527]), a stranger whom he treats with kindness, nourishes with food, and teaches to play. The imagined wish-fulfillment here is that nurturing kindness, parentlike, familial well-wishing, the desire for the good of another, should precede sexual desire and maturity. Hence the focus on the child. The angel and the cur—Nell and Quilp—shall die, but Swiveller and the Marchioness (who is just Nell's age) live. It's a pre-Freudian, post-Freudian dream: where superego and id were, there the healthy ego shall be. The incest taboo and family longings shall lead to happy matings. The oppressed love-child becomes the wife—the love-child whose education depends on Dick's reformation and on his common humanity and paternal sense of responsibility.

In Dickens and *The Old Curiosity Shop* comic and erotic faith meet in the companionship of child and man and in the regeneration of equanimity, pleasure, and exuberant language through the redeeming reconciliation of different generations with their incongruous drives. That union, however, is a highly unstable amalgam; and in both the happy ending of the Sphinx and the sacrificial ending of Nell we can see spawning the comic desperation of Lewis Carroll, the fatalistic, unmasking insight of Freud, the incest-obsession of the familial Joyce of *Finnegans Wake*, and that terrible tragicomic progeny of Victorian child-worship, Nabokov's *Lolita*. Dickens's subject of the tribulations, abuses, and idolizing of the child is now open.

The Crisis of Representation in
Dombey and Son

ROGER B. HENKLE

'DOMBEY AND SON' (1848) IS THE PIVOTAL NOVEL in Dickens's career. It comes after the early successes of the sentimental and comic novels; it is the first of the great social novels of his midcareer; and it marks a moment of crisis in his attitude toward his art and toward middle-class experience. There had been a relatively long stretch between *Dombey and Son* and its predecessor *Martin Chuzzlewit*, and we know from John Forster's accounts that it was a period in which Dickens reexamined his own craft after *Chuzzlewit*'s choppy reception, began to sour on the English middle-class culture forming around him, and toyed with an autobiography—addressing questions about his own past, about the experiences that formed his own subjectivity.[1]

Structurally, *Dombey and Son* seems to abort itself about a third of the way through. It opens with the birth of little Paul Dombey—the son of the title—and remains essentially absorbed with Paul's "progress" until his early death. The last days of Paul are rendered in such powerfully evocative and sentimental terms that readers can be drained by them. Yet after the compelling involvement in Paul's poignant life, we are abruptly obliged to shift our interests to another story, and it takes some shunting around of new and old characters before we can pick up the threads of a new set of relations. We seem to fall upon a dead spell in the narrative in which, like Paul's bereaved father Dombey, we need to reorganize ourselves emotionally—as the novel's plot seems obliged to do. Such an apparent dislocation, however, signifies something other than authorial indecision; it marks Dickens's realization that the old novelistic strategies of his previous successes can no longer serve to represent the new experience of the mid-Victorian period. It registers an engagement on new terms with another set of issues: the conjunction of the discourses of adult sexuality and middle-class economic desire, and the ambiguous role of art in rendering them. It identifies, in fact, a crisis of representation in the nineteenth-century realist novel.

I

Dickens customarily works through the tensions and contradictions of ideology in terms of familial relations. Father-daughter, mother-son, sister-brother combinations seek to represent, often in vexed, even perversely twisted terms, the configurations of power and desire that undergird the essential relations of the ascending middle-class capitalist social structure of mid-Victorian England. *Dombey and Son* is no exception; the novel begins at the heart of the family, with the birth of Paul and the almost immediate death of his mother. Dickens's protagonists are often motherless, but never does a character's life define itself so essentially through the maternal. Paul can never lift his mind and imagination beyond the trauma of that separation. His life is linked through a series of substitute mothers: first Polly Toodles, who is brought in to nurse him, then his sister Florence, in whom the maternal powers of the novel are invested, then Mrs. Pipchin. That life is in essence a short trajectory to a return to his mother, whom Paul imagines that he sees in his dying fantasy: "Now the boat was out at sea, but gliding smoothly on. And now there was a shore before him. Who stood on the bank! . . . 'Mama is like you, Floy. I know her by the face!'"[2]

As his last image suggests, Paul embodies within the novel the quality of oceanic feeling—an erasure of all distinction and a merging and flowing of identity that has been associated with the pre-Oedipal, the maternal. In his last night at Dr. Blimber's School, Paul's sensibility, which refuses to respond to the categories of modern life, dissolves all distinctions of class, status, age, and gender, creating an ambiance of affection and (because everyone is conscious that Paul is soon to die and can never be a creature of this world) of intense sentimentality. He represents a special order of feeling, one that is contrasted to the mode of thinking of his father, which defines itself on the basis of *difference*. The principal realm of differentiation is gender-coded, as the narrator reminds us when he observes that prior to Paul's birth, Dombey had spoken as if he had no issue. There was a daughter, Florence, to be sure, "but what was a girl to Dombey and Son! In the capital of the House's name and dignity, such a child was merely a piece of base coin that couldn't be invested (31)." To a certain extent, Dombey is only perpetuating the old patriarchal scheme that had ruled family dispositions for centuries. But he is also a figure of the new competitive bourgeois order that is rising to hegemony in the 1840's. He is a business-man, not a man of title or blood. It is especially telling, then, that such a figure reasserts gender discrimination so insistently throughout the novel. It implies a sensitiveness about masculine prerogative that goes beyond issues of power, as we shall see, and a pervasive self-doubt among the entrepreneurial males of the mid-nineteenth century about the premises of their own subjectivity. Dombey is one of many figures in the literature of the time whose impotence reflects middle-class anxieties about the role and nature of the man without an established social pedigree.[3]

The novel begins, then, opposing two kinds of mentality, two dis-courses: Paul's "maternal," nondifferentiating way of thinking, and Dom-bey's ethos of the competitive male. The distinction is illustrated in a scene in which Paul and his father sit silently together, "Mr. Dombey entertain-ing complicated worldly schemes and plans; the little image [Paul] enter-taining Heaven knows what wild fancies, half-formed thoughts, and won-dering speculations" (93). Dombey's is the mentality of the age's aggressive middle class: projective in its thinking, solidly based in materiality, full of "schemes and plans." Paul's mentality is adrift in fancy, half-formed and wandering. That conflict between the two modes of thinking dominates the world of the first third of the novel. The narrative oscillates, for in-stance, between the commercially determined sphere of the Dombeys and that of a pair of social anachronisms from the old seafaring days, Sol Gills and Captain Cuttle. Gills, his shop of nautical instruments and curiosities about to go to the bankruptcy auction block, observes in a puzzled way, "But competition, competition—new inventions, new inventions—altera-tion, alteration—the world's gone past me. I hardly know where I am myself; much less where my customers are" (41). This impression of hardly knowing where one is—an acute disorientation of one's own sense of sub-jectivity—proves to be symptomatic of the victims of the remarkable social and economic changes of the early Victorian period. The recourse of such characters is that taken by Dickens himself in his early fiction: an attempt to ground subjectivity and to organize the narrative of individual experi-ence through the discourse of the fairy tale.

II

The world of this novel does, in fact, seem to begin in a state of en-chantment. A curious spell is upon the land, freezing characters into their grotesque malformations. Even the Dombey mansion lies under the baleful power: "No magic dwelling-place in magic story, shut up in the heart of a thick wood, was ever more solitary and deserted to the fancy. . . . The spell upon it was more wasting than the spell that used to set enchanted houses sleeping once upon a time" (311). The customary promise of the fairy tale, of course, is that the curse will be lifted by mysterious help or luck. Sol Gills assuages his despair by dreaming of a fairy-tale life of good fortune for his ward, Walter Gay. And when Walter rescues Florence, who has been briefly kidnapped by the witchlike Good Mrs. Brown, the fairy-tale allusions tumble forth: "Walter picked up the shoe, and put it on [Florence's] little foot as the Prince might have fitted Cinderella's slipper on. He hung the rabbit-skin over his left arm; gave the right to Florence; and felt, not to say like Richard Whittington—that is a tame comparison—but like Saint George of England, with the dragon lying dead before him" (77–78).

Although we customarily think of the fairy tale as a way of educating us emotionally in the reality of gender division and generational difference, of providing us with a means of coming to terms with anxieties of sexuality and separation, the fairy-tale elements operate auratically in *Dombey and Son*. They evoke an emotional state, a quality of affect, in which ego boundaries are obscured. Dickens evokes the modal qualities of the fairy tale in order to plunge us back into the mentality of childhood, when we seemed to have a more innate sense of ourselves, when everything seemed to be quickened by how *we* felt about it, how *we* defined it. For Paul, it is forever the time in which he is bound into his mother and his loss of and desire for her. And thus the fairy tale would presumably serve as the "narrative mode" of the sensibility that the novel associates with Paul. There are no boundaries to his subjective state. Wherever he goes, he seems to dissolve all life into a realm of pure affect—of pathos or intense affection. And as is so often the case in Freud's description of the register of affect in dreams, the scenario of the emotional state rarely produces its own thematic coherence. Situations are magically poignant, or happy, or uncanny—and that is all we can say about them.

In a memorable scene, Paul sits for hours with Mrs. Pipchin in her boardinghouse that resembles an ogre's castle: "The good old lady might have been—not to record it disrespectfully—a witch, and Paul and her cat her two familiars, as they all sat by the fire together. It would have been quite in keeping with the appearance of the party if they had all sprung up the chimney in a high wind one night, and never been heard of any more" (107). Although the fanciful description contributes to the cumulative effect of Paul's strangeness, it stands in isolation from the narrative around it. It is a simile that teases us into the possibility of interpretation, but never undertakes it. It is a piece of a story—some tale that we must have heard and that we are ready to hear—but no more story follows.

The fairy tale, then, plays a special kind of role in the early episodes of *Dombey and Son*. It seems to be a means of registering affect, and through that of suggesting the quality of the more emotionally intense— and, in some cases, psychically unbounded—subjectivity that we associate with childhood. It does not provide, in most instances, a symbolic narrative for organizing the experiential world and for giving it meaning. In this novel, therefore, the fairy tale does not perform its usual function of registering and interpreting the socialization of the individual. It relinquishes much of its power as a narrativizing code.

Also, the fairy tale seems to have lost its other great aesthetic power: its ability to *transform* experience. As Sol Gills observes, the world of the 1840's is undergoing "alteration," symbolized in the novel not only by competition, but most dramatically by the building of the great railroads, which produced not only physical change, but also dislocations in people's sense of time and space. Stagg's Gardens, a run-down neighborhood in Camden Town, figures these processes, for it is being razed to make way for a railroad; when we see it in the early part of the novel, it is an image of inchoateness:

Everywhere were bridges that led nowhere; thoroughfares that were wholly impassable; Babel towers of chimneys, wanting half their height; temporary wooden houses and enclosures, and fragments of unfinished walls and arches, and piles of scaffolding, and wildernesses of bricks, and giant forms of cranes, and tripods straddling above nothing. There were a hundred thousand shapes and substances of incompleteness, wildly mingled out of their places, upside down, burrowing in the earth, aspiring in the air, mouldering in the water, and unintelligible as any dream. (65)

The fancy cannot put this vision together in its own terms; it cannot make it intelligible. Later in the novel Stagg's Gardens will be described again, when it is put together, made complete as the head of a streamlined new railroad line. It will be made intelligible as a function, a creation of the railroad itself. The steam engines, we are told, bubbled and trembled, "as if they were dilating with the secret knowledge of great powers yet unsuspected in them, and strong purposes not yet achieved" (218–19). That new world of power, forward projection, economic efficiency—the world of Dombey, in other words—carries through the process of transformation. What had once seemed only to be possible within the realm of the imagination is now exceeded by the powers of the economic order. It is almost as if the great magic that reigned in the art of the earlier Dickens novels is now itself in jeopardy.

III

In Paul's last hours two qualities of imagination war against each other. Tonight, "his fancy had a strange tendency to wander to the river, which he knew was flowing through the great city; and now he thought how black it was, and how deep it would look, reflecting the hosts of stars—and more than all, how steadily it rolled away to meet the sea." But when day begins to dawn again, the concrete experiential world fills his mind: "[H]e pictured to himself—pictured! he saw—the high church towers rising up into the morning sky, the town reviving, waking, starting into life once more. . . . Familiar sounds and cries came by degrees into the street below" (221). One vision has the indistinct flow and indeterminacy of the auratic, "fancies and half-formed thoughts"; the other is tied to objects, sounds, and movements of the material world. Since this passage occurs shortly before the death of Paul, the text seems to be telling us that the latter vision will prevail: Paul's sensibility had never been fixed to a concrete object or set of objects. It lacked materiality; it was disengaged from the world of experience that *Dombey and Son* purports to represent: "At his own bedroom window, there were crowds of thoughts that came on, one upon another, like rolling waves . . . where the clouds rose and first began; whence the wind issued on its rushing flight" (193). As lyrical as such musings are, their otherworldliness detaches them from the richly detailed and grounded social text that is one of the salient qualities of a Dickens novel. Dickens's force lies in his full realization of his world, and Paul's vision seems to draw the imagination away from that world. Our eyes, as readers, are lifted above the scene spread before us; like Paul we seem to be lost in a reverie. We have the sense that the impressions unfold in our minds; they do not arise from what our eyes are asked to see, nor are they transpositions from the mind of the character, Paul. On the contrary, in moments such as this, we seem to see *through* Paul, as if he were not there, or as if he were (as so many of Dickens's "spiritual" characters are) a focusing lens for us.

Throughout, in fact, Paul is rendered as something almost impalpable. While Dombey looms in the novel as opaque solidity, his son is small and pale and sickly, at times almost lost from sight. Dombey's palpability symbolizes his own reification, his "objectness," as we shall discuss later, but Paul is, contrastingly, a slight mark upon the social text, characterized by his diffidence, his quizzical nature, his translucence. Paul never quite comes into being in the physical world of the novel; as his positioning in the fairy-tale mentality implies, he represents the unformed self of childhood.

Because the sentimentality that Paul embodies in the novels stands against that crass, stultifying materialism that is being imposed by the new competitive economic order, Dickens problematizes his own vision through his rendering of Paul's role. As passionately as the author denounces a materially grounded imagination, and as stubbornly as he resists the notion that human subjectivity is a construct of the experiential world, the first part of *Dombey and Son* elaborates a text in which there is almost no site of an alternative subjectivity. Indeed, what we are being asked to fix our eyes upon as readers—"the rolling waves," "where the clouds rose and first began," "where the wind issues on its rushing flight"—is absence.

Dickens's great power as a novelist up to the time of *Dombey*—and his great popular success—comes from his ability to inscribe for his audience a relation to the text that covers that place of absence. Dickens is a master of narrative suture: he inscribes readers into the discourse so that they are invited to look at and respond to the objects being depicted (the actions, characters, scenes), and yet remain aware, often unconsciously, that their point of observation is being determined and manipulated by the narration. His readers are sensitized to the fact that their lines of sight, and also their values and their emotional and cognitive responses, are being shaped. Dickens relies on this rhetorically created position of his readers to go about transmitting qualities of compassion and family feeling that he assumes they share and that he wants to shore up against the inroads of competitiveness and materialism.

It is precisely through this "suturing" that Dickens constructs and transforms the subjectivity of readers. It places them in a position, as observers of the novel's action and judges of its values, that confirms and develops their own ideological and psychological being. Literature's unique power as an instrument of ideology (or as a site for the contestation of ideological formations) lies in its capacity to interpellate individual readers—to invoke them as people of certain values, certain social positions, status, and dispositions—and then to naturalize that self-identification through their responses to fictional characters and actions.

In the early sections of *Dombey and Son*, then, the novel appears to finesse both the failure of Paul to attain a subject position and the difficulty of establishing the mentality that Paul embodies as a real social force by relying on the sutured presence of the reader as a source of sentimentality and affective response. That had been, after all, Dickens's tactic in his earlier novels. Paul's death is one of the most sentimentalized episodes in the Dickensian canon—comparable to the death of Little Nell. Yet Little Nell's case carried the day for *The Old Curiosity Shop*; it sustained the whole novel. Paul, on the other hand, disappears from the scene early; sentimentality is no longer enough. What is sentimentality, after all, if not an emotive overflowing that stands in for presence, that tries to center feeling and desire without its being able to pinpoint the subjective source or focal point for them? Affect sweeps over and seeks to replace any comprehension of the motives or even objects of the desire, any comprehension of the relation of this feeling to one's need or one's sense of self. Dickens is no longer satisfied with that particular rhetorical affect.[4]

IV

Specifically, Dickens is ridding himself of the discourse of a debased Romanticism. It was Romanticism that situated the conception of the integral self in the recollections of a past state of being that seemed to be united with God and nature, and that was often most intensely registered in childhood. As Dickens turns, after the death of Paul, to a new set of characters and to a new sphere of action, he applies the deadly knife of his parodic powers to the distorted Victorian remains of Romantic rhetoric. Dombey, devastated by the loss of his male heir, surrenders himself to the scheming of impostors, such as Major Bagstock, who promise to bring him into "Society." The major introduces Dombey to Edith Skewton Granger, a stunning, haughty young woman who will become Dombey's second wife, and to her shambles of a mother, Mrs. Skewton, who, though "not young . . . was very blooming in the face—quite rosy [from excessive makeup]—and her dress and attitude were perfectly juvenile" (280). At one of their first meetings, Mrs. Skewton carries on as if she were the very soul of Wordsworthian sentiment. "Why are we not more natural?" she asks. "Dear me! With all those yearnings, and gushings, and impulsive throbbings that we have implanted in our soul, and which are so very charming, why are we not more natural?" Music, she insists, has "so much heart in it—undeveloped recollections of a previous state of existence—

and all that—which is truly charming" (288, 290). Begging later on for "more of the poetry of existence," she complains that the problem of the time is that "we are dreadfully real" (373). As grotesque and bogus as these expressions are, coming from the mouth of one of Dickens's most preposterous comic figures, they show up at an uncanny moment in the text. Right on the heels of the demise of Paul and his vision, at the moment when the novel is turning its attention to adult figures in the modern world of ambition and commerce—and when issues of sexuality emerge for the first time—such relentless travesties of the Romantic ideal signal to us the author's own need to clear away a tenor of thinking that has become itself debased. It is a purging so that something new can happen.

For the new era *is* "dreadfully real." The new world of Victorian experience requires a vision that is more empirically responsive than Paul's. And that vision must somehow construct new narrative formulas and means of interpretation, for it is clear that new discourses are abroad in the land, foremost among them the projections of power:

Away, with a shriek, and a roar, and a rattle, from the town, burrowing among the dwellings of men and making the streets hum, flashing out into the meadows for a moment, mining in through the damp earth, booming on in darkness and heavy air, bursting out again into the sunny day so bright and wide; away, with a shriek, and a roar, and a rattle, through the fields, through the woods, through the corn, through the hay, through the chalk, through the mould, through the clay, through the rock, among objects close at hand and almost in the grasp, ever flying from the traveller, and a deceitful distance ever moving slowly within him: like as in the track of the remorseless monster, Death! (275–76)

That is the steam engine train, the symbol of modern industry, the great transformer of Stagg's Garden (as if it were the new genie of the imagination), the creator of a new sense of time and space, and even of human stimulus.[5] The train symbolizes something more: the projective mentality that we associate with the middle class in a capitalist growth phase. The class is characterized by its disposition to think ahead, to plan for the future, to save and to invest—Dombey's way of thinking.

We would seem, then, to have fixed upon a discourse that articulates the nature of contemporary experience far better than a diffused mélange of fairy-tale wish-fulfillment and sentimentalized Romanticism. That railway journey occurs at the textual break following Paul's death. But we see also the contradictions inherent in the ideology that informs the discourse. The projective mentality as embodied in Dombey is unfeeling; and as exhilarating as the immense power and forward thrust of the railway is, it lacerates the countryside. It is like the projection of Death.

The task at hand is now twofold. It is first one of conceptualizing the mentality and the way of living that are determined by ideology—for ideology emerges as dispositions, practices, and everyday relations. It is also a matter of perceiving how the ideology affects representation—how it shapes or confounds the novelistic powers. The two are interlocked. Dombey, for instance, appears to be a nineteenth-century characterization of the *homo economicus* that Ian Watt defined in his chapter on *Robinson Crusoe* in *The Rise of the Novel*.[6] The ascetic puritanism that Max Weber and others found so congenial to capitalism—a rigorous self-discipline in attending to one's economic affairs and the conviction that hard work and the amassing of wealth serve the glory of God—has rigidified, Dickens suggests, in the course of the century. Dombey retains the lonely self-absorption; he lives by the belief that financial power signifies character; he treats those around him as commodities. But his behavior is no longer defined by the disciplined rationalism of the earlier individualism, and his rigor has turned to stiff-necked pride. The novel's narrator pauses often to brood upon Dombey:

> It was not in the nature of things that a man of Mr. Dombey's mood, opposed to such a spirit as he had raised against himself, should be softened in the imperious asperity of his temper; or that the cold hard armour of pride in which he lived encased, should be made more flexible by constant collision with haughty scorn and defiance. . . . [His nature] draws support and life from sweets and bitters; bowed down before, or unacknowledged, it still enslaves the breast in which it has its throne; and worshipped or rejected, is as hard a master as the Devil in dark fables. (538)

Dombey, like Dickens's capitalist tycoon Merdle in *Little Dorrit* and Anthony Trollope's Melmotte in *The Way We Live Now*, is a man self-enslaved, baffled by his wretchedness, knocking about in his own emptiness. It is significant that he has inherited his economic power; he is the son of him who amassed the fortune, the second generation. The self-made entrepreneurs, the great builders and venture capitalists so celebrated in the later eighteenth and early nineteenth centuries, lie between the Crusoes and the Dombeys. Dombey is a creature of advanced capitalism, unable to command his own course in the economic market, controlled instead by the caprices of trade, the vagaries of creditor confidence, and the treachery of his competitors. He is, as Norman Russell has pointed out, one of a number of such figures in the literature of early Victorianism,[7] but the social and psychological process through which this characterization of capitalist power was reached is mystifying. As we shall see, this is one of the instances in the novel in which the ideology of Victorian competition/capitalism appears to contain an inexplicable gap in representing its own genesis.

V

One way of accounting for such characterizations is through the breakdown of the patriarchal order, which, in the previous century, had rested largely in the aristocracy and landed gentry. Dombey is preeminently a failed father; the loss of his only son is the more symbolic because its signifies his failure to sustain the male line that had been the backbone of the patriarchy. Culturally, men like him should be the successors to the Old Order, figures of the ascendent middle class whose money was acquired in commerce, and who will be the foundations of new paternalistic leadership. But the Old Order is slow to surrender power in the nineteenth century, and the bourgeois male finds it difficult to justify himself in his own mind. He considers himself an impostor; he inherits no tradition or prerogative or easy assumption of authority through which to confirm his right to govern and command. So central are those anxieties of Dombey's self-construct that they are symbolized in the novel as sexual failure: sterility and impotence. He is depicted as one incapable of real passion: in instances where he should feel desire, he experiences only the dread of being shamed. The nature of his marriage to Edith is transparent; there is no sexual consummation, and he is figuratively—if not literally—cuckolded by Carker. Consequently, when Edith runs away from him, his primary response is paranoia: "The world. What the world thinks of him, how it looks at him, what it sees in him, and what it says—this is the haunting demon of his mind" (682). As if to underscore this, he huddles immediately with Major Bagstock, a lurid pastiche of blustering male lasciviousness—the kind of fellow who winks and leers and makes jokes about sexual conquests and failures. Thus, ironically, the mentality that premises itself on gender differentiation—the Dombey mentality—is represented as having no *sexual* element.

The symbol of the railroad stands in an intriguing relationship to this syndrome, for though the railroad is quite clearly a figuration of potency, even phallic in its forward thrust and penetration, it is a reification of the sexual.[8] It is an asexual abstraction of maleness, much as Dombey himself is: the phallicized power has been detached from desire and thus from subjectivity. Consequently, it can be as readily envisaged as the power of death as of transformation; this is proved when a train grinds Carker to pieces, wreaking Dombey's revenge for him—a scene cast in horrifically carnal terms: the train "spun him round and round, and struck him limb from limb, and licked his stream of life up with its fiery heat, and cast his mutilated fragments in the air" (743). The Dionysian railroad crushes sexuality.

There is an attempt in this novel, in scenes such as the one in which he seems to be part of the train's trajectory, to transpose Dombey and the railroad, as a means of moving toward some measure of interpretation of whatever social forces they both represent and toward some understanding of where they came from, where they might go. The tycoon and the railroad, however, become a problematic nexus of symbols for those, like Dickens, who seek to find the means of interpreting the ideology of their time. The nexus defies interpretation because there is no way to inscribe them in a construction of subjectivity. The railroad is simply dehumanized force and movement. As we can see in the cited description of it, the railroad erases the coherence of human consciousness as objects and places fly by the rider, and he experiences "a deceitful distance moving slowly within him." Although there are earnest efforts within the early Victorian period to account for the capitalist tycoon, such as Samuel Smiles's popular book *Self-Help*, the figure remains in much of the fiction a psychologically obscure phenomenon, especially those like Dombey who are of the second generation. The problem is crucial in the realist novel of the period because the primary enterprise of that novel is to weave social phenomena into the process of constructing subjectivity. The thrust of the bourgeois ideology, after all, is to establish the individual as the center for understanding and meaning. Thus literary characterization has a function beyond the depiction of various social types; it has to be a site on which a subjectivity that comprehends the experiential world can be constructed and elaborated upon. We have seen how necessary that is in the instance of little Paul, who could not provide such a site.

A corresponding problematic unfolds with respect to the characterization of Dombey. The emptiness of Dombey becomes a motif throughout much of the novel. He is most often seen brooding alone in his study, unable to comprehend his own balked and obscure feelings, let alone communicate them. What is so striking about these set pieces is that he is always *being seen*. Either the reader is invited by the narrator to observe

Dombey in his loneliness, or Florence is pictured watching Dombey, afraid to speak to him, yet trying to engulf him in her devotion and love, as if to make him become human. As his own fear of what "the world" will think of him implies, Dombey does not exist except in the observation of other people. Thus, when he hits Florence, whose gaze had been the only hope of humanizing him, he essentially ceases to exist: "She only knew that she had no Father upon earth, and she said so, many times" (650). And thus it is that in the depths of his despair, Dombey has no self at all. For some time after his financial ruin, he lives in isolation, unseen, in his study. Toward the end, he glimpses in the mirror "a special, haggard, wasted likeness of himself" (801), imagines his own death, and begins to fantasize obsessively on the trickling of his blood out the study doorway into the hall of the mansion. He foresees people walking though it. Gradually, the spectre in the mirror takes on awful reality:

> He glanced at it occasionally, very curious to watch its motions, and he marked how wicked and murderous the hand looked.
> Now it was thinking again! What was it thinking?
> Whether they would tread in the blood when it crept so far, and carry it about the house among those many prints of feet, or even out into the street.
> It sat down, with its eyes upon the empty fireplace, and as it lost itself in thought there shone into the room a gleam of light; a ray of sun. It was quite unmindful, and sat thinking. Suddenly it rose, with a terrible face, and that guilty hand grasping what was in its breast. (801)

The absence of a centered subjectivity has reached its full symbolic figuration at this point. It is an Other, a mirror image that acts. But just as Dombey's image in the mirror is about to reflect the stabbing of himself, he is interrupted by a "wild, loud, piercing, loving, rapturous cry," from Florence. Her entry reconstitutes Dombey's being, for he is brought once again into her realm of sight. She can now ultimately redeem him into humanity as the recipient (object) of her sutured subjectivity and its compassion.

The other symbolic characteristic of the portrait of Dombey is his stiffness. He looms, particularly to Florence, as a solemn wooden figure, massive as the heavy furniture that fills the dark mansion. He is inflexible in all company, "gloomy, sullen, irksome, and unyielding," unable to articulate himself into social movement. Dombey's sheer mass, his rigidity, his resistance to movement and change, epitomize a recurrent motif of the novel itself: the difficulty of changing things with kinetic energy—the difficulty of transformation. We see it in the description of Dombey's mansion: "Gorgon-like," the archway "curling and twisting like a petrifaction," curtains "drooping heavily . . . like cumbrous palls" (311). We observe it in the panoply of paralyzed or rheumatically crippled or disjointed characters in the book. The powers of imagination appear to have reached an impasse; again and again they encounter beings and objects that they do not seem to be able to transmute or bring to life. It is almost as if the agonies Dickens complained of in composing *Dombey and Son*—what he called the "convulsions of Dombey"—were manifesting themselves in the struggles of the book with its material.

VI

The difficulties apparently confronting the imagination as it tries to rework the hard metal of post–industrial revolution experience signify a problem with representation itself. Confronted, as we have noted, with the absence of a base on which to construct subjectivity (and with it an interpretive center) in the character of Dombey, Dickens once again shifts that burden onto the observer—the presence that "reads" Dombey and that in a sense creates his being and situates it within a value system. As we noted, we as readers share with Florence Dombey the position of being a constant observer of him. That shared position creates a kind of transference between us and Florence, and it foregrounds the process of suturing, since we see her doing what we are doing. Dickens intends that, of course, because Florence is presumably the transmitter of value in the novel, the heroine whose constancy, unwavering compassion, and pluckiness (even in the face of neglect and abandonment) imply an integral, developed subjectivity. She fulfills in the text the complex function of being an emblem of subjectivity, but as an observer, an outsider like us, who is woven into the subtext of giving meaning to Dombey and the experience he stands for. The redemptive heroines in Dickens's novels often function in this way; Esther Summerson in *Bleak House* and Little Dorrit provide other examples.

To be sure, Florence is a major character in the novel in her own right, and has her own tale, ending in a happy marriage to Walter Gay and the raising of a family that will be the hope of the future (and into which the debilitated, essentially helpless Dombey is invited). But she is excluded from the vital activity of the new social order. Throughout much of the novel, Florence is a virtual captive in the Dombey mansion, gazing through the windows at the world outside. And when she does flee into that world, she is only briefly (but nightmarishly) exposed to its tumult, and then rescued from it by Captain Cuttle. All the subsequent scenes involving Florence take place (in a sense) out of the main arena of contemporary social action—out of the "real world," in other words. Florence is assigned to a realm of childlike romance, in which she marries the boy of her dreams without the slightest hint of sexual passion, and in which she is surrounded by cute little people, such as Toots and Susan Nipper, Captain Cuttle and Sol Gills. It is regression again to the puerility of the fairy tale, contrasting sharply in terms of dramatic energy and psychological complexity to the other sphere of the text, where Edith, Carker, and Dombey—all figures of the adult experiential world—drive to their breathless conclusions.

Such a treatment of Florence inevitably undercuts the value system that she brings into the novel. Florence represents the maternal, not in the pre-Oedipal formulation of the earlier sections of the book (although she certainly plays her part in them), but now presumably as the maternal qualities of the adult, gender-discriminate sphere. Happily married, the mother of two children, a source of domestic stability, she is in a normative adult position in the culture. Yet how she came to that position is something that even the text finds "a marvel":

Thus living in a dream wherein the overflowing love of her young heart expended itself on airy forms, and in a real world where she had experienced little but the rolling back of that strong tide upon itself, Florence grew to be seventeen. . . . A child in innocent simplicity, a woman in her modest self-reliance, and her deep intensity of feeling; both child and woman seemed at once [to be] expressed in her fair face and fragile delicacy of shape, and gracefully to mingle there. (624)

Although Dickens describes a natural moment of passage, his elision here and elsewhere of any awakening to sexuality or desire in Florence, and his generally coy and evasive account of her courtship with Walter, mask his almost congenital uneasiness as an artist in trying to portray sexuality in his female redemptive/maternal figures. That uneasiness goes beyond Victorian decorum, for he is not otherwise reluctant to represent passion. It betrays his ambivalence toward those figures. Such ambivalence manifests itself in the preoccupation of the text with the awful mother (Mrs. Skewton, Good Mrs. Brown) or the absent mother (Florence's mother and Edith). The role of motherhood appears to be highly vexed, and all the more so because of the daughter-mother reversal that Florence herself must enact in serving as mother to her own father. The normative quality of the maternal is unstable here, as in all of Dickens's works.

In addition, we cannot ignore the fact that Florence has been a victim of the social order that Dombey inhabits. The fact that the redemptive values that are to be sutured in must come from the victims and the powerless, from the children and little people of no economic or apparent social consequence in society, suggests that the very code of middle-class values is being synthesized from the bottom up. Dickens is one of the many influential voices in nineteenth-century England who attempted to formulate bourgeois discourse through an extrapolation from the Other, from the urban poor, the old and anachronistic, the lesser bourgeoisie, from children and women. Whatever the many and complex reasons for this particular synthesis, its effect is a mystifying of the concrete relations and processes of mid-Victorian ideology. Such a formulation necessarily produces the kinds of contradiction we are accustomed to find in the representation of Victorian women, and it occludes the insufficiency of the culture's understanding of its own class construction, particularly of the dominant male figures such as Dombey.

VII

The difficulties of rendering subjectivity in *Dombey and Son* become both more clear and more complex when we look at the other key figures in the novel: Carker and Edith. These two characters represent other forces and relations in the social and economic world of the 1840's. Carker, for instance, occupies a different position in the commercial world than Dombey does, for Carker is the manager of the firm Dombey and Son, a man who has had to claw his way up the corporate ladder, thriving by his wits and inspired by his ambition. His drive for power is fueled in part by his resentment of and lack of respect for those in power. In this he embodies what Dickens considers to be the disturbing qualities of the new breed emerging into the economic world.

His counterpart, Edith Granger, who joins him in the ruin and humiliation of Dombey, represents another facet of the changed socioeconomic circumstance. She is a stunning beauty who has been completely commodified. As if to herald the onset of the consumer society of the second half of the nineteenth century, she exists purely in the realm of market exchange.

"I am a woman," she said . . . "who from her childhood has been shamed and steeled. I have been offered and rejected, put up and appraised, until my very soul has sickened. I have not had an accomplishment or grace that might have been a resource to me, but it has been paraded and vended to enhance my value, as if the common crier had called it through the streets." (724)

Her mother sells her in marriage to Dombey, and neither party to the bargain need be disabused about the lovelessness, the purely commercial character of the arrangement.

"[H]awked and vended here and there . . . until . . . I loathe myself" (382), as she says, she demonstrates the particular psychic trauma that Dickens assigns to the commodification of women in modern society. Like another woman who sells her beauty to the highest bidder, Lady Dedlock of *Bleak House*, Edith turns against herself. The narrator speaks of "her remarkable air of opposition to herself" (290), and in a candid moment, she describes her pride as one that "has been galled and goaded, through many shameful years, and has never recoiled except upon itself; a pride that has debased its owner with the consciousness of deep humiliation . . . [that] like all else belonging to the same possessor, has been self-contempt, mere hardihood and ruin" (585–86).

The strength of this psychic energy—for Edith and Carker stand out in the text for their often melodramatically rendered intensity—reveals Dickens's awareness of the avid depth of his culture's engagement with commodification itself. His portrayal of Edith suggests that this engagement is a deeply destructive element in the formation of many women; it renders the construction of subjectivity in such women impossible: "I was a woman—artful, designing, mercenary, laying snares for men—before I knew myself" (381), Edith cries out. It also suggests that there is a considerable psychological engagement of the society itself in commodification, for Edith seethes with sexual energy, and if the site of libidinal energy in a text is any locus for the driving forces that seek representation, then the conjunction of the economic energies engaged in commodification and those of sexual desire can be identified as a crucial preoccupation of *Dombey and Son*.

On the surface, at least, the form those sexual energies take is determined by gender. Edith makes them into a canker; they torment her in ways that prevent her from developing her other capacities. They denature her own emotions, and seem to be directed inwards. In James Carker they take the shape of pure desire. In him as well the sexual is a factor of his economic impulses, but here the governing dynamic is acquisitiveness. Lust manifests itself as an exercise of power over a desired object. Looking at Edith, he reflects that "he would have sold his soul to root her, in her beauty, to the floor, and make her arms drop at her sides, and have her at his mercy" (729).

Desire defines Carker, because, like so many of Dickens's villains, he seems to have no origins. His sheer avarice comes out of nowhere. We learn that he has a family: a sister and brother whom he has essentially shut out of his life, and who live simple lives, the brother a symbol of those left behind in the hard race for financial success. But Carker resolutely closes off his past as if to deny the experience that made him. Almost all Dickens's novels, as Raymond Williams has noted, engage in a search for the missing links of the past, for a source that explains the current state of evil.[9] It is an effort to account for the forces that drive the selfish competitive world—an effort to penetrate across the mysterious gaps that the bourgeois ideology constructs for itself. Experience is, in fact, a kind of lost text of the new social order; there is no clear history of actions that would have shaped motive and desire. On the contrary, the shift that Dickens records is away from a society grounded in actions as the definers of being, toward one that writes itself as a new text. That presumably lends significance to the story of Florence's husband Walter Gay, who proves his mettle by going to sea, that old crucible of character developed through actions, before he begins his admirable movement up the economic ladder. Walter, however, never comes to life in the novel; he represents only a boyish fascination with the ideal of a subjectivity founded on adventure. It is Carker who seems to embody the new phase of capitalism, for he attains power through access to information: "Frequently when the clerks were all gone, the offices dark and empty, and all similar places of business shut up, Mr. Carker, with the whole anatomy of the iron room laid bare before him, would explore the mysteries of books and papers, with the patient progress of a man who was dissecting the minutest nerves and fibres of his subject" (605).

The fellow clerk Morfin tries to account for Carker's manipulations of the firm's destiny by saying, "in the midst of many transactions of the House, in most parts of the world: a great labyrinth of which only he held the clue: he had had the opportunity, and he seems to have used it, of keeping the various results afloat, when ascertained, and substituting estimates and generalities for facts" (714). We are entering upon a new sphere of business, Dickens is saying, a time in which realities give way to the manipulation of commercial and legal fictions. The empirical mentality of the middle class has now moved on to the weighing and measuring of textualized matter, of information rather than experience.

VIII

What does this mean for the artist of such a phase? If *Dombey and Son* is to be an attempt to represent the new social order—one of several such novels by an author who is himself a product of empiricism—will it not, as is so often the case with art, be affected by the formal qualities of its subject matter? This would seem to be more clearly a possibility in a novel that has explicitly forsaken one mode of representation—the sentimental discourses of Dickens's earlier work—for one that will more truly come to terms with the contemporary social and economic situation. Such speculations take on more substance when we discover that Carker and Edith are the only "artists" in the novel. As if to reveal the pattern of his own literary anxieties, Dickens ironically inscribes the hands and the eyes of the artist into the two figures who are most deeply implicated in the practices of economic desire and consumption.

Carker proves to be not only a calculating student of data and information, a master of the texts of commercial fictions, but a consummate reader of people. Dombey lets it drop that Carker "is a very creditable artist himself" (373), and Edith at one point trembles and recoils, realizing "that he read her life as though it were a vile book, and fluttered the leaves before her in slight looks and tones of voice which no one else could detect" (502). It is all the more ironic that Carker is, as Edith's intuition implies, a voyeur. He is a great watcher of the people he wants to write into his own text: while "gentle Florence tossed on an uneasy sea of doubt and hope . . . Mr. Carker, like a scaly monster of the deep, swam down below, and kept his shining eye upon her" (385). The metaphor tells us that Carker's realm of insidious creation occurs beneath the surface, in the dark currents of sexuality and the unconscious.

Carker is more than an observer; he is a grand schemer of the novel. No one plots his own melodrama as assiduously as he does. No one possesses the mysterious powers of insight and control that enable him not only to write the discourses of Dombey and Edith but to hold hapless Rob the Grinder in virtual mesmeric thrall. No matter that his is an evil text. No matter that he too cannot construct a subjectivity through which to give meaning to his text's discourse. His text is the source of energy, sexuality, movement. When we are in the presence of Carker and Edith we are held in the illusion of creative power, of change, of inscription of the new acquisitive mentality. We are engrossed in the mirage of representation—the author hinting to us the elements of voyeurism, sexual desire, exploitation, and manipulation that would make up the art of the realistic novel of the contemporary economic/social order.

The further dimensions of the crisis of representation—which has preoccupied the entire book, and which is a measure, it seems, of the book's complexity—emerge in the moment during Dombey's "courtship" of Edith when she does a watercolor for him, and Carker reflects upon it:

Thinking, perhaps, as he rode, that even this trivial sketch had been made and delivered to its owner, as if it had been bargained for and bought. Thinking, perhaps, that although she had assented with such perfect readiness to [Dombey's] request, her haughty face, bent over the drawing, or glancing at the distant objects represented in it, had been the face of a proud woman, engaged in a sordid and miserable transaction. (379)

The commodification of Edith and the commodification of art come together in this scene. We are presented with not only the incipient commercialization of art (likely to be on the mind of an author of best-sellers keenly attuned to his market through the process of publishing a book such as *Dombey and Son* in monthly numbers) [10] but the aesthetic implications of an art so inscribed into the commercial world. In bargaining away herself, and bargaining away her painting, Edith is selling beauty in both cases.

The modern age, in its redetermination of aesthetic categories, threatens the abstract concept of beauty itself. The railroad train throws out of kilter all the harmonies of the human relation to the movement of travel and to the environment through which one passes. It even denies the rider his experiential connection to the means of travel, which Thomas De Quincey notes, measures the drama of stagecoach passage in the "dilated nostril, spasmodic muscles, and thunder-beating hoofs" of the horses. [11] It will be decades before an aesthetic of industrial sights and objects will acquire respectability in painting. Fiction, in contrast, is boldly making art out of the ravaged and corrupted conditions of the new urban environment, especially in the hands of men like Dickens. It makes this art, however, with a certain degree of ambivalence, as if it sensed it was a party to the despoliation of some preexisting, more integral, comelier world.

Thus *Dombey and Son* broods over the desecration of beauty—not only through the commodification of Edith but also in the despoliation of Alice Brown. Alice is the mirror image of Edith (she is, in fact, the child of Edith's uncle), and she was in her early days as spellbinding a beauty as her cousin. She too was trained while young to vaunt herself a commodity on the market, but because *her* mother became a derelict, Alice was used badly, by none other than Carker himself, who picked her up like "a toy" and then discarded her. She came before a cruel judge on a minor offense, and was sentenced to transportation under harsh conditions of servitude. She returns eventually to England, but possessed now of only the hardened remnants of her fine looks. Her death at the end of the novel is a heavily overdetermined moment in the text, juxtaposed against Florence's happiness, and set out as one of the last dramatic episodes of the story. Alice's mother laments the wasting of beauty itself: "My handsome gal . . . Oh! is the likeness gone, and is it my gal—only my gal—that's to change so! . . . for all she's so quiet now; but she'll shame 'em with her good looks yet. Ha, ha! *She'll* shame 'em, will my handsome daughter!" (784–85).

The narration underscores the dimensions of her death: "Nothing lay there, any longer, but the ruin of the mortal house on which the rain had beaten, and the black hair that had fluttered in the wintry wind" (786). It is an emblematic moment; one of those powerful set-pieces for which Dickens is famous. She is natural beauty—and at one time innocence—desecrated by the twin influences of the new urban condition, that by-product of the industrial ethos, and by Carker, a figure of economic acquisitiveness, desire, and a new and deeply troubling visual and, yes, "authorial" presence.

It is going too far to read a sense of complicity on Dickens's part, as an artist experimenting with the means of rendering this new order, in the despoliation of beauty. Yet the text surely records his uneasiness, as he searches for the appropriate modes of representation of the actualities he apprehends. The novel even hankers after the old Romantic "verities" that it had travestied earlier on, by reminding us that Carker had been characterized by his inability, keen though he was in other ways, to observe Nature around him. And Florence is invoked at the last for her capacity to sustain the constancy that Dickens would like to associate with the auratic qualities of art—the uniqueness, immutability, and integral subjectivity that composes aura. But that serves only as a coda, for *Dombey and Son* has already undertaken its major and complex reconsideration of representation.

Impersonal Violence: The Penetrating Gaze and the Field of Narration in *Caleb Williams*

JOHN BENDER

MY SUBJECT IS THE VIOLENCE HABITUATED WITHIN certain techniques of impersonal narration typical of realist prose fiction. I want to point to issues at once broad, complex, and by no means intuitively obvious. In developing them here, however, I concentrate mainly upon William Godwin's attempt, in his novel *Caleb Williams*, at a radical critique of the machinery of character and conscience as socially, legally, and governmentally constructed during the Enlightenment—a critique ultimately overwhelmed from within by the technology it assailed.

I

I begin with three quotations, the first from Jonathan Swift's Hack in "A Digression on Madness." Both Swift's dichotomy between ordinary vision and the scientific gaze and his metaphor fusing female skin and foppish clothing—his feminization of the body under the knife of scientistic inquiry— emerge as uncannily prophetic:

The two Senses, to which all Objects first address themselves, are the Sight and the Touch; These never examine farther than the Colour, the Shape, the Size, and whatever other Qualities dwell, or are drawn by Art upon the Outward of Bodies; and then comes Reason officiously, with Tools for cutting, and opening, and mangling, and piercing, offering to demonstrate, that they are not of the same consistence quite thro. . . . therefore, in order to save the Charges of all such expensive Anatomy for the Time to come; I do here think fit to inform the Reader, that in such Conclusions as these, Reason is certainly in the Right; and that in most Corporeal Beings, which have fallen under my Cognizance, the *Outside* hath been infinitely preferable to the *In*: Whereof I have been farther convinced from some late Experiments. Last Week I saw a Woman *flay'd*, and you will hardly believe, how much it altered her Person for the worse.

Yesterday I ordered the Carcass of a *Beau* to be stript in my Presence; when we were all amazed to find so many unsuspected Faults under one Suit of Clothes: Then I laid open his *Brain*, his *Heart*, and his *Spleen*; But, I plainly perceived at every Operation, that the farther we proceeded, we found the Defects encrease upon us in Number and Bulk: from all which, I justly formed this Conclusion to my self; That whatever Philosopher or Projector can find out an Art to sodder and patch up the Flaws and Imperfections of Nature, will deserve much better of Mankind, and teach us a more useful Science, than that so much in present Esteem, of widening and exposing them.[1]

Swift's contempt for deluded rationalist projectors leads him to prefigure, from an opposite political perspective, a counter-Enlightenment rebel like William Blake, and to offer a satiric anticipation of Godwin's political idealism. Swift's Houyhnhnms in fact distilled for Godwin an ideal of society governed by orderly thought and practice—that is to say, a society inhabited by Godwin's peculiar brand of individually autonomous rationalism, by benevolence, and by honesty, rather than by institutions and contractual rights.[2]

This counter-Enlightenment current surfaces, too, in poststructuralist thinking, for example, in Jacques Derrida's appreciation of the thought of Emmanuel Lévinas, entitled "Violence and Metaphysics":

Incapable of respecting the Being and meaning of the other, phenomenology and ontology would be philosophies of violence . . . [connected with] the ancient clandestine friendship between light and power, and the ancient complicity between theoretical objectivity and technico–political possession. . . . The heliological *metaphor* only turns away our glance, providing an alibi for the historical violence of light: a displacement of technico–political oppression in the direction of philosophical discourse.[3]

The metaphor of "enlightenment," which we inherit from the eighteenth century, is one of those "heliological metaphors" that conceals the impersonal violence involved in the scientistic framing of objects—in effacing mysterious otherness by infiltrating autonomous bodies with knowledge, by "flaying" them with light's probing rays. When the form of knowledge known as realist narrative infiltrates the bodies and minds it represents, as it progressively does in the eighteenth-century novel, its "technico-political possession" dominates and mutilates—symbolically dissects and even castrates—these bodies whether the instrument is the anatomical knife in the impartial hands of Reason that exposes flaws in the carcass of Swift's Beau, or the penetrating gaze of clinical inquiry, or the novelistic depiction of consciousness. Caleb Williams is no more than a representative victim of enlightened enquiry.

The third quotation comes from a preface that Godwin wrote nearly forty years after *Caleb Williams*'s publication. He thematizes the metaphor of dissection, also a favorite of his novelistic predecessors:

I began my narrative . . . in the third person. But I speedily became dissatisfied. I then assumed the first person, making the hero of my tale his own historian. . . . [This] was infinitely the best adapted . . . to my vein of delineation, where the thing in which my imagination revelled the most freely, was the analysis of the private and internal operations of the mind, employing my metaphysical dissecting knife in tracing and laying bare the involutions of motive. . . . I rather amused myself with tracing a certain similitude between the story . . . and the tale of Bluebeard. . . . Falkland was my Bluebeard, who had perpetrated atrocious crimes. . . . Caleb Williams was the wife, who in spite of warning, persisted in his attempts to discover the forbidden secret; and, when he had succeeded, struggled fruitlessly to escape the consequences, as the wife of Bluebeard in washing the key of the ensanguined chamber, who, as often as she cleared the stain of blood from the one side, found it showing itself with frightful distinctness on the other.[4]

Later, I shall recur to this belated preface by Godwin. For now, let me just point out that he views his assumption of Caleb's first-person voice as a metaphysical dissection and that he feminizes Caleb as the last in the sequence of Bluebeard's murdered wives. The context of this passage includes Godwin's review of the fictional analogues on which he depended and clearly places Caleb in a long line of novelistic cadavers whose authors were, as Godwin says, "employed upon the same mine as myself, however different was the vein they pursued: we were all of us engaged in exploring the entrails of mind and motive" (340). Hogarth already had conceived such exploration as the literal dissection of criminal innards illustrated in the final plate of his *Four Stages of Cruelty* and had visually likened the process to a juridical trial—the scene of action more prevalent than any other in *Caleb Williams*.[5]

II

It is time to turn to certain framing propositions. A first set concerns the social and psychological significance of the emergence of the third–person narrative form known as *style indirect libre* (free indirect discourse), a technical innovation historically specific to the later eighteenth century that enables the presentation of consciousness through seemingly untrammeled, all–seeing, impersonal narration. As Dorrit Cohn says, free indirect discourse is a device "for rendering a character's thought in his own idiom while maintaining the third-person reference and the basic tense of narration."[6] It is the characteristic mechanism for securing the illusion of transparency that distinguishes the realist novel from the later eighteenth century onward. Transparency is the convention that both author and beholder are absent from a representation, the objects of which are rendered as if their externals were entirely perceptible in a unified field of vision and their internality fully accessible. Flaubert condensed the basic principle into a vivid formulation: "The illusion (if there is one) comes . . . from the *impersonality* of the work. . . . The artist in his work must be like God in his creation—invisible and all-powerful: he must be everywhere felt, but never seen." Free indirect discourse disperses authoritative presence into the very third-person grammar and syntax through which the illusion of consciousness is created. The technique's emergence in narrative fiction correlates historically with the projection of impersonal authority in the penitentiary prison as epitomized by Jeremy Bentham's *Panopticon*. Bentham's idealized plan revealed that the operational fact of the penitentiary is what he called the "principle of inspection," not the person of the inspector. The point is that the inspector-keeper is not really omniscient, or even really a person, but rather that the transparency of penitentiary architecture forces the prisoner to *imagine* him as such. Reformation hinges upon the conviction that omniscience enfolds being.[7]

Both free indirect discourse and Bentham's "principle of inspection" correlate, further, with Adam Smith's identification of the sympathetic interchange of "I" and "other" as the fundamental psychic mechanism establishing conscience and character through the introjection of social norms as individual values. Thus, by a central irony, the sensation of sympathy founds an order of power. Smith, who named this internalized representation of the third person the "impartial spectator," himself sometimes employed narrative devices very similar to free indirect discourse. He presents his construction as a natural universal, whereas I view it as a description of the dominant behavioral ideology or social system of post-Enlightenment culture. Later, in my analysis of *Caleb Williams*, I will show how Godwin attempted to restage the very mechanisms of this ideology to expose it as a system of domination.[8]

Smith's contemporary Goldsmith allows us to see the embodiment of the "impartial spectator" in literary culture, and to uncover the dispersed and secret assertions of omniscience in the seemingly private voice of the individual. *The Vicar of Wakefield*, though written during the 1760's in the first person and not self-evidently part of the prehistory of free indirect discourse, nonetheless reaches toward this technique. Certain passages in the novel can be understood as third-person narration reinscribed *as if* from the first-person perspective of the vicar.[9] The first-person subject emerges as a remarkably permeable web spun of individual sensations but *structured* by the impersonal geometry of sociopsychic organization. In hindsight, this fact has startling political implications for Goldsmith's case, since not merely his specific advocacy of penitentiary confinement but the dispersed, impersonal grounding of his narration cut across the grain of his articulate philosophy as a nostalgic country conservative with longings—à la Bolingbroke—for the concentration of authority in the highly individual person of a paternalistic king.

Godwin presents the obverse case: he is a utopian anarchist whose attack on personified authority in *Caleb Williams* also is staged within a field of narration that profoundly contradicts his enterprise. So compelling is the teleology of representation as configured in the realist novel that Godwin not only recast the ending of his story in conformity to its dynamic, but he proceeded thereafter to a wholesale rewriting of *Political Justice*. This rewriting, as well as further insertions in *Caleb Williams*, indicate that the novel became a conflictual scene within which Godwin's initial belief in radically individualistic virtue could not maintain itself. His thought remained in the current of rational dissent, but was enveloped within a delineation of moral being that emerged as increasingly hegemonic from the 1760's onward and that established a dialectic between a psychologized inner world of subjective reflection and an abstracted social order introjected through sympathetic identification with representative individuals. The gaze, and of course the spectatorship attendant upon it, are primary media within which this dialectic operates but the broader issues at stake concern the *vraisemblable*—the appearance of reality— within which post-Enlightenment culture constructs character and social relations.

Contemporary discussion of the gaze as a mechanism embraces ranges of generalization too vast and subtleties of distinction too refined for complete exposition here. But some opening to the topic is required by way of a second set of framing propositions. Especially relevant in this context are concerns about sexual domination brought forward in the work of Laura Mulvey and other feminist film theorists, and questions about the history of the gaze raised by Michel Foucault.[10] They have assisted in historicizing the gaze as an ideologically laden cultural procedure that works to stabilize social forms by representing the political order as if it arose naturally from individual perception and psychology. This procedure establishes subjective character as a function acting at the conjucture of a double or collateral gaze that stabilizes the Other within a fictionalized field of vision and knowledge, so as, finally and paradoxically, to introject its image as an impersonal gaze that fixes the subject within a moral, social, and political order. This gaze is figured metaphorically and ideologically as a neutral, natural perspicuity that spontaneously opens objects in its field to analytic yet painless dissection.

Foucault has outlined a history of the medical gaze that moves from a clinical phase focused on the description of symptomatic surface to an anatomical phase that opens the body's interior to analytic pathology. Loosely but suggestively correlative would be Norman Bryson's contrast between Renaissance painting, where the gaze both predicates bodily surfaces in the field of vision and situates the viewer's body at the point of comprehension, and later European painting in which the gaze is disembodied and analytically sequenced.[11] Foucault's chapter title, "Open Up a Few Corpses," like his discussion of Sade and the metaphorics of light in the conclusion to *The Birth of the Clinic*, points to the piercing quality of the gaze. As Bryson says, "The *regard* attempts to extract the enduring form from fleeting process; its epithets tend towards a certain violence (penetrating, piercing, fixing), and its overall purpose seems to be the discovery of a second . . . surface standing behind the first, the mask of appearances" (93). We recur, then, to the medical imagery Godwin himself used because it carries the correct (if usually submerged) implication that the gaze is an instrument that violently, albeit precisely, cuts open the body in the act of mapping its functions. This gaze is charged with sexual energy because it penetrates and wounds the body, which it characteristically genders female.

Film studies, the history of science, and speculative art history offer richly elaborated theories of the gaze. Comparatively novel, however, is my correlation of contemporary ideas about the violence latent in the gaze with the eighteenth-century British school of benevolist moral thought— especially Adam Smith's—and with the narrative mode of free indirect discourse. The only current thinking I know about that explicitly links violence with sympathy appears in David Marshall's *The Surprising Effects of Sympathy* and in a few extraordinarily suggestive pages in Leo Bersani's and Ulysse Dutoit's *The Forms of Violence*. Bersani and Dutoit suggest, in the context of psychoanalysis rather than eighteenth-century moral theory, that "there is a certain risk in all sympathetic projections: [namely, that] the pleasure which accompanies them promotes a secret attachment to scenes of suffering or violence" because any form of sympathetic identification with suffering must be considered to contain a "trace of sexual pleasure, and that this pleasure is, inescapably, masochistic." Psychoanalysis provides a more detailed account, but, as Marshall suggests, the text of Smith's *Theory of Moral Sentiments* implies some linkage between the pleasures of sympathy and sadomasochistic identification.[12]

III

I need to insist that my aim is not to produce a single unified reading of *Caleb Williams*. Instead, I consider *Caleb Williams* as a fractured text, conflictual and dynamic at its very core, a text most usefully imagined as a residue of intellectual and representational struggle, rather than as the embodiment of a single set of purposive intentions or the outcome of a teleological development in thought.[13] This struggle involves contestants that the rules of criticism—despite the presence of a book like Ian Watt's *The Rise of the Novel*—have traditionally consigned to separate leagues: political thought and narrative technique. Godwin criticism abounds in treatments of both but not in studies of their interaction. If we look at the two together, especially under the rubric of violence, we can see that the variously revised texts of Godwin's treatise and novel exhibit at least two sets of interrelated symptoms having to do first with Godwin's political critique and second with the narrative field he constructs.

Before specifically treating the textualization of these symptoms in *Caleb Williams*, I must offer a brief plot summary. With the hero, we enter a story long after many important events have transpired. Caleb, a bookish young man of humble birth, becomes upon his parents' death secretary to Falkland, a melancholy aristocrat of broad accomplishment who once relished society but now is reclusive. After an incident where Falkland threatens to trample Caleb when the secretary accidentally comes upon him moaning and hastily locking a mysterious trunk, the youth elicits the patron's story from his steward, Mr. Collins. We encounter this long narrative in Caleb's third-person retelling—itself lodged within the novel's retrospective first-person account of actions beginning with Caleb's entry into Falkland's household.

The polished Falkland had innocently fallen afoul of his neighbor Mr. Tyrrel, a brutal country squire. After many perceived slights and real reprimands from Falkland, Tyrrel redirects his anger at his own dependent niece, the naive Emily Melville. He punishes Emily's admiration for Falkland by forcing her engagement to an odious fiancé and then, upon her flight, casting her into debtor's prison for not paying her keep during her residence in his house. Emily of course dies. Falkland's condemnation so infuriates Tyrrel that he beats him up before a county assembly. The same evening Tyrrel is secretly murdered. Falkland, having denied his guilt before an admiring public and having allowed a farmer and his son to be executed for the crime, retires into the solitary reflection that is disrupted by Caleb's arrival on the scene.

The curious Caleb, actuated by a magnetic sympathy and convinced of Falkland's deed, employs observation, innuendo, and sly questioning to reach the firm conviction of "guilty." When a household fire presents the chance, Caleb breaks open that mysterious trunk and is apprehended by Falkland, who confesses to the terrified secretary after extorting an oath of secrecy and bondage. Caleb flees, and is apprehended and indicted for theft upon planted evidence. After twice escaping prison in the manner of Jack Sheppard, and then joining and fleeing a well-governed band of thieves, he feels himself under universal surveillance because his story has been widely circulated by folktale and criminal broadside. He undertakes a series of disguises before being captured in London by a seemingly omniscient agent named Gines. He breaks the oath of secrecy but no magistrate will countenance his accusation and he is returned to prison. Released, and seemingly free when Falkland declines to appear against him, Caleb begins a new life in Wales only to have it destroyed when Gines seeds the town with an old broadside. Debarred from exile and informed that Falkland intends England to be his lifelong prison, Caleb resolves to assail his patron with a full and circumstantial written narrative—that is, with the novel we are reading—and to accuse Falkland once more on his home ground. A dramatic postscript concludes the action. I want to defer that, however, in order to discuss the symptoms mentioned above and to notice how Godwin's staging of the novel manifests them.[14]

The first range of symptoms has to do with Godwin's sociopolitical critique and indicates that he initially arranged *Caleb Williams* as a contention between two systems of moral and political order, both of which he hoped to discredit because both were working hegemonically in the society of his day to maintain corrupting institutional forms. Roughly speaking, Falkland and Caleb figure forth an opposition between the two: on the one hand, an aristocratic system preoccupied with class honor and actuated by shame; and on the other a contract system propelled by sympathy and actuated by guilt.[15] The year previous, in the 1793 version of *Political Justice*, Godwin had powerfully argued instead for a society in which all institutions would be supplanted by autonomous private judgment equally exercised by all members. What he called "political justice" opposed party politics and questioned even republicanism, because he viewed all forms of government as giving "substance and permanence to our errors."[16] Rather, justice was for Godwin "a rule of conduct originating in the connection of one percipient being with another" and politics was "the adoption of any principle of morality and truth into the practice of a community."[17] Godwin strives to maintain this utopian ideal as an alternative to any institutional formation.

Godwin founds individual judgment in the human capacity to make reasoned comparisons among perceptions, which refer themselves in turn to sensations. A virtuous community assists the process by transmitting its forms through practice, education, discussion, and literature—but *not* through formal institutions, which by their nature lend authority to error. He insists upon the role of education in training autonomous judgment, and upon communal discussion in calibrating it to specific situations, but rejects its maintenance through mechanisms of shame or guilt. Both the old system based upon honor and the newer one based upon sympathetic introjection are political in the bad sense because they personify judgment as an enforcing third person rather than founding it upon the analogous but independent percipience of individuals. The one holds this spectator externally, the other introjects and holds it internally, but both situate individual morality in the regard—in the gaze—of others rather than in one's own integrity. Both deny what Rousseau called *amour de soi*: that crystalline openness of self that he equates with true sentiment, and which, as Mark Philp says in his study of *Political Justice*, constitutes in Godwin's view the "moral independence . . . required for genuine happiness and genuine concern for others."[18]

I divide into two clusters the second range of symptoms—that is, the ones having to do with formal narrative features. They indicate that Godwin fundamentally undermined his project from the beginning because narration as he undertook it reproduced the constructions of character he was assailing, and precluded any stable delineation of autonomous private judgment of the kind he idealized.

The first cluster of symptoms points to a fundamental contradiction in narrative practice: even though, as Godwin indicated in his 1832 preface, he abandoned his initial conduct of narration in the third person in order, as he says, to make "the hero of my tale his own historian," the purpose, as Godwin says, was in fact to wield his "metaphysical dissecting knife . . . in exploring the entrails of mind and motive" (339–40). In truth, not only is the nominally first-person account of fact in *Caleb Williams* shot through with knowledge about past events and motives that no single individual could possibly possess; the field of narration is fractured by sentences that render consciousness in encoded free indirect discourse of the kind I have elsewhere pointed out in Goldsmith. By "encoded" I mean that the first-person form is maintained while the grammatical instance of communication—the speech act—is of the third person. Ann Banfield has argued that such discourse is historically produced and can take place only in written narration.[19] Godwin's entry into the grammar of omniscient presence, even or perhaps especially for purposes of fiction, replicates the very structure of domination he is assailing.

The second cluster of symptoms reveals that Godwin persistently frames his narration as a progression of images or tableaus that reproduce the violence of the gaze as a demand that the individual submit to external authority. Possibly because Godwin was straining to intensify conventional narration in order to propel his audience into awareness of a new kind of identity, or possibly because his virtually exclusive focus on two male characters throws the gender-laden phenomenology of realist narrative into prominence, he pushes toward the extreme instance of the European tendency (described by Bersani and Dutoit) "to isolate and to immobilize the violent act as the most significant moment in . . . plot development." In arguing that "a coherent narrative depends on stabilized images; [and that] stabilized images stimulate the mimetic impulse," they observe that "our views of the human capacity for empathetic representations of the world should therefore take into account the possibility that a mimetic relation to violence necessarily includes a sexually induced fascination with violence."[20]

I shall turn, then (working under the symptomatic rubrics just traced, and in the same order), to ways in which *Caleb Williams* both exhibits apprehensions about sympathetic identification and narrative violence and is captured by their spell.

IV

Godwin obviously attacks the aristocratic code of honor, which always has been understood as his chief target, but the novel also works to indict the newer orthodoxy of sympathy. Caleb's transparent subjectivity makes plain that the sympathetic equation, no less than Falkland's aristocratic *amour propre*, holds up the opaque mask of appearance that Rousseau condemned as merely artificial social form. But Caleb's sympathy is no neutral or innocent alternative; it is an irrational and exploitative byproduct of political power, experienced as a real psychological state, though itself produced in masquerade. When he decides, as he says, to "place myself as a watch upon my patron," he confesses to "a strange sort of pleasure in it." This pleasure is directly aroused by Caleb's fear of authority: "To do what is forbidden always has its charms, because we have an indistinct apprehension of something arbitrary and tyrannical in the prohibition." The more domineering the object, the more intense the "enjoyment [and] the more the sensation was irresistible. . . . The more impenetrable Mr. Falkland was determined to be, the more uncontrollable was my curiosity" (107–8). This "magnetical sympathy," as Caleb calls it (112), propels him to the first climax of the action when Falkland, sitting as justice of the peace on a case analogous to his own, flees the scene, thus convincing the closely observant secretary of his patron's guilt. If Caleb's "involuntary exclamations" and the feeling that his "animal system had undergone a total revolution" were not sexually explicit enough, he cries "I had had no previous conception . . . that it was possible to love a murderer" (129–30). Once the fire and Caleb's burglary of Falkland's trunk have followed with a haste that smacks of allegory, he justifies his "monstrous" act by claiming that "there is something in it of unexplained and involuntary sympathy" (133). A more scathing depiction of the sympathetic construction of character would be hard to imagine.

Now, let us move to specific instances of the two clusters of formal symptoms previously outlined, treating first the novel's actuation of plot through immobilized tableaus and then the technical forms of its narration. The first third of the novel, containing Caleb's retelling of Mr. Collins's narrative, replicates in hyperconcentrated form Godwin's comprehensive organization of plot as a sequence of stablized tableaus, many of them violent. This narrative explicitly inspires Caleb's sympathetic identification and establishes it as the motive force of the main action. In fewer than one hundred pages we encounter more than a dozen such tableaus: a duel narrowly averted during Falkland's grand tour of Italy; a standoff between Falkland and Tyrrel at a country ball; a call upon Tyrrel meant by Falkland to substitute rational expostulation for the duel they seem headed toward (which visit ends with veiled mutual threats); Falkland's rescue of Emily from a fire during which he orders adjacent houses destroyed and can be seen to walk across a burning roof; Tyrrel's and the fiancé's threat of Emily's despoilage in a forced marriage; her flight in the manner of Clarissa; her wasting illness, imprisonment, and death; Falkland's verbal assault on Tyrrel and, of course, their final altercation ending in Tyrrel's murder; a hearing on Falkland's arraignment; and the execution of innocent parties. Caleb's fictional mimesis of this history recapitulates for readers the profound sympathetic engagement the young man is said to have experienced upon hearing Mr. Collins's version.

So compelling is the mechanism that establishes Caleb's destructive fascination with Falkland that it assumes control of the novel. In order to assure the reader's identification with his hero, Godwin establishes in this opening Collins/Caleb narration a paradigm of concentrated plot deployment that structures the balance of the work. He thus authorizes in *Caleb Williams* a whole a pattern of identification that, in the early segments of the novel, he had used to unveil the awful dynamic of power underlying the sympathetic construction of character. Godwin's revisions show his defensive response to this fact. In the third edition, that of 1797, the interpolated fourth paragraph of chapter 1 specifies Caleb as a person whose fascination with sequences of cause and effect propagated "an invincible attachment to books of narrative and romance." "I panted," he says,

for the unravelling of an adventure, with an anxiety, perhaps almost equal to that of the man whose future happiness or misery depended on its issue. I read, I devoured compositions of this sort. They took possession of my soul; and the effects they produced, were frequently discernible in my external appearance and my health. (4)

This paragraph attempts to reinscribe susceptibility to narrative as a pathological trait of Caleb's (not to mention as a vector of bodily penetration) and thus to exempt readers from any taint produced by their own engagement with Godwin's novel.

In the end, however, Godwin cannot novelistically produce a subject capable of sustaining the utopian autonomous private judgment he so forcefully advocated in the 1793 *Political Justice*. In many ways it appears that Godwin framed Caleb's third-person narration of Mr. Collins's story within the larger first-person context of the novel to act out the illusion of mastery conferred by the false sense of first-person autonomy based upon sympathetic introjection. This mastery is a juridical illusion, because the very power it confers to construct one's own version of another subjectivity derives from the maintenance of an "impartial spectator" within a permeable self.[21]

Interestingly, the two passages in Caleb's third-person retelling of the Collins story that come closest to free indirect discourse and hence to sympathetic illusionism both thematize a sense of powerlessness on the part of the entered subject. These are our only points of access in the novel to reflections by Tyrrel and Falkland, who otherwise remain opaque precisely because they mark one pole in an opposition with transparency that Godwin in general maintains. The first occurs when Tyrrel, thwarted by Emily's flight and condemned by Falkland for persecuting tenant farmers, "recollected all the precautions he had used . . . and cursed that blind and malicious power which delighted to cross his most deep laid schemes":

To what purpose had heaven given him a feeling of injury and an instinct to resent, while he could in no case make his resentment felt? It was only necessary to him to be the enemy of any person, to insure that person's being safe against the reach of misfortune. What insults, the most shocking and repeated, had he received from this paltry girl! And by whom was she now torn from his indignation? By that devil [Falkland] that haunted him at every moment, that crossed him at every step, that fixed at pleasure his arrows in his heart, and made mows and mockery at his insufferable tortures. (80)

After these reflections, Tyrrel immediately proceeds to his destruction of Emily by imprisonment.

The other passage comes after Tyrrel's furious public assault on Falkland, whom he knocks to the ground and kicks. Falkland's reflections appear in the text as follows:

Every passion of [Falkland's] life was calculated to make him feel it . . . acutely. . . . [His] mind was full of uproar. . . . He wished for annihilation, to lie down in eternal oblivion, in an insensibility, which compared with what he experienced was scarcely less enviable than beatitude itself. Horror, detestation, revenge, inexpressible longings to shake off the evil, and a persuasion that in this case all effort was powerless, filled his soul even to bursting. (96)

These passages might be read as ironically intended signs of Caleb's delusion that he can enter Falkland's, or any other, mind. But in fact, information Caleb could not possibly possess, and encoded episodes that verge on free indirect discourse, both covertly invade—even capture—the first-person account that makes up the balance of the novel.

Key instances of such encoded first/third-person introspection occur, for example, during Caleb's earlier and later episodes of imprisonment. I present them in simultaneous translation into quasi free indirect discourse by inserting into Caleb's first-person narration brackets that contain the third-person pronouns:[22]

I [Caleb] recollected with astonishment my [his] puerile eagerness to be brought to the test and to have my [his] innocence examined. I [He] execrated it as the vilest and most insufferable pedantry. I [He] exclaimed in the bitterness of my [his] heart. . . . why should I [he] consign my [his] happiness to other men's arbitration? (182)

Or again later,

My [His] resolution was not the calm sentiment of philosophy and reason. It was a gloomy and desperate purpose; the creature, not of hope, but of a mind austerely held to its design, that felt, as it were, satisfied with the naked effort, and prepared to give success or miscarriage to the winds. (278)

The surprising consequence of Godwin's representational strategy is that his thought appears to have been overtaken in some considerable measure by the allied forces of the grammar that governs his field of narration and the propulsion derived from a plot suspensefully and climactically structured into images stabilized by the gaze of covert omniscience. Both mechanisms engender sympathetic identification by replicating the violence upon which they are predicated.

V

In the dramatic postscript that concludes the first edition (1793), Godwin rewrote the original climax he had intended for the novel, enacting not his initial plan for Caleb's defeat and probable destruction by the malice of Falkland but showing, rather, the capacity of the young man's sympathetic identification with the anguish of his haughty patron to inspire both Falkland's confession and his spontaneous death. The remorse that instantly descends upon Caleb follows inevitably in the system of sympathetic representation, like guilt after an exultantly violent sexual fantasy. The new ending closes with the novel's most famous lines: "I began these memoirs with the idea of vindicating my character. I have now no character that I wish to vindicate: but I will finish them that thy story [Falkland's] may be fully understood" (326).

Just about everyone agrees that the revised ending makes for a more powerful narrative than the unpublished original, which leaves Caleb scribbling away like the ravingly incoherent Clarissa after her rape. In that ending, the feminizing logic of the gaze was overtly thematized but there was no magical reversal, no fixated tableau where, in the manner of Bluebeard's wife, the victim becomes keeper of the perpetrator's violence. But paradoxically, the most successful readings of the novel (those of Myers and Philp, for example) do not respond to Caleb's lines about lack of character. On my account, this gap in response occurs because these lines reassert the structural logic of the novel in face of the overwhelming triumph of its narrative momentum. But the fame of Caleb's final lines also speaks a truth—the dissonant truth that the novel's conceptual order lives in contradiction with its mode of representation.

On my analysis, then, *Caleb Williams* is best understood as the textual residue of a struggle to define the price paid for that moral progress which other critics attribute to Caleb. Myers argues, for example, that he learns to appreciate the essential humanity of sympathetic understanding, while Philp maintains that he gains the kind of autonomous private judgment Godwin values above all else. This moral progress, like the narrative that produces it, is typically experienced as *real* when in fact it is merely *realistic* and, in truth, deeply fractured. *Caleb Williams* reveals the idea of moral progress to be historically specific and ideologically laden—a product of a certain kind of violently fixated narrative structuration implicit in sympathetic spectatorship.

No doubt one could construct a linear reading that found Caleb, as first-person narrator, to be distorting the real meaning of sympathetic identification. Certainly the first published version of 1793 left open the possibility of a radical reading that would leave Caleb in the delusionary state of *believing* that he at last had reached the highest ideal of humankind in his sympathetic union with Falkland while in fact recording the truth that he has no character at all. Such a reading of the 1797 version, profoundly contradictory as it remains, is far more difficult to support. Godwin's strenuous efforts in the revised editions of 1796 and 1797 to incorporate passages toward the end of the novel that extol the impartial spectator and that found the idea of humanity itself on sympathic identification make it quite clear that he is trying ex post facto to clarify the novel and to redeem it from the fractious struggle of its original production. What had been Caleb's investment in the new orthodoxy has become Godwin's investment. Godwin, as Mark Philp shows, clearly changed his mind in the course of his novel's initial composition. The remarkable fact is that he responded so powerfully to the narrative logic of sympathetic introjection that he also entirely rewrote *Political Justice* for its second and third editions to bring it, much more closely than before, into conformity with that main line of British moral thought from which he had so carefully established a distance in 1793. Disquisitions on sympathy and the impartial spectator figure importantly among these additions.

VI

I close by returning, however briefly, to the body. The stringent economy of a short essay allows only a passing glance at the myriad ways in which Falkland and Caleb each employ the gaze as an instrument to waste away the body of the other. Falkland fades into a corpse well before his death and Caleb, after his long flight, must literally be strip-searched by Gines in order to be identified. At one point Caleb, dreaming that Falkland has sent an assassin, awakes to behold the "Amazonian" hag who cooks for the band of robbers that is hiding him. She wields a butcher's cleaver that sinks into the bedpost in an attempt to halve his skull. Her "glance" no less than her strength all but overwhelm him and, when he prevails in the struggle, she threatens to dash his entrails into his eyes (231). This same economy permits no more than mention of Godwin's addition in 1796 of a new third paragraph of chapter 1 concerning the strength and flexibility of Caleb's youthful body—for the purpose, I believe, of counterbalancing the powerful feminization his field of narration had worked upon his hero.

Instead of accumulating further examples from the text, I turn in conclusion to a spellbinding recollection of the terrifying eighteenth-century machine placed on exhibit in London for five shillings per view during the year 1733 by the surgeon Abraham Chovet: it was a

new figure of Anatomy which represents a woman chained down upon a table, suppos'd opened alive; wherein the circulation of the blood is made visible through glass veins and arteries; the circulation is also seen from the mother to the child, and from the child to the mother, with Histolick and Diastolick [sic] motion of the heart and the action of the lungs.[23]

I have been suggesting that we ourselves may take for granted another kind of anatomizing that survives from the eighteenth century because to some degree we still live within its canon. I refer, of course, to realism as a cultural practice.

James and Stevenson: The Mixed Current
of Realism and Romance

GEORGE DEKKER

IN "THE ART OF FICTION" (1884), HENRY JAMES celebrates the novel's "immense and exquisite correspondence with life" (79).[1] He asserts
the primary claims of observation, first-hand and adult; hence of contemporary experience and the example of the French realist novelists; of the
"work" of art. In "A Humble Remonstrance" (1884), written in "genial
rejoinder" (101) to James's essay, Robert Louis Stevenson protests that
there is a radical disjunction between art and life as we normally experience
it. He argues for the priority of imagination and the child's perspective;
for universal experience and the models provided by romancers of all times
and places; for the "play" of art. If the pattern of oppositions sounds familiar, so it should. This debate of the 1880's clearly updates a controversy
about the nature and merits of fictional realism and romance that "novelists" and "romancers" had been carrying on for nearly a century and a
half.[2] In turn, James's contributions to the controversy have probably done
more than anybody else's to make it seem worth continuing and to shape
its terms for modern criticism. Although Stevenson's critical writings have
not survived their occasions, the examples of his bravest romances and
braver life challenged James to move beyond the realist canons of "The Art
of Fiction" and work toward a synthesis that would incorporate the romance values of play, imaginative freedom, and what he was later to call
"the finest feelings."

To understand Stevenson's role in the development of James's fictional
theory, we must try to see him as James saw him rather than as he appears
from the diminishing perspective of the 1990's. Few interpreters of James's
criticism appear to have made this imaginative effort or to have reflected
much on the rich trove that survives from the James-Stevenson relation-

ship.[3] Besides the two manifestoes of 1884, there are over forty letters written between 1884 and 1894, two long essays on Stevenson that James published in 1888 and 1900, and numerous allusions demonstrating that Stevenson's ideas and example haunted and influenced him to the end. My aim here is not to survey these materials in any detail but rather to explain more fully how James and Stevenson differ in "The Art of Fiction" and "A Humble Remonstrance"; to isolate from James's writings to and about Stevenson that special quality which, for James, made him so deeply appealing and significant—so "great" as a man and author; and to contend that the preface to *The American* (1907), James's most influential and controversial statement about the realism-romance polarity, is itself best read as a Romantic ode in prose, with distinct Stevensonian reverberations.

I

James replied to "A Humble Remonstrance" with a warm personal letter in which he expressed his appreciation of Stevenson's "suggestive and felicitous" remarks and his conviction that "we agree . . . much more than we disagree." Disclaiming complex or covert aims, James assured Stevenson that "The Art of Fiction" was "simply a plea for liberty." While we may be sure that rather more was involved and that Stevenson was not taken in by this disarming encapsulation, the frequent appearance both of the words "liberty" and "freedom" and of their opposites ("proscription," "a priori," "prescription," "suppression," "dogma," etc.) suggests that James's plea for liberty is both important in itself and at the root of much else in the essay. Indeed, as Leo Bersani and others have argued, it is at the root of nearly everything James wrote.[4]

The first of the two major liberties James claims for the novelist is freedom from the restrictive and trivializing expectations of the Anglo-American reading public. Against the popular conception of the novel as a form of entertainment dedicated to supplying predictably cheerful endings and matter suitable for "young people," he argues that the novelist's high artistic "cause" is the same as that of the painter, while the novelist's commitment to finding and telling the truth about life is as uncompromising as the historian's or philosopher's (56). "Experiment," which links the novelist's with the scientist's investigations of life, is another key word. But the one that echoes through the essay almost as persistently as "freedom" and its cognates is "serious."

James probably intended this array of lofty analogies and verbal repetitions not so much to browbeat squeamish or philistine readers as to brace fellow novelists against their pressures—and also, of course, against those of compromising editors. He had often experienced these pressures himself, as in 1877 when *Atlantic Monthly* editor William Dean Howells protested against the unhappy ending of *The American*. James's response was very much in the spirit of "The Art of Fiction" and, as we shall see, the more interesting because he was later obliged to eat his brave words. If he had ended his novel with the marriage of Christopher Newman and Madame de Cintre, he wrote Howells, "I should have made a prettier ending, certainly; but I should have felt as if I were throwing a rather vulgar sop to readers who don't really know the world and who don't measure the merit of a novel by its correspondence to the same."[5]

Allusions to the once-powerful "Evangelical hostility" to fiction help us to place "The Art of Fiction" with other passionate (and rhetorically cunning) "defenses" of the seriousness and moral value of literature, such as Sidney's "An Apology for Poetry" or Shelley's "A Defense of Poetry." It belongs as well to another familiar nonfictional genre, the romantic manifesto, in the claims it makes for a second major liberty for the novelist: freedom from the restrictive artistic formulas devised by critics on the basis of past performances by other writers. As Ian Watt explains in *The Rise of the Novel*, romanticism and novelistic discourse were intimately related through their emphasis on individualism and originality, and their resistance to "those elements in classical critical theory which were inimical to formal realism."[6] The polemic of "The Art of Fiction" is squarely in this tradition.

The immediate occasion of James's essay was a public lecture, delivered earlier in 1884 and also entitled "The Art of Fiction," by the popular novelist Walter Besant. Although Besant expressed a suitably elevated sense of the greatness of the novel form, his lecture's approach to questions of "art," like that of other briskly professional progeny of Horace's *Ars Poetica*, was predominantly commonsensical and prescriptive: keep a notebook; young ladies brought up in quiet country villages should not write about garrison life; "If you have tried the half-dozen best publishers, and been refused by all, realize that the work *will not do*."[7] James's approach is so different that we may wonder why he recycled Besant's title. In his opening remarks, James displays some uneasiness about "so comprehensive a title" (53), but claims to find a "pretext for my temerity" in Besant's usage—a deferential gesture that is itself an ironic pretext. So far from a timid following of example, James's "copying" is a decisive act of appropriation that says, in effect, that the entire job must be done over again. It says, too, that the well-meaning Besant did not understand the meaning of the words—"Art" especially—that *he* had had the temerity to use.

For James, "Art" principally means that which cannot be reduced to practical tips or generic axioms to be passed on from the elder to the rising generation. Starting from the radically individualistic premise that the ways novels can be "interesting" (the only "general responsibility" to which they can be held) are "as various as the temperament of man, and . . . successful in proportion as they reveal a particular mind, different from others," he defines the novel as "a personal impression of life" (62). This definition accords precisely with Ian Watt's dictum that the "primary criterion" of the novel is "truth to individual experience."[8] On this showing, traditional generic distinctions, such as that between the novel and romance, can have "little reality or interest" (71) or are positively misleading, since each novel must be a new beginning with its own laws of development. Lest this privileging of the unique personal impression seem less a liberation from the dead hand of the past than a crippling limitation for writers who have seen little of the world, James explains that the direct experience that both he and Besant call for includes, indeed is inseparable from, imaginative experience. "When the mind is imaginative—much more when it happens to be that of a man of genius—it takes to itself the faintest hints of life, it converts the very pulses of the air into revelations" (66). No less "Romantic" in thought and vocabulary is his corollary claim that the product of this imaginative extension of experience is "a living thing, all one and continuous, like every other organism, and in proportion as it lives will it be found, I think, that in each of its parts there is something of each of the other parts" (69). Thus understood, the novelistic work of art might well be said to "compete with life" (55, 68). James's plea for artistic liberty culminates in a celebration of the "splendid privilege" of the novelist to work with a form that has "so few restrictions" that "the other arts, in comparison, appear confined and hampered" (84). Such is the plenitude of novelistic fiction, open to all manner of seeing and rendering life, that "talents so dissimilar as those of Alexandre Dumas and Jane Austen, Charles Dickens and Gustave Flaubert, have worked in this field with equal glory."

Very much in the same pluralistic spirit is James's judgment earlier in the essay that *Treasure Island* is "delightful . . . it appears to me to have succeeded wonderfully in what it attempts" (80). However, a thoughtful reader would be hard pressed to find firm ground in "The Art of Fiction" for judging Dumas or even Dickens or Austen equal to the author of *Madame Bovary*, or for taking the author of *Treasure Island* seriously. Despite James's paean to the imagination and the catholicity of taste he displays, his essay consists mainly of an eloquent restatement of the doctrines of contemporary French and American exponents of novelistic realism. It is out of their window in the House of Fiction that he is looking when he maintains that the measure of success for novelistic fiction is its "closeness of relation" (75) to life, its ability to let us "see life *without* rearrangement," and when he ventures that "the air of reality (solidity of specification) seems . . . the supreme virtue of a novel" (67). Wishing to steer clear of the implication that the novelist is a mere transcriber or copier of life's surfaces, he allows that "Art is essentially selection" (75); but wary on the other hand lest selection be construed to legitimize censorship, he insists that "it is a selection whose main care is to be typical, to be inclusive." In sum, a work of fiction is most a novel, and better for being so, when it is a novel in the tradition of Balzac.

To this tradition *Treasure Island* obviously did not belong, but the novel with which James chose to compare it, Edmond de Goncourt's *Chérie* (1884), just as obviously did. *Chérie* invited the comparison inasmuch as it too featured a child protagonist, but it was written for an exclusively adult audience and in fact carried the documentary procedures of French realism to an unprecedented extreme. Conceiving his role as a novelist to be that of "a historian of those who have no history,"[9] Goncourt had announced in the preface to *La Faustin* (1882) that his next novel would be a study of a young girl's psychological and physiological development, and appealed to his female readers to become his collaborators by writing to him anonymously about their intimate experiences in growing up. Rightly seeing himself among "the bringers of the new,"[10] Goncourt claimed in the preface to *Chérie* that the result of this collaboration was a novel lacking in incidents, reversals, and intrigue, but abounding in interior drama and having its destined place in the evolution of the novel from the adventure romances of the early nineteenth century to what would eventually supersede the novel form itself, "a book of pure analysis."[11]

Although James saw the evolution of the novel somewhat differently and believed that *Chérie*, like other Goncourt experiments, was more interesting in theory than practice, he had assimilated much of that theory and, as Ezra Pound in his generation also would, wished to honor the elderly French novelist as a major spokesman for the Make-It-New approach to writing. In juxtaposing *Chérie* with *Treasure Island*, then, James was implicitly invoking a historical and critical schema that left scant room for Stevenson's "delightful" little novel. Explicitly, however, he only expressed the reservation that in the case of *Chérie* he could appeal to his own experience to say "Yes" or "No" (80). "I have been a child, but I have never been on a quest for a buried treasure, and it is a simple accident that with M. de Goncourt I should have for the most part to say No."

To which Stevenson promptly rejoined: "If he has never been on a quest for buried treasure, it can be demonstrated that he has never been a child. There never was a child (unless Master James) but has hunted gold, and been a pirate. . . . Elsewhere in his essay Mr. James has protested with excellent reason against too narrow a conception of experience; for the born artist, he contends, the 'faintest hints of life' are converted into revelations" (94). Both here in "A Humble Remonstrance" and in other essays Stevenson contends that the imaginative child, trailing clouds of glory, is a primitive literary artist ("the born artist" precisely) and therefore a proper touchstone for literary theorists.

This thesis is stated more vulnerably in "A Gossip on Romance," written before "A Humble Remonstrance" but published as its preliminary and companion piece in Stevenson's 1887 collection of essays, *Memories and Portraits*: "The dullest of clowns tells, or tries to tell, himself a story, as the feeblest of children uses invention in his play; and even as the imaginative grown person, joining in the game, at once enriches it with many delightful circumstances, the great creative writer shows us the realisation and the apotheosis of the day-dreams of common men. His stories may be nourished with the realities of life, but their true mark is to satisfy the nameless longings of the reader, and to obey the ideal laws of the day-dream." [12] Thus broadly and unqualifiedly formulated, Stevenson's theory of fiction is undeniably escapist. Nor can it help to explain why one writer, perhaps Stevenson himself, fits the category of "great creative writer" whereas another, say, a scriptwriter for *Dallas*, does not. However, our immediate concern is not with the adequacy of Stevenson's theory but simply with what it was and how it differed from James's. How are the fundamental relationships between writer, reader, narrative form, and "the realities of life" reconstituted when James's model of the novelist as a specially imaginative adult observer is replaced by a daydreamer who combines a child's capacity for shared imaginative play with an adult's awareness of the "realities of life"?

"Shared" may be the key word. James stresses a novelist's freedom to differ in his view of life and art not only from other novelists but from readers as well, conceding readers the same freedom to differ but not one iota more. Indeed, the readers posited in "The Art of Fiction" are mainly characterized as obtuse, sentimental, and interfering, more likely to be satisfied consumers of Besant's *All Sorts and Conditions of Men* than of *The Portrait of a Lady*. As might be expected of a writer who reached a far wider audience than either Besant or James, Stevenson's emphasis falls on the bond of experience that reader and author share as people who have learned to read and write, who have become aware of some of the realities of life, but who have not outgrown a basic human need to play roles and make up stories.

This bond being granted, the art of fiction becomes (at least at one level) very practically rhetorical. Counting upon the reader, like himself, to have "ardently desired and fondly imagined" a life of adventure in youthful daydreams, the "cunning and low-minded" author of *Treasure Island* "addressed himself throughout to the building up and circumstantiation of this boyish dream. Character to the boy is a sealed book; for him, a pirate is a beard in wide trousers and literally bristling with pistols. The author . . . himself more or less grown up, admitted character, within certain limits, into his design; but only within certain limits" (94). To be "more or less grown up" is, for Stevenson, to strike the right balance between survival of the child's expansive imaginative faculty and acquisition of the adult's understanding of limits and character. As James was later to emphasize, this balance is crucial to Stevenson's limited but distinguished achievement as a fictionalist. A mature moralist and literary technician, he was also one of the preeminent Victorian mythmakers, and had a profound intuitive understanding of the contending forces central to the Freudian scheme of human development. Like Mark Twain, he conducts his boy heroes, Jim Hawkins and David Balfour, on journeys of adventure such as they (and all children) might have vaguely imagined for themselves; but he is always aware, and always makes his adult readers aware, of ranges of experience beyond the boys' ken—of the drives, motives, and designs that lie behind a beard in wide trousers.

But the balance achieved in his practice depends in his theory on qualifiers grudgingly conceded or hastily tacked on. Shorn of these qualifiers, Stevenson's is a projective theory of fiction, a sort of nursery version of Northrop Frye's. For him, the great fictionalist is the writer who does the best job of reimagining and retelling what are, at bottom, the same old stories—in short, and in traditional terms, a "finder" rather than a "maker." This is the underlying reason why, at the outset of "A Humble Remonstrance," he (misleadingly) maintains that "what both Mr. James and Mr. Besant had in view" was not the art of fiction but rather "the art of narrative" (87). Since the stories being narrated anew in novels (as likewise in narrative poems or prose romances such as *Morte D'Arthur*) are known to everybody, James's individualistic definition of the novel as "a personal impression of life" (62) is far wide of the mark. In some ways far more old-fashioned than James, in others he strikes us as much more modern—even modernist. Thus he deals with James's mimeticism by allowing that "circumstantiation" (what Frye would call realistic displacement) is necessary, but he is scornful of James's contention that the novelist can or should try to "compete with life." Life, he rejoins, "is monstrous, infinite, illogical, abrupt, and poignant; a work of art, in comparison, is neat, finite, self-contained, rational, flowing, and emasculate" (92). At points where he implicitly concedes that novelistic fiction has a correspondence with the life we wakefully experience rather than the one we dream, his emphasis falls on the principles of rigorous selection, abstraction, and simplification—principles common to all the arts, and readily endorsed by James, but scarcely *the* hallmark of the novels James most admired or that he wrote himself.

Although pointedly eschewing any organic analogy, Stevenson agrees with James that after his own fashion the novelist can compete with life by creating a work of art with its own wholeness and unity: "For the welter of impressions, all forcible but discrete, which life presents, it substitutes a certain artificial series of impressions . . . all aiming at the same effect, all eloquent of the same idea, all chiming together like consonant notes in music" (91). The analogy with music appears likewise in "A Gossip on Romance": "The right kind of thing should fall out in the right kind of place; the right kind of thing should follow; and not only the characters talk aptly and think naturally, but all the circumstances in a tale answer to one another like notes in music."[13] Stevenson was a poet as well as a prose writer, and had a wonderful ear for the variety and music of English. James, whose ear was more limited, took little pleasure in vocal or instrumental music but was deeply responsive to the visual arts. In Stevenson's fiction, characters are likely to overhear; in James's, they always see.

When, years later, James complained that *Catriona* "subjects my visual sense, my *seeing* imagination, to an almost painful underfeeding" (239), Stevenson responded:

I *hear* people talking, and I *feel* them acting, and that seems to me to be fiction. My two aims may be described as—

        1*st*.   War to the adjective.

        2*nd*.   Death to the optic nerve.

Admitted we live in an age of the optic nerve in literature. For how many centuries did literature get along without a sign of it? (241)

This pithy manifesto of 1893 seems to recall the advice to the novice fictionalist with which he concluded "A Humble Remonstrance": "In this age of the particular, let him remember the ages of the abstract, the great books of the past, the brave men that lived before Shakespeare and before Balzac" (100). Of course he was right that, in fiction, the nineteenth century was to an unprecedented degree the age of the particular and the optic nerve; the massing of visual details was essential to novelistic realism in the tradition of Balzac. His reasons for mistrusting this development were similar to Wordsworth's for deploring the "tyranny" of the eye, "most despotic of our senses."[14] The eye, riveted on a host of distinct external particulars, had the power to hold in thrall both the heart that bonded human to human and the imagination that unified both natural scenes and works of art. Stevenson had what James called the "*hearing* imagination" (239) and, for many conscious and unconscious reasons, he preferred to analogize fiction with music, of all arts the least directly mimetic and most dedicated to making the right things fall out in the right places and "answer to one another" like ideal writer to ideal reader and dream to dream.

How was it, then, that writers so opposed in background, temperament, theory, and fictional practice soon became fast friends and mutual admirers? Part of the answer has to be that, although they had less in common than James wished to acknowledge, they were probably further apart in their aims and methods when they wrote "The Art of Fiction" and "A Humble Remonstrance" than at any other point in their careers. Although we tend to think of the later Stevenson principally as the romantic rover of the South Seas, his tendency in fiction after *Kidnapped* (1885) was to move gradually in the direction of more realistic treatment and more adult subject matter—to become increasingly preoccupied with what lay behind "a beard in wide trousers."[15] Adult sexuality, although handled discreetly and sometimes even coyly in *The Master of Ballantrae* and *Catriona*, achieves a new importance in those novels and becomes central in *The Beach of Falesa* and the great fragment *Weir of Hermis-*

ton. Whereas the author of *Treasure Island* had no need of James's "plea for liberty" and did not mention it once in "A Humble Remonstrance," he was forced to permit his candid treatment of relations between natives and white traders in *The Beach of Falesa* to be bowdlerized. Now he lamented: "This is a poison bad world for the romancer, this Anglo-Saxon world; I usually get out of it by not having any women in it at all" (266). As for James, neither before nor after 1883–86 was he nearly so committed to the precepts and procedures of post-Balzacian realism. Never after *The Bostonians* and *The Princess Casamassima* (both 1886) did he write a novel that smacked so strongly, if intermittently, of Daudet, the Goncourts, and even Zola.   .

James once declared that Stevenson was "the sole and single Anglo-Saxon capable of perceiving . . . how well [James's fiction was] written" (188). Although doubtless a sincere expression of the admiration they felt for each other as literary craftsmen, this praise probably says more about James's low opinion of contemporary critics than about his confidence in Stevenson's overall judgment of fiction. In letters to James, Stevenson expressed keen if usually vague appreciation for many of his works, but clearly preferred *Roderick Hudson* (1875) above the rest. In truth, greatly though he admired James's technical skills and moral insights, Stevenson sometimes found his fiction hard going, and succeeded in liking it only by misreading it. James must have been baffled by some of his friend's enthusiastic preferences. What did he make of Stevenson's "falling in love" with Olive Chancellor (*The Bostonians*) and Adela Chart ("The Marriages"), two of his most astringent studies of female psychology?[16] He was obviously distressed by Stevenson's impatient judgment that *The Portrait of a Lady*—so rich in visual detail, so subtle in its leisurely exposure of motive and relation—was "BELOW YOU to write and me to read" (166). This outburst was singular, however, in all senses of the word, and Stevenson was generally able to cope by recalling the romantic novels of James's youth, by misreading the later ones, or by transferring his disapproval to other targets.

A fascinating example of the transference strategy is the short section he added to the *Memories and Portraits* version of "A Humble Remonstrance." Shifting attention from James, Stevenson identifies Howells as "the bondslave, the zealot" of the "school" of realist fiction who "thinks of past things as radically dead" and also "thinks a form can be outlived." Summing up his objections to realist doctrine, he contends that "the danger is lest, in seeking to draw the normal, a man should draw the null, and write the novel of society instead of the romance of man." Sadly, claims Stevenson, Howells was "of an originally strong romantic bent—a certain glow of romance still resides in many of his books, and lends them their distinction." [17]

Stevenson's remarks about Howells's unfortunate development away from romance partly repeat and partly reverse ones Howells himself had made in 1882 about James's development. In a major midcareer assessment of the James *oeuvre*, Howells commented that the early stories had

a richness of poetic effect which he has since never equalled. . . . Looking back to those early stories, where Mr. James stood at the dividing ways of the novel and the romance, I am sometimes sorry that he declared even superficially for the former. His best efforts seem to me those of romance; his best types have an ideal development, like Claire Belgarde and Bessy Alden and poor Daisy and even Newman. But, doubtless, he has chosen wisely; perhaps the romance is an outworn form, and would not lend itself to the reproduction of even the ideality of modern life. I myself waver somewhat in my preference—if it is a preference. [18]

Regarded as literary criticism, Howells's performance here is comically indecisive and inept; and it is easy to see why James soon responded by firmly rejecting the distinction between novel and romance, and why Stevenson just as firmly redrew it as a distinction between the "romance of man" and the mere "novel of society." But Howells's images of dividing ways and wavering, besides suggestively recalling major tropes of Scott and Hawthorne, accurately register the tensions experienced by the many nineteenth-century readers and fictionalists who wanted, please, more of both—more of realism *and* more of romance—and got them, too.

Instructed as much by Stevenson's life as by anything he or Howells wrote, James began to think more deeply about the meaning and value of romance, in life, in fiction, than ever before. From Stevenson too he learned, or relearned, that play could be "serious" as well as "delightful" and was essential to creative work.

II

In his final delirium, after suffering two strokes, James supposed himself to be one of the favorite subjects of his recreational reading—Napoleon Bonaparte—and dictated letters concerning the decoration of imperial apartments in the Louvre and Tuileries. So far from being ravings, these letters are coherent, dignified, commanding: the assumption of the Emperor's persona is complete. We naturally wonder how far they disclose unconscious longings for power and status on the grandest possible scale, and also how they are linked with other, much less connected utterances recorded near the end:

Individual souls, great . . . of [word lost] on which great perfections are If one does . . . in the fulfillment with the neat and pure and perfect—to the success or as he or she moves through life, following admiration unfailing [word lost] in the Highway—problems are very sordid.

One of the earliest of the consumers of the great globe in the interest of the attraction exercised by the great R.L.S. [Robert Louis Stevenson] of those days, comes in, afterwards, a visitor at Vailima and [word lost] there and pious antiquities to his domestic annals.[19]

The fitful outcroppings of a broken mind can prove almost nothing and are cited here only because the occasion and the seeming lack of connection between Napoleon, Stevenson, and Henry Adams (the "visitor at Vailima") make even more striking the connections they actually would have had for James in his right mind. For him, Napoleon and Stevenson were alike "great" inasmuch as each turned his life into a romance by making reality conform to the requirements of his imagination. Adams and Stevenson, on the other hand, typified temperamental opposites: *il penseroso* with a debilitating streak of morbidity, who left James depressed and dispirited; *l'allegro* with a strengthening admixture of sanity, who restored his sense of fun and play and braced him for living and working.

When Adams passed through London in 1891 after visiting Stevenson in Samoa, James wrote to a mutual friend that "I like him, but suffer from his monotonous disappointed pessimism."[20] His experience with Stevenson was as different as possible. Words he uses recurrently to characterize his friend are "romantic," "charm," "boy," "fun," "happy," and "genial." In his first letter to Stevenson, he writes: "The native *gaiety* of all that you write is delightful to me, and when I reflect that it proceeds from a man whom life has laid much of the time on his back . . . I find you a genius indeed" (102). The conjunction of "gaiety" and "genius" confirms our hunch that when James refers earlier in the letter to Stevenson's "genial rejoinder," he is using "genial" as Coleridge and Wordsworth did to suggest that the true spring of creative activity was "Joy"—the "genial spirits" of "Tintern Abbey" and "Dejection: An Ode."

The other word he applies to Stevenson with consistently double significance is "happy," meaning both cheerful and felicitous. In a passage describing Stevenson's peculiar combination of "jauntiness" and care for style, he comments that Stevenson's "sense of a happy turn [of phrase] is of the subtlest" (131). Other examples are "his happiest [= best] work" (140) and the "impression . . . of deepening talent, of happier and richer expression" (268). But surely the most moving and revealing usage occurs in the letter James wrote to Edmund Gosse immediately after they learned of Stevenson's death: "I'm not sure that it's not for *him* a great and happy fate; but for us the loss of charm, of suspense, of 'fun' is unutterable."[21]

From "happy" and "fun" it is but a short hop back to "boy" and "play." James was fond of children and their games, and made them the subject of some of his finest later fiction. But throughout his career and, as we have seen, especially during the 1880's, he reacted strongly to the trivializing forces of the literary marketplace and its audience of "young people" by insisting the writing and reading of fiction were or should be deeply serious adult activities. Therefore, however much he liked children or his friend Louis, he was never entirely at ease with the writings Stevenson addressed partly or mainly to children, much less with any suggestion that authors were all children at heart.

In his first full-length essay on Stevenson's writings, James emphasizes the balance Stevenson claimed for himself: "He describes credulity with all the resources of experience, and represents a crude stage with infinite ripeness. . . . Sometimes, as in *Kidnapped*, the art is so ripe that it lifts even the subject into the general air; the execution is so serious that the idea (the idea of a boy's romantic adventures) becomes a matter of universal relations" (132). This is all very handsome, but phrases such as "crude stage" and "lifts even the subject" suggest that although the "execution" is serious the "idea" or "subject" is not. Again, to say of *Treasure Island* that "it is all as perfect as a well-played boy's game" (154) and that it is "in its way a classic" may strike us as a very just summation and one with which Stevenson would have been well satisfied, but the qualifications implicit in his phrasing suggest that James continued to have doubts about the ultimate seriousness of an art so frankly and happily committed to the value of "make-believe."

Those doubts he retained to the end. Meanwhile, distinguishing between the art of fiction and the art of living, he rejoiced in Stevenson's refusal to accept the limiting "reality" of an invalid condition. In his long review essay on *Letters to His Family and Friends* (1899), James remarks that Stevenson "was so fond of the sense of youth and the idea of play that he saw whatever happened to him in images and figures, in the terms, almost, of the sports of childhood" and then quotes Stevenson on the subject of his near-encounters with death: "I keep returning, and now hand over fist, from the realms of Hades. I saw that gentleman between the eyes, and fear him less after each visit. Only Charon and his rough boatmanship I somewhat fear" (259). This is but one example of Stevenson's "imagination always at play, for drollery or philosophy, with his circumstances." In turn, Stevenson's "desperate larks" (184) in the remote South Seas inspired James to draw playful metaphors of his own out of the diverse realms of erotic play and the big top: "You are indeed . . . the wandering Wanton of the Pacific. You swim into our ken with every provocation and prospect—and we have only time to open our arms to receive you when your immortal back is turned to us in the act of still more provoking flight" (187). In a later letter, James refers to his friend's "projects—and gyrations! Trapezist in the Pacific void!" (241).

In James's eyes, Stevenson's greatest game was to convert "that splendid life, that beautiful, bountiful thing . . . into a fable as strange and romantic as one of his own" (248). From 1887 onwards James recurs again and again to the idea that, at great risk and against great odds, Stevenson "in a singular degree, got what he wanted, the life absolutely discockneyfied, the situation as romantically 'swagger' as if it had been an imagination made real" (269). As James well knew, Stevenson's actual "situation" was nearly as full of hardships, deprivations, and indignities as the one experienced by David Balfour in *Kidnapped*. And yet, like David's adventure in the Scottish Highlands, Stevenson's in Samoa *was* "romantically 'swagger,'" too. The crucial difference was that David neither imagined boldly nor sought his great adventure, whereas Stevenson did both, taking charge of his life in a way that compelled James's admiration. It is perhaps worth remarking that James's own "escape" to Europe had been similarly purposeful and productive—and, while outwardly deficient in "swagger," was also a romantic adventure.

Was it James's conclusion, then, that Stevenson lived a greater romance than any he ever wrote? Yes; but to say so is rather to affirm the greatness of the life as James saw it than to imply that he had major reservations about Stevenson's talent and achievement as a fictionalist. For while James was growing in appreciation of the function and value of Stevensonian play, Stevenson was maturing as a man and writer, until in *Weir of Hermiston*, left unfinished at his death, he became the sort of fictionalist James could unreservedly admire. *Weir*, so completely adult and "serious" and yet so inventive and "romantic," left nothing at odds between Stevenson the writer and James the reader, between play and work. "The Pacific," wrote James, made him, 'descriptively,' serious and even rather dry; with his own country . . . he was ready infinitely to play. . . . In *Weir* especially, like an improvising pianist, he superabounds and revels, and his own sense, by a happy stroke, appeared likely never more fully and brightly to justify him; to have become even in some degree a new sense, with new chords and possibilities. It is the 'old game,' but it is the old game that he exquisitely understands. (274)

In this moment of enthusiasm for the "happy" way Stevenson plays "the old game," James seems ready even to reverse the valence of "serious."

Stevenson—or Stevenson much more than any other "influence"— made James understand that to be *homo sapiens*, or even *homo faber* very successfully, a person had likewise to be *homo ludens*. As Johann Huizinga's classic study *Homo Ludens* explains, play enters constitutively into a range of central human activities—recreational, erotic, artistic, religious; enters, indeed, into the very creation of a human order. "First and foremost," says Huizinga, "all play is a voluntary activity. . . . By this quality of freedom alone, play marks itself off from the course of the natural process. It is something added thereto and spread out over it like a flowering, an ornament. . . . Play casts a spell over us; it is 'enchanting,' 'captivating.'"[22] These extracts distill the essence of Stevenson's significance for James and have an important bearing on his efforts after "The Art of Fiction" to reconsider the relationship between realism and romance. The "quality of freedom" in play and by extension in romance is also a quality essential to moral and artistic action. Perhaps the charge should not be that romance is escapist but that realism is defeatist?

James's first essay on Stevenson is a crucial document in the history of his rethinking the relationship between realism and romance. In it he re- states the generic premise of "The Art of Fiction": "The breath of the novelist's being is his liberty; and the incomparable virtue of the form he uses is that it lends itself to views innumerable and diverse" (149). Al- though he doesn't say so, it is obvious that he would still resist any attempt to "separate" the novel from the modern prose romance. The novel form as he envisages it can subsume both the "novel of society" and the "ro- mance of man"—and more. Now, however, James's plea for liberty works in favor of that elusive quality (as distinct from fictional genre), "ro- mance": "The doctrine of M. Zola himself, so meagre if literally taken, is fruitful, inasmuch as in practice he romantically departs from it." James's point about Zola is the point that Stevenson had made earlier about How- ells. Now James's emphasis falls on the leavening effect of romance rather than on the "truth of detail" and "solidity of specification" (67) likewise so abundantly present in Zola and so resoundingly endorsed as "the supreme virtue of a novel" in "The Art of Fiction." James is beginning to associate romance in fiction positively with imaginative freedom and play: here it is the genie in the Naturalist machine.

Stevenson, James dryly remarks, "does not need to depart" from a theory in order "to pursue the romantic." What he doesn't remark, but clearly means, is that Stevenson's theory is in its way just as meager as Zola's and equally fruitful when he departs *realistically* from it. On several occasions later in the essay James explains how Stevenson creates an "indescribable mixture of the prodigious and the human, of surprising coincidences and familiar feelings" (155). In *Kidnapped* especially we find "the author's talent for seeing the actual in the marvellous, and reducing the extravagant to plausible detail" (158). Over "the whole business," James says, is the "charm of the most romantic episode in the world—though perhaps it would be hard to say why it is the most romantic, when it was intermingled with so much stupidity." As for Stevenson's enthusiasm for romances of adventure in the tradition of Alexandre Dumas, James comments: "He makes us say, Let the tradition live, by all means, since it was delightful; but at the same time he is the cause of our perceiving afresh that a tradition is kept alive only by something being added to it. In this particular case—in *Doctor Jekyll* and *Kidnapped*—Mr. Stevenson has added psychology" (152). Since James's generosity to R.L.S. the novelist is at the expense of R.L.S the theorist, it is but fair to note that Stevenson himself had previously claimed that "true romantic art . . . makes a romance of all things. . . . *Robinson Crusoe* is as realistic as it is romantic; both qualities are pushed to an extreme, and neither suffers." [23]

James offers a patch of ground for romance in realist fiction when he argues that the novelist "who leaves the extraordinary out of his account is liable to awkward confrontations" in an "age of newspapers," for the "next report of the next divorce case . . . shall offer us a picture of astounding combinations of circumstance and behaviour." While Stevenson doubtless would have agreed with this argument, he patently had something more in mind when he contrasted the romance of man with the novel of society. For him, as James well knew, the "extraordinary" also meant things of rare value and importance. James explains: "even if he did not wave so gallantly the flag of the imaginary and contend that the improbable is what has most character, he would still insist that we ought to make believe. He would say we ought to make believe that the extraordinary is the best part of life, even if it were not, and to do so because the finest feelings—suspense, daring, decision, passion, curiosity, gallantry, eloquence, friendship—are involved in it, and it is of infinite importance that the tradition of these precious things should not perish."[24]

This inward paraphrase of Stevenson's credo as a romancer also lists many of the personal qualities James associated with his friend. They were qualities, too, that he celebrated in his own bravest heroes and heroines, and the reference to precious things perishing inevitably makes us look ahead to the doomed heroine of *The Wings of the Dove* and back to the "finest" people in James's life who contributed to his conception of Milly Theale—preeminently Minny Temple but also Alice James and "the great R.L.S."

III

When he returned to *The American* in the course of revising and prefacing his fictions for the New York Edition, James also returned to ideas and motifs that belong especially to his dialogue with Stevenson. The rambling, elliptical, and yet wonderfully resourceful argument of the preface to *The American* is an extension of that dialogue. At first glance, these reminiscences are surprising, since *The American* antedates the friendship and apparently was not among the novels by James that Stevenson most appreciated. But it was reworking this novel, reflecting on the nature and origins of its chief strengths and weaknesses, that inspired James to rejoin the romance versus realism debate. Other fictionalists—notably Balzac, George Sand, and Hawthorne—contributed to his reflections on the subject, but it was Stevenson's life and writings that had most directly and movingly exemplified romance for him and prompted his own deepest thinking about it. So it was almost a matter of course that the principal negative and positive qualities associated with romance in his writings to and about Stevenson should reappear in this preface: the jejeune, escapist, and potentially dangerous nature of romantic make-believe; the creative freedom of play; the case for the extraordinary (or the "finest feelings"); the "fruitful" mingling of realism and romance.

But if the qualities James associates with romance remain essentially the same, the form he now employs to define and relate those qualities is quite different from that of a manifesto such as "The Art of Fiction" or a midcareer assessment such as his 1888 essay on Stevenson. All of the New York Edition prefaces combine personal reminiscence, theoretical pronouncement, and more particularized analysis of fable and treatment in the novel under discussion. However, they vary fairly widely in tone, length, and focus; as might be expected, analysis tends increasingly to displace reminiscence as James comes to deal with more recent works. The prefaces to the early novels—*Roderick Hudson, The American, The Portrait of a Lady*, and *The Princess Casamassima* are all romantically rich in nostalgic recollections of the settings and personal circumstances in which the novels were written. But the preface to *The American* is "Romantic" likewise in a more historically specific and revealing sense. Because of its fluid associative shifts between past and present and its complex, ambivalent weighing of the gains and losses involved in the transition from innocence to experience, it is, of all the prefaces, closest in structure and feeling to a Romantic ode such as Coleridge's "Dejection: An Ode," Wordsworth's "Ode: Intimations of Immortality" or "Tintern Abbey." Indeed, when James refers to "Gray's beautiful Ode" (1057), that is, "Ode on a Distant Prospect of Eton College," he invokes the chief eighteenth-century prototype of such odes.[25]

James delighted in the poetry of his century; on Daniel Mark Fogel's reckoning, "by far the greatest number of explicit allusions in James are to the English Romantic poets."[26] Questions of direct influence aside, the main topic of the preface is a twofold "Wordsworthian" antithesis between the claims of realism and romance (particularly in *The American* but more generally, too) and between a remembered younger self who supposed he was practicing realism and an elder self who recognizes that it was romance all along. The second, then versus now, antithesis dominates the beginning of the preface as, in images reminiscent both of "Tintern Abbey" and "Resolution and Independence," James summons up scenes where the "story" came to him and the novel itself was written: "the long pole of memory stirs and rummages the bottom, and we fish up such fragments and relics of the submerged life and extinct consciousness as tempt us to piece them together" (1058). Portraying his 33-year-old self as an "artless" babe in the woods, he recalls "the habit of confidence that . . . a special Providence . . . despite the sad warning of Thackeray's "Denis Duval" and of Mrs. Gaskell's "Wives and Daughters" (that of Stevenson's "Weir of Hermiston" was yet to come) watches over anxious novelists condemned to the economy of serialisation. . . . And yet as the faded interest of the whole episode becomes again mildly vivid what I seem most to recover is, in its pale spectrality, a degree of joy, an eagerness on behalf of my recital" (1053).

Reminiscences at once nostalgic and ironic lead to a richly nuanced contrast between "the free play of . . . unchallenged instinct" (1057) in his youthful "surrender to the . . . projected fable" of *The American*, and the "free difficulty" which he now perceives to be inseparable from the "free selection—which is the beautiful, terrible *whole* of art" (1061). The idea that selection is the *whole* of art is distinctively Stevensonian, and, sure enough, James's meditation on it prompts recollection of Stevenson's dictum on a related topic: "Robert Louis Stevenson has, in an admirable passage and as in so many other connexions, said the right word: that the partaker of the 'life of art' who repines at the absence of the rewards . . . might surely be better occupied." In the passage James apparently has in mind, Stevenson explains why "the lights seem a little turned down" in some of his later, less popular writings dealing with social injustices in America and the South Pacific: "What I wish to fight is best fought by a rather cheerless presentation of the truth. The world must return some day to the word duty, and be done with the word reward. There are no rewards, and plenty duties."[27]

The then-versus-now scheme of the preface can be reduced to the following key words and phrases:

THEN	NOW
bliss of ignorance	awakened critical sense
rewards	duties
free play	labor
bondage of ease	free difficulty
Providence/muse/surrender	free selection
romance	realism

Although this abstract seems overly schematic, it accords with James's dictum in the preface to *Roderick Hudson* (1907) apropos the antithetical heroines of that novel: "One is ridden by the law that antitheses, to be efficient, shall be direct and complete" (1052). Clearly, we are dealing with a Jamesean version of the Fortunate Fall in which the artist protagonist, graduating from a passive state of delusive ease and freedom, takes charge of his own destiny. He then experiences a fate resembling that of the heroes and heroines of many of James's own novels, including Christopher Newman—except in the crucial particular that at the end of the day they have their "duties" while he has his "rewards" in the form of the novels themselves and the power to write more of them. For him the fall is fortunate indeed, and it cannot matter much if there is an untrespassable chasm between his present and his former self. Or so we might suppose, reading

James rhapsodize about the "constant nameless felicity" of the mature writer of fiction, "with the toil and trouble a mere sun-cast shadow that falls, shifts and vanishes" (1061). James's triumphant progress over the years from romance to realism is mainly a matter of growing up. Thus far, the Stevenson who figures positively in the preface to *The American* is the later, "grown-up" Stevenson, author of *Weir* and realistic critic of Anglo-American imperialism.

The famous definition of romance James gives in this preface is couched in the familiar terms of freedom and constraint:

> The only *general* attribute of . . . romance that I can see . . . is the fact of the kind of experience with which it deals—experience liberated, . . . disengaged, disembroiled, disencumbered, exempt from the conditions that we usually know to attach to it and . . . drag upon it, and operating in a medium which relieves it, in a particular interest, of the inconvenience of a *related*, a measurable state, a state subject to all our vulgar communities. (1064)

James's argument is developed by means of an extended metaphor whose vehicle is not fully revealed until, like a magician, he suddenly produces a toy:

> The balloon of experience is . . . tied to the earth, and under that necessity we swing, thanks to a rope of remarkable length, in the more or less commodious car of the imagination; but it is by the rope we know where we are, and from the moment that cable is cut we are at large and unrelated: we only swing apart from the globe—though remaining as exhilarated, naturally, as we like, especially when all goes well. The art of the romancer is "for the fun of it," insidiously to cut the cable, to cut it without our detecting him. What I have recognized then in "The American" . . . is that the experience here represented is the disconnected and uncontrolled experience—uncontrolled by our general sense of "the way things happen"—which romance . . . palms off on us. (1064)

"Disconnected," "uncontrolled," and "palms off" make romance sound irresponsible, escapist, and deceitful. Small wonder that Michael Davitt Bell, commenting on the same passage, says that "for James, then, the essence of romance lies in its moral irresponsibility."[28]

Clearly, James still harbors some of the suspicions of romance that, with varying degrees of sophistication and intelligence, realists and moralists have always had. The irony here is that the novel whose unhappy ending he had defended against Howells as realistic now fails on precisely those grounds. Although he obviously exaggerates the extent of his ingenuousness at the time he wrote *The American*, it is true that his acquaintance with the European aristocracy was then comparatively superficial and that his picture of the haughty Bellegarde family disdaining rich Christopher Newman is largely a projection of democratic myth. From the later and more worldly perspective of the author of *The Golden Bowl*, the representation of the Bellegardes' behavior is so patently "uncontrolled by our general sense of 'the way things happen' " that it appears false and immature. If *The American* is the product of such guileless "surrender to . . . the projected fable," and if it is also an example of romance, what adult interest can the book or the genre have?

Yet despite his misgivings about romance and about *The American* in particular, James in his old age found a place in the New York Edition canon for the novel and also a place in his scheme of good things for "fun" and "play" and, above all, "freedom." He obviously feels some nostalgic good will toward his prelapsarian self and finds he can experience "the joy of living over . . . the particular intellectual adventure" of writing that romance. If this return to his former self is possible, perhaps travel in the opposite direction is, too. Perhaps, after all, the child is the father of the man.

Which brings us back to Stevenson. When James referred to the "habit of confidence" that a serializing novelist persists in feeling "despite the sad warning" of Thackeray's, Gaskell's, and Stevenson's last works, he cannot have forgotten the questions Stevenson himself asked in "AEs Triplex": "Who, if he were wisely considerate of things at large, would ever embark upon any work much more considerable than a halfpenny post card? Who would project a serial novel, after Thackeray and Dickens had each fallen in mid-course?" [29] If Stevenson had been more "wisely considerate" than romantically aspiring, he would have achieved far less and would not have left the great fragment of *Weir*. So the Arcadian innocence of the "confident" young romancer who wrote *The American* may have been practical wisdom on at least one count.

Upon reexamination, many of the negative qualities James associates with childhood and romance can be seen to have a strong positive valence as well. The exhilarating balloon ride is a "genial" experience; the sense of "fun," expansion, and gravity overcome is psychologically refreshing and valuable. This ride through space may remind us of his earlier image of Stevenson's "gyrations" as the "Trapezist in the Pacific void!"—an image of soaring, of performance for sheer joy in the exercise of skill and energy and freedom. And of course James's playful metaphors are themselves supreme examples of such performance. No doubt about it, among the many things he is doing in this preface James is reaffirming the Stevensonian message that to be *homo sapiens* one must also be *homo ludens*.

And play has a moral as well as a recreational dimension. Huizinga explains that "play only becomes possible, thinkable and understandable when an influx of *mind* breaks down the absolute determinism of the cosmos. The very existence of play continually confirms the supra-logical nature of the human situation."[30] Stevenson was the player *extraordinaire* whose writings and life (for a time) defied all the determinisms of his age, including those of Henry Adams and "the School of Balzac." James, although a friend of Adams and one of the most persistent champions of the French realists, could never accept their pessimistic determinism.[31] Therefore, while heeding the threatening sound of "uncontrolled" and "disconnected," we do well to remember that "liberty," "liberated," and "freedom" usually have the most positive connotations in James's moral/aesthetic vocabulary. Moreover, as Peter Brooks has recently argued, *The American* is centrally and at many levels—generic as well as moral and psychological—*about* the quest for freedom.[32]

Positive connotations are surely present when James speaks of "experience liberated . . . from the conditions that we usually know to . . . drag upon it." Happily for the novelist, the "life of art," of the genial creative imagination, confers a power of "free selection" rarely available in ordinary life. To be sure, for the artist as for others freedom entails risks and labor and the paradoxical necessity of either using or forfeiting it. But without a larger measure of freedom than is usually present in life or represented in realistic fiction, there can be little scope for artistic creation *or* for moral action—or for what James calls "the finest feelings."

There is no clearer instance of such feelings being realized in fiction than the "last view" James gives us of the hero of *The American* turning from the perfidious Bellegardes and, despite his power to do them harm without danger to himself, acting with "practical, but quite unappreciated, magnanimity . . . a strong man indifferent to his strength and too wrapped in fine, too wrapped above all in *other* and intenser reflexions for the assertion of his 'rights' " (1055). According to James, it was at the moment he imagined Newman's *unconstrained* magnanimity that his "conception unfurled . . . the emblazoned flag of romance" (1057). It is impossible to say whether James at this point recalled his figure of Stevenson waving "so gallantly the flag of the imaginary," but his account of Newman's "extraordinary" behavior makes no apology for the experience represented being "uncontrolled" but seems rather to endorse Stevensonian romantic principle. What we recognize here is the moral, the supremely responsible face of romance.[33]

Perhaps it was, finally, as a moral rather than as an aesthetic exemplar that James prized Stevenson above all. When he names the novelists of "largest responding imagination before the human scene" (1062), he does not mention Stevenson, even though his ghost may be said to haunt this preface. His ghost is present not least when James explains that the interest of such a novelist is greatest "when he commits himself" in the directions both of romance and realism "by some need of performing his whole possible revolution, by the law of some rich passion in him for extremes . . . of Scott, of Balzac, even of the coarse, comprehensive, prodigious Zola, we feel . . . that the deflexion toward either quarter has never taken place. . . . His current remains therefore extraordinarily rich and mixed, washing us successively with the warm wave of the near and familiar and the tonic shock . . . of the far and strange." Here James seems to be echoing and brilliantly elaborating Stevenson's contention that "true romantic art . . . makes a romance of all things. . . . *Robinson Crusoe* is as realistic as it is romantic; both qualities are pushed to an extreme, and neither suffers." Although James himself had emphasized the admixture of realism in Stevenson's fictions, it is obvious that there was a marked "deflexion" toward romance in most of them and that, in James's eyes, this made Stevenson a lesser novelist than one whose current remained *extraordinarily* rich and mixed.

In life, however, the "deflexion" meant a career that exemplified "the finest feelings" and bravely repudiated the deterministic certainties of the age. Far better than most of their contemporaries, James was able to see beyond the surface glamor and "swagger" to the essential fineness and moral achievement of Stevenson's life. But because James was as much of as apart from his time, he was also able to join wholeheartedly in the general apotheosizing of a man who, in defiance of "that gentleman" Hades and of gravity itself, had raised, levitated, himself from his invalid's couch to shine as *the* romantic literary hero for the era. Stevenson himself anticipated this fate in his figure of the man who "reckons his life as a thing to be dashingly used and cheerfully hazarded . . . keeps all his pulses going true and fast, and gathers impetus as he runs, until, if he be running towards anything better than wildfire, he may shoot up and become a constellation in the end."[34] "There he is—" wrote James in 1899, "he has passed ineffaceably into happy legend" (277).

Joycean Realism

WILLIAM M. CHACE

AS THE NINTH EPISODE ("SCYLLA AND CHARYBDIS") of *Ulysses* begins, the time is 2:15 on the afternoon of June 16, 1904. The place is the office of the Director of the National Library on Kildare Street in Dublin. The occasion is the most auspicious one that Stephen Dedalus will have all day to express his beliefs about the necessary constituents of fiction, the fiction that he hopes someday to be able to write, and the fiction that we now know Joyce *was* able to write after he became more capacious and more generative than the Stephen he once was.

Stephen's explanation of himself that afternoon as a fiction writer— like Joyce's rise as a novelist—is made against considerable resistance. In order to set forth his ideas, he must combat not only the stolid traditionalism of his auditors, but also his own chronic skepticism. When, after reaching a climax of explanation and defense, Stephen is asked by John Eglinton if he believes his own theory, he promptly answers "No" and then to himself says "I believe, O Lord, help my unbelief."[1] Joyce had to argue against the conception of the novel as it had hitherto been written if he was to succeed in producing *Ulysses* and Stephen has to argue against himself if he is to win the day in the library.[2]

Stephen's argument, constructed with ingenuity, irony, and implausibility, is based on his belief that the great artist must achieve a position of absolute, godlike independence. In *A Portrait of the Artist as a Young Man*, he had argued that the artist, "like the God of the creation, remains within or behind or beyond or above his handiwork, invisible, refined out of existence, indifferent, paring his fingernails."[3] The artist is seen as wholly self-sufficient, free of all dependencies, particularly to fathers of any kind (church or country). From that position he can generate the world he will people, color, and organize into plots and destinies. When, in "Scylla and Charybdis," John Eglinton fatuously announces that Shakespeare is both the ghost and the prince in *Hamlet*—that he is "all in all" (174: 1018–19)—Stephen is quick to add in excited agreement that:

The boy of act one is the mature man of act five. All in all. In *Cymbeline*, in *Othello* he is bawd and cuckold. He acts and is acted on. Lover of an ideal or a perversion, like José he kills the real Carmen. His unremitting intellect is the hornmad Iago ceaselessly willing that the moor in him shall suffer. (174: 1020–24)

Once unencumbered from such loyalties and bonds, Shakespeare can become both Iago and Othello and indeed everyone else in that play and in all remaining 36 Shakespearean plays. With such arguments, Stephen gives his auditors in the National Library a version of Shakespeare that separates him entirely from the rest of humankind ("Man delights him not nor woman neither" [175: 1030]) and establishes his equivalency to God through his superior imagination, an imagination so vast that nothing in the world can surprise it:

He found in the world without as actual what was in his world within as possible. . . . The playwright who wrote the folio of this world and wrote it badly (He gave us light first and the sun two days later), the lord of things as they are whom the most Roman of catholics call *dio boia*, hangman god, is doubtless all in all in all of us, ostler and butcher, and would be bawd and cuckold but that in the economy of heaven, foretold by Hamlet, there are no more marriages, glorified man, an androgynous angel, being a wife unto himself. (175: 1041–52)

The trouble with this theory of unencumbered creativity, a trouble that Buck Mulligan immediately exploits, is its solipsism. It negates the authority of the world to exist in its own right. Mulligan, who is as clever as Stephen and who energetically represents Stephen's own bitter cynicism, grasps that fact and responds to the theorizing he has heard by presenting a play for the library auditors, a play he calls:

—*Everyman His Own Wife*
or
A Honeymoon in the Hand
(a national immorality in three orgasms)
by
Ballocky Mulligan.

Mulligan's response to Stephen's theoretical constructions is, while witty, not devastating. Stephen has already anticipated the solipsistic dangers he faces and has been constructing something else that will serve to offset or balance them. The episode is, after all, about balance, about navigating between extremes, about the way in which Odysseus once had to sail between the devouring six-headed monster Scylla and the whirling maelstrom Charybdis.

The answer Stephen provides to devouring solipsism is drawn from what his Jesuit training has instructed him to call "composition of place" (155: 163), a term from the *Spiritual Exercises* (1548) of Ignatius Loyola. Loyola's lessons tell Stephen

that in the contemplation of meditation of a visible object as in contemplating Christ our Lord, Who is visible, the composition will be to see with the eye of the imagination the corporeal place where the object I wish to contemplate is found.[4]

Stephen transforms Loyola's injunction to "see the place" into a novelistic injunction to himself to provide "local colour. Work in all you know. Make them accomplices" (154: 158). The imagination must become corporeal, must descend from mind to the world as it is. When Stephen says, "Ignatius Loyola, make haste to help me" (155: 163), he recognizes his dependency on the given circumstantiality of the world. Such recognition had also come to him earlier in *Ulysses*, in the second episode, "Nestor," when he had told Mr. Deasy that God is "a shout in the street" (28: 386), a manifest and not an abstract thing, phenomenal and not noumenal. The memory of that rejoinder to Deasy now echoes in Stephen's mind as he rehearses the strategies of his argument and as he proceeds to define his own species of realism:

Unsheathe your dagger definitions. Horseness is the whatness of allhorse . . . God: noise in the street: very peripatetic. Space: what you damn well have to see . . . Hold to the now, the here, through which all future plunges to the past. (153: 85–89)

Like the Odysseus who sailed before him, Stephen must navigate between extremes. He must move between the dangers of a theory defending solipsism (the artist need not pay his respects to the world or even grant it a real existence) and a theory saying that the artist can create something only by reassembling the given pieces of the world as he finds them. As he moves, he implicitly poses for us questions that Joyce, composing *Ulysses*, faced again and again. The answers he gave to those questions shaped the literary realism that became his own: Does the artist create or does he rearrange? Does imagination really exist or is it only the unhappy result of bad memory and a confused recollection of the actual world? Does the world exist or is it only a deformed and secondary product of the imagination?

When Joyce wrote to George Antheil that "I am quite content to go down to posterity as a scissors and paste man for that seems to me a harsh but not unjust description,"[5] he was denigrating, as he often did, his own creative imagination. But the attractiveness of Joyce's modesty vanishes when a reader confronts the consummate originality manifest in *Ulysses*. The book is clearly the act of an extraordinary imagination, one so powerful that Joyce is rightly seen as a revolutionist of the novel, but it is an imagination never disengaged from actual circumstances. Joyce maintained a loyalty to both Daniel Defoe, who grounded everything he wrote in details, and William Blake, who was convinced of the supremacy of mind over all the tiny details it is forced to survey. (Joyce had enthusiastically lectured on both authors in Trieste in 1912.)

When Stephen imperiously claims in "Eumaeus" that "Ireland must be important because it belongs to me" (527: 1164–65), he cannot be taken seriously. But what can be taken seriously is the problem that the Joyce who wrote the book faced: How at once to *possess* that which you create and to *respect* its autonomy? How can something be both imagined and real? Since the writing of *Dubliners*, Joyce had been devoted to fictional realism ("he is a very bold man who dares to alter in the presentment, still more to deform, whatever he has seen and heard").[6] Must that devotion yield, in *Ulysses*, to some larger demand issuing from the imagination and from the inherent properties of fiction which Joyce discovered he could unleash?

Joyce is often quoted telling Frank Budgen that "I want to give a picture of Dublin so complete that if the city one day suddenly disappeared from the earth it could be reconstructed out of my book."[7] Perhaps some such reconstruction could be effected, but the recovered city would now have to include certain entities not known to any "real" Dubliner living in the "real" world of 1904. There would be, for instance, a dark, "sinewless and wobbly," cuckolded Jewish advertising canvasser carrying an old potato and a cake of lemon soap in the pockets of his black suit. There would be an ample and faithless woman, "fulfilled, recumbent, big with seed," luxuriating in her thoughts while that dark man sleeps upside down beside her. And there would be the house that both of these people, who happened to have been nonexistent in Dublin in 1904, were inhabiting, a house actually vacant of people on that "real" day in that "real" year.

In addition to such presences, the recovered Dublin would be accessible only through certain verbal and linguistic conventions, ones wholly in the control of James Joyce. Latter-day archaeologists would not be given a city, but a city in words, *Joyce's* Dublin, and they would have to address themselves to the fact that the medium of his transmission is never perfectly transparent. What would they do, while attempting to reconstruct the Ormond bar of 1904 and wanting to be sure to capture the ambience of such a place, when they encountered:

—*Come . . . !*
It soared, a bird, it held its flight, a swift pure cry, soar silver orb it leaped serene, speeding, sustained, to come, don't spin it out too long breath he breath long life, soaring high, high resplendent, aflame, crowned, high in the effulgence symbolistic, high, of the etherial bosom, high, of the high vast irradiation everywhere all soaring all around about the all, the endlessnessnessness . . . .
—*To me!*
Siopold!
Consumed. (226–27: 744–54)

And what might such archaeologists, properly interested in recovering the "Nighttown" area of Dublin (a slum razed in the 1940's, and now transformed into Corporation housing), do when coming across this kind of Joycean description:

The Mabbot street entrance of nighttown, before which stretches an uncobbled tramsiding set with skeleton tracks, red and green will-o'-the-wisps and danger signals. Rows of grimy houses with gaping doors. Rare lamps with faint rainbow fans. Round Rabaiotti's halted ice gondola stunted men and women squabble. They grab wafers between which are wedged lumps of coral and copper snow. Sucking, they scatter slowly, children. The swan-comb of the gondola, highreared, forges on through the murk, white and blue under a lighthouse. Whistles call and answer. (350: 1–9)

In both instances, the written medium would impede rather than help the archaeologist, for that medium would not be governed by the demands of documentary realism (caviar to the archaeologist) but by overriding stylistic imperatives, the first musical and the second impressionistic. And would the early evening weather of June 16, 1904, be faithfully recaptured for a latter-day meteorological archivist by a passage such as this:

The summer evening had begun to fold the world in its mysterious embrace. Far away in the west the sun was setting and the last glow of all too fleeting day lingered lovingly on sea and strand, on the proud promontory of dear old Howth guarding as ever the waters of the bay . . . (284: 1–4)

In this last passage, the curious archaeologist would encounter a more conventional prose but nonetheless one modulated by a diaphane of sentiment and shopworn expressions; he would be given language but he would not be given meteorology. What indeed is a "mysterious embrace" other than a cliché, and what function has it other than the literary and the satirical? To ask such questions, and thus to expose Joyce's prose for what it is—language—is to reinforce the truth that even the realism to which he was notably so faithful is constantly subject to the more forceful demands of fictional language in all its capacities, only one of them being traditional realism.

To trace the evolution of *Ulysses* is to see, then, how Joyce's understanding of realism flourished as the book grew. After the first six episodes had established the identities of both Stephen Dedalus and Leopold Bloom in a style that would not be unfamiliar to readers of *A Portrait of the Artist as a Young Man*, Joyce apparently began to perceive the underutilized properties of the verbal medium that had been supporting his realism. He then liberated that medium from the exclusive service it had been paying to tradition. The results, small at first, are to be seen everywhere in the book. An example is the sentence at the conclusion of the eighth episode, "Lestrygonians": "His hand looking for the where did I put found in his hip pocket soap lotion have to call tepid paper stuck" (150: 1191–92). That sentence, though fitted out with irregular syntax, is a faithful rendering of what is happening (Bloom is looking for the lemon soap, which he almost immediately finds in his hip pocket stuck to some paper, while he is at the same time recalling that he will have to call again at Sweny the chemist's to pick up the lotion of oils and waters for Molly [69: 490–93]). The syntax represents Joyce's fusion of the realism of third-person narrative description and the realism of first-person psychological revelation—*monologue intérieur*. And thus he would maintain his fidelity to fictional realism, but he would also thus incorporate his growing awareness that such realism could include more voices than one.

Another complex product of this same kind of awareness can be seen in a pair of phrases from the tenth episode, "Wandering Rocks": "As said before he ate with relish the inner organs, nutty gizzards, fried cods' roes. . . ." (221: 519–20) and "Bloom ate liv as said before" (223: 569). Both expressions are, of course, *true* of Leopold Bloom; we know them to be faithful descriptions of his dietary preferences because they are echoes of the very first thing we learn of him in the fourth episode, "Calypso": "Mr Leopold Bloom ate with relish the inner organs of beasts and fowls.

He liked thick giblet soup, nutty gizzards, a stuffed roast heart, liverslices fried with crustcrumbs, fried hencods' roes" (45: 1–3). Fictional realism of the most scrupulous sort is maintained in the two latter sentences. At the same time, however, that realism is being pressed into service at the behest of a narrator who is not only the observer of what is to be seen *out there* in the imagined real world but is also the supervisor of what is to be seen *in there* in the already created text. Realism is being enlarged to take note of the extant products, on the page, of what realism has been able to accomplish thus far in the book. Fiction, as Joyce was letting it become in *Ulysses*, was to be documentary of both the world it imagined it saw and the language of its seeing. As Richard Brinkmann has noted, literature can become "the *realisation* of the subject, realism equals the realisation of the subject and of its reality in the text."[8]

A further example of such expansion should be noted. In the eighth episode, "Lestrygonians," Bloom apparently is made to think: "In Gerard's rosery of Fetter lane he walks, greyedauburn" (230: 907–8). The phrase is a recreation of Stephen's musing about Shakespeare in "Scylla and Charybdis": "In a rosery of Fetter lane of Gerard, herbalist, he walks, greyedauburn" (166: 651–52). Robert Martin Adams, presuming that Joyce would not implant in Bloom's mind thoughts about Shakespeare's relationship to the supervisor of gardens for Queen Elizabeth's secretary of state, is troubled by this echoing. Assuming that such thoughts could properly belong only to Stephen, Adams complains that Bloom, whose knowledge of Shakespeare is rudimentary, could not be aware of Gerard's rosery, for, as he says, "Joyce never enforces thematic parallels of this sort so crudely as by transferring one man's thoughts into another man's head."[9] But the fact is that he does exactly that, again and again, and does so with increasing vigor and inventiveness (as we shall see) as the book moves into its later episodes.

Joyce's fictional realism came to accept the fact that the supervisory narrator, who knows the thinking of everyone in the book, is free to distribute the record of that thinking or activity wherever he wants. By so doing, he interposes himself between the "action" and the reader— something done, after all, by every writer of fiction, implicitly or explicitly, since the beginning of the art. The result, in *Ulysses*, is apparently to reduce the consequentiality and weight of the fictional personages and to augment the importance of the writer who has set them in motion. That might seem disturbingly radical, but only to readers who prefer to suppress their knowledge that all fictions and all characters, realistic or not, are inventions wholly controlled by *ego scriptor*, a most imperious entity.

To argue that Joyce exploited the dimensions of fictional realism in these ways is to reinforce the notion that realism perpetually offers itself to writers as a medium to suffer redefinition. As a kind of "loose, baggy monster," it is not necessarily of the nineteenth century, even though that century has exerted a kind of proprietary claim upon the genre of lengthy, circumstantially rich, and substantially credible novels. As J. P. Stern has said, realism is not of *any* century, because it

is not a single style and has no specific vocabulary of its own, except in contrast to styles and vocabularies employed by other modes of writing in any given age. It is not a *genre*, nor a *Weltanschauung*, but rather a disposition of mind and pen, something like a humour—in brief a *mode of writing*. As a mode it makes its appearance in all kinds of cultural situations yet is identical with none.[10]

Elsewhere Stern enumerates the attributes of realism that make it, at any time, what it perennially is: it possesses an interest in "the riches of the represented world," a "weightiness and resistance to ideals," a "consequential logic and circumstantiality," and "a creative attention to the visible rather than the invisible, an unabating interest in the shapes and relations of the real world, the world that works."[11] To these attributes of such fiction should be added another crucial component, first lucidly defined by Ian Watt, namely, its continuing task of providing both a "realism of description" and a "realism of assessment." The novel, literary realism's truest vehicle, must be engaged in the world as it is, being objective in its demeanor and yet forthcoming in its analytical awareness. Watt argues that the novel cannot descend into simpleminded *chosism*, a world of unmediated objects and phenomena: "if the new genre was to challenge older literary forms it had to find a way of conveying not only a convincing impression but a wise assessment of life."[12]

And to these attributes may yet be added two others, also described by Stern, namely, that insofar as all fictions combine "mimesis" and "imagination," or what Stern calls "matching" and "making," fictional realism is characteristically weighted in favor of the former: "every matching involves a making, but the two are not one and the same thing. In realism the balance is on the side of the matching";[13] and that insofar as the fictional realist must observe both the social milieu in which events take place and the psychological environment surrounding them, he must achieve a "middle distance" allowing him bifocal vision: "that middle distance which places individual people and their institutions in one working perspective ('gets them all into the picture') gives the realist a sharper and finer view than the view of his uncreative contemporaries."[14]

While these criteria make for a necessary definition of realistic fiction, and while against their force any kind of fiction may be gauged to determine the quality of its realism, the criteria are not exhaustive. Realism seems always to be outstripping the constraints into which categorization places it. Stephen Heath, arguing that realism is a kind of "utopia of writing" which is not so much realized as it is aspired to, says that it continually challenges the documentable reality from which it springs. "It must be grasped in and against the modes, meanings, orders of . . . reality," for, as he says, it "is not a property of reality nor of any given literary form; it is always to be fought for, achieved."[15] Some latter-day fictional narratives—by Samuel Beckett, Gertrude Stein, William Burroughs, Italo Calvino, and others—apparently exist to question the very definitions of fiction implicit in the works that have preceded them; these latter works are constantly working to subvert the stability of those prior definitions. But what remains in fictional realism, the property about whose presence neither Watt, Stern, nor any other commentator would be likely to disagree, is its aim to tell the truth, to touch bedrock, or, to quote Heath, to provide

intelligibility, the real made sense; it is there to provide knowledge and truth . . . realism is never intended as a simple copy of reality—whatever that could mean—but always . . . as a demonstration of reality, getting through to what it really is.[16]

Several years ago, in commenting on the rarefied developments of Henry James's late style, Watt clearly made the same point by remarking that James had made "a supremely civilised effort to relate every event and every moment of life to the full complexity of its circumambient conditions."[17] Joyce would have seconded such an aspiration, but he would have added the innovative amendment that one of those "conditions" was the medium of prose expression itself. James was not so innovative—perhaps owing to his "supremely civilised" demeanor—for he limited the linguistic freedom of his characters and constrained the stylistic play they were offered. His presiding consciousness does not entertain a multitude of voices, but *one*, the unforgettably Jamesian. *That* voice becomes, in its implacable way, one of the "conditions" of every great James novel. For Joyce, on the other hand, a novel was an opportunity to set into play an array of voices, each with the power of description, each with the power of assessment. Both writers enriched the tradition they inherited, the one by intensifying the authority of the central narrative consciousness, the other by deregulating that consciousness and letting its authority flow to the characters it had put into existence.

These observations now permit us a return to *Ulysses* and to the four final episodes of the book, "Circe," "Eumaeus," "Ithaca," and "Penelope," sometimes seen as destructive of any form of realism. "Circe" has all about it the look of a play: characters appear and are given lines, stage directions are provided, asides delivered, and some consequential action taken (e.g., the "smashing" of a "chandelier" and a fight between Stephen and two British soldiers). But the "look" of a real play is all we get, for the action is mostly internal and textually self-referential. The bulk of "Circe" is hallucinatory, only about one-tenth of it being firmly footed on actions and talk that everyone concerned—the reader, the characters, and the author—would agree "really" takes place. We are, that is, in the minds of those who make up *Ulysses*, sometimes in Bloom's mind, sometimes in Stephen's, but a great deal of time in the mind of the book itself.

The "unconsciousness" of the previous episodes of the book is, in fact, the real subject in "Circe," for in it the book exposes its own latent content while its characters are concurrently being revealed through hallucinations somehow not making an impact on them. Neither Bloom nor Stephen seem in any way "transformed" by the traumatic events of "Circe," but those events, if real, would have been profound enough to have left their marks everywhere in the three concluding episodes. Yet no such marks exist, and thus "Circe" seems a moment in *Ulysses* when the astounding is set free, but when the characters are immunized to its dangers. One indication of the fact that *Ulysses*, and not its characters, is the main "dreamer" or "hallucinator" in "Circe" is that many things are thought of in it that the character to whom they are attributed could have no way of thinking about or even knowing. For instance, Bloom and "The Nymph" (i.e., Molly) refer to "Nebrakada" (451: 3463) but the reference is clearly to "Nebrakada feminum," a phrase thought of by Stephen, and Stephen alone, in "Wandering Rocks" (200: 861); the fictitious Mother Grogan turns out to be a nemesis of Bloom and throws her shoe at him (400: 1717) but she is unknown to Bloom and he to her, her only previous appearance in the book being by name in "Telemachus" (11: 357), an episode empty of Bloom; the Very Reverend John O'Hanlon, the canon of the Star of the Sea Church in "Nausicaa" and known to Gerty MacDowell but not to Bloom, elevates and exposes a timepiece which sounds three "cuckoos" (383: 1133–35) in a hallucination seemingly attributed to Bloom; and, most striking of all, articles that have no power of consciousness at all (a cap, a doorhandle, a buckle, buttons, etc.) are each given *their* hallucinations.

One basic way of explaining what is happening in the episode, then, is to say that it is composed of three essential components: *reality*, that is, the material of novels that conform to the principles of traditional realism; *heightened reality*, that is, the material of novels that reveal the inner workings of the minds of their characters in an effort to expose their consciousness on all its levels and to reflect that consciousness in the stylistic coloration and atmosphere surrounding those characters; and *unreality*, that is, the material of fiction that, by suspending the principles of traditional realism, shows the purely imaginary as it supplants while it reveals the truth of things.[18]

Traditional realism grants prestige to a certain kind of prose, Watt describing it as one restricting "itself almost entirely to a descriptive and denotative use of language," its aim being "to make the words bring [the] object home to us in all its concrete particularity."[19] Realism, as he says, involves "the adaptation of prose style to give an air of complete authenticity,"[20] his clear implication being that the novel, a mirror to the world, should treat reality so that it may emerge as purely itself. Were fictional realism considered from that traditional point of view, "Circe" must certainly be seen as beyond the pale. But if Heath's understanding of the underlying properties of realism ("intelligibility, the real made sense . . . a demonstration of reality, getting through to what it really is") is invoked, the episode becomes quite real indeed.

That is because "Circe," while it most certainly does not use language in any traditional way, is a monumentally concentrated effort to get at the reality both of Bloom's life—his temptations, his guilt (both real and imagined), his fantasies—and of the book in which Bloom has been placed—*its* anxieties, suppressions, concealments, and fantasies. At what point, then, and by virtue of what principles, can one say that its prose is *not* realistic, that no mirror reflecting its reality has been provided? At what point can one say that the primary duties and capacities of realism have been abrogated? To make realism a term meaningful only for represented characters in fiction, and not for the medium of that representation, is to withhold from realism one of its greatest capacities for growth and power. Just as we know that self-consciousness cannot be withheld from human beings, Joyce's lesson is that the language of fiction constitutes the self-consciousness of realism and cannot be withheld from it.

To turn to "Ithaca" is to encounter the episode that, in some ways, is the fullest possible realization of traditional realism. It is saturated in data, dense with facts. If realism embeds us in the circumstantial, this, then, is the moment in literary history to which all realism has been aspiring. "Ithaca" apparently tells us "everything": Bloom's weight (158 lbs.) and the size of his collar (17), the arrangement of the furniture of his house, the evidence confirming Boylan's presence in that house hours earlier, the dates of the two earlier meetings of Bloom and Stephen, the circumstances of Bloom's three baptisms, the contents of his library, his budget for the day, his posture in the marital bed, and the facts of the history of complete carnal intercourse between Bloom and Molly. This, and much else, about two central personages of the book and about the world in which they and we live, we learn.

But the quantity of data disgorged by the episode gives us the spectacle of realism unmonitored, realism liberated to pursue data unchecked by any traditional regulation. A small ocean of some 440 words is gushed out to describe the qualities of water (549–50: 185–228) and another 140 or so words are spent to show the relation of the planet Earth to other celestial bodies, including the star Sirius, some 10 light-years distant (573: 1042–56). If the globally aqueous and the celestially distant present one kind of extreme in the episode, however, the exiguous and the laconic form the other. In response to the inquiry about Bloom and Dedalus, "Did either openly allude to their racial differences?" one word sits on the page: "Neither" (557: 525–26). In response to the important question, "What two temperaments did they individually represent?" four true but all too curt words answer back: "The scientific. The artistic" (558: 559–60).

At moments in the episode, then, we are given "the whole truth" and at other moments "nothing but the truth." But to ask for more, to ask for "the Truth" in this episode, is to inquire, as readers, after something else—a something else we do not get. It is to ask for information appropriate to the fullness of our human need to see life in its proper perspective and proportion. That we get only intermittently in "Ithaca," for its narrative authority seems to be a kind of computing machine stripped of the cognitive and epistemological savvy we have learned to expect from fiction. What we sometimes think we will find in fiction is Stern's "the middle distance." But the perspective we find in "Ithaca" seems both inappropriately large, including too much of the vastness of water and of the heavens, and inappropriately small, with too much of the trivia of everyday life. We are told, for instance, that *When We Were Boys*, a book in Bloom's library, has an envelope bookmark at page 217 (582: 1370–71). That is true and it is inconsequential.

To acknowledge the micro-reductions and macro-expansions to which

Joyce brings realism in *Ulysses* is to grasp how faithful, in all his errancy, he nonetheless is to its fundamental principles. He still is dedicated to truth-telling, large and small. And thus he has one kind of disproportion continually confronting another and opposite kind: on the same page where the immensity of the constellation Orion "with belt and sextuple sun theta and nebula in which 100 of our solar systems could be contained" meets with "a cat" (573: 1049–50, 573: 1035) there stands the narrator, and with him Bloom the intermediary. A balance is thus achieved, and just as the movement of Bloom's emotions in this episode is toward equanimity, so the episode itself works to establish a midcourse between extremes:

I am writing *Ithaca* in the form of a mathematical catechism. All events are resolved into their cosmic, physical, psychical, etc. equivalents, e.g. Bloom jumping down into the area, drawing water from the tap, the micturition in the garden, the cone of incense, lighted candle and statue so that not only will the reader know everything and know it in the baldest and coldest way, but Bloom and Stephen thereby become heavenly bodies, wanderers like the stars at which they gaze.[21]

To "know everything" is to know it both *sub specie aeternitatis* and temporally, both from far away and from close within, and thus, as Joyce demonstrated, the aperture of fiction had to be opened more fully than ever before so that we could see more clearly.

But if Joyce's lesson in this episode is that the medium of truth-telling must be reengineered if more of the truth is to be told, and if the general lesson of *Ulysses* is that realism must examine its own methods of procedure if it is not to risk naiveté, "Ithaca" also prompts us to recognize that truth-telling is forever in the hands of unreliable truth-tellers. Joyce questions what appears to be omniscience as it has been represented in traditional fiction by giving us an apparently objective narrator who, in a series of catechetical interrogations and responses, sprinkles some error into much truth. There was, for instance, no prolonged summer drouth in Dublin in the spring of 1904 (548: 171); as usual, it was wet. At least 162, and not just 72, BTUs are required to raise a pound of water from 50 F. to 212 F. (551: 270–71). The arithmetical calculations involving the respective ages of Bloom and Stephen (555–56: 447–61) include a small but important error. If Bloom were 5'9" and weighed 158 lbs., had a neck size of 17" and well-developed abdominal muscles, his chest could not have measured 28" to 29.5" (593: 1818). Other such small but observable errors can be found in "Ithaca," an episode in which "the reader will know everything." Last, but not least, the episode (601–2: 2133–42) provides the names of some two dozen men putatively the occupants, at one time or another, of Molly's bed. Yet the list is implausible in most cases and ridiculously wrong in others; scholars more numerous than all those alleged lovers have persuasively shown that she simply could not, and would not, have slept with all those named.

Into the crevices, then, of Joyce's catechetical formulas there creeps, or there is planted, error. We might say by way of explanation that Joyce simply forgot, or nodded, like Homer, in his work. Perhaps, but the nod about the suitors is sustained for an inordinately long time. A more plausible explanation comes from computer-based theories of knowledge and "artificial intelligence"—namely, that Joyce is exposing the illusion of so-called "perfectly objective" knowledge. It will contain small glitches because the very nature of any kind of knowing (ultimately a property exclusively of human beings) means that it will wind up including the sorts of errors of which humans alone are capable. There always must be "garbage out" (GO) because humans like Joyce inevitably put "garbage in" (GI).[22] Hence realism, properly understood and properly maintained, must show itself to be fully cognizant of the human nature of its preparation.

If traditional realism presumed for its stability the presence of a narrator situated in "the middle distance," and if that narrator was thought to superintend, in a kind of authorial equanimity, the full sway of conflicting forces he or she had set in motion, "Ithaca" is the moment in *Ulysses* when the subject of equanimity and its achievement is taken up. Joyce thought that he had finished the book with that episode, and he told Robert McAlmon that it constituted a "tranquilising spectrality" and Harriet Shaw Weaver that it was "in reality the end."[23] The book gets to be completed because Bloom himself establishes balance through his return to Molly's side in bed, but, more important, because he has achieved victory over his emotions. In order to do that, he must move through the "antagonistic sentiments" of "envy, jealousy, abnegation" (602: 2154–55), doing so in a variety of ways, including the ingeniously grammatical. He is able to put the entire subject of the liaison of Molly and Blazes Boylan in a new light—and a happier one for himself—by simply rewording it, a transfiguration involving

the natural grammatical transition by inversion involving no alteration of sense of an aorist preterite proposition (parsed as masculine subject, monosyllabic onomatopoeic transitive verb with direct feminine object) from the active voice into its correlative aorist preterite proposition (parsed as feminine subject, auxiliary verb and quasimonosyllabic onomatopoeic past participle with complementary masculine agent) in the passive voice . . . (604: 2217–23)

Thus what was once the dreadfully brutal "he fucked her" is softened into "she was fucked by him." The deed is now seen by Bloom as mutual; Boylan loses his place at the head of the sentence and is shunted into a prepositional phrase; the passive voice ameliorates the direct force of the action. Once this grammatical transition is completed, Bloom himself is able to perform, with Molly as the object of *his* affections, an act of love (after his own fashion) and then he falls asleep.

Were this moment in *Ulysses* not crucial to its resolution, emotionally and psychologically, Bloom's rewriting of the relationship between Molly and Boylan would not matter very much. But his seizure of narrative responsibility gives him the equanimity he must have to "come home," to be "the centripetal remainer" (577: 1214), and to be the Odysseus-like hero who now can secure his deserved sleep: "He rests. He has travelled" (606: 2320). It is a Bloomesque triumph, one based on his adroit manipulation of the linguistic possibilities that realism, in its variety, had at the ready to describe his marital situation. Bloom opts for a "lesser," a more benign realism, and in so doing illuminates not only the fact that the genre is protean but also the fact that narrative responsibility is not, *pace* Adams, always the exclusive property of the narrator. It is Bloom who gets to describe the relationship between his wife and another man, and it is Bloom who is able to find in his own account something innocuous enough to allow him to sleep.

Such rewriting is, in fact, an element constantly alive in *Ulysses*. If we turn, for instance, to those passages in "Eumaeus" suggesting that Bloom and Stephen are in the process of discovering their "consubstantiality" of relationship—of being "father" and "son"—we find that such an interpretation is wholly in the hands of a narrator who, apparently objective in his treatment of events, is actually quite partial:

Mr B. and Stephen, each in his own particular way, both instinctively exchanged meaning glances, in a religious silence of the strictly *entre nous* variety . . . (514: 594–96)

Though they didn't see eye to eye in everything a certain analogy there somehow was as if both their minds were travelling, so to speak, in the one train of thought. (536: 1579–81)

The language here is Bloom's; he is the one persuaded that congruence of thought has been established. Stephen shares not at all in such an understanding, nor is there any substantial evidence that the ultimate presiding consciousness of the book, James Joyce, does either. "Consubstantiality" might be no more than what the anxious Bloom would want it to be, and what his words, dominating the discourse in *Ulysses* at this point, would make the book say.

As these instances demonstrate, *Ulysses* is a book whose author repeatedly and gladly defers to the created sensibilities of his characters to provide, by way of free indirect discourse, the definition of the events in which they participate. Those events, thus colored, are no less "real" than any other events in any other novels, and that is because Joyce was persuaded that reality is a function of the observing glance. Hugh Kenner has denominated this phenomenon "the Uncle Charles Principle: *the narrative idiom need not be the narrator's*" and has called this "something new in fiction, the normally neutral narrative vocabulary pervaded by a little cloud of idioms which a character might use if he were managing the narrative."[24] But the phenomenon had been detected earlier by Watt in his explication of the first paragraph of James's *The Ambassadors*, with Watt saying of the later Jamesian novels that "we do not quite know whether the awareness implied in a given passage is the narrator's or that of his character."[25]

Hence "parallax." That phenomenon is a way of telling us that as the situation of the witness to events changes, so apparently do the events—and hence their meaning. Molly's adultery gets to be what Bloom makes of it; Stephen gets to be what Bloom makes of him (a forlorn young man in need of guidance) but at other times what the men of the National Library make of him (a disdainful young man in need of better arguments); Bloom becomes an apotheosis, "ben Bloom Elijah" (283: 1916), by virtue of the elevated language concluding "Cyclops," an episode also including narrative language ("Cute as a shithouse rat" [279: 1761]) denigrating the "same" Bloom. C. H. Peake correctly remarks that "the events of the day derive such meaning and consequence as they have from the part they play in various modes of experience" and that such experience "is made up of numerous, dissimilar and often irreconcilable ways of looking at life, so different in kind that each demands a different kind of literary representation."[26] True—and all these representations are realism writ large, realism made more capacious by virtue of the fact it gets written out of an omniscience that can be modulated by the character it describes.

Traditional realism was broadened in myriad other ways in *Ulysses*. By the time, in 1921, that Joyce came to the writing of "Penelope," he was prepared to pay his final homage to the demands of realism, and that he did by distributing a wealth of factual data within an episode that is, at first inspection, a fluid and lyrical anthem. One powerful indication of the richness of information contained in that last episode is that John Henry Raleigh's *The Chronicle of Leopold and Molly Bloom* (1977), a tracing of the two characters' respective lives, addresses, jobs, meetings, and so on, draws about half of its content from the 37 pages making up "Penelope." What appears at first to be a rhapsodic review of the day, the days before, and all the past years is actually an account laden with dates, place names, and with resolutions of documentary problems elsewhere unsolved in the book. "Lunita Laredo" is the name of Molly's mother (627: 848); *The Moonstone* is the first of Wilkie Collins's novels that Molly has read (622: 653); Boylan is to return to 7 Eccles Street next Monday, the 21st, again at four o'clock (615: 332–33); and Bloom, it is disclosed, once got into great difficulties with his boss Joseph Cuffe in the cattlemarket, a situation from which, Molly believes, she alone could have extricated him (619: 510–11). These and many other exact particularities give rigid texture to what otherwise would be pure rapture.

Joyce's much-noted letter to Frank Budgen about the episode can easily be misread:

Penelope is the clou of the book. The first sentence contains 2500 words. There are eight sentences in the episode. It begins and ends with the female word *yes*. It turns like the huge earth ball slowly surely and evenly round and round spinning. Its four cardinal points being the female breasts, arse, womb and cunt expressed by the words *because, bottom* (in all senses bottom button, bottom of the glass, bottom of the sea, bottom of his heart), *woman, yes*. Though probably more obscene than any preceding episode it seems to me to be perfectly sane full amoral fertilisable untrustworthy engaging shrewd limited prudent indifferent *Weib. Ich bin der Fleisch das stets bejaht.*[27]

The words not normally heeded here—"sane" and "full" and "shrewd" and "limited" and "prudent"—are the words issuing from Joyce's loyalty to the realism sometimes thought to have been surrendered in "Penelope." When we say that Molly is fluid, solvent, alogical, digressive, inclusive, maternal, unambitious, apolitical, solipsistic, generous, and recumbent, we are granting her the characteristics she will need if she is to enjoy symbolic and mythic status in the book. Those qualities she rightly deserves. But if we neglect to observe that she happens also to be made of grittier stuff—local and specific—we will allow the purely abstract to define her. And liberation from the abstract, as Watt long ago noted, is one of the central achievements of fictional realism. Thus Molly, in whose words the book ends, is Defoe's Moll Flanders reborn, with Moll's strength and untrustworthiness, her sanity and shrewd character, her indifference, all made to come to life again in this Gibraltar-born "Gea-Tellus." Molly is, in all her particularity, Joyce's final vindication of the realism from which he is sometimes thought, erroneously, to have fled. Both the substance and the possibilities of that "most independent, most elastic, most prodigious of literary forms,"[28] as Henry James once called it, are alive in *Ulysses*. From "nationality, language, religion," as *A Portrait of the Artist as a Young Man* tells us, he aspired to flee, but never from realism. The book seizes both what realism once was and what, with the enlivened consciousness of the language in which it could now speak, it could now become.

The Making of *Crime and Punishment*

JOSEPH FRANK

DOSTOEVSKY'S 'CRIME AND PUNISHMENT' BEGAN WITH the idea for a long short story whose initial kernel was outlined in a letter, written somewhere between September 10 and 15, 1865, to the powerful editor M. N. Katkov. His monthly journal, *The Russian Messenger* (*Russki Vestnik*), was the outlet for both Turgenev and Tolstoy and the most prestigious publication of its kind in Russia; but Dostoevsky, who had carried on quite bruising polemics with Katkov in the early 1860's, had never published anything in its pages. Unable to pay his hotel bill in Wiesbaden, where he had lost all his money at gambling, he turned as a last resort to an editor whom he considered his personal foe and asked for an advance on a proposed contribution after all other appeals elsewhere had failed.

The idea, as he cautiously informs his old opponent,

so far as I can judge, in no way contradicts [the policy] of your journal; quite the contrary. The action is contemporary, set in the present year. A young man, expelled from the university, petty bourgeois in origin and living in the midst of the direst poverty, through light-mindedness and lack of steadiness in his convictions, falling under the influence of the strange "unfinished" ideas that float in the air, decides to break out of his disgusting position at one stroke. He has made up his mind to kill an old woman, the wife of a titular counsellor, who lends money at interest. The old woman is stupid, stupid and ailing, greedy, takes as high a rate of interest as a Yid, is evil and eats up other lives, torturing a younger sister who has become her servant. "She is good for nothing." "Why should she live?" "Is she at all useful for anything," etc. —These questions befuddle the young man. He decides to kill her in order to bring happiness to his mother living in the provinces, rescue his sister, a paid companion in the household of a landowner, from the lascivious advances of the head of this gentry family—advances that threaten her ruin—finish his studies, go abroad, and then all his life be upright, staunch, unbendable in fulfilling his "humane obligation to mankind," which would ultimately "smooth out" his crime, if one can really call a crime this action against a deaf, stupid, evil, sickly old woman who does not herself know why she is on earth and who perhaps would die herself within a month.

Dostoevsky then goes on to explain that, by accident, the crime will be committed successfully, and that "no one suspects or can suspect him [the criminal]." (This last point in the final text, of course, will be considerably weakened to a lack of "conclusive" evidence; suspicion against Raskolnikov actually begins from the day after the deed has been done.) With the passage of time, however, "the entire psychological process of the crime is unfolded. Insoluble problems confront the murderer, unsuspected and unexpected feelings torment his heart. Heavenly truth, earthly law take their toll and he finishes by *being forced* to denounce himself." Dostoevsky explains that his character will find the isolation from other people unbearable and that the criminal himself will end up actually *morally demanding* his own punishment. Finally, citing several instances of recent crimes committed by students and reported in the newspapers, Dostoevsky remarks that he is convinced "my *subject* is not at all eccentric . . . especially that the murderer is an educated and even a well-inclined young man."[1]

This passage contains Dostoevsky's original statement of his intention, much of which is retained in the final version. But at some point whose date remains uncertain, this idea for a long short story was amalgamated with another of Dostoevsky's literary projects: the plan for a long novel to be called *The Drunkards*, which, so far as is known, had been conceived independently. A year before his letter to Katkov, Dostoevsky had tried unsuccessfully to obtain an advance for this project from several editors; but his notebooks contain no material that can be identified with it (except for three or four sentences that read like a possible epigraph). It is generally believed, and seems quite plausible, that the Marmeladov subplot in *Crime and Punishment* contains material originally destined for *The Drunkards*; but since there is no reliable evidence, this can be only a conjecture.

The final stage in the planning of this novel, which, as we can see from Dostoevsky's numerous sketches of the action, had continued to grow far beyond its initial dimensions, occurred at the end of November 1865. According to letters written to two correspondents, Dostoevsky decided at this time to shift from a first-person narrator telling his own story to a third-person omniscient narrator standing outside the events he was describing. "By the end of November," Dostoevsky wrote his old friend Baron Wrangel, "much had already been written and was ready; I burnt it all; now I can admit this. I didn't like it (what I had written) myself. A new form, a new plan swept me away, and I began all over again."[2] In fact, Dostoevsky did not discard as much of his original manuscript as this letter might lead one to believe; many pages were kept and simply transferred from the first to the third person.

Crime and Punishment, as we can see, thus only emerged as the result of a complicated process of expansion, rethinking, and recasting; and we shall attempt in the following pages to describe the course of this process so far as it concerns the problems of thematic structure and narrative perspective. There is, of course, much more to be said about the origins of the book from the points of view of both literary history and the ideology of Russian radicalism; but my concern here will focus more narrowly on the creative process through which the novel received its definitive shape and form.

I

In the splendid complete edition of Dostoevsky's writings published in the Soviet Union, the editors have reassembled the disorderly confusion of the notebooks that Dostoevsky kept while working on *Crime and Punishment* and have printed them, so far as possible, in a sequence roughly corresponding to the various stages of composition. Dostoevsky, as we know, was in the habit of casually flipping open his notebooks and writing on the first blank space that presented itself to his pen; and since he also used the same pages to record all sorts of memorabilia, the extraction of this material was by no means a simple task. As a result of these meritorious labors, however, we now possess a working draft (unfortunately only a fragmentary one) of the story or novella as originally conceived, as well as two other versions of the text. These have been distinguished as the Wiesbaden edition, the Petersburg edition, and the final plan involving the shift from a first-person narrator to the indigenous variety of third-person form invented by Dostoevsky for his purposes.

The Wiesbaden version coincides roughly with the story that Dostoevsky described in his letter to Katkov, and a draft of six short chapters has been reconstructed from his notes. Written in the form of a diary or journal, the events it records correspond more or less accurately to what eventually became part II, chapters 1–6 of the definitive redaction. The action of this part of the novel begins with Raskolnikov's return to his room after the murder, where he first restores the axe to the house porter's lodge from which it had been taken. Then he conceals his plunder in a hole in the wallpaper and frenziedly tries to erase bloodstains from his clothes. Utterly worn out by nervous tension and illness, he falls into a feverish sleep until awakened by a summons from the local police station. He drags himself to the station in terror, learns that the summons is merely about a debt to his landlady, but faints from physical weakness combined with fright when he hears talk about the murder between two police officials. This collapse arouses suspicion and, fearing a search of his room, he hurries home to remove the spoils of his crime, which he hides under a large stone near a public urinal for workmen. Losing consciousness for four days, he awakens to find himself in the care of his friend Razumikhin and the recipient of money from his mother. But finding the presence of others, and particularly the spontaneous effort to aid him, irksome and burdensome, he slips out of his room unobserved and goes to a café where he turns to newspaper accounts of the crime and encounters the police clerk Zametov; at this point the manuscript breaks off.

What strikes one about Dostoevsky's six chapters is how much of the later text they already contain. Here are almost all the secondary characters in their final form: the sympathetic and simple peasant girl Nastasya, an amused and astonished observer of the goings-on of the city folk among whom she has been cast; the rowdy, boisterous but pure-hearted ex-student Razumikhin, who comes of a noble family and is also penniless; the two police officials, one peaceable and kindhearted, the other vain, irritable, and explosive; the elaborately gowned German brothelkeeper Luisa Ivanovna, preposterously striving to assert the impeccable decorum maintained in her establishment; the dandified and corrupt police clerk Zametov; the self-important young doctor, an acquaintance of Razumikhin's, who has a special interest in nervous diseases and has come to advise about the narrator's condition. The details of the murder are given retrospectively, and it is not clear whether Dostoevsky, as one commentator assumes, had begun with a depiction of the murder itself now missing from the available manuscript. It is difficult to see how this event could have been recounted by an I-narrator as disturbed and agitated as Raskolnikov; and it is equally plausible, if not more so, to assume that the murder was initially intended to be shown only as refracted through the narrator's account of his past. [3]

This first draft concentrates entirely on the moral/psychic reactions of the narrator after the murder—his panic, his terror, his desperate attempts to control his nerves and pretend to behave rationally while consumed by a raging fever and constantly at the mercy of his wildly agitated emotions. What continually haunts him, in moments of lucidity, is his total estrangement from his former self, from his own past, and from the entire universe of his accustomed thoughts and feelings. And it gradually dawns on him that he has been severed from all this by one stroke—the stroke that killed the repulsive pawnbroker, and, by a horrible mischance, her long-suffering and entirely blameless sister Lizaveta, who, to make matters worse, is said to have been pregnant. This emphasis, of course, corresponds to the original motivation given by Dostoevsky for the criminal's surrender: "The feelings of isolation and separation from humanity which he felt immediately after committing the crime wear him down."

This theme dominates in the early draft and is expressed in three scenes of a growing order of magnitude. The first takes place at the police station, when the narrator, offended at being treated discourteously, snaps back at the police official for his rudeness. In a marginal note, Dostoevsky adds the narrator's reflections: "Yes, I was trembling with indignation and nothing could distract me; I even forgot everything. To be sure I was still saying it all from old habit (but all the same how could I) not yet understand everything. My God, did I think that I could (really), that I had the right to breathe freely, and that everything had already been taken off my chest, only because all the traces had been hidden?"[4] The narrator, an educated person and ex-student, had responded to official insolence with the same anger as he would have done in the past, still oblivious of the total change in his relations to others: no longer could he morally assert a right to be treated with respect, weighed down as he was by the terrible burden of the crime he had committed.

This realization only comes to the narrator by hindsight; but a much more instant recognition occurs when, after concealing the spoils of the crime, he decides to pay a visit, on the impulse of the moment, to his friend Razumikhin. Something very odd occurs as the narrator climbs the stairs—something which, as he writes, "I don't know quite how to put into words." For he felt a sensation that "if there is [now] for me on earth something [especially] hard [and impossible] then it is to talk and have relations . . . with other [people, as before, I don't know how, in short, to express exactly what I felt then, but I know it]. . . . And (the consciousness of all that) was my instant of the most oppressive anguish for perhaps all that month, in which I went through so much endless torture" (134). Dostoevsky drew a circle around this paragraph in the manuscript to mark its importance; for it indicates the moment at which the narrator realizes that even the simplest and most ordinary human relations have now become impossible for him.

The final epiphany of this experience occurs in a sequence that begins when the narrator, quitting Razumikhin and walking through the busy streets on the way home, is lashed by the whip of a passing coachman whose path he was blocking. "The whip's blow made me so furious that, having jumped to the railings, I angrily ground and (gnashed) my teeth"; he also is aware of the laughter of the onlookers who had witnessed this insulting chastisement. "But as soon as I realized what the point [of the laughter—J.F.] was [then the rage in me immediately disappeared. It seemed to me that it was no longer worthwhile concerning myself with that]" (137). Just as in the police station, his first reaction was one of outraged pride; but he realizes almost at once how inappropriate such a response was in his present predicament. "The thought came to me immediately that it would have been a lot better (perhaps even good) if the carriage had crushed me (completely)" (137). These words may well be the origin of what later occurred to Marmeladov, who in fact dies after being crushed by the wheels of a carriage.

Among the onlookers was a merchant's wife and her little daughter, who slip a twenty-kopek piece into the narrator's hand because "the blow had awakened their pity for me." Clutching the coin, the narrator walks toward the Neva in the direction of the Winter Palace while gazing at the cupola of St. Isaac's Cathedral and "all that splendid panorama" (138). In the past, as a student, he had walked by the same vista many times and had always felt that "despite this unexampled splendor and this astonishing river, this whole view was worth nothing" because there was "a (complete) coldness (and deadness) about it . . . a quality that destroys everything . . . an inexplicable cold blows from it." Even this negative impression, however, which Raskolnikov had previously assumed he had a right to feel, now falls away from him; and as he stands in the place that he knew so well, "suddenly the same (painful) sensation which oppressed my chest at Razumikhin's half an hour ago, the same sensation oppressed my heart here . . ." He realizes that "there was no reason for me (any longer) to stop here or anywhere . . . Now I had something else to concern me, something else, but all those, all those former sensations and interests and people were far away from me as if from another planet" (139). As he lingers at the railing of a canal, he lets the twenty-kopek piece slip into the water, thus symbolizing his break with all those emotions and values of the past. The same scene and gesture will be used in the novel, where it will also take on the richer significance of a rejection of the moral values embodied in the act of charity. Although the effects of such estrangement are clearly intended to dominate in the resolution of the action, they are reinforced by other episodes. One is the narrator's half-dream, half-hallucination, kept almost unchanged in the novel, which reveals both his own self-revulsion at the crime and his fear of pursuit. Lying in bed, he suddenly hears "a terrible cry" and opens his eyes; slowly he realizes that it is one of the police officials he has just met who is beating the landlady on the staircase. "I had never heard such unnatural sounds, such yelling, grinding of teeth, sobs, curses, and bellows . . . What is it all about, I thought, why (is he beating her), why? Fear like ice penetrated me to the core. . . ." Believing all this to be real, the narrator asks Nastasya about the frightening occurrence; but he is told that nothing of the sort had happened—it had all been a delusion, despite the narrator's conviction that he had been fully awake. "A yet greater tremor seized me," he writes, presumably at this evidence of his derangement; and when Nastasya tells him "(that) is the blood in you crying out," she takes this bit of folk-wisdom literally, while to the narrator (and the reader) the word "blood" immediately evokes the crime (140–41). Such an experience, added to his estrangement, was surely meant to provide further incentive for the narrator's eventual confession.

II

Why Dostoevsky abandoned his story can only remain a matter for speculation, but one possibility is that his protagonist began to develop beyond the boundaries in which he had first been conceived. All through the Wiesbaden text, the narrator is crushed and overcome by the moral/psychic consequences of his murderous deed; but just at the point at which the manuscript breaks off, he begins to display other traits of character. Instead of fear and anguish, he now exhibits rage and hatred against all those who have been looking after him in his illness and decides to slip away from their oppressive care. The conversation about the murder at his bedside, he explains, "made me feel unbearable malice . . . and what is more remarkable still is that during these agonies, this terror, I never thought a single time with the slightest personal compassion about the murder I had committed" (103). Here is an entirely different character from the one previously portrayed, and Dostoevsky may have stopped writing at this point because his figure had begun to evolve beyond his initial conception. In some notes for the immediate continuation of this version, he jots down: "Recovered. Cold fury, calculation. Why so much nerves?" (151). This last phrase is presumably a scornful question of the narrator addressed to himself.

Once Dostoevsky had begun to see his character in this light, alternating between despair and "cold fury," it became increasingly difficult to imagine a purely internal motivation for his self-surrender; and this may have led Dostoevsky to fuse the story with his previous idea for the novel called *The Drunkards*. An early plan already includes "the episode with the drunkard on Krestovsky" (91), and references to "Marmeladov's daughter" now appear in all the outlines of the action. "He [the narrator] went to the daughter. Like a prostitute. Then the daughter herself came. The daughter helps the mother. Takes the money. Pity for the children" (93). It is this note of pity that the Marmeladovs introduce into the narrative, or rather, since the narrator also pities the plight of his mother and sister, a totally different manner of expressing pity than the one he has chosen.

Once the narrator has committed the crime, it is now he who feels a need for pity that he cannot imagine being offered except by a Sonya capable of loving and forgiving even her ignominious father. One note shows how important pity has now become for Dostoevsky's character: "Who will then take pity?" he asks himself. "No one? No one? I am a base and vile murderer, laughable and greedy. Yes, precisely, is such a one to be pitied? . . . Is there someone to take pity? No one, no one! And yet this is impossible" (84). Of course it is Sonya who will "take pity," but what is explicitly articulated here will remain implicit, though perfectly discernible, in the final text, and it is what underlies Raskolnikov's irresistible impulse to turn to her with his confession.

"The civil servant's daughter," as Sonya Marmeladova is initially labeled, now becomes linked with the narrator's decision to give himself up, though Dostoevsky has great difficulty imagining how this act will take place. One alternative envisages him evoking a "picture of the golden age" and then asking: "But what right have I, a vile killer, to desire happiness for people and to dream of a golden age? I want to have that right. *And following this* (this chapter) he goes and gives himself up. He stops by only to say good-bye to her . . ." (90). Another note sketches a different scenario of the same sort of resolution: "Mother, sister, the story of the love. Why can't I become a Gaas [a saintly Moscow doctor who aided convicts—J.F.]? Why is everything lost? The baby. Who will forbid me to love this baby? Can't I be good? Prayed. Then *the Dream*. [There is reason to believe that this dream contained a vision of Christ—J.F.] The next day he went [to confess—J.F.] . . . In the evening the civil servant's daughter brought to him . . ." (93).

Such sentimental resolutions, however, clashed too obviously with the manner in which the narrator has begun to evolve. "About the mother and sister. No, for you, for you, my dear creatures! But people are base" (102). This denigration of mankind as a whole, not only its more "useless" specimens, now begins to appear more and more frequently. For example: "(The misfortunes of his father, mother). How nasty people are! Are they worth having me repent before them? No, no, I'm going to remain silent" (80). Or again: "How disgusting people are! And just now the letter from his mother. (That keeps him from becoming embittered)" (80). Most important of all, Dostoevsky now links such misanthropy with the motif of power: "How low and vile people are . . . No: gather them up into one's hands, and then do good for them. But instead [he is thinking of his confession—J.F.] to perish before their eyes and inspire only sneers" (81).

All these notes portray the character's own thoughts and feelings, but in others Dostoevsky sets down instructions for himself; and these indicate that he has begun to see how these two divergent aspects of his protagonist might be shown as more than a simple alteration of mood. "N. B. *Important*. After the sickness, a kind of cruelty and complete justification of himself, and when that was shaken, the letter from his mother" (154). This observation is indeed "important" because it suggests a significant character change after the murder and the resulting illness; now a "kind of cruelty" comes to the surface that was not evident before, a new aspect of personality, previously hidden, unexpectedly emerges. Another note reveals all the weight that Dostoevsky attributed to this discovery. "So that there is then a *coup de maître*," he writes with pardonable pride. "At first there was danger, then fear and illness, and his whole character did not show itself, and then suddenly his (whole) character showed itself in its full demonic strength and all the reasons and motives for the crime become clear" (88). The handling of the character is thus conceived not so much in terms of any deep-seated alteration as, rather, the bringing to light of potentialities always present but hitherto remaining in the background.

III

There has been a perpetual quarrel in Dostoevsky criticism over whether the motives finally attributed to Raskolnikov are or are not contradictory. At first, his crime seems to be the result of his Utilitarian logic set in motion by his own economic straits, the desperate plight of his family, and a desire to aid others with the spoils of the murder. A bit later, we learn about the article in which he has justified the right of "extraordinary people" to step over the moral law in order to bring benefits to humanity as a whole. In the confession scene with Sonya, however, Raskolnikov gives as his motive simply the desire to obtain power for himself alone, solely to test whether he is entitled to take his place among those superior individuals who possess the innate right to overstep the moral law. These alternate explanations certainly seem to clash with each other if we take them independently of the unfolding evolution of Raskolnikov himself. The notes we have been citing, however, indicate that Dostoevsky was acutely aware of the emergence of *new* aspects of Raskolnikov's character as the plot action proceeded, and he structured the novel in conformity with this metamorphosis—which leads to the disclosure of differing sides of Raskolnikov's "theory" to correspond with his continually altering view of himself and his motivations as he gradually comes to understand them.

It is this revelation of latent aspects of his personality that leads to the character's own self-questioning of what he had imagined his motives to have been, and to his ultimate recognition of what they truly were. As Dostoevsky writes in another note: "N. B. His moral development begins from the crime itself; the possibility of such questions arises which would not then have existed previously" (64). Another entry, entitled "the chief anatomy of the novel," is often cited to prove Dostoevsky's indecisiveness on this crucial question; but, in my view, it rather indicates what he considers the answer to be. "After the illness, etc. It is absolutely necessary to establish the course of things firmly and clearly and to eliminate what is vague, that is, explain the whole murder one way or another, and make its character and relations clear" (58). The phrase "one way or another" would seem to confirm the worst suspicions about Dostoevsky's lack of clarity; but a marginal jotting keyed to the word "murder" shows exactly the opposite to be true. For this reads: "pride, personality, and insolence" (58). These are the forces unleashed in Raskolnikov by his Utilitarian logic; and the murder teaches him to what extent they are irreconcilable with, and have in fact swept aside, the humanitarian aims to which he had presumably been committed.

Dostoevsky, as we have seen, speaks of Raskolinkov's character as suddenly exhibiting "its full demonic strength"; other references change this significantly to "satanical pride" (49). These phrases may seem little more than shorthand notes of the author to himself, but in fact the latter designation opens up an important perspective on the ideological context in which Raskolnikov was being elaborated. For the same phrase had been used three years earlier in Turgenev's famous novel *Fathers and Sons* (or, more accurately, *Children*) to describe the main protagonist Bazarov; and in the furious controversy that had broken out over the book, which one faction of the radical intelligentsia considered a defamation of their ideals, the chief spokesman of those radicals supporting Turgenev, Dimitry I. Pisarev, had proudly accepted Bazarov as a perfect delineation of a new generation. As for "satanical pride," Pisarev hastened to declare that "this expression [for Bazarov] is very felicitously chosen and is a perfect characterization of our hero."[5]

What is important about Pisarev's article, however, is not so much this telltale phrase as the fact that one can find in it exactly the same notions that lie at the root of Raskolnikov's own ideas. "Thus Bazarov everywhere and in everything," Pisarev had written, "does only what he wished, or what seems to him useful and attractive. . . . Neither over him, nor outside him, nor inside him, does he recognize any regulator, any *moral law*, any principle" (italics added). Nothing, Pisarev went on to declare, "except personal taste prevents him from murdering and robbing, and nothing except personal taste stirs people of this stripe to make discoveries in the field of science and social existence."[6] The equation of murder and robbery with discoveries in the field of science and with significant social changes could not be closer to the theory developed in Raskolnikov's famous article *On Crime*; and one also finds in Pisarev's pages Raskolnikov's notorious distinction between "ordinary" and "extraordinary" people. The first live in contented tranquillity, and only some sort of "material catastrophe" jolts them into movement; but the second, an insignificant minority, are those "dissatisfied with life in general, or with some special form of life in particular," and it is this "insignificant minority" (i.e., the Russian radical intelligentsia) who attempt to change the world. The mass, Pisarev notes sadly, "does not make discoveries or commit crimes; other people think and suffer, search and find, struggle and err on its behalf—other people eternally alien to it, eternally regarding it with contempt and at the same time eternally working to increase the amenities of its life."[7]

These words define the ideas and attitudes of Raskolnikov so perfectly that one can only wonder at the general failure to make the specific connection between the article and the novel, even though some Russian critics have uneasily noted the resemblance; one reason for this failure is probably Pisarev's own famous analysis of *Crime and Punishment*, in which he vehemently maintained that Raskolnikov's ideas were totally dissimilar to those current among the radical student youth. All the same, it seems obvious that once Dostoevsky had embarked on his plan to explore the moral/psychological dangers of radical ideology—"the strange 'unfinished' ideas that float in the air"—he began to develop Raskolnikov along the lines indicated by Pisarev as typical of the new generation (the older radical generation, or at least their dominant ideas, are parodied in the ridiculous, obtuse, but well-meaning and kindhearted Lebezyatnikov). Moreover, besides the evident persuasiveness of this linkage once the novel and the article are brought together, there is more direct evidence that Dostoevsky had Pisarev in mind when supplying Raskolnikov with his ideological baggage. There is a specific allusion to Pisarev's ideas in the early version of a speech by Luzhin, the unscrupulous businessman who wishes to marry Raskolnikov's sister Dunya. In this note, he is still called Chebilov, but the content of his words is identical with those of the preening suitor in part II, chapter 5. And this homily, it should be noted, is recognized by Raskolnikov as expressing the identical pattern of ideas that had led him to the murder. Chebilov says to Raskolnikov, *"Tant que* I've put my affairs in good order, I am useful to others, and therefore, the more I am an egoist, the better it is for others. As for the old beliefs: you loved, you thought of others, and you let your own affairs go down the drain, and you ended up being a weight around the neck of your neighbors. It's simply a matter of arithmetic. No, you know, I like the realities of the new generation, the shoemaker and Pushkin; and although I do not agree with them in part, still the general tendency" (48). This last sentence unmistakably refers to Pisarev, who had launched the slogan of "Realism" as a social doctrine in 1864, and, following Bazarov, had resoundingly declared a shoemaker to be more useful than Pushkin. It was manifestly within this specific ideological framework that Dostoevsky was now conceiving the peripeties of Raskolnikov's career and interweaving these ideas with his psychology.

IV

Crime and Punishment came to birth only when, in November 1865, Dostoevsky shifted from a first-person to a third-person narrator; and this was the culmination of a long struggle whose vestiges can be traced all through the early stages of composition. Some of the problems of using the first person are already apparent from the earliest version, whose first chapter is supposedly written five days after the murder has taken place (on June 9). The narrator dates the beginning of his diary as June 14 because, as he explains, to have written anything earlier would have been impossible in view of his mental and emotional confusion. Indeed, even when he begins to write, this same state of confusion continues to plague him, and Dostoevsky reminds himself to remember that in "all these six chapters [the narrator] must write, speak, and appear to the reader in part as if not in possession of his senses" (82).

Dostoevsky thus wished to convey the narrator's partial mental instability, while at the same time using him as a focus on the external world and also conveying the reactions induced in him by his crime as the action proceeds. All this posed serious difficulties, and the manuscript version shows Dostoevsky's constant uncertainty about how to hold the balance between the narrator's psychic disarray and the needs of his story. He writes, for example, in the first chapter: "I had already started up the stairs, but [suddenly] I remembered the ax. I don't understand how I could even for a single moment have forgotten about it; [it was after all necessary]. It tortures me now. It was the last pressing difficulty I had to take care of" (107). Dostoevsky crosses out the last three sentences because they obviously show a narrator reflecting on actions that had taken place in the past; and such reflections indicate a composure that the writer was not yet supposed to have attained.

This problem of time-perspective bothered Dostoevsky from the very start, and he moves the second chapter back several more days, to June 16, in order to give his narrator more time to come to his senses; but such an expedient could only be a temporary stopgap. The distance between past and present was still not great enough, and this led to an inevitable clash between the situation in which the narrator was immersed and his function as narrator. As Edward Wasiolek has rightly pointed out, "Raskolnikov is supposed to be . . . fixed wholly on his determination to elude his imaginary pursuers. But the 'I' point of view forces him to provide his own interpretations, and, even worse, his own stylistic refinements. Every stylistic refinement wars against the realism of the dramatic action" (101). As a result, there are serious doubts about the verisimilitude of a narrator presumably in a state of semi-hysteria who yet is able to remember and analyze, to report long scenes as well as lengthy dialogues, and in general to function as a reliable observer. This problem was only made more acute when the Marmeladovs entered the picture, and fragments of the drunkard's monologues begin to appear among the notes.

There is ample evidence that Dostoevsky was acutely aware of this issue, and the first expedient he thought of is indicated by a brief note: "The *story* ends and the *diary* begins" (79). Since no trace of such a dual form can be found, this idea was probably abandoned very quickly; but one understands how Dostoevsky's mind was working. He wished to separate a recital of events, set down by the narrator after they had been completed, from another account of the same events written by someone still caught in their flux; this would have eliminated the disturbing clash between one and the other so noticeable in the Wiesbaden version. The same purpose inspires the next alternative, the Petersburg version, which is entitled "On Trial," and whose author is now in the custody of the legal authorities.

In this text, the narrator begins: "[I am on trial and] I will tell everything. I will write everything down. I am writing this for myself, but let others and all my judges read it, [if they want to]. This is a confession (a full confession). I am writing for myself, for my own needs and therefore I will not keep anything secret" (23). This draft continues with Marmeladov's monologic recital of his woes (preserved almost verbatim in the eventual novel); and by this time the schema of events has been recast so that this scene clearly precedes the murder. Most important, though, is that the position of the narrator, sitting in jail and sadly contemplating his errors, allows him both to respond and to reflect without unduly straining credibility. But even in this plan, the time gap between the termination of all the events and the narrative is very small (roughly a week), and Dostoevsky remained uneasy; after all, the narrator can hardly be completely tranquil since the trial has not yet taken place.

The notebooks thus contain a third possibility, which is attached to a near-definitive outline of the action concerning Raskolnikov during the first two-thirds of the novel. "*A New Plan*," Dostoevsky announces, "*The Story of a Criminal*. Eight years before (in order to keep it completely at a distance)!" (54). The phrase in parentheses indicates just how preoccupied Dostoevsky was with this issue of narrative distance, and how clearly he saw all of the problems involved. In this new plan, the narrator would be writing after the conclusion of his prison term (eight years), and what was probably the subtitle would indicate the profound moral alteration induced by the passage of time; the narrator now calls *himself* a criminal, no longer maintaining that the murder could not be considered a "crime" at all. In any event, the narrator is now so far removed from his previous self that it would require only a short step to shift from an I-narrator to the third person.

V

This shift, however, did not occur all at once, and Dostoevsky debates the reasons for it in pages that, being contiguous to those just cited, were probably written almost simultaneously. "Rummage through all the questions in this novel," he admonishes himself, and then proceeds to do so. "If it is to be a confession," he muses, "then everything must be made clear to the *utter extreme*. Every instant of the story must be entirely clear." The recognition of this necessity leads Dostoevsky to some second thoughts: "*For consideration*. If a confession, then in parts it will not be chaste (*tselomudrenno*) and it will be difficult to imagine why it was written" (52). The use of the term "chaste" in this context is rather odd; but it seems to refer to the question of why the narrative has been written at all. Why should the narrator have wished to engage in so lacerating an act of self-exposure? At this point, Dostoevsky comes to the conclusion that his narrative technique must be altered. "But the subject is like this. The story from oneself (the author), and not from *him* (the character)" (52). What Dostoevsky means by "subject" is left ambiguous; but he may be thinking about his conception of a main character who reveals unexpected aspects of himself after the crime of which, previously, he had not been fully aware. If, in a first-person narration, "everything must be made clear *to the utter extreme*" at every instant, then it would be difficult to obtain such an effect of self-surprise; at best it could be referred to and explained, but hardly presented with full dramatic impact. Taken in conjunction with the problem of justifying his narrative, such considerations would explain why Dostoevsky, despite his desperate economic straits, could not resist making a fresh start and transferring to a third-person narrator.

But there still remained the question of exactly what kind of narrator this should be. Contemporary narratologists have hailed, as a recent triumph of their discipline, the discovery that authorial narrators are not just loose, amorphous presences who know how to spin a yarn; they are, rather, integral parts of the text with distinct profiles and attitudes that decisively shape the novelistic perspective. Dostoevsky, as it turns out, was fully conscious of this important truth, and he tries to define exactly the stance that his authorial narrator will adopt. No such problem had arisen earlier because, since the narrator was the central character, everything had been presented from his own point of view—which meant by someone who, though guilty of a terrible crime, would inevitably arouse a certain sympathy because of his altruistic impulses, his inner sufferings, and his final repentance. What sort of third-person narrator could play the same role in relation to the reader? As Dostoevsky pondered the choice between the first and third person, he wrote: "But from *the author*. Too much naïveté and frankness are needed" (52). Why this should be so is hardly self-evident; but Dostoevsky's elliptical notes leave open the possibility that he may still have been thinking about some sort of confessional novel which, even if cast in the third person, would involve the total identification of the narrator with the main protagonist. This would help explain the emphasis of the next sentence, which insists on the *separation* of the author from the character. "An *omniscient and faultless author* will have to be assumed, who holds up to the view of all one of the members of the new generation" (52).

The narrator will thus be undertaking a specific historical task: to exhibit for scrutiny an example of the very latest Russian type, the successor to Bazarov and the other "new men" of Russian literature. But Dostoevsky may have felt that such a narrator would be *too* coolly detached, too "omniscient and faultless" to serve his purposes ("faultless" translates the Russian *ne pogreshayuschim*, which contains the strong moral connotation of sinlessness). He therefore alters his narrator, in another notation, merely to a "sort of invisible but omniscient being, *who doesn't leave his hero for a moment*, even with the words: 'all that was done completely by chance'" (53; italics added). By attaching the narrator as closely as possible to the protagonist's point of view, Dostoevsky retains the advantages of I-narration, which automatically generates the effect of identification and sympathy created by all inside views of a character; and he reminds himself to maintain such inside views, as far as possible, even when moving from the direct portrayal of consciousness into summary and report. At the same time, he retains the freedom of omniscience necessary to dramatize the process of Raskolnikov's self-discovery, to reveal the character gradually, to comment on him from the outside when this becomes necessary, and to leave him entirely when the plot-action widens out.

This narrative technique fuses the narrator very closely with the consciousness and point of view of the central character as well as other important figures (though without, as Mikhail Bakhtin was inclined to maintain, eliminating him entirely as a controlling perspective). Dostoevsky had used a similar narrative approach earlier in *The Double*, and such a fusion was by no means unprecedented in the history of the novel (in Jane Austen, among others); but in *Crime and Punishment* this identification begins to approach, through Dostoevsky's use of the time shifts of memory and his remarkable manipulation of temporal sequence, the experiments of Henry James, Joseph Conrad, and later stream-of-consciousness writers such as Virginia Woolf and James Joyce. Brilliantly original for its period, this technique gives us the superbly realized masterpiece we know, whose masterly construction and artistic sophistication can only cause us to wonder at the persistence of the legend that Dostoevsky was an untidy and negligent craftsman. Some light on this legend may be cast by the remark of E. M. de Vogüé, a novelist himself, who wrote with some surprise in 1886 of *Crime and Punishment* that "a word . . . one does not even notice, a small fact that takes up only a line, have their reverberations fifty pages later . . . [so that] the continuity becomes unintelligible if one skips a couple of pages."[8] This acute observation, which expresses all the disarray of a late nineteenth-century reader accustomed to the more orderly and linear types of expository narration, helps to account for the tenacity of this critical misjudgment; but it has now been replaced by a more accurate appreciation of Dostoevsky's pathbreaking originality.

VI

Once having decided to recast his novel in this new form, Dostoevsky began to rewrite from scratch; but he did not, as he told Wrangel, burn everything he had written earlier. On the contrary, he was easily able to integrate sections of the earlier manuscript into his final text—especially those scenes in which his narrator had acted as an observer and reporter—by simply shifting them from the first to the third person. The remainder of Dostoevsky's notes concern the finished novel and need not be discussed here. There is, however, one additional question on which they help to throw some light.

The writing of the novel went smoothly and steadily except for a clash with the editors of *The Russian Messenger*, about which, regrettably, very little is known. Dostoevsky refers to it in a letter to A. P. Milyukov in which he explains that Katkov and his assistant N. A. Lyubimov had refused to accept the initial version of the chapter in *Crime and Punishment* containing the famous scene in which Sonya reads the Gospel story of the raising of Lazarus to Raskolnikov. "I wrote [this chapter]," Dostoevsky confides, "with genuine inspiration, but perhaps it's no good; but for them the question is not its literary worth, they are worried about its *morality*. Here I was in the right—nothing was against morality, and *even quite the contrary*, but they saw otherwise and, what's more, saw traces of *nihilism*. Lyubimov declared firmly that it had to be revised. I took it back, and this revision of a large chapter cost me at least three new chapters of work, judging by the effort and the weariness; but I corrected it and gave it back."[9] By the time this letter was written, the revision had already been completed.

Since the manuscript that Dostoevsky turned in to Katkov has unfortunately been lost, it is very difficult to determine just what the editors had objected to in the original. The only other information available is a remark made at the end of the century (1889) by the editors of *The Russian Messenger*, who, in publishing Dostoevsky's letter, commented that "it was not easy for him [Dostoevsky] to give up his intentionally exaggerated idealization of Sonya as a woman who carried self-sacrifice to the point of sacrificing her body. Feodor Mikhailovich substantially shortened the conversation during the reading of the Gospels, which in the original version was much longer than in the printed text."[10] It seems clear, then, that Dostoevsky had initially given Sonya a much more affirmative role in this scene which led to what Katkov considered her unacceptably "exaggerated idealization."

What Katkov found inadmissible may perhaps be clarified by a passage in Dostoevsky's notebooks, where Sonya *is* presented occasionally as the spokeswoman for the morality that Dostoevsky wished to advocate. In one scene, for example, she explains to Raskolnikov that "in comfort, in wealth, you would perhaps have seen nothing of human unhappiness. The person God loves, the person on whom he really counts, is the one to whom He sends much suffering so that he becomes aware of himself and sees more things, for in unhappiness one distinguished the suffering of people better than in happiness" (47). Immediately following this speech, Raskolnikov retorts bitterly: "And perhaps God does not exist" (47). This reply is included in the Gospel-reading chapter, and we may assume that Sonya's words were meant for the same context; it is quite possible that other speeches of the same kind in the notes were also included in the rejected version.

If so, it is not difficult to understand why the worthy editors of *The Russian Messenger* might have been upset. For Dostoevsky is in effect depicting a prostitute as the inspired interpreter of the Gospels, the expositor of the inscrutable purposes of Divine Will. Moreover, if the logic of Sonya's words is taken literally, it would mean that God had ultimately brought about, for his own ends, her degradation and Raskolnikov's crime; the traces of "nihilism" detected by the editors may well have been caused by such a bold reversal of the ordinary standards of social morality and the opening it could provide for an implicit accusation against God Himself. Indeed, exactly such an accusation will soon be made by the tubercular Ippolit Terentyev in *The Idiot* and later by Ivan Karamazov. If these speculations have any validity, they may help to clarify why Dostoevsky was accused by his editors of blurring the boundaries between good and evil. "*Evil* and *good* are sharply separated," he assures Lyubimov, "and it will be impossible to confuse or misinterpret them. . . . Everything you spoke about has been done, everything is separated, demarcated and clear. *The reading of the Gospels* is given a different coloring" (42). Katkov probably did Dostoevsky an artistic service by insisting that he shorten Sonya's loquacity; and there is some indication that in the end Dostoevsky felt this himself. For in returning the proofs in mid-July he remarked: "I do not finally regret *all* of the cuts. For twenty years I have painfully felt, and seen more clearly than anyone, that my literary vice is: *prolixity*, but I can't seem to shake it off." There is, however, nothing prolix about *Crime and Punishment*, whose masterly craftsmanship stems from the acute artistic self-awareness so amply illustrated in the preceding pages.

Faulkner's Muse: Speculations on the Genesis of *The Sound and the Fury*

THOMAS C. MOSER

IN 1933, FIVE YEARS AFTER COMPOSING HIS first masterpiece, Faulkner wrote about its conception: "I, who had three brothers and no sisters, . . . began to write about a little girl": Caddy Compson. "I was trying to manufacture the sister which I did not have." For Caddy's youngest brother Benjy, "all knowing must begin and end," Faulkner said, "with that fierce, panting, paused and stooping wet figure which smelled like trees." For Faulkner himself, in 1957, Caddy still remained "my heart's darling. That's what I wrote the book about."[1]

In light of the intensely personal quality of these remarks, I cannot help asking if anyone "in real life" inspired Caddy's creation? The answer lies surely in the phrase quoted above: "the sister . . . I did not have." In early childhood, Faulkner acquired a sister-substitute in the little girl next door, Estelle Oldham. In 1918, however, he lost her in marriage to an older man, Cornell Franklin. Almost immediately two things happened: Estelle became pregnant and poetry poured out of Faulkner. He spent the rest of his life, I would argue, attempting, through his writing, to make reparation for that loss. For the first decade he was largely, but not wholly, unsuccessful. Although most of that time his medium was poetry, his breakthrough came (appropriately enough for this present volume) through fiction. His apprenticeship was so long, it seems to me, not just because he was learning his literary craft but also because he kept denying the full truth about the loss he was trying to put down on paper. Although he would sometimes come close to understanding it, he refused, until writing *Father Abraham* (in 1927) and *The Sound and the Fury* (in 1928), to reconstruct his whole emotional situation. That is, his mourning for Estelle continued to be cripplingly incomplete. He could not bear to admit how desperately he loved her, how deeply wounded he was by her departure, and how much he needed her presence. He declined to acknowledge, also, how much hostility he felt over her desertion. More particularly, Faulkner resisted understanding the significance to himself of Estelle's pregnancy and the extent of his own responsibility for their separation. It would take ten years of writing for him to understand the events of the spring of 1918; it would take ten years of living in the world for Faulkner to become "sole owner and proprietor" of Yoknapatawpha County—including another failed love affair, this time a brief one with Helen Baird in 1925; the collapse of Estelle's marriage in 1927; and the vital period of 1927–29, during which Estelle's prolonged divorce proceedings and her unexpected availability coincided precisely with the writing of *The Sound and the Fury*.

It is my contention, then, that Estelle was crucial to the creation of Caddy, as well as to a host of beloved, and hated, female creations who appear in Faulkner's works both before and after her. I would go further and assert that he linked Estelle, more even than his mother, with that mysterious, animating inner force that I would term his personal muse.

Estelle's enormous influence on Faulkner manifests itself in three distinct areas. First, the informing idea of *The Sound and the Fury*—Quentin's and Benjy's love for, and loss of, their sister Caddy—strikingly reconstructs Faulkner's passion for Estelle from their early childhood to their separation in 1918. Second, the implicit subject of virtually all of Faulkner's writing from 1918 through *The Sound and the Fury* is his obsession with that real-life loss. Third, the significant periods of Faulkner's early creativity and despair coincide with Estelle's comings and goings and her two pregnancies during that decade. In short, I believe that *The Sound and the Fury* was a story struggling to get out almost from the time that Estelle Oldham married Cornell Franklin, and left Oxford and Faulkner.

The purpose of this essay, then, is to articulate the causal connections between Faulkner's relationship with Estelle from her 1918 marriage to its 1927 collapse and his literary production during the same period. Further, I shall demonstrate that Faulkner's private anguish over Estelle and his creative development came to a climax in 1928 with *The Sound and the Fury* and that Estelle was the key element in his miraculous creation of Caddy.[2]

I

In the fall of 1903, when six-year-old Billy Falkner (as his family spelled the name) had been living in Oxford only a year, six-and-a-half-year-old Estelle Oldham moved into the same block. From the beginning, their relationship was an extraordinarily close one. Unlike Billy's austere mother, Miss Maud, and his tomboy first cousin, Sallie Murry Wilkins, Estelle was always "feminine": she liked to play with dolls, wear her hair long, dress up, and play the piano. Despite Billy's addiction to sports and the out-of-doors, he adored hearing her play and she loved to hear him read poems aloud, first others', then his own. Estelle took to Billy and instantly announced (she said, after his death) that she was "going to marry him."³

Moreover, Billy's and Estelle's seems to have been an idealized brother-sister relationship, in which they played, without competition, parent-child-sibling-beloved to each other. Being with Estelle was a vital refuge to Faulkner because his own home life was apparently beset by anxiety. He was intensely, conflictedly dependent upon his mother. Everyone who knew them testifies to their extreme closeness. Her first-born, Billy, looked like her—with a small frame, thin lips, dark eyes, folded eyelids—and not at all like his large father, Murry. A frustrated painter, Billy's mother passed on to him both her artistic talent and her passion for literature. (Billy once drew for her a picture of himself, seated beside her, reading before the fireplace.) Miss Maud generally inspired affection and admiration among her women friends and her children, yet she had some very unendearing ways. She ruled her husband with an iron hand and managed to make them both unhappy. When, through no fault of his own, Murry lost the important railroading job he loved and did well, she vetoed his scheme to go cattle-ranching in Texas and forced him instead to tie his fortunes to his father in Oxford, where he did not flourish. She made of his dryings-out in a sanitorium near Memphis an edifying spectacle for their little sons. Late in life she told Faulkner (he says) that she "never did like" her husband.⁴

How much loving care, one wonders, went into her intense attachment to her firstborn? Jay Martin highlights the curious fact that she "rocked" her chronically colicky infant in a straight chair by raising up and banging down on its front legs. To make him stand straight, she strapped his shoulders so tightly to a board that he leaned backwards as he walked. Miss Maud seems, moreover, to have done little to alleviate Billy's strong feelings of sibling rivalry. The births of the second and third brothers (in 1899 and 1901) were accompanied by severe illnesses in the oldest. The birth of the fourth and last son, in August 1907, was, in the view of one Faulkner biographer, the hardest of all on him.⁵ At the time of that pregnancy, Miss Maud was burdened by the terminal illnesses of both her mother-in-law, who died in December 1906, and her mother, who died in June 1907. The union of Eros and Thanatos could scarcely have been more evident; and the sensitive Billy could not have dodged the awful truth that, for all her contempt for her alcoholic husband, Miss Maud was still, however unwillingly, letting him make love to her.

Faulkner himself was a conspicuously moody child. No doubt some of his early sorrow reflected the dampening presence of his father, who was not only inadequate, but personally hostile to him. (He called Billy "Snake Lips" in recognition of his resemblance to his mother. Although much could be, and has been, said about the father-son relationship, it is beyond the scope of this paper.) But surely the main source of Billy's melancholy was his intense relationship with the overwhelmingly possessive Miss Maud. Faulkner's early, persistent attachment to Estelle was his chief way of saying No to Mother.

As Estelle grew up, she became one of the most popular girls in the district. A superb dancer, she was the "butterfly of the Delta" and "pretty as a little partridge."[6] Billy, on the other hand, was unprepossessing, shy, morose, and a reluctant dancer. Yet, according to Estelle's recollection, they always assumed they would marry eventually. Even after Estelle was pressured into an engagement to Cornell Franklin, a University of Mississippi law graduate five years her senior, she still felt so committed to Billy that she offered to elope with him. They may even have bought a marriage license. However, Billy, just past twenty, had no job prospects and not even a high school diploma. Small wonder, then, that when he honorably informed Estelle's parents of their intentions to wed, they objected strenuously, and Cornell Franklin claimed his bride. (Small wonder, too, that Miss Maud deeply disapproved of Estelle then, and probably ever after.) Although Faulkner blamed Estelle for betraying him, he must have known that the fault lay largely in his own failure of nerve.

In any case, when Estelle named her wedding day, April 18, 1918, Faulkner's world, in the words of his brother John, "went to pieces."[7] He fled to New England to Phil Stone, his best friend and a Yale law student. Faulkner's pain was no doubt exacerbated by the news that Estelle became pregnant immediately. (She had a daughter February 8, 1919.) Temperamentally melancholy, Faulkner seems, after Estelle's marriage, to have become more so. His friends sometimes feared suicide, and he himself on one occasion predicted he would die within a year.

But he didn't; instead, he wrote. In the next section, I will turn to

Faulkner's first literary efforts after Estelle's marriage; but I want to remind the reader of a few key elements in *The Sound and the Fury*. A young woman, beloved since childhood by her older and youngest brothers, becomes pregnant by an unknown lover. On April 25, 1910, she marries, without love, an older, affluent suitor and leaves her Jefferson, Mississippi, home. Some five weeks later, in Cambridge, Massachusetts, her older brother, a Harvard freshman, drowns himself. Early in 1911, the sister has a baby daughter, who is soon returned to Jefferson. The youngest brother, a congenital idiot, remains at home in a state of dumb, unassuageable grief over the loss of his beloved, eternally young sister. Art, it seems, has been roughly inspired by life.

II

Faulkner's writing prior to his artistic breakthrough falls into two phases. The first, primarily poetic phase begins to flourish with his departure from Oxford in 1918 and ends with Estelle's return in December 1924. The second, primarily fictional phase begins with his January 1925 move to New Orleans, his friendship with the Sherwood Andersons, and his meeting Helen Baird. It ends in Oxford in early 1928. Faulkner's first serious poems were written soon after Estelle's marriage. "Lilacs," the most biographically significant, was essayed in the latter half of 1918 while Faulkner was an RAF cadet in flight training in Toronto. Combining aerial warfare, fauns, nymphs, and female menace, "Lilacs" features three downed pilots. The death of the first ("John the poet") results fantastically from female seduction in the form of nympholepsy—that Romantic longing for ideal beauty, as embodied in a naked, momentarily glimpsed female figure, which informs much of Faulkner's early work. One spring dawn, John takes off in his faun-like, "little pointed-eared machine," "stalking . . . a white wanton," her "whiteness mirrored in a lake." Just as John overtakes his nymph at the edge of a "cloud forest" and feels "her arms and her cool breath" like a "red rose on white snows, the kiss of Death," a bullet strikes his left breast. The second pilot, James, tells of his death on a bombing run. The third, unnamed pilot surprisingly reveals that, though "shot down—last spring," he is "not dead." He has, like Faulkner, been grievously injured in the spring. The experience is so dreadful that he finds himself among dead pilots and ministering women as unreal as "figures on a masque." Though he is alive, his mind has been so afflicted he "scarcely speaks."[8]

Here, at the very outset of his literary career, Faulkner is working with characters who are to become the dead and damaged officers of his first novel, *Soldiers' Pay* (Lieutenants Powers and Mahon), and his third novel, *Flags in the Dust* (John and Bayard Sartoris). More important, John the poet achieves his fullest development in the nympholeptic Quentin, with his branch-side erotic encounters with Caddy—as well as his watery union with Little Sister Death. The third, silent pilot achieves his fulfillment in the mute Benjy's childhood recollections of Caddy stooping over him in the branch. Equally important, "Lilacs" initiates the fundamental autobiographical lie that pervades Faulkner's work prior to *The Sound and the Fury*: he blames his hero's grievous wound not on the disappointment of love but on the destruction of war. This lie also pervaded Faulkner's personal life. As the returned RAF veteran who not only never saw combat but probably didn't even fly, he frequently claimed to have been wounded in the war; he sometimes walked with a limp; and he attributed his severe headaches to a silver plate in his skull. (Sensibar persuasively associates such behavior with that of pathological impostors.)[9]

The Marble Faun, Faulkner's amazing poetic outburst dated on the first anniversary of his Estelle-inflicted wounding, carries psychological denial far further than does "The Lilacs." When Faulkner at last published the poem sequence in December 1924, he dedicated it to his mother, and yet concluded the volume with "*April, May, June, 1919*." In light of his pained responses to the births of his brothers, the news of Estelle's lightning pregnancy, the February birth of her child, and the planned arrival of mother and baby in June for a long visit must have been deeply disturbing. Although the only known prepublication version of *The Marble Faun* is dated April 1920, my guess is that Faulkner showed the first version to Estelle during that summer visit of 1919 and sent the 1920 typescript to her via her mother and sister, who visited Estelle in Honolulu that next May. Reiterating Faulkner's emphasis on Estelle's first anniversary, this early version consists of a cycle of twelve numbered poems. Four of them are named for the seasons of the year, and "Spring" (eclogue I) vividly imagines Estelle's situation: "brooding spring . . . is quick with child, and sad."[10]

In an October 1924 essay, Faulkner says that when he first wrote poetry, his "mental life" was "completely and smoothly veneered with a surface insincerity—obviously necessary . . . to support intact my personal integrity."[11] Even though Faulkner had historical precedents for using a delicate creature encased in stone as his poetic speaker, the choice was also personally appropriate. His notorious moodiness and his tendencies to silence, apparent deafness, and immobility make his choice of speaker only too plausible. Even Faulkner's best Oxford friends never knew whether he would acknowledge their salutation. On his return home from Canada, Faulkner is remembered as "standing still as a statue in the railroad depot." When "he moved a little," an observer commented: "Damned if it ain't alive." [12] The emblem of the marble faun raises questions recalling "Lilacs." Is he alive or not? How did he come into his parlous state? Faulkner's treatment is inconsistent; he does not maintain his *donnée*. On the one hand, Faun sadly acknowledges that he is a "prisoner," and sighs for life, freedom, change. On the other hand, Faun is not always "marble-bound"; sometimes he runs about. Three times Faun rages against his "impotence" as if it weren't inherent in his marble condition. Yet he expects somehow to grow old, his eyes to grow "dim" and himself "dumb" (isn't he now?). Then he'll no longer be driven by "nameless pain / To . . . know again." Why "again?" Clearly, *something happened* to turn the faun to marble— but that event is not in the poem sequence. At the same time, Faun rages constantly against the inevitable passing of time, the remorseless cycle of conception, parturition, and death, the relentless roll of the seasons.

Although Estelle is almost surely the source of Faun's dilemma, not even Faulkner's awareness that her imminent return inspired the writing can allow him to think of her presence in the poem sequence. Perhaps the only way he can imagine their relationship is as this "marble-bound" creature watching her amid the nymphs of summer kneeling to braid their "short blown hair" before slipping "into the pool." Yet even though Estelle is not an identifiable character in this poem that sorrowfully celebrates the seasons of her pregnancy, she is unconsciously present everywhere in the imagery. To Estelle and her fictive avatars Faulkner would later apply phrases such as these: the guttering gold "flames of roses," the "poised dancers" of poplars, the "silver light" of fountains; as well as Summer's "dreaming knees," Winter's "silver symphonies," and above all "cruel White Spring." Yet Spring can be sympathetic, too, "brooding" and "sad" like Faun; "watching" like him the "immortal dance"; and sitting, like Caddy, "clad . . . in her dampened hair."

On September 29, 1919, Estelle left Oxford for Hawaii, bearing Faulkner's RAF copy of Swinburne, with an inscription "so passionate" that Estelle tore it off before rejoining her husband. [13] After a year's study as a special student at Ole Miss and the writing of a few lyrics plus further work on *The Marble Faun*, Faulkner, in September 1920, became a founding member of a drama group, the Marionettes; later that fall he wrote a symbolic dream-play in prose and verse using the group's name as his title. Faulkner hand-lettered and illustrated several copies; one he dedicated to Estelle's daughter: "To 'Cho-Cho,' a tiny flower of the flame." [14] *The Marionettes* is a vital document because it features for the first time a glamorous, vulnerable heroine obviously based upon Estelle, and a hostile mother-figure, reflective of Miss Maud. Its double-hero not only recalls Faulkner's own dilemma but also looks back to the pilots of "Lilacs" and forward to Benjy and Quentin.

Like the Marble Faun, an immobilized male figure sits under poplars. But Pierrot is fixed there for a human reason. He's in a drunken stupor because he has lost his beloved Marietta. Her empty slipper (like Cinderella's—and like Caddy's) lies at his feet. The action of the play—the Shade of Pierrot seducing Marietta—presumably takes place in Pierrot's dream. Significantly, Marietta is simply reenacting her own mother's seduction, pregnancy, and death: "From her grave / There sprang a flower," which, says Marietta, "was I." Warned against dancing, Marietta still cannot resist Shade's song, joins him in the moonlight, strips by the pond, and elopes with him over the garden wall. She returns later, still youthfully beautiful, but sad, her jade gown and Chinese brocaded scarf recalling Estelle's glamorous Oriental clothes. The last page depicts her lying dead before mournful Pierrot. In light of Faulkner's dedication to Cho-Cho and the unmistakable resemblance to Estelle of his drawings of Marietta (pointed out by Sensibar), the mother-daughter pattern in the play is clearly crucial. It reminds us both that Caddy's daughter Quentin follows in her mother's footsteps and that Caddy plays both nurturing mother to Benjy and erotic seductress to Quentin. It is astonishing, moreover, that Faulkner would so early have envisioned a bereft male possessed of his absent love's empty slipper.

Besides bringing a doomed and fatal woman into his imaginary *fin de siècle* garden, Faulkner emphasizes the destructiveness of his hero's quasi mother, the moon. At Pierrot's birth, his "foster mother" afflicts him with "moon madness." Whenever the moon is full, he must "seek some one to come and play." Obligingly, the moon entices out a playmate for her foster son. Moon-inspired love leads to death, and Marietta predicts the "moon will play my body when I die." So far as mothers are concerned, this brief play bristles with breasts. As graphic artist, Faulkner painstakingly delineates Marietta's nipple in a silhouette and later borrows from Beardsley's *Salomé* for a terrifying topless frontal view. And breasts are everywhere in the language. Most strikingly, and violently, the "moon is like a dismembered breast upon the floor of a silent sea." Marietta's breasts are appropriately lunar and aged: they look "like twin moons . . . dead for a thousand years." According to one member of the drama group, Faulkner surprised them by talking frankly of the acceptability of incest.[15] All these maternal moon images certainly suggest Faulkner's sense of his mother's powerfully threatening influence upon his sexual feelings.

University studies did not occupy Faulkner for very long. Early 1921 found him at work on what was to be the most ambitious and successful literary effort of his private apprenticeship: a poem sequence characteristically titled *Vision in Spring.* Its source is obvious. Estelle was returning in March for a second long visit, and her childhood lover was responding as he had two years before. So that summer of 1921 Faulkner presented Estelle with a typed, 88-page booklet, hand-bound, containing 14 numbered poems, some titled, some not. (The last is called "April.") The influence of Estelle's return is implicit in various ways in most of the poems: "Time / Ticks . . . my heart / In which a faint last long remembered beauty hides."[16] Sensibar rightly calls Estelle the muse of these love poems; and Poem X, "The Dancer," is dedicated in another typescript "to V. de G. F." (i.e., to Cho-Cho, Victoria de Graffenreid Franklin). Poem XI, untitled in *Vision in Spring* but called "Marriage" in other typescripts, is striking in the explicitness of its treatment of Estelle, her husband, and Faulkner. Faulkner flagrantly portrays Cornell Franklin listening, as he himself long did, to Estelle playing the piano. Faulkner even writes the first half and last quarter of the poem from the husband's point of view. Though "Laxly reclining," the husband is sexually excited by the golden firelight "spurting" over his wife's presence. "His eyes like hurried fingers fumble and fly" around her dress's "narrow bands" and "trace the line" of her "back and thigh." He imagines her mounting the stairs, her knees "supple" and her skirts "swirling." His wife, meanwhile, having acceded to his request to "Play something else," feels herself become a flower "cast / Upon a river" and transported to a moonlit setting like that of *The Marionettes.* She dreams "Through springs and springs, back to a certain . . . shattered spring" that she seeks "to build into a whole again." Her section of the poem concludes with her seeing, through pain-darkened eyes, "a face / Now purged of hunger, quiet with time and space." But to her husband the firelight is a "thunderous surf," and his eyes again seek her shoulder straps. The poem ends with the husband's sexual fantasy being unhappily realized. On the way to the bedroom, the wife pauses, shivers, and "hates him as he steadily mounts the stairs." Thus, in this gift booklet made for Estelle, Faulkner portrays her as detesting her husband's attentions; as wishing to reconstitute their ruined spring; and as appreciating his calm and unpossessive love.

If spring 1921 had found Faulkner creating *Vision in Spring* in response to Estelle's arrival, autumn would have plunged him into deepest gloom. Cornell arrived to take his wife away, this time all the way to Shanghai. Faulkner was not to see her for more than three miserable, largely unproductive years. His first reaction repeated that of spring 1918: he went immediately to the northeast, to New Haven and New York—but for less than three months. At Phil Stone's behest, he returned to Oxford in December to become the university postmaster, a job he loathed. Except for revising *Vision in Spring* and *The Marble Faun*, writing a few short prose pieces, and assembling, in 1923, a sheaf of twelve short poems, not all of them new, he seems to have done little creative work. It was a protracted moratorium, like the pause in Sutpen's house-building in *Absalom, Absalom!* Faulkner did socialize with Stone and other friends and even, early in the period, in Stone's words briefly "fancied he was in love" with Stone's "pretty little" stenographer, who rejected him.[17] Faulkner cured himself of the infatuation by imagining her in the unromantic act of defecating. Carvel Collins, the pioneering Faulknerian, tentatively yokes this infatuation, despite an admitted "timing" problem, with perhaps the most important and intriguing episode in this period: Faulkner's "extreme emotional disturbance" of the spring of 1924.[18] But surely, if it's spring, it must be Estelle. Moreover, the most important event of this period for her would have been the birth of her son Malcolm, on December 3, 1923. Two pieces of evidence suggest that knowing his mother-sister-substitute had not only gotten pregnant but produced a male offspring was deeply troubling to Faulkner. First, he wrote a friend in late September 1924 that *"for nearly a year* he has felt a powerful presentiment that he soon will die."[19] Second, one of Faulkner's 1923 poems is called "Pregna[n]cy," and it is not a happy piece. The words "Rain and fire and death" are set above the pregnant woman's door and remain "in her heart." Moreover, her "harried / Body [is] wrung to a strange and bitter lyre." Once, however, her body's music was "pure strings simply married," and her "thin and happy sorrows" were wedded together.[20] Marriage and pregnancy are clearly curses; however much richer their complex music may be than the simple tunes of virginity, only in the latter state was the woman truly whole.

If the months after Malcolm's birth found Faulkner emotionally disturbed and creatively blocked, autumn 1924 saw him productive again. Between September and December, he wrote, reworked, or revised a dozen poems (five from the 1923 batch) and put them, along with an October essay, into a typescript entitled *Mississippi Poems*. Two reasons for Faulkner's recovery suggest themselves: he resigned from the postmastership, and Estelle was coming home. Nevertheless, although writing had been Faulkner's characteristic response to Estelle's returns, the nature of that response changed significantly. "Mississippi Hills: My Epitaph" makes clear that, although Mississippi spring will continue to "shake and break" the poet's sleep and he will return home, the poet is leaving for a long time. The poem thus reflects Faulkner's firm decision, taken with Stone's blessing, to try Europe in order to further his literary career. Particularly striking is the hostility evoked in a sonnet not included in the Mississippi group, but dated December 9, 1924, and addressed to Cleopatra. While granting that she is the "race's splendor," the poet seems relieved that "she is dead and safely tombed." "Ay, Cleopatra's dead, and . . . wombed," but still she's the castrator and devourer who "breaks [man's] vine, and slowly eats the fruit."[21]

Yes, Estelle was back in Oxford, "in the early days of December," says Joseph Blotner. "She still loved him," Blotner goes on. "In that way nothing had changed."[22] *Except* that Faulkner was, for the first time, fleeing upon Estelle's arrival. Indeed, the New Orleans *Times-Picayune* of December 16 reported that Faulkner was preparing to spend the winter months writing in England and Italy. Faulkner's willingness to go could simply confirm his October essay's boast that his "interest" in "philanderings" and "fornication" was "waning." Or his eagerness to be gone could mean that he feared that Estelle's presence would be irresistible.

III

Although Faulkner left Oxford for a year, shifted his emphasis from poetry to prose, and fell in love with Helen Baird, still his most persistent and fruitful literary subject during the three years before *The Sound and the Fury* remained the loss of Estelle in 1918. It is perfectly true that he dedicated his second novel, *Mosquitoes*, to Helen and made two gift booklets for her. Yet in tandem with giving Helen literary keepsakes, Faulkner made similar significant presentations to Estelle and Cho-Cho. Besides, Estelle figures importantly in virtually everything Faulkner wrote between 1925 and 1928: in the New Orleans prose sketches, in all three novels, and in significant pieces of unpublished prose. Moreover, Faulkner had written, well before meeting Helen, several brief fictional pieces that prefigure the first three novels and *The Sound and the Fury*. "Moonlight," dated by Faulkner as early as 1919, deals with George and Cecily, who reflect himself and Estelle and who subsequently appear in *Soldiers' Pay*. Also, a scene featuring a penknife looks forward to the great moment by the branch when Quentin proposes a murder/suicide pact to Caddy. "Adolescence," an early 1920's story, contains a puritanical old woman reminiscent of Miss Maud and a pair of innocent childish lovers who relate as siblings. The girl's family, like the Oldhams (and the Compsons), make their daughter take a suitable husband. The girl, like Caddy, has three brothers and "in an access of pity" comforts the youngest, kneeling at her feet.[23] Finally, two closely related poetic prose works, "The Hill" (1922) and "Nympholepsy" (early 1925), at once render the lonely, melancholy spirit of Faulkner at this time and through their imagery foreshadow the peripatetic Quentin on his last day.

Faulkner ultimately put his early 1925 New Orleans newspaper sketches into a handsome, hand-lettered gift book for Estelle. Also, several of the 1925 magazine pieces either vividly recall his loss of her or strikingly prefigure *The Sound and the Fury*. Nevertheless, *Soldiers' Pay* and the unpublished *Elmer* fragment are the most important documents of 1925. *Soldiers' Pay* puts into novelistic form two poetic subjects originating in the year of Estelle's marriage: from "The Lilacs" comes the aviator shot down in the spring; from *The Marble Faun* comes the immobilized, melancholy protagonist surrounded by burgeoning life. And from *The Marionettes* of 1920 Faulkner takes the idea of the heroine ignoring the unconscious hero in order to run off with his double.

Soldiers' Pay highlights the complex relations between life and art, their mutuality and the mixing and fusing of their causes and effects. For the first time, Faulkner was attempting to depict in a fictionally "real" world his relationship with Estelle. This shift to fictional representation is consistent with two significant personal acts: Faulkner had the gumption to vacate Oxford upon Estelle's arrival; he had the imagination to fall in love with someone else (but someone who, significantly, was not very interested in him). Helen's appearance as potential real-life rescuer may have made possible the fictional creation of Lt. Donald Mahon's rescuer, Mrs. Margaret Powers. Or maybe creating Margaret helped Faulkner to fall in love with Helen. Yet Helen is not a "source" for Margaret as she is for certain female characters in Faulkner's next three fictions: *Elmer, Mosquitoes,* and the gift book *Mayday.* In truth, both the grave, loyal Margaret and the flighty, unfaithful Cecily are derived chiefly from Estelle. Indeed, *Soldiers' Pay,* set in spring 1919, mainly recalls Faulkner's situation in 1918–19. George Farr, hard-drinking small-town drugstore cowboy and enthralled lover of Cecily, recalls both the 1918 Faulkner and his rival, Cornell Franklin; Donald Mahon reflects Faulkner's postwar pathological persona of the wounded flier. Thus Faulkner's first novel, written while he unsuccessfully pursued Helen, seems inspired by the wish both to put into perspective his 1918 loss of Estelle and to escape the world of poetic fantasy dominated by her memory. Desirable, maternal Margaret partially prefigures Caddy before her fall; Cecily previews Caddy after it; puzzled, almost mute Donald looks forward to Benjy; George fitfully plays Quentin.

Now, one reason—beyond the author's inexperience in the genre— for *Soldiers' Pay's* artistic inferiority to *The Sound and the Fury* is its deep personal dishonesty. In *Soldiers' Pay,* as in "Lilacs," Faulkner tries to blame the war for the hero's suffering: Donald loses Cecily because a head wound has horribly disfigured his face and rendered him comatose; ultimately Donald dies of his war injuries. Nevertheless, the novel's characters reflect Faulkner's 1918 personal disaster and simultaneously suggest his 1925 feelings about it. Cecily's looks, personality, and situation all recall Estelle's. The very word used by Estelle's daughter, Jill Faulkner Summers, to describe her—"flighty"—appears in *Soldiers' Pay.*[24] Again, Summers's description of her mother as "manipulative" applies only too well to Cecily. With her glamorous silk garments, short torso, long legs, and hair like a halo (94), she certainly looks like Estelle. Cecily's popularity, especially on the dance floor, is Estelle's hallmark. And then Cecily's situation of having been long engaged to one man while being wooed by another, whom she ultimately marries, parallels Estelle's dilemma. Faulkner, however, so identifies with both of Cecily's suitors that George Farr does not so much reflect Cornell Franklin as he doubles Donald Mahon.

One reason to believe Faulkner left Oxford to escape Estelle is his hostile portrait of Cecily. Both the narrator and the characters label her shallow, silly, theatrical, and temperamentally if not physically promiscuous. Yet Faulkner cannot remain unreservedly hostile. As one character admits: "Yes, she is pretty. And silly. But—but pretty" (206). Moreover, he portrays Cecily, for all her apparent fragility, as a natural force. In her delicate way, she embodies the energy investing the universe. If Caddy smells like trees, Cecily resembles poplars, both because she is so slender and because she endures: "There was something so fragile . . . yet strong withal as a poplar is strong through very absence of strength" (80). But if Estelle seems thoroughly to inform Cecily, she is, paradoxically, not wholly absent from Cecily's hated rival Margaret. That is, Faulkner presumably set out to prove that he, the wounded hero, does not need the faithless Estelle by creating a fantasy-figure to rescue him. Yet that figure resembles the 1925 Estelle: still in her twenties, once married to a man she did not love, and now indifferent to small-town gossip about her kindness to a taciturn RAF veteran.

Both Donald and his successful rival are surely alter egos for Faulkner. Although he sometimes ridicules George, he empathizes utterly with George's terror at the prospect of losing Cecily. On the other hand, he wonders, as Faulkner must have done in the face of Estelle's visits, "if he could bear to see her" (213). At last, Cecily phones George, telling him, "Come to me, now" (270), an undisguised fantasy of Estelle's permanent return—to be realized four years later. Yet when the fictive couple return from their honeymoon, George looks "morose and thunderous"—Faulkner's prophetic sense of the cold reality attending the fulfillment of his dreams (306)?

Soldiers' Pay's chief fantasy, however, involves Donald. A fantasy of revenge, it asks: What if our poor hero is proposed to by a woman who had previously rejected him, and what if he then marries a far more caring woman, but what if he does not really know either and heartbreakingly dies on them? Still, the fantasy is flawed by its reliance on the war as a *deus ex machina*. The flaw is underlined by Donald's difference from Benjy: the former can remember nothing; the latter cannot help remembering. Presumably the reason Donald cannot remember how he was shot down (and why therefore he cannot die) is that Faulkner knows that Donald was *not* shot down over Flanders. Until Faulkner can fully, creatively accept that Estelle shot him down and that it was the worst wound of his life, he cannot write a great novel.

Nevertheless, Donald does at last die, and the death seems artistically appropriate. Why is that? First, those war wounds of a "forgotten spring" (292) are castration strokes: two "shocks at the base of his skull" and a blow to the hand on the "control column" (294, 293). Second, in light of the works to come, it is surely Cecily's pregnancy that kills Donald: subsequent pregnancies will bring down the Sartoris twins and Quentin Compson (not to mention Darl Bundren, Joe Christmas, and Thomas Sutpen). The language Jill Faulkner Summers uses to describe her father strikingly recalls *Soldiers' Pay*: "He didn't really care about people."[25] Donald Mahon, too, "never cared about anybody" (126). Perhaps, though, Donald and his creator instead cared too much for their women, cared so much that they could scarcely bear to think about them.

In the fifteen months following completion of *Soldiers' Pay*, Faulkner wrote three fictions and a number of poems inspired by Helen Baird. Ostensibly serious works, they seem to me the least authentic creations of his early period. Although the fictions are supposed to be funny, only *Mosquitoes* is genuinely so. Even its humor tends to be vitiated by the pretentious dialogue about art. Significantly, the poorest of the lot, *Elmer*, was written far from Oxford, in Paris; whereas writing *Soldiers' Pay* was sandwiched between February and June visits to Oxford and Estelle. Moreover, the locales of these Helenic works are emphatically not Mississippian. Still, *Elmer* ought to be relevant. Faulkner's most patently autobiographical work, it contains recognizable portraits of Faulkner's parents, of Helen Baird and her mother, of Estelle and her husband, and of Faulkner the artist. Although everyone is so trivialized as to make *Elmer* no significant step toward *The Sound and the Fury*, nevertheless Elmer's sexual and companionate ideal, his older sister Jo-Addie, is an obvious prefiguration of Caddy, and Faulkner's inability to finish *Elmer* may indicate his indissoluble bond with Estelle.

On the surface, Faulkner treats with contempt all Elmer's loves except his sister. Elmer, moreover, seems far less committed than was his creator to his two major love affairs—with Myrtle (inspired by Helen) and Ethel (inspired by Estelle). Although Faulkner intended Elmer to marry Myrtle, he does not get that far, does not, that is, imagine himself winning Helen. In fact, the love affair most fully reflected is that between Faulkner and Estelle. As in *Soldiers' Pay*—and unhistorically—the unwed Estelle-character, Ethel, becomes pregnant by the Faulkner-hero, Elmer. In *Soldiers' Pay*—again unhistorically—the Estelle-character weds that lover, whereas in *Elmer*, as in real life, she marries another, just before her true love leaves for Canadian military service. Finally, and again unlike *Soldiers' Pay*, *Elmer* follows history further, to the time, well after the war, when the hero not only fantasizes wresting his beloved and their five-year-old child away from her husband, but also actually calls upon mother and child.

Although Faulkner treats the Elmer-Ethel relationship almost farcically, seriousness and pain keep peeping through, especially in the final, unfinished episode in the manuscript, a strange, highly charged scene depicting Elmer, Ethel, and their child alone together at Ethel's. The scene is heavy with Ethel's attractiveness. When she opens the door, "an old magic" touches Elmer. When their little boy drops his ball, Ethel recovers it "with a careful and conscious grace to which temporary abnegation of self lent a sort of splendor."[26] (Once again, the gesture prefigures Caddy bending over Benjy.) This final scene is rife, too, with mysterious hints of sexual complications. Elmer's last words, to ask whether Ethel's maid stays all day, imply his wish to remove the child so he and Ethel can make love. In short, it is hard to see how Faulkner could have extricated Elmer so completely from his renewed relationship with his old flame Ethel as to permit him plausibly to marry his new love Myrtle. Faulkner was apparently too emotionally involved with his memories of Estelle to let a fictional version of their affair end trivially.

Mosquitoes, the least characteristic of Faulkner novels, differs from *Soldiers' Pay* and *Elmer* in three vital respects: it contains no obvious Estelle-character, no pregnancy, and no wounded hero. (After his rejection by Ethel, Elmer is painfully injured by a hand grenade.) Yet, just beneath the surface, the author of *The Sound and the Fury* struggles to emerge: *Mosquitoes* points toward the creation of the Compson family; Estelle's presence makes itself felt at crucial moments. The key to the novel is Patricia Robyns. Despite her superficial resemblance to Helen Baird, she belongs to that line of Faulknerian nymphs inspired by Estelle. She moves with the quickness of a bird, stands "straight as a poplar," recalls flames, and is literally flighty: twice, clasping Gordon's wrists, she feels herself "flying."[27] She is very much a sister, with a devotion to her brother that is explicitly sexual. But Josh, with his "cold gaze," relates to her not as Quentin does to Caddy but as Jason does. "You ought to beat hell out of her," he advises his aunt, prefiguring Jason's advice to his mother concerning Caddy's daughter (217).

But who, then, in *Mosquitoes* would anticipate Quentin and Benjy? Patricia's two male admirers, Gordon and David, of course. For all Faulkner's attempts to make the sculptor Gordon into a strong, silent type, he is really an old softie. His first extended speech is to ask someone to fetch him "a bottle of milk" (13). And if Faulkner does not emphasize a sibling relationship between Gordon and Patricia, he doubles Gordon and her brother Josh, insisting in similar phrasing upon their being fellow sculptors. Like Faulkner himself and like his previous wounded heroes, Gordon doesn't dance and has a "silver faun's face" (152). Like earlier Faulknerian lovers, Gordon is literally narcissistic. He thinks of Patricia while "staring down into the water" at his own reflection (47). When Gordon disappears from the yacht immediately after Patricia goes off with the steward, David, Gordon's friends wonder if anyone nowadays drowns "himself for love" (227). Patricia's aunt instantly has a "vision of floating inert buttocks" (217). (It is presumably to avoid this ignominious end that Quentin buys the flatirons.) But *Mosquitoes* is a comic novel, and Patricia inflicts no permanent harm on Gordon.

Nevertheless, she certainly does a job on poor David, converting his "young lean splendor" (159) into the shambles that will become Benjy. Almost from the first, David's devotion to Patricia looks subhuman; witness his "dumb yearning eyes" (171), "passive abjectness of a dog" (166), and "beastlike longing" (216). But it is after he alone is permitted, like Benjy, to see Patricia naked that David becomes his spitting image. In the most memorable episode in the novel, the terrible trek through the swamp, on which David becomes Patricia's beast of burden, his mouth is soon "drooling" (205) and capable of making only a "harsh, awkward sound" (212). It is, however, the reader's last view of David that most strikingly prefigures Benjy as it also looks clear back to Pierrot in *The Marionettes*: sitting "in the pallid moonlight . . . alone and quite motionless" and holding "a single slipper, cracked and stained, . . . yet seeming still to hold in its mute shape something of that hard and sexless graveness of her" (235).

As Gordon, Patricia, Josh, and David partially anticipate the Compson children, Patricia's aunt is a premonition of Mrs. Compson—in her "silliness" (154), in her hypocritical frailty, and especially in her concerns with appearance and respectability. She worries about Gordon's possible suicide only because of the "position it puts me in, . . . I live here, I have a certain . . ." (238). She spies on all sexual activities; and like earlier aged maternal figures, presumably inspired by Miss Maud, she is repeatedly associated with the moon, a consistently "weary" and "waning moon of decay and death" (156, 287), "a tarnished implacable Venus" (133).

With her flirtatiousness and skimpy garb, Patricia, like Caddy, attracts lots of male attention. David, this time like Quentin, even gets to feel "her heart thumping against his palm" (162). Later, she seems to offer herself sexually to him: "I'd like to do something for you. . . . Anything, just anything" (213). And David, again like Quentin, refuses. Still, Patricia's great divergence from Caddy, and from Estelle, lies in her keeping her virginity. Yet Faulkner seems to question even this crucial fact through images and actions. Probably the most striking aspect of David and Patricia's grueling trek is the relentlessness of the mosquitoes. Their "invisible fire" (188) surely means for Faulkner, who pictures Patricia as a "flame" (187), the pain of female sexuality. Further, Patricia's suggestion that their childish expedition is a sort of elopement (172) reminds us that Estelle offered in 1918 to run off with Faulkner. Faulkner connects the mosquito bites with Patricia's sexuality by drawing merciless attention to her "blood-flecked stockings," "bloody legs" (179), "splotched flashing legs" (190). In the subsequent light of Mr. Compson's and Quentin's revulsion toward menstruation, of Temple Drake's horror at her rape-induced dripping blood in *Sanctuary*, and of the convict's reluctant presence at childbirth in the swamp in "Old Man," Faulkner's fixation on Patricia's blood could have to do with menstruation or criminal assault or parturition. Although all three are probably involved, Patricia's actions point particularly to the last. The way she sits "huddled in the road . . . trying to draw her bloody legs beneath her brief skirt" and then lies "suddenly flat, writhing her back in the dust, clutching [David's] hand" (179), surely implies childbirth as Faulkner's dominant fantasy here. In short, even in *Mosquitoes*, which seems so far from Estelle and even further from Faulkner's central creative idea of a sad, frustrated lover (Gordon), a dumb, frustrated lover (David), and an unhappy young woman symbolically bearing an illegitimate child, this idea manages vividly, if momentarily, to glimmer through.

IV

The last three prose works written before *The Sound and the Fury* embody Faulkner's creative pattern beautifully: Estelle looms large, and so does childbearing, in *The Wishing Tree, Flags in the Dust*, and *Father Abraham*. Even back in the time of his apparent effort to escape her and win Helen, Estelle was never wholly absent from Faulkner's life. Thus, in February 1925, just before beginning *Soldiers' Pay*, he wrote a birthday poem for Cho-Cho and contrived to be in Oxford later in the month when Estelle returned from visiting in-laws. In June, the month when he wrote *Soldiers' Pay*'s final draft in Helen's presence in Pascagoula, Faulkner also visited Oxford, saw Estelle, and presumably showed her the manuscript.

On January 25, 1926, two days before inscribing Helen's copy of *Mayday*, he wrote a fresh inscription in Estelle's newly bound, 1921 copy of *Vision in Spring*. When *Soldiers' Pay* appeared on February 25, Faulkner duly inscribed a copy to Estelle. And when she returned to Oxford in March from Shanghai, her stay of only four months strongly suggesting marital problems, Faulkner was there. But when Estelle took her children to Monteagle, Tennessee, to escape the summer heat, "It was time," says Blotner, "for Bill Faulkner to leave Oxford, again, too."[28] He was, that is, back to his old habit of vacating Oxford when Estelle did. Helen, let it be said, was still in Europe, and Faulkner spent the summer in Pascagoula, finishing her book, *Mosquitoes*, and continuing to aver his love for her. In September, Faulkner briefly visited Oxford, where he must have heard that the Franklins were talking divorce but that Estelle had agreed to return to Shanghai for a final attempt at reconciliation. Although Faulkner spent the fall in New Orleans working on his Sartoris and Snopes manuscripts, he apparently made a special trip to Oxford to give Estelle a going-away present. At least, the beautiful hand-bound, hand-lettered booklet, *Royal Street: New Orleans*, is dated, "Oxford—Mississippi—29 October 1926." The gentlemanly language of the dedication ought to have been reassuring to one embarking upon a painful mission: "To Estelle, a Lady, with Respectful Admiration."[29] Faulkner returned to Oxford at Christmas, to stay; Estelle and the children returned in January, also to stay. The Shanghai divorce would be final in two years.

But far and away the gift booklet most germane to Faulkner's creativity is the one he made for Cho-Cho's eighth birthday, and dated February 5, 1927. *The Wishing Tree* begins with the birthday girl giving birth to a boy artist:

It was like there was . . . [a] little balloon inside her, getting bigger and bigger and rising and rising. Soon it would be at her mouth, then it would pop out and jump right up against the ceiling. . . . What can it be? she wondered, . . . "It's your birthday," a voice said near her. . . . There, standing beside the bed, was a strange boy, with a thin ugly face and hair so red that it made a glow in the room.[30]

Symbolically, Faulkner is reenacting Estelle's momentous pregnancy of 1918–19: it brought forth first Cho-Cho and then Faulkner, the magical maker of *The Marble Faun* (and so much more!). Yet throughout his early work that creativity celebrates loss and smacks of mortality—and so it does in most of the masterpieces, with one notable exception to which *The Wishing Tree* strikingly relates. This birthday dream-vision has to do not only with balloons but circuses and horses. The boy magician first leads the little girl through mist like a "big tent" (12). He then supplies her and her companions with ponies "no larger than a squirrel" (13). And when her little brother wants to "go to a circus," their nanny concurs, in language anticipating the wonderful beasts in *Father Abraham* and *The Hamlet*: "Spotted hawses, and folks spanglin' through the air . . . [and] a band" (27). *The Wishing Tree* ends happily, of course, with the little girl waking to find her mother there and a bluebird in a wicker cage to remind her of her adventure with the boy-magician. But the moment has sad reverberations as well. The mother's "grave unhappy eyes" are surely, as Blotner says, an allusion to Estelle—and to such fictional heroines as Margaret Powers, Elmer's Ethel, and Narcissa Benbow. The birthday girl's mother is "leaning over her" and her "hand came on her forehead" (81–82). The gestures both recall the girl comforting her brother in "Adolescence" and look forward only a year to Caddy comforting Benjy. "When she did so," Faulkner later said, "the entire story . . . seemed to explode on the paper before me."[31]

When Faulkner wrote *The Wishing Tree*, he was also writing his most ambitious work to date, *Flags in the Dust*. The time was his thirtieth year, and events were moving so swiftly as to make his problems with women more acute than they had been since 1918. By January 1927 Estelle was committed to divorce, and Helen was on the brink of marriage. Meanwhile, Miss Maud had altered not a whit in her hostility to Estelle. In *Flags in the Dust*, Faulkner deals with all these affectional problems of his past and present; he even envisions two possible horrific outcomes if he should marry Estelle. Faulkner dramatizes these problems through three interconnecting relationships: Bayard Sartoris, Bayard's great-aunt Miss Jenny, and his beloved, Narcissa Benbow; Horace Benbow, Horace's sister Narcissa, and his beloved, Belle Mitchell; Byron Snopes and Byron's fantasy-beloved, Narcissa. Although Horace the aesthetic lawyer may owe something to Phil Stone, and although Byron Snopes's rural heritage is far from Faulkner's, all three male characters are most importantly portraits of the artist. And although Narcissa as Bayard's rescuer may owe something to Helen, she and the married Belle chiefly recall 1918 and 1927 versions of Estelle. And finally, although Miss Jenny may superficially suggest Faulkner's widowed aunt, she most importantly reflects Miss Maud.

Thus, Bayard's situation resembles Faulkner's on his return from the war. Horace's involvement with Belle and Narcissa resembles Faulkner's dilemma with Estelle and Helen while writing the novel. And Byron is a marvelous distortion of the 1918 Faulkner as lowly bank clerk losing Estelle to a well-heeled rival. In addition to containing these biographical resemblances, *Flags in the Dust* exhibits, to an unusual degree, Faulkner's tendency to double his characters. Through numerous verbal echoes, he connects Bayard, Horace, and Byron; he similarly equates Narcissa with Belle. The effect is to telescope the five young lovers into their creator and his muse. Limitation of space prevents full documentation of these doublings. Let me concentrate here, as elsewhere, on Estelle and childbirths.

Faulkner's presentation of Bayard recalls his 1918–19 image of himself as half-dead, marblelike, nympholeptic, needing to be rescued, and doomed by his beloved's pregnancy. Curiously, Bayard's memory is dominated by the death of his twin brother the previous July, rather than by the deaths of his own first wife and infant in October. Indeed, Bayard has been "in hell" ever since the death of John, who was, like the dead flier in "Lilacs," a poet.[32] It is the shooting down of his twin and not the death of his wife that allegedly makes Bayard so morose and self-destructive. Still, a biographical truth may lurk in this fantasy: putting Estelle into the Compson family as the second child has the effect of eliminating the second Faulkner brother, "Jack" (Murry). The fact that Bayard loses his first love to pregnancy tends to yoke her with Estelle. As usual, the pregnancy proves lethal for a male protagonist—not, however, to Bayard, who merely takes a tracer in the gut, but to his twin, who has to leap out of his flaming plane. His death resembles a drowning and hence prefigures Quentin's: "[He] smacked on . . . a bunch of cloud . . . right on his belly like . . . gut-busters in swimming" (239).

Although Bayard's memories of his first wife initially constitute his erotic ideal, they are replaced by images of Narcissa: "two eyes round with grave astonishment, winged serenely by two dark wings of hair" (134). This picture recalls young Estelle, whereas Narcissa beside Bayard's bed after his near-death by drowning recalls grave Margaret tending Donald. Faulkner skips the actual marriage and first portrays the married couple on a coon hunt after Narcissa has become pregnant. Narcissa is revolted by the raccoon's "pink, baby-like hands" and "skull-like grin" (273); she flees as Bayard begins its decapitation. Thereafter, Bayard goes coonhunting alone every night, rekilling his baby-substitutes and sometimes avoiding until dawn the marital couch. Although Faulkner alleges that the "ghost" (282) lying between the lovers belongs to Bayard's twin, the barrier is surely Narcissa's lethal fetus, delivered the very day of Bayard's fatal, self-destructive plane crash in Chicago.

The night before, by an unrealistic but psychically appropriate coincidence, Bayard's "wife's brother's husband-in-law" (354–55) turns up in Chicago. That is, Horace Benbow's wife's ex-husband sits near Bayard in a drunken stupor. The presence of Horace's predecessor on the eve of Bayard's death is just right because Faulkner constantly doubles Bayard and Horace. Seven years older than Bayard and Narcissa, the fashioner of exquisite glass sculptures, and ambivalently attracted to an old flame now married and the mother of an eight-year-old daughter, Horace corresponds strikingly to Faulkner in 1927.

In general, Faulkner treats Belle harshly, emphasizing her plumpness and unattractive legs (more like Helen than Estelle), her selfishness and manipulativeness (probably true of the young Estelle). Most striking is Belle's coarse, self-absorbed sexuality, rarely accompanied by the charm so often attributed to Estelle. Of course, every novelist has the right and duty to conceive his or her characters in complete freedom and to allow these to grow according to their inner fictive reality. But Faulkner seems to me to protest too much, to make Belle at times unbelievable by having her treat Horace so meanly. Still, Faulkner cannot hate Belle unreservedly. In a melodramatic love scene at the piano, interrupted by Little Belle, her mother's "bent head and her back" look "tragic and still, somehow young" (181).

Marriage to Belle means the spiritual end of Horace. Indeed, her "sultry imminence" is "like the odor of death" (194). Neither of the grooms can win. Bayard dies, literally, six months after leaving home and writing, sporadically, not to his wife but to his mother-substitute, Aunt Jenny. Horace dies too, but metaphorically, while writing frequent letters to his nurturant sister Narcissa, in script that, like Faulkner's, is "practically illegible" (339). Insofar as Faulkner is imagining two possible outcomes to marrying Estelle, his view is consistently dark. As Belle remarks to Horace before their marriage, "You'd make a rotten husband" (181).

Although yoking fatalistic Horace and self-destructive Bayard may seem appropriate, it is surely unfair to equate the grave and tranquil Narcissa, who smells of jasmine, with the smouldering, discontented Belle, who emanates "tiger-reek" (190). Still, if Belle is explicitly "dirty," Narcissa, as the object of Byron Snopes's anonymous obscene letters, feels "filthy" (59)—and enjoys it. She saves all the letters, hides them with her underwear, and will take no steps to apprehend the sender. The brilliantly named Byron is young Faulkner carried to a hilarious extreme. His lithograph of a topless Indian maid parodies the *Marionettes* drawings. When he realizes that Narcissa is getting "married, married," he complains in language like Faun's that she is "flouting him with his own impotence" (249). The evening of Narcissa's marriage finds him moving, like Quentin, amid "massed honeysuckle," forcing a screen with his penknife, and then lying on Narcissa's bed "making smothered, animal-like moanings" (254, 255) that prefigure Benjy, as do the references to his "drooling mouth" (250). Ultimately, Byron suffers the ritual wounding that is the guerdon of most Faulknerian lovers (including the castrated Benjy) when he crashes into Narcissa's "glassed flower pit" (256) and badly cuts his leg. He binds his wound with his shirt and drinks long from the lavatory tap, as Quentin is soon to do between his bloodying at the picnic and his death in the river.

Despite its manifold flaws, *Flags in the Dust* worthily anticipates *The Sound and the Fury*. Although Caddy is a far more moving reconstruction of Estelle than are Narcissa and Belle, at least Narcissa acts maternally toward her brother Horace and her quasi brother Bayard. And different as Horace is from Quentin in age and experience, he seriously anticipates the latter. In returning to Belle Horace knows, as Faulkner must have known in 1927, that he is reliving his past: "the world was opening out before him fearsome and sad and richly moribund, as though he were again an adolescent, and filled with shadowy shapes of dread and of delight not to be denied" (190).

One might argue that so hostile a portrait of Estelle as Belle's casts doubt on the very idea of Estelle as Faulkner's muse. But besides the contemporaneous *Wishing Tree*, the supreme evidence of Estelle's importance to Faulkner's creativity lies in the fictional fragment *Father Abraham*. Written in the same period as *Flags in the Dust*, but utterly eschewing the Great War, *Father Abraham* is, as its editor says, "more successful" than anything Faulkner wrote before *The Sound and the Fury*.[33] It is also the creative germ of Faulkner's 1940 masterpiece, *The Hamlet*. *Father Abraham* is vital to my present purpose chiefly because of Eula Varner's seminal role. In her plumpness and passivity, Eula of course appears quite different from the slender, electric Estelle. Yet her effect is strikingly similar: "A body . . . richly disturbing to the male beholder" (16). Long after she has married Flem, hers is the "still disturbing image of [a] silkclad wife" (13). Young Eula, with precisely Belle's eyes "like cloudy hothouse grapes" (16), is a "very popular girl" (18). But unlike Belle's tiger-reek, "the odor of Eula's washed and scented flesh is terribly sweet to the young men" (17). "Quite a few" ride to church on Sunday to look at her and spend the afternoon

with her, "rife and richly supine on the porch swing, showing no par-
tiality" (16, 17). Eula attends "all the dances and picnics and meetings and
allday singings within ten miles, and with the best young blood of the
countryside she drove homeward beneath the moon" (18).

Ben Wasson, an old friend of Faulkner's, first met Estelle in 1916, paying a "Sunday afternoon . . . call" with a "group of my SAE [fraternity]
friends":

I was awed . . . by Estelle, whose popularity had become a legend. . . . I had never
before met so "alluring" a woman. . . . She was flirtatious, a trait she never lost . . .
and was, . . . I'm sure, more popular with men than with women. Not that she
cared. . . . Altogether she was seductive.[34]

Now what happens to Eula is roughly what happened to Estelle in
1918–19. Eula marries an older, ambitious man, leaves town with him,
bears a daughter, returns a year hence with the child to her parents' house
("still rifely . . . disturbing to the male beholder" [22]), and is subsequently
joined by her husband. Faulkner, of course, imaginatively distorts reality
in finding the formula to release his creativity, a formula that works variously in *The Sound and the Fury*, *Sanctuary*, *As I Lay Dying*, and *Light in
August*. Although Faulkner had earlier approached the formula, he had
not quite found it before. Thus like Cecily and Ethel, Eula gets pregnant
before her marriage but unlike Cecily marries another swain. Eula's pregnancy is signalized by "one of the young bucks" precipitately departing
for Texas. Next day, Eula marries Flem Snopes, and two days later "another young man" also heads for Texas (18, 19). This last, neat fillip not
only looks forward to Quentin's pathetic claim to have deflowered Caddy,
but also recalls Faulkner's flight to New England in April 1918 and his later,
unpersuasive claim to have fathered several bastards. Clearly, Faulkner's
creative imagination cannot accept Cornell Franklin as the father of Cho-
Cho (and must have exulted in making him into Flem!). Incidentally, not
only Eula and Caddy but also Temple Drake, Dewey Dell, and Lena Grove
are deserted by their first sexual partners. In *Soldiers' Pay*, *Flags in the Dust*,
and all but one of the masterpieces succeeding *Father Abraham*, a female's
sexual activity heralds the violent death of a male. Even in the comedies
Father Abraham and *As I Lay Dying* a good deal of hilarious maiming
ensues: Henry Armstid's broken leg, and Vernon Turpin's face full of
splinters; Cash's broken leg, and Jewel's burnt back.

Still, the damage wrought by Eula's return is trivial compared with
the benefits—spring, the circus, poetry:

Then it was April. Peach and pear and apple were in bloom . . . and the turned earth smelled like calves in a clean barn. . . . Thus the world, and on a day Flem Snopes came up the road in a covered wagon . . . followed by a score of horses. . . . "Startin' you a circus, Flem?" (22–23)

When the horses run free in the moonlight, the result is explicitly poetic: "Strophe and antistrophe, clear and remote" (61). Lest there be any question as to the ultimate source of this excruciatingly beautiful spring night of "moon drenched china-berry trees" (59), Uncle Billy Varner explains. The night reminds him of the time when he could lay his ear on his wife's "'nekkid belly . . . and year Eula a-scroungin' inside her.' . . . The earth dreamed on, mysterious, rapturous, like a chord hushed, like an unborn chord held in suspension: the grave and tragic rhythm of the world" (62–63). Faulkner uses that musical figure recurrently in his earliest poetry. For if Estelle's marriage, pregnancy, and return deeply pained him, they stimulated his creativity then, and their memory continued to do so: "in an apple tree like a resurgent phantom of old forgotten springs . . . a mockingbird sang" (29). *Father Abraham* thus seems even more important psychobiographically than artistically. In this last and best, if fragmentary, early work, Faulkner for the first time fully accepted the following truth: his muse's most significant act, to have belonged to another and borne a child but then to have come back, changed and yet not changed, this was to be the chief source of his creativity. Compared to all this, the Great War was an irrelevancy.

Faulkner, then, was able to write *The Sound and the Fury* when he knew that he was going to have, for better or for worse, to embrace that glamorous symbol of maternal and sisterly loss who had first entered his life a quarter of a century before. He surely knew, too, that embracing Estelle meant embracing Oxford and Miss Maud, who was to last almost as long as Faulkner. The conventional wisdom is that Estelle and Faulkner lived unhappily ever after. Yet marriage to her certainly did not prevent the production of a string of the greatest American novels of this, or any, century. In fact, actual publication of *The Sound and the Fury* itself did not occur until nearly four months after the wedding. (They were married June 20, 1929; the novel came out October 7, 1929.) [35] Like *Soldiers' Pay*, that masterpiece bears no dedication. Estelle had to wait for her husband's seventh book, *These Thirteen* (1931): that wonderful collection of short stories is dedicated "To Estelle and Alabama" (their short-lived first offspring). Faulkner could think of his muse only in terms of motherhood and loss.

Emma Watson: Jane Austen's Uncompleted Heroine

JULIET MCMASTER

UNLIKE *Sanditon, Denis Duval*, or *The Mystery of Edwin Drood*, Jane Austen's *The Watsons* was not interrupted by its author's death. It remained a fragment for some other reason, for it was written in the middle of Jane Austen's career, after the drafts of *Northanger Abbey, Sense and Sensibility*, and *Pride and Prejudice* had been written (though not published) and before *Mansfield Park, Emma*, and *Persuasion*. There was time for the author to complete, revise, and publish it, as she did her other novels; but for some reason about which we can only speculate, she set it aside and never took it up again.[1] Much of the existing criticism of *The Watsons* is addressed to this mystery. Critics have tended to look in the fragment for the reasons for its failure (assuming from its noncompletion that it *is* a failure), rather than to examine the quality of what is there. I would like to reverse this tendency, for as I read it, *The Watsons* is a piece of what promised to be a successful and beautiful work, and a worthy addition to the Jane Austen canon.

The reasons adduced for the noncompletion of *The Watsons* may be divided into the biographical and the artistic, and both have a bearing on the quality of the work. *The Watsons* was probably written in 1804; the watermarks establish that it could not have been written before 1803, and Austen family members attest to its having been abandoned in 1805. At that time Jane Austen was faced with a series of difficulties that are likely to have interfered with her writing. She was living in Bath, which she disliked; her novel *Susan*, sold to a publisher in 1803, had still not emerged; her dearest friend, Mrs. Lefroy, died from a riding accident in December 1804, and her father died unexpectedly in January 1805. "We can understand the pressure of circumstances that made it difficult to continue the story," writes B. C. Southam, "which was, anyway, proceeding unsatisfactorily."[2] Her biographer, John Halperin, also suggests that the biographical circumstances adversely affected the quality of the fragment. "What we do know is that Jane Austen, buffeted in quick succession by the deaths of a valued friend and beloved father, and living now in a household of widows and spinsters . . . pushed aside the morbid, sordid story she was working on . . . and never took it up again. It belonged to too painful a time, and she put it out of her mind."[3] He does not demonstrate that it is morbid or sordid.

Most prominent among the voices that have adduced artistic reasons for the abandonment of *The Watsons* has been that of Q. D. Leavis. According to her theory, *The Watsons was* finished, for it was essentially made over into *Emma*, as *First Impressions* was made over into *Pride and Prejudice*.[4] A different version of this theory of Jane Austen as a thrifty novelist who wasted nothing has more recently been presented by Joseph Wiesenfarth,[5] who argues that Emma Watson becomes not Emma Woodhouse, but Jane Fairfax in the same novel, and that most scenes and characters in *The Watsons* were cannibalized and used up in other novels, so that there was not enough left of it to make a new novel, even had Jane Austen decided to return to it in happier years. Margaret Drabble considers much of *The Watsons* has been used in *Pride and Prejudice*,[6] and David Hopkinson finds that Emma Watson has been "subsumed" into the characters of subsequent heroines.[7]

But these cases, however cogently argued, are not convincing: they simply don't *feel* right. Emma Watson and Emma Woodhouse are entirely different from one another, and they inhabit totally different worlds, even if there is an invalid father and a vulgar, domineering woman in each. The first-time reader of *The Watsons*, I think, far from having a sense of déjà vu and checking off each character and incident as having been used in one of the completed novels, is more likely to be struck with the *difference* between *The Watsons* and the other novels. Here we have a number of new departures, including the concentratedly dramatic method, the shabby-genteel setting, the development of a charming child character, and an unusual degree of specificity about food, clothes, and living quarters. Hints within the fragment, and the notes we have on Jane Austen's intentions for its completion, suggest that it would have broken further new ground, including the dramatized death of the heroine's father, a sojourn in an attorney's vulgarly pretentious home in Croydon, and a consideration of the sexual viability of fifty-year-old women. Such material can hardly be said to have been exhausted in the completed novels.

More serious among the charges that *The Watsons* is an artistic failure is the objection to its heroine, most fully articulated in Marvin Mudrick's influential study of 1952. Emma Watson labors under the serious handicap of being too good. She has too little to learn, and therefore leaves no room for the operation of authorial irony. Her point of view, says Mudrick, is "solemnly coincident with the author's. Emma Watson serves, then, as chief agent in the author's resolute unironic simplification of the moral problem."[8] A. Walton Litz's reading of *The Watsons* is more sympathetic, but he shares Mudrick's objection to Emma: "In *The Watsons* Jane Austen is so intent on the social discriminations she is making that, for once, she fails to give us a double vision of her heroine. Her view is completely coincident with that of Emma Watson."[9] B. C. Southam has more to add to the damning praise of the heroine: "sensitive, intelligent, spirited, charitable, affectionate and high-principled, the possibilities for her development are limited. She is perceptive with others and has almost nothing to learn about herself."[10]

These are heavy charges. (We know that moral credits in a personal account often transfer as debits in the account of a fictional character.) It should be noted, however, that *Mansfield Park*, a completed novel that some have claimed to be Jane Austen's greatest achievement, has also had its detractors; and the objections to it and to Fanny Price have been very like those to *The Watsons* and its heroine. Critics who object to Emma Watson as too good, I think, take the erring heroines—Catherine Morland, Marianne Dashwood, Elizabeth Bennet, and Emma Woodhouse—as their models of the essential Austen heroine. They tend for the nonce to overlook the principled and right-judging heroines—Elinor Dashwood, Fanny Price, Anne Elliot. Mudrick, whose subject is Jane Austen's use of irony, predictably most admires the novels with the most erring heroines, *Pride and Prejudice* and *Emma*. Southam, in objecting to Emma Watson as an authorial mouthpiece, admits that "In other of the novels . . . Elinor Dashwood, Henry Tilney, and Mr. Knightley serve this end, as well as participating fully in the action. But they are not placed at the heart both of the action and of the experience of the work, as Emma Watson is."[11] Elinor may be a debatable case, but Fanny Price and Anne Elliot undoubtedly *are* placed centrally in both their novels, though Southam seems not to think of them here. We need to remember that in her whole oeuvre Jane Austen relied on both kinds of heroine, the erring and the right-judging.

And if we are ready to accept Fanny and Anne as satisfactorily fulfilling their particular roles, then Emma Watson is not out of line. They too, though morally admirable from the beginning, have their necessary progresses to achieve. Fanny Price, for instance, remains morally static; but she has to develop socially in order to make her goodness effective. Emma Watson's progress—and she has one mapped out for her—is to be, like Fanny's, rather a social than a moral one. And, again like Fanny, she is not immune from authorial irony, though it is an irony less dazzling than that which operates at the heroine's expense in *Pride and Prejudice* and *Emma*.

I

The critic who undertakes to examine the thematic structure of an uncompleted work has a delicate task. Such an effort must necessarily be grounded partly on speculation; but the speculation itself may be soundly based. To use a geometrical analogy: suppose you have the arc of a circle, and want to deduce the whole. The first thing is to find the center of the circle. And that can be done by drawing two or more chords in the arc, and bisecting them at right angles. The center of the circle should fall where all these lines meet. Once the center is found, the tracing of the full circle can be reasonably accurate. And the larger the arc in relation to the whole circle, the better are the chances that the center will be true.

To apply this geometrical metaphor to my own procedure: *The Watsons* as a fragment clearly is my arc, and the circle will be my diagram of the whole shape that the novel was intended to take. But what must be my chords? How many can I fit into my arc, in order to ensure a reasonable degree of accuracy for my center?

As my chords I propose to use certain aspects of *The Watsons* that we recognize as being techniques more fully developed in the completed novels: the thematic arrangement of minor characters, for instance, and the use of repetition to create a significant motif. Small things that happen twice begin to make a pattern, to make a chord that can be made to point at something. Trifles light as air, fallings from us, vanishings, can thereby furnish intimations of integrity: and my airy circle can be completed. The thematic structure I postulate will still be only a circle on paper, a diagram, and very far from a completion of the novel itself. But criticism is of its nature diagrammatic. We inscribe our geometrical figures on paper, in the flat. But the works of Jane Austen and her like, the real characters, are spheres, globes, worlds. They happen in three dimensions.

II

In *The Watsons*, as Litz recognizes, Jane Austen "squarely confronted her major theme: the conflict between the free spirit and social-economic imperatives." [12] Emma Watson, who has been brought up by her aunt and uncle to assume that she will be the heiress to a comfortable fortune, and therefore not subject to the humiliations of the poor spinster who must catch a husband, suddenly finds herself dropped back into her father's impoverished family "without a sixpence" (352), [13] and placed in automatic competition with her desperately husband-hunting sisters. This situation of having come down in the world, and of being thrust into immediate intimacy with brothers and sisters who are virtual strangers to her, places particular strains on a character who is particularly anxious to behave properly. The decisive passage that announces the direction that her development is to take (like the pronouncement on Emma Woodhouse that "the real evils indeed of Emma's situation were the power of having rather too much her own way, and a disposition to think a little too well of herself" [*E*, 5]) comes early in the novel, in conversation with her eldest sister Elizabeth.

" . . . I suppose my Aunt brought you up to be rather refined." [says Elizabeth to Emma.] "Indeed I do not know.—My conduct must tell you how I have been brought up. I am no judge of it myself. I cannot compare my Aunt's method with any other persons, because I know no other."—"But I can see in a great many things that you are very refined. I have observed it ever since you came home, & I am afraid it will not be for your happiness. Penelope will laugh at you very much." "*That* will not be for my happiness I am sure.—If my opinions are wrong, I must correct them—if they are above my situation, I must endeavour to conceal them." (318)

The passage contains some difficulties, because Elizabeth, not being refined herself, is not very clear on what she means by refinement. But it provides, clearly, a major thematic pivot for the novel that is to be. When we hear an Austen heroine declare, "My conduct must tell you how I have been brought up. I am no judge of it myself," we know that here is room for development. It is a heroine's business to know how to judge her own conduct; or if she doesn't know already, to learn. And in this very passage we see an example of the excessive "refinement" that Elizabeth is trying to put her finger on. Emma reverts from free and open discourse to a circumspect evasion: "I cannot compare my Aunt's method with any other persons, because I know no other." In fact Emma is very well able to judge conduct and upbringing, both her own and other people's, as her subsequent confident and accurate judgments show; but here there is a momentary freezing-over of the developing intimacy between the sisters, and Emma produces a proper little sentiment of the kind that the decorum-conscious Mrs. Edwards would approve. She is, of course, morally scrupulous and verbally precise: "If my opinions are wrong, I must correct them—if they are above my situation, I must endeavour to conceal them," she says, a reaction that Southam calls "admirable but colourless," and considers as one more proof that Emma "has almost nothing to learn about herself."[14] But are opinions *meant* to be subject to class divisions? And *should* good opinions be "concealed?" The interaction of class and morality, and the bearing of one upon the other, are matters to be more fully explored.

To wind up her concessions about her opinions and her refinement, and to respond to Elizabeth's warning that Penelope will laugh at her for them, Emma says primly, "But I doubt whether Ridicule—" and leaves her sentence unfinished. We may infer that she means, "Even if my opinions need revising, I doubt whether ridicule will be an effective means." From the author of *Pride and Prejudice*, such a sentiment may well suggest a propriety that will have its fall. Unfortunately Penelope never appears, so that we cannot follow through the suggestion that Emma's refinement will be subjected to the testing of mockery. But we are given some intimation that Emma Watson, like Mr. Darcy, may have to learn to be laughed at.

In her sensitive study of *The Watsons*, Margaret Drabble recognizes that "refinement" is to be a key issue in the novel, and cites Emma's excessive embarrassment at the visit of Lord Osborne and Tom Musgrave as an example of "misplaced" refinement. Emma is painfully and "fully sensible of all that must be open to the ridicule of Richer people in her present home"; she could usefully take a lesson from her less refined sister Elizabeth, whose "simpler Mind, or juster reason saved her from such mortification" (345). Here, clearly, is an explicit judgment on Emma's hypersensitivity. And Margaret Drabble speculates, "The plot would surely have provided some more interesting examples of false and true refinement."[15]

The fragment as it stands, however, provides several instances—and in the process some of that irony at Emma's expense that some critics have found to be so sadly lacking. The irony is of a restrained and gentle kind, like that applied to Fanny Price in her self-pity at being neglected while Mary Crawford gets a riding lesson from Edward: "She began to think it rather hard upon the mare to have such double duty; if she were forgotten the poor mare should be remembered" (*MP*, 68). In Emma's case the focus is on her propriety. She is one whose disapproval modulates swiftly into shock, especially noticeable in the face of Elizabeth's laconic calm about the matters that shock her sister: "You quite shock me by what you say of Penelope," cries Emma (316), and "To be so bent on Marriage—to pursue a Man merely for the sake of situation—is a sort of thing that shocks me" (318). Emma produces refinements of sensibility on Elizabeth's behalf that Elizabeth herself has long outgrown. "A heart wounded like yours can have little inclination for Matrimony," she says tenderly, after hearing of her sister's disappointment over Purvis. But Elizabeth herself does not rise to this heroism of sentiment, and responds in her down-to-earth manner, "Not much indeed—but you know we must marry" (317). Emma's delicacy is occasionally a liability to her: her refinement has its cost in comfort and peace of mind. On two occasions Tom Musgrave, who loves to pique people's curiosity, tantalizes her with hints about flattering comments on her by other men:

"If it were not a breach of confidence, replied Tom with an important look, perhaps I might be able to win a more favourable opinion of poor Osborne.—" Emma gave him no Encouragement, & he was obliged to keep his friend's secret. (340)

Here Emma's refinement in resisting the dangled bait is endorsed, and the garrulous and indiscreet Tom is properly put in his place. A confidence is not to be infringed. But later in a similar situation we see Emma subjected to the same kind of gentle irony for her refinement as Fanny Price is for her displaced pity for the mare. On this occasion it is not only Lord Osborne's opinion of her—for him she cares relatively little—but Howard's also that Tom is ready to reveal:

"I fancy you must have a little cheek-glowing now & then Miss Emma. Were not you rather warm last Saturday about 9 or 10 o'clock in the Eveng—? I will tell you how it was—I see you are dieing to know.—Says Howard to Ld Osborne—" At this interesting moment he was called on by the others to regulate the game . . . & his attention was so totally engaged . . . as never to revert to what he had been saying before:—& Emma, tho' suffering a good deal from Curiosity, dared not remind him. (358–59)

Here, clearly, is irony at the expense of Emma's "refinement." Anyone else in that situation would simply wait her chance and then bring Tom back to the subject. Anne Elliot, for instance, who is certainly sufficiently refined, in similar circumstances is frankly "all curiosity," and the narrator indulgently comments, "No one can withstand the charm of such a mystery" (*P*, 187). But Emma, who is understandably intensely anxious to know what Howard thinks of her, must pay the price of her hyperrefinement. As Elizabeth had warned her, "I am afraid it will not be for your happiness" (318).

On another occasion we are allowed to smile at Emma's vacillations on the matter of why Howard has not come to visit along with Lord Osborne:

> Among other unsatisfactory feelings it once occurred to her to wonder why Mr Howard had not taken the same privilege of coming, & accompanied his Lordship—but she was willing to suppose that he had either known nothing about it, or had declined any share in a measure which carried quite as much Impertinence in it's form as Goodbreeding. (347–48)

Her feelings here are in fine play with her propriety. Her perfectly understandable pique at his not coming must be allayed by adducing for him a motive of noble delicacy.

An appropriate crisis for Emma's refinement is the issue of whether to ride home from the Edwards' house in Tom Musgrave's curricle. Catherine in *Northanger Abbey* has to learn that for a girl to ride unchaperoned in a man's vehicle is "not at all the thing" (*NA*, 104); but Emma knows this already. Her trial is different:

> Emma felt distressed; she did not like the proposal—she did not wish to be on terms of intimacy with the Proposer—& yet fearful of encroaching on the Edwardes', as well as wishing to go home herself, she was at a loss how entirely to decline what he offered. (339)

Knowing what is proper, she has to find a way of delivering the right signals to her hostess to prompt the offer of a carriage, without absolutely asking for it. In this crisis she succeeds admirably, managing to get on the same wavelength as the punctilious Mrs. Edwards; and the carriage is forthcoming.

Her sister Elizabeth highlights Emma's hypersensitivity. As we have seen, the opening conversation between them exemplifies both Emma's refinement and Elizabeth's happy lack of it. The older sister is down-to-earth and laconic, where the younger is inclined to cherish high-flown sentiments.

"Is Sam. attached to Miss Edwards?" [asks Emma]—"Did not you know *that*?"—"How should I know it? . . . It is not likely that circumstances of such delicacy should make any part of the scanty communication which passed between you & me for the last 14 years." "I wonder I never mentioned it when I wrote . . ." (320–21)

What are "circumstances of such delicacy" to Emma are only ordinary items of news to Elizabeth, to be included or forgotten in letters, but certainly not to be avoided. Similarly, while Emma suffers agonies of "mortification," Elizabeth with her "juster reason" is refreshingly free from embarrassment when Lord Osborne and Tom Musgrave catch the sisters at their early dinner (345). As Jane Bennet's generous propensity to think well of everybody contrasts with Elizabeth Bennet's prejudice, so Elizabeth Watson's sensible realism brings out Emma's overdeveloped delicacy.

Refinement, then, like sense, sensibility, pride, and prejudice, or like "firmness" in *Persuasion*, is a quality that has its degrees and fine gradations. Emma's refinement is a virtue, and part of what constitutes her value; but it also has its excesses, and in the higher reaches of her refinement and propriety Emma, like Jane Austen's other heroines, becomes accessible to our judgment and our laughter. We recognize a delicacy that exceeds the circumstances, a clinging to propriety at the expense of sense and of acceptable self-expression. Such moments create the necessary vibration of response: we may look *at* her rather than *through* her, sharply assessing her rather than feeling and judging *with* her. The irony is not lacking after all.

However, for all her careful observance of the rules of propriety, Emma has it in her, from the first, to be refreshingly direct and spontaneous. And in the fragment as we have it, it is in the moments when she allows her feelings to carry her that she is most effective as a moral agent. The glorious scene of her rescue of little Charles Blake in the midst of his bitter throes of disappointment sets the tone: "Emma did not think, or reflect;—she felt & acted" (330). By offering to be his partner after Miss Osborne has broken her engagement to dance with him, Emma, from his stricken state with "crimson'd cheeks, quivering lips" restores him to "all his first delight" (330–31). Jane Austen creates a number of such moving rescues. Notably, Harriet is rescued on the dance floor by Mr. Knightley after being slighted by Elton: "Oh! it was such an inexpressible obligation!" Harriet recalls fervently,—"The very recollection of it, and all that I felt at the time—when I saw him coming—his noble look—and my wretchedness before. Such a change!" (*E*, 342). Anne Elliot is likewise rescued by Wentworth from the rambunctious little Walter, and is similarly moved.[16] But in both these instances the woman is the one rescued. In the case of Emma Watson and Charles Blake, Emma is the active one, the rescuer, deservedly carrying all before her in an act as heroic as any performed by Jane Austen's heroines. And it is one that instantly brings its own reward: Emma not only wins the devotion of young Charles, but she is noticed and admired by the company, and becomes a Cinderella in the eyes of the local prince, Lord Osborne.

With Lord Osborne, too, she is an effective moral agent as much by virtue of her unguarded and direct pronouncements as by her restraint and refinement—though he is undoubtedly attracted by her refinement too. The combination of her keen sense of propriety and her bravely forthright pronouncements performs a kind of moral magic that we see in process. Lord Osborne plays Cymon to Emma's Iphigenia: the oafish lout exerts himself to become worthy of the refined woman. He has been blurting out some male chauvinism of the day about how "A woman never looks better than on horseback," and insisting that all women should therefore ride, regardless of expense, when he draws her pointed reproof:

" . . . Female Economy will do a great deal my Lord, but it cannot turn a small income into a large one."—Ld Osborne was silenced. Her manner had been neither sententious nor sarcastic, but there was something in it's mild seriousness, as well as in the words themselves which made his Lordship think. (346)

Such a consummation is not easily achieved: clearly Lord Osborne is not accustomed to thinking, and doesn't do it readily. Emma has had to be irritated beyond her usual restraint in order to make so pointed a remark; according to her own social standards, reference to one's income, especially to its meagreness, is scarcely proper. But her frank avowal brings him face to face with social realities, and makes him respect her. By momentarily setting aside the refinement that makes her his superior, she jolts him into an awareness of a condition other than his own. And his moral growth is enacted before us: "when he addressed her again, it was with a degree of considerate propriety, totally unlike the half-awkward, half-fearless stile of his former remarks" (346). George Eliot was later to dramatize a similar relation, when she shows how the trivial and "supercilious" Stephen Guest exceeds himself, and takes huge moral strides in order to fit himself for Maggie Tulliver.

Emma Watson, as a heroine who knows both how to think and reflect, *and* how to feel and act, is appropriately at the center of a novel in which the conflict and interplay of feeling and propriety is a theme as central as sense and sensibility or pride and prejudice in other novels. Ian Watt has memorably demonstrated how Jane Austen creates and disposes her minor characters in such a way as to play a set of variations on the moral concern central to the novel, so that in *Sense and Sensibility* we can see "almost the whole of Jane Austen's *dramatis personae* as highly unsatisfactory representatives of the two concepts which she has aligned against each other."[17] In *The Watsons* Emma is similarly surrounded by minor characters who play variations on the central concepts.

Mrs. Edwards, described by Tom as "too nice a judge of Decorum" (334) and, less respectfully, as "that stiff old Mrs. E" (333), is a character who has received no critical attention, but she is as memorable and pointed a creation as Lucy Steele or Lady Catherine de Bourgh, who similarly reflect facets of the moral traits of the major characters. Mrs. Edwards is the caricature of Emma's refinement as Lady Catherine is the caricature of Darcy's pride or Lucy Steele the travesty of Elinor's sense. We are introduced to her as a lady with "a reserved air, & a great deal of formal Civility" (322). At almost any appearance, she continues to illustrate herself as the embodiment of propriety. Since Emma is under her wing at the ball, she is schooled in advance about the details of correct form at the assembly. At the break for tea,

Miss E[dwards] gave her a caution to be at hand, in a manner which convinced her of Mrs. E[dwards]'s holding it very important to have them both close to her when she moved into the Tearoom; & Emma was accordingly on the alert to gain her proper station. (332)

("On the alert to gain her proper station" is one of the many pregnant phrases in *The Watsons* that carry a load of social implication beyond their immediate context. In one sense each Austen novel is all about a heroine who is largely on the alert to gain her proper station.) When Emma accidentally infringes Mrs. Edwards's unspoken rule, and becomes temporarily separated from her party, she receives the chilly reminder, "We had quite lost you—said Mrs. E[dwards],—who followed her with Mary, in less than five minutes.—If you prefer this room to the other, there is no reason why you should not be here, but we had better all be together" (333–34). And the next morning, when Emma receives a note from her sister, we are reminded again of her hostess's decorous formality: "Emma was beginning to read rather *before* Mrs Edwards had entreated her to use no ceremony" (338). Although Emma's refinement is analogous to Mrs. Edwards's ceremonious civility, such a moment of close contiguity illuminates the heroine's engaging leavening of spontaneity. Mrs. Edwards devotes herself entirely to stultifying social rituals that can be the death of individual expression. Her daughter Mary, we hear, "seemed . . . to have caught something of the stile of the Mother who had brought her up" (322). When Emma is first left alone with them, it is not surprising that a gathering of these representatives of refinement is not a very convivial one: "some very, very languid remarks on the probable Brilliancy of the Ball, were all that broke at intervals a silence of half an hour" (323). At this extreme end of refinement, feeling is subsumed in social formality, and the virtue becomes a vice.

Emma's sister Margaret Watson is a character who has signally failed to integrate the selfish desires of the individual with the controlled responses of the social being, a disintegration that Jane Austen symbolically represents by giving her two voices and two appearances:

Margaret was not without beauty; . . . but the sharp & anxious expression of her face made her beauty in general little felt.—On meeting her long-absent Sister, as on every occasion of shew, her manner was all affection & her voice all gentleness; continual smiles & a very slow articulation being her constant resource when determined on pleasing.

She was now so "delighted to see dear, dear Emma" that she could hardly speak a word in a minute. (349)

Subsequently we are usually informed as to whether Margaret's speeches are delivered in "the tone of artificial Sensibility" or in "a sharp quick accent, totally unlike the first" (351). Margaret, with a strong sense of what she wants, finds herself in a society that provides few gratifications for portionless unmarried ladies. She slavishly accepts the society's superficial standards, and tries to adjust her behavior to fit its demands. But her limited intelligence can produce only an alternation of transparent affectation with thwarted fretfulness. "Wrong-headed folly, engrafted on an untoward Disposition" (361) is the summary characterization of Margaret at the end of the fragment. The "engrafted" again suggests the forced and unnatural relation of the individual to the social role, and the alienation of the self.

Tom Musgrave, on the other hand, shows no such conflict. As the antihero, he stands in relation to Emma Watson as Frank Churchill stands to Emma Woodhouse: each has the heroine's faults in a more emphatic form, and is perfectly satisfied with them. As Emma Watson is in danger of being too refined, of subsuming her self in a set of social responses, Tom Musgrave is the perfectly adapted social animal. Social sanctions—as provided by acceptable models like the Osbornes—are his be-all and end-all. If on a sunny day Miss Osborne told him it was raining, he would probably put up his umbrella. His behavior, his emotions, and even his perception of reality are ruled by his need for the approval of his gods, the local aristocracy. When Margaret, angling for a compliment, praises Emma's appearance, and prompts him, "I think even *you* must be a convert to a brown complexion," we have a little history of his mental process:

He hesitated; Margaret was fair herself, & he did not particularly want to compliment her; but Miss Osborne & Miss Carr were likewise fair, & his devotion to them carried the day. "Your Sister's complexion, said he at last, is as fine as a dark complexion can be, but I still profess my preference of a white skin. You have seen Miss Osborne?—she is my model for a truly feminine complexion, & she is very fair."—"Is she fairer than me?"—Tom made no reply. (357)

In this little crisis Tom must pick his way carefully, and he performs very creditably. He must pay a tribute to Emma's complexion, because Lord Osborne admires her, and he must announce his belief in Miss Osborne as the standard of perfection. And he manages, by neglecting her question, to withdraw the apparent compliment to Margaret, who currently stands nowhere in his view of the established pecking order. It is notable that in all these carefully weighed responses, his actual preference on the abstract question of whether a fair complexion is better than a brown one does not figure at all.

   Tom is a perfect specimen of what Thackeray was later to define as the snob, who in the presence of a very great man "can be as humble as a flunkey, and as supple as a harlequin."[18] He is Lord Osborne's attendant toady. And though he is a much more intelligent and accomplished man than Lord Osborne, he makes himself entirely available as the dogsbody of Osborne castle, being ready to dance attendance on every member of the family. He won't join the dance until they arrive, and (in spite of his predilection for dancing) considers it incumbent on him to leave when they leave. He chooses his dancing partners at Lord Osborne's behest, and is ready to be the middleman in procuring him the girls he likes. Jane Austen has conveyed with some ingenuity the way he contrives to live his life at second hand. He has constructed an image of himself—one that he believes matches the Osborne requirements—as a dashing, fashionable young fellow who keeps late hours, drives fast horses, and breaks female hearts; and he spends all his energies in living up to this image. His real self scarcely has a chance to appear while he is so busy enacting the image. And yet Jane Austen has managed to suggest, even in the fragment as it stands, that he *has* a real self somewhere, folded away in a drawer perhaps, like Peter Pan's shadow; and that he may some day produce it, shake it out, and put it on—and even that he would look quite presentable in it if and when that day arrives. In the meantime, however, he is partial and contrived, a mere social role. He is like Mr. Elton in his courtship of Emma Woodhouse, whose constant refrain is "Exactly so!" Tom makes it his whole business to live up to the social expectations of an aristocratic blockhead.

Mary Edwards, who seems destined to be the heroine of a subplot, is not one of the strongly marked characters of *The Watsons*. But her lack of definition is itself a characteristic, and signals her relation to the main theme. She is her mother's daughter, and she, like Emma, shows signs of being too refined. "Mary Edwards is rather prim & reserved," complains Elizabeth, who can't discover whether she responds to Sam Watson's love: "I do not always know what she wd be at" (321). Emma too finds her reticent and uncommunicative (322–23). Mary is apparently rather overwhelmed by her two domineering parents. However, we are provided with an important clue to her feelings in the pregnant little exchange on Emma's family resemblances:

The discussion led to more intimate remarks, & Miss Edwards gently asked Emma if she were not often reckoned very like her youngest brother.—Emma thought she could perceive a faint blush accompany the question, & there seemed something still more suspicious in the manner in which Mr E[dwards] took up the subject.—"You are paying Miss Emma no great compliment I think Mary, said he hastily." (324)

A knowledge of Jane Austen's other novels makes the implications of this passage quite plain: Mary is inclined to be in love with Sam Watson, as signaled by her blush, her avoidance of his name, and her searching for his likeness in his sister's face. (Elizabeth Bennet similarly looks for a resemblance to Darcy in Lady Catherine and believes that Bingley searches her own face for a likeness to Jane [*P&P*, 162, 262].) But Mary's parents are far from favoring such a match, and they announce their opposition, plainly enough to be understood, by denying any likeness between Emma and Sam. "The Father is decidedly against him, and the Mother shows him no favour" (341), Emma is able to report to her sister, on the basis of this conversation. Parental opposition is not the only obstacle to the love of Mary and Sam. She is also courted by the confident Captain Hunter, who has a way of carrying all before him. And yet the favorable signs of her feeling for Sam seem a reliable indication that here is her true love. Her history, it seems, will be one of exceeding her socially dictated submission to her parents, and discovering the force of her own feelings. She and Sam will surely be happily united at the end, despite parental reservations and the forceful maneuvering of Captain Hunter.

The hero, the clergyman Mr. Howard, seems to have a similar development mapped out for him. In the fragment as it stands, his character is
one of the weakest features; and had Jane Austen decided to finish the
novel she would surely have filled in his role, even in his early appearances,
with a little more specificity. But his lack of definition, like Mary's, is no
doubt strategic: like her and like Emma, he blends in with his social sur-
roundings, being so fully adapted to his social role that his individuality is
partly subsumed. He does not adopt a vivid new role as Tom Musgrave
does, and therefore he is rather bland. But this, again, is itself a notable
trait. He is a hero calculated to appeal to the refined Emma Watson: "an
agreeable-looking Man," with "a quietly-chearful, gentlemanlike air . . .
which suited her" (330, 333). And he has "unexceptionable" manners (335).
His few appearances in the fragment further inform us that he has "a sensible, unaffected, way of expressing himself" (335), that he is properly attentive to the invalid Mr. Watson, and that, when preaching, "He reads
extremely well, with great propriety & in a very impressive manner; & at
the same time without any Theatrical grimace or violence" (348). That is
about all we learn of him, aside from Emma's bravely declared predilection
in his favor. But we do have surprising information from Jane Austen's
nephew, in his *Memoir*, about her intentions for Howard:

Mr. Watson was soon to die; and Emma to become dependent for a home on her
narrow-minded sister-in-law and brother. She was to decline an offer of marriage
from Lord Osborne, and much of the interest of the tale was to arise from Lady
Osborne's love for Mr. Howard, and his counter affection for Emma, whom he
was finally to marry. (362–63) [19]

Here is matter for a May morning! Chapman as editor found the news
that Howard was to be sought by Lady Osborne simply incredible, and he
firmly declared that "Lady Osborne" is "Doubtless a slip for *Miss Osborne*.
Lady O. was 'nearly fifty'" (363n). In *The Watsons*, however, being nearly
fifty does not disqualify a woman for marriage. Emma's aunt, Mrs. Turner,
whom Mr. Edwards remembers as a "fine woman . . . about 30 years ago"
(325), also has a coltish tooth, and has just made an imprudent marriage to
the dashing Irish Captain O'Brien. And in the same passage in which we
hear of Lady Osborne's age, we are also told, "Of the females [including
her daughter, Miss Osborne], Ly. Osborne had by much the finest person;—tho' nearly 50, she was very handsome, & had all the Dignity of
Rank" (329). Taken in conjunction with the information provided in the
Memoir, this suggests a particular and unusual trial for the hero. His

unexceptionable manners and gentlemanliness will make him peculiarly prone to be governed by a titled patroness, a woman of power, rank, and presence to whom he owes debts of gratitude as well as of respect. We do not know to what extent he will become entangled with her; but apparently he will need to shake loose the shackles of social restraint in order to follow the devices and desires of his own heart, and marry Emma. Howard too, then, in the completed novel as I project it, would be a character who will learn to assert himself and follow his feelings in the teeth of propriety and social obligation.

III

If among the characters an enlightened individualism is endorsed over an unquestioning acceptance of authority and social sanctions, so society in the aggregate is viewed in unusually hostile terms. Certain social abuses identified in the completed novels appear in *The Watsons* in a concentrated form. To exemplify:

In the completed novels, especially *Pride and Prejudice*, Jane Austen draws attention to the unjustly difficult plight of the single woman who is not in possession of a good fortune; here she makes it a keynote. "You know we must marry," says Elizabeth Watson simply; " . . . it is very bad to grow old & be poor & laughed at" (317). And Emma Watson is the heroine with the bleakest outlook of all.

In the completed novels, especially *Emma* and *Persuasion*, Jane Austen shows herself sensitive to social snobbery; here snobbery is rampant. From the opening sentence about the winter assembly we are alerted to the value system of the town of D: "sanguine hopes were entertained that the Osbornes themselves would be there" (314). "The Osbornes themselves," for the local society as for Tom Musgrove, are looked to as the standard of excellence, in spite of their very visible lapses in courtesy and community spirit. They expect and receive almost universal deference, and do virtually nothing to deserve it. Mrs. Edwards acknowledges that "they add nothing to the pleasure of the Evening, they come so late, & go so early;—but Great People always have their charm" (323). They, like Sir Walter Elliot in *Persuasion*, are perfect examples of snobbery, according to Lionel Trilling's definition: they have "pride in status without pride in function."[20]

If the Osbornes are the big-time snobs, Mr. and Mrs. Robert Watson of Croydon carry on the habits of false pride and false adulation in the lower strata. Their judgments are all made on the basis of status; feelings, or even intelligent moral assessment like Emma's, don't enter into their response to the newly returned sister:

> Mrs R[obert] W[atson] eyed her with much familiar curiosity & Triumphant Compassion;—the loss of the Aunt's fortune was uppermost in her mind, at the moment of meeting;—& she cd. not but feel how much better it was to be the daughter of a gentleman of property at Croydon, than the niece of an old woman who threw herself away on an Irish Captain.—Robert was carelessly kind, as became a prosperous Man & a brother; more intent on . . . inveighing against the Exorbitant advance in Posting, . . . than on welcoming a Sister, who was no longer likely to have any property for him to get the direction of. (349)

When Emma moved to her brother's home after her father's death, we would presumably have become more fully acquainted with the habits of Croydon. It is quite a pleasure to see the small-time snobs put down by the big-time snobs, in the discussion of which game to play after tea. "Speculation . . . is the only round game played at Croydon now," announces Mrs. Robert, "—we never think of any other." But Tom Musgrave trumps that card. "Vingt-un is the game at Osborne Castle; I have played nothing but Vingt-un of late. . . ." One cannot but rejoice in the narrator's comment, "Mrs Robert offered not another word. . . .—She was quite vanquished, & the fashions of Osborne-Castle carried it over the fashions of Croydon" (358).

In the world of *Persuasion* the snob Sir Walter Elliot comes to seem peripheral, almost an anachronism, as the more healthy meritocracy of the navy gains prominence; but the Osbornes, the Robert Watsons, and the meanly based adulation and status-seeking that surround them seem destined to remain central for most of *The Watsons*. As a result, the social vision, even in the fragment as we have it, seems surprisingly close to Thackeray's satirical view in *The Book of Snobs*: "behold the state of society, viz., Toadyism, organized:—base Man-and-Mammon worship, instituted by command of law: — SNOBBISHNESS, in a word, perpetuated."[21]

In such a society Emma Watson, the heroine of refinement, will have a sufficiently difficult task. She brings with her into the beginning of the novel, as we have seen, a capital of already acquired "refinement"; and we see this already effectively at work—for instance, in the reformation of Lord Osborne. But her refinement is also "above [her] situation," and it must be further tested, refined, and redefined as the novel progresses. Her trials at the Robert Watsons' on the one hand, and as the rival of Lady Osborne on the other, will call for heroic feats of discrimination and restraint, and also, perhaps, for some uncalculated outbursts of feeling; for true refinement is an attribute far more positive than mere restraint; and Emma's most decisive and effective action in the fragment as we have it occurred when she "did not think, or reflect; — she felt & acted."

As a novel in which the heroine's refinement is to be tried and tested, and her spontaneity applauded; in which the hero must learn to shake off social obligation in order to win his love, and the antihero must get his just deserts for a slavish toadying to rank; in which propriety and decorum are viewed as faultily excessive, and feeling as all too absent in a society that is obsessed with getting and spending—as such a novel, *The Watsons* bids fair to being the most Romantic of Jane Austen's works. Its opening incident is a version of "Cinderella." Feeling is endorsed over propriety, the individual over society. The child is enlightened, and a source of wisdom.[22] Rank and authority are hostilely conceived as corrupt and corrupting. And the world is definitely too much with us. Jane Austen is not likely to provide us with a completely and unqualifiedly romantic document; but then neither do the Romantic poets themselves, if it comes to that. *The Watsons*, however, is as close as she gets.

The fragment, though it endorses a passionate exceeding of restraint, is nevertheless as controlled and precise in its language as the other novels. As always, Jane Austen can command the exact and revealing phrase. In a memorable reading of *Sense and Sensibility*, Tony Tanner finds in Marianne's "muffled scream" an epitome of the conflicts embodied in that novel and its heroines.[23] *The Watsons* also includes phrases of a beautiful significance and economy; and several of them are oxymorons that contain the rival claims of passion and restraint, individual commitment and social accommodation, which are enacted in the novel at large. Mrs. Robert Watson regards the impoverished Emma with "Triumphant Compassion" (349). Compassion for a fellow human being is clearly negated by the delight of being able to look down on her. When Mr. and Mrs. Edwards are launched into one of their ritual marital arguments about his whist club, we are told that he responds to her complaint about his lateness "with sturdy pleasantry" (325). The phrase exactly renders that strained phase of human relations in which some slight subterfuge, some assumption of a cheerfulness that is not really felt, is the only resource for avoiding dissent and open hostility. Mr. Edwards's pleasantry, his native talent for and enjoyment of social relations, is a genuine entity; but at such a moment, while he represses his personal irritation at his wife's routine querulousness, the structure of his habitual social accommodation just audibly creaks. Similarly, we hear that when they leave the ball the Osbornes feel constrained to notice Emma: "From Miss Osborne & Miss Carr she received something like a jerking curtsey as they passed her" (336). How that gracious social gesture of respect and community, the curtsey, is modified and nullified when it becomes "jerking"! The phrase conveys a history of grudging friendliness, of forced spontaneity, of the best in arranged human intercourse soured by individual envy and malice. In *The Watsons* the gracious formal gesture is too often negated, the courtesies are indeed jerking. And the heroine who can exceed conventional refinement by a spontaneous and unconventional act such as asking a little boy to dance with her is the heroine who is best qualified to learn and display true refinement.

"The finest and noblest book of men in war": Frederic Manning's *Her Privates We*

JOHN HENRY RALEIGH

ERNEST HEMINGWAY SAID OF FREDERIC MANNING'S *Her Privates We*:[1] "It is the finest and noblest book of men in war I have ever read. I read it over once a year to remember how things really were so that I will never lie to myself nor to anyone else about them."[2] By this time in his life, 1942, Hemingway was lying to himself at a great rate and had convinced himself that he had been in infantry combat during World War I. So he continued on to say that each year in July, the month in which he got his "big wound," he rereads Manning's novel (which was probably not true either).[3] He is then once more transported back to the ranks before daylight, "waiting there, dry-mouthed, for it to start." Nothing can spoil the praise, however, "finest and noblest." The English military historian Cyril Falls said of the Manning novel, "Here indeed are the authentic British infantry men."[4] Similar tributes could be cited from T. E. Lawrence, E. M. Forster, Arnold Bennett, T. S. Eliot, Ezra Pound, and others. The present essay will discuss *Her Privates We* under three rubrics: its authenticity; its literary and philosophical orientation; and its psychological descriptions of men at war and its speculations on the meaning of World War I.

I

The first thing to be remarked about *Her Privates We* is that it is solidly authentic historically, something that cannot be said of all World War I novels. For example, the soldiers of *Her Privates We* spend a relatively small amount of time in action or under fire. When the novel opens, the first stage of the Battle of the Somme (July and August) is over, and we are given a retrospect in the consciousness of the protagonist, Bourne, describing what it was like to be in that tragic affair (a total of eleven pages). Throughout the whole middle part of the novel, Bourne and his outfit are behind the lines and moving about the French countryside, although they are sometimes under fire. In chapter 12—now it's October—they move up to the front once more and do a tour of duty in the trenches, plus a rest period. The climax and denouement come in the last three chapters, 16, 17, and 18: Bourne and his fellows participate in the Battle of the Ancre—by now it is November. They are back in the trenches and under fire; they go on the attack; and finally in chapter 18 a small group engages in the night raid in which Bourne is killed. This distribution of time that Manning provides for his soldiers appears to approximate the historical reality. For example, Charles Carrington in *A Subaltern's War* says, based on a diary he kept for 1916, that he spent 65 days in the trenches (18 percent of that year); 36 days in supporting positions and under fire (9 percent); 120 days in reserve position (28 percent), 73 days for rest (20 percent); and another 72 days (20 percent) for various contingencies: going to school, in hospital, and so on.[5] As an officer, he got leave every six months (leaves did not come this often for the men). In addition, he noted that he moved 80 times during the year and stayed in any one place only a week or ten days. It is impossible to correlate exactly Carrington's actual experiences to Manning's imaginative recreation of the temporal pace for the men of war of 1916, but I think they are roughly analogous—a relatively small percentage of time in action and under fire, and never very long in any one place.

Again, the rock-bottom reality for the troops of World War I, the only unalloyed virtue, as thousands of testimonies said, was comradeship. Without this (and rum, as many participants also averred) the men could not have carried on. So at the center of the fable of *Her Privates We* are three "pals": Bourne, Shem, and Martlow, all enlisted men in His Majesty's Army. This is "the little platoon," "the band of brothers," the dependables, the ones who would disobey the usual order for an attack, which said that one must disregard fallen comrades and push on with the fighting, and would aid the wounded instead. Just as at the end of the novel, when Shem, wounded, and Martlow, dead, are both forever separated from Bourne, Weeper Smart, a great, grotesque tragicomic creation of Manning's, becomes Bourne's "pal," and volunteers for the night raid only in order to look after Bourne. "'If tha go'st, a'm goin,' he said solemnly."[6] "'A can look after mysen, aye, an' thee too, lad. You leave it to me'"

(242). When Bourne is hit, he shouts at Weeper to go on, but Weeper will not leave his fallen comrade, and carefully carries back on his huge shoulders the dying body of his friend (D.O.A., as it turns out). A. E. Montague, in remarking on the tendency of the British troops to form into small informal units and on the fact that in such small and close relationships no one could escape judgment, said, "They had domesticated the Day of Judgment."[7] Manning said the same thing: "There is an extraordinary veracity in war, which strips man of every conventional covering he has, and leaves him to face a fact as naked and as inexorable as himself" (40). By the same token the death of a pal in an attack can turn the still-living friend into a berserk killer of the enemy, as it does Bourne when he witnesses Martlow fall dead in the mud at Ancre.

Still, if this is the most powerful and binding of the human relations that are forged by war, it is also one of the most fleeting and unenduring, for the simple reason that members of the "little platoon" are always disappearing, by reason of death or wounding or transfer or whatever. So Bourne, when he is parted forever from his two friends, reflects: "They had been three people without a single thing in common; and yet there was no bond stronger than the necessity which bound them together. They had never encroached on each other's independence. If the necessity [i.e., war] had been removed, they would have parted, keeping nothing of each other but a vague memory, grateful enough, though without substance" (232).

The most interesting thing about Manning's trio is that while Bourne is upper-class, and is continually pressured by the officers and the noncoms of his regiment to apply for officer's training, Martlow and Shem (who is Jewish) are lower-class. So while Bourne speaks the King's English (and carries with him Connington's translation of Horace), his friends speak Cockney and other lower-class dialects. Through a reminiscence of Martlow in chapter 18 about his mother and father and his family life we are given a masterful vignette of familial existence of the English urban lower-class. Bourne's background is never fully fleshed out, but at a mail call in chapter 15, Shem receives one letter, Martlow a parcel and a letter, and Bourne gets fourteen letters and parcels (some no doubt from Fortnum and Mason). These facts alone speak volumes. When the regimental chaplain urges Bourne to go for an officer, saying that he would then have friends of his own kind, Bourne responds with a long and interesting analysis of his anomalous relationship to the two Cockneys. The central point of his discourse is that there are two kinds of male bonding: friendship, which requires stable conditions and shared interests, and "comrade-ship," which is forged in desperate circumstances. "I have one or two par-ticular chums, of course; and in some ways, you know, good comradeship takes the place of friendship. It is different; it has its own loyalties and affections; and I am not so sure that it does not rise on occasion to an intensity of feeling which friendship never touches" (79). Again: "No, it is not friendship. The man doesn't matter so much, it is a kind of imper-sonal relation, a kind of enthusiasm in the old sense of the word. Of course one is keyed up, a bit over-wrought. We help each other" (80). And Bourne has other reasons for staying in the ranks: he prefers its anonym-ity; as a man in the ranks one lived in a world of men, full of flexible movement and human interest, while an officer was part of an inflexible and inhuman machine; the men are bound together more closely, and even most strongly by the trivial experiences they have shared. Thus for these reasons and for others, "comradeship" is at the heart of *Her Privates We*, as it is of most English memoirs of the Great War.

As a counterpoint to the theme of "comradeship" Manning intro-duces early on one Miller, a deserter—"he had deserted them" (81). Miller had deserted before the Somme and had been captured at Rouen. This fact introduces one of the leitmotivs of the book, both deadly serious and highly comic, for Miller keeps escaping and being recaptured. Every time he is recaptured, he is exhibited as a coward to the troops, is then incar-cerated, and escapes once again. Once we actually see him, a "degenerate face," "cunning," maybe "insane" (193). We last hear of Miller in the last chapter, and, sure enough, he has escaped once more, his army career now having risen to "heroic proportions." So Sergeant-Major Tozer, a tough, resolute warrior, one of the stalwarts of the company, says: "That bugger deserves to get off" (240). But the supreme irony of the Miller affair is that Miller will probably be alive at the end of the war while Bourne and Martlow, and hundreds of thousands of others, will be dead. Thus after one of the Miller "exhibitions"—the coward shown to the brave and en-during—Bourne speculates on what will probably be Miller's final destiny. He will be sentenced to be shot, but the sentence will be commuted to penal servitude for twenty years. Then the execution of that sentence will be deferred to the end of the war, since men could not be allowed to choose jail as an alternative to military service. Come the peace a general amnesty would be declared that would cover all cases of this kind, "and the tragedy, but for the unspeakable humiliation they had just witnessed, became a farce" (168).

The second great social fact of the British Army is the pervasive existence in it of the well-known English class system, separating the forces
into officers and men. On the basis of the evidence of *Her Privates We* it
would seem that however unfair and unjust was the class system in peacetime, it was a powerful asset in war. The officers considered themselves
responsible for their men and the men looked up to and respected their
officers—that is, the good officers, of which there are quite a few in *Her
Privates We*. This relationship appears also to be no less than the historical
truth. In his *Memoirs of a Fox-Hunting Man*, Siegfried Sassoon remarks on
how many good officers there were—he was one himself—in the British
Army. The existence of many capable and respected officers is, in fact, the
theme of R. C. Sherriffs's essay "The English Public Schools in the War."
Sherriffs explains that after most of the officers of the regular British Army
were killed in 1914, the army had to bring into existence a whole new cadre
of officers and decided that the graduates of the English public schools
would have had inculcated in them just the virtues that would make good
officers. And, according to Sherriffs, this was to be the case; most of them
proved worthy of their trust:

> Without raising the public school boy officers onto a pedestal it can be said with
> certainty that it was they who played the vital part in keeping the men good-
> humored and obedient in the face of their interminable ill treatment and well-nigh
> insufferable ordeals. . . . They won the trust and respect of their men, not merely
> through their willingness to share the physical privations, but through an under-
> standing of their spiritual loneliness.[8]

That is to say, the notions of service and of a sense of responsibility for
those below you, of dedication to the job at hand, no matter how onerous,
that constituted the moral ethos of the public school world did, in fact,
carry over to the field of battle. It should be added that Sherriffs was
himself an officer, a lieutenant in charge of thirty men, and served, among
other engagements, in the terrible carnage in 1917 in the battle called "Passchendaele," yet another instance when in a welter of mud and blood the
English suffered horrendous casualties. Sherriffs himself was wounded at
Passchendaele.

The respect and affection that so many British officers earned from
their men is highlighted by the contrast to World War I documents, fictional or historical, generated by other cultures. There is, for example, the
historical contrast to the French Army, sections of which—we shall never
know how many men were involved—mutinied in 1917. Sherriffs referred

to this and added that there was never a suggestion of rebellion in the British ranks.

It is not that there were no pangs or pains or anomalies in the class relations as dramatized by Manning. For example, one of the less-assured officers, Mr. Rhys, sometimes tries to get in personal touch with the men, but he fails: "Only a very great man can talk on equal terms with those in the lower ranks of life. He [Rhys] was neither sufficiently imaginative, nor sufficiently flexible in character, to succeed" (149). The men respected him but when he spoke of patriotism, sacrifice, duty, they turned away.

Bourne has a sort of reverse class relationship to one of the best officers, Captain Marsden, precisely because of the intricacies of the class system (although Bourne is of Marsden's class in civil life, he is not an officer but a ranker in the army). While the conventions that separated officers from men were relaxed to some extent on active service, they tended to become more rigid between men of the same class if they were of different ranks. Thus Marsden usually speaks to Bourne in a rather cold manner. The little episode dramatizing these anomalies occurs in chapter 17, and is too complex to describe in detail, but there is a misunderstanding between Bourne and Marsden, upon which Sergeant-Major Tozer, one of the pillars of the company, who likes Bourne, tries to intervene on Bourne's behalf, telling a lie in the process. This makes the whole affair even more complicated, socially speaking: two middle-class men in an ambiguous relationship and having a difference of opinion, with a lower-class non-com intervening on behalf of the middle-class man who is a ranker. In any event Captain Marsden finally forces Bourne to go out on a night mission— once more Sergeant-Major Tozer tries, unsuccessfully, to prevent this—in which he will be killed. One might almost say that Bourne dies because of the intricacies, rigidities, and ambiguities of the class system.

Finally, in additional support for the authenticity of *Her Privates We*, there was published in 1983 Lyn Macdonald's *Somme*, a multiple view of that battle from the perspective of the men in the trenches, the whole text being studded with transcripts of descriptions by the men who had actually fought the battle. Macdonald relied not only on published texts, for example, *The History of the 16th Battalion*, but obtained accounts, oral and written, from old soldiers as well. In her bibliography she lists some 320 veterans, with their ranks and regiments, with whom she conversed. She did not use all of these testimonies in her book, naturally, but a rough count of the testimonies she does quote shows a distribution as follows: 10 officers, the highest rank being a major; 31 non-coms, sergeants and corporals; and 35 of the troops, enlisted or conscripts. In other words, the reader is mostly (although there are also quite a few quotations from General Haig's *Diary*) in the consciousness of "her privates we." This convergence between a work of fiction, *Her Privates We*, and a historical work, *Somme*, each detailing the same battle and telling its story from more or less the same perspective and point of view is, I believe, unique; at least, I know nothing else like it. In fact, Macdonald wrote the introduction to the Hogarth Press edition of *Her Privates We*. Macdonald actually talked with or corresponded with a sergeant in the King's Shropshire Light Infantry, the outfit that Manning had enlisted in and had said in a letter was the "finest regiment in the Army,"[9] but the sergeant does not appear in her text.

First, for some differences. Macdonald concentrates on the battle itself and describes only intermittently life in the rear, while much of Manning's novel takes place in the rear. Thus too her cast of characters keeps changing, as the same witnesses could not have participated in all the actions of which the long-drawn-out Somme campaign was composed. Moreover, she has transcribed whatever oral reminiscences she heard, as opposed to written evidences, into upper-class English, while we know that much of that oral testimony from non-coms and privates must have been in Cockney or other dialects. This is one of the real triumphs of Manning's novel, its use of Cockney and other dialects (an example has been given above in the quotes from Weeper Smart). When Cyril Falls said that in *Her Privates We* are the "authentic" British infantrymen, I think he meant that not only was exhibited the admirable "spirit of the troops" of those brave and enduring men but that we hear their "authentic" voices as well. Or as David Jones has put it: as Latin is to the Church, Cockney is to the Army.

Differences aside, we are in the same universe in both works, the fictional and the historical, the salient facts of each being twofold: incredible human hardships and sheer human pain and terror being undergone by men of equally incredible powers of endurance, resilience, and spirit. Manning early in *Her Privates We* put the central antithesis succinctly: "Power is measured by the amount of resistance which it overcomes, and, in the last resort, the moral power of men was greater than any purely material force, which could be brought to bear on it" (10). If anything, the horrors and grisly terrors of *Somme* outweigh, both in substance and number, those of *Her Privates We*, one of the reasons being, of course, that in *Somme* we are constantly in the line of fire. But that is not the only reason. Manning simply does not dwell constantly on suffering, pain, and death, as do many war novels such as Barbusse's *Under Fire*, for the simple reason that this was only a part of the total experience.

One more authentic touch should be mentioned. So far I have been describing human relationships in *Her Privates We*, but as is well known, the denizens of the trenches were not all humans. And the happiest, sleekest, most well-fed, most agile, driest, cleanest, and most free creature in the trenches is a rat, seen by Bourne near the end of the novel:

> [A] rat came hurrying, with a quick dainty movement of its twinkling feet, towards him. Seeing him, it stopped, a few yards from the parapet, its muzzle twitching sensitively, sat up, sleek and well fed, to stroke its whiskers with its forepaws; and then, avoiding the puddles and shell-holes, turned aside in a direction parallel to the trench, not taking a straight path, but picking its way delicately along the ridges, as though to keep his feet dry. (226)

Shortly after this we learn why this "good fellow" is so sleek and well fed. The men are speculating on how long a dead soldier has been dead; the remark is, "No sir, 'e couldn't 'ave been dead long, because the rats 'adn't begun on 'im" (229).

II

Her Privates We is also, along with David Jones's *In Parenthesis*, exceptional among Great War narratives for the depth and scope of its literary and philosophical dimensions and its general cultural sophistication. Even the name "Bourne" has several significances. Literally, it is the name of the town in Lincolnshire where Manning lived at times before and after the war. But it has allegorical and symbolic significance as well. I have emphasized above the generally warm relationships between officers and men, but it was, of course, not all sweetness and light by any means, and Manning-Bourne's heart is always with the men, for the final, ultimate burdens are theirs. He once speaks of "the chain of responsibility" of the British Army, which means that "all responsibility for the errors of their superior officers, is *borne* [emphasis added] eventually by private soldiers in the ranks" (166). Obviously too "Bourne" means, in the modern sense of the word, a stream, a goal, a destination. And finally that destination is death: "The undiscovered country, from whose bourn / No traveler returns" (*Hamlet* III.i).

As the title indicates, *Her Privates We* is permeated with Shakespeare, the two different titles—*The Middle Parts of Fortune* and *Her Privates We*—being taken from the well-known interchange between Hamlet and

Rosencrantz and Guildenstern, with its sexual punning about the unreli-
ability of that strumpet, Fortune. Each of the eighteen chapters has a
Shakespearean epigraph, and the wheel of the meaning of the novel, introduced by its two titles, comes full circle in chapter 18 (in which Bourne is
killed) where the Shakespearean epigraph is: "Fortune? O, most true; she
is a strumpet," all this prepared for by the well-known Shakespearean
phrases prefacing chapter 1: "By my troth, I care not; a man can die but
once, we owe God a death . . . and let it go which way it will, he that dies
this year is quit for the next" (Feeble in *Henry IV, Part Two* III.ii). I shall
confine myself to a few general observations about the epigraphs. First,
the quotes are not all as obvious as the ones I have so far cited, and,
obviously, Manning did not take his Shakespeare from Bartlett but drew
on a wide and deep acquaintance with the plays. Nor are they all serious
and solemn. For example, chapter 3, which is to describe a drinking bout,
is introduced by Iago (*Othello* II.iii.2) telling Cassio that an Englishman
can drink any Dane or Dutchman or German under the table. Chapter 9,
when Bourne translates for a young French woman a love letter written to
her in English by an English soldier, is prefaced by Henry V speaking to
Kate: "but thy speaking of my tongue, and I thine, most truly falsely, must
needs be granted to be much at one" (*Henry V* V.ii). On the other hand,
some of the Shakespearean quotations are soul-chilling enough. Chapter 16, when Bourne and his cohorts go into action at Ancre, is prefaced
by Williams speaking to Bates and King Henry on the eve of battle: "We
see yonder the beginning of the day, but I think we shall never see the end
of it. . . . I am afeard there are few die well that die in a battle" (*Henry V*
IV.i).

In their totality, the quotes come from the plays as follows: *Henry V*
(5); *Henry IV, Part Two* (3); *King Lear* (2); *Antony and Cleopatra* (2);
Hamlet (2, plus the two titles); *Henry IV, Part One* (1); *Othello* (1); *As You
Like It* (1—Rosalind is speaking); and *Julius Caesar* (1). Suffice it to say
that many Shakespearean warriors are heard to speak, from a monarch
warrior, Henry V, to officers such as Iago and Falstaff, to foot soldiers
such as Feeble and Williams.

It should be added that all this Shakespeareanizing in *Her Privates We*
is not at all malapropos or inauthentic for the British Army in World War
I. In *The Great War and Modern Memory* Paul Fussell cites two British
soldiers at the Somme who, fearful of what they faced, recited speeches
from *Henry V*; he also speaks of "the unparalleled literariness of all ranks
who fought the Great War."[10] Indeed, the same penchant hung on in

World War II, and Eric Larrabee in *Commander in Chief* tells of British officers quoting *Henry V* to each other on D-Day:

> He that outlives this day, and comes home safe,
> Will stand a-tiptoe when this day is named.
>
> (*Henry V* IV.iii) [11]

Manning's relationship to modern literature and its characteristic techniques is muted but real. For example, the twentieth-century literary habit of saturating one's work with symbols, à la *The Wasteland* and *Ulysses*, is followed temperately by Manning. Thus he designated as the proper symbols of modern war mules, "grotesque, stubborn, vindictive animals" (60). It was true that during the Great War the mule stood up much better under battlefield conditions than did the more gentle and sensitive horse. Again during a "prick-inspection," with pants dropped, Bourne looks down at his boots and thinks that if the sword is the symbol of battle, boots are the symbol of war, and being saturated in the King James Bible he thinks of the Biblical phrase "the warrior's boots that stamped in the tumult" (142). Choosing boots as the proper symbol for World War I has also much justification. The army had only a few sizes and they were almost never a proper fit for any individual. The long marches meant aching, blistered, bloody feet, and one of the first concerns of a good officer was to inspect the feet of his men and try to ameliorate their often pitiful state. In *Memoirs of an Infantry Officer*, Sassoon said that good boots were your best friend because "your feet were your fortune."

The philosophy or outlook or belief of the man who composed *Her Privates We* is difficult to penetrate and formulate because he was so skeptical and so widely read in both ancient and modern literature, and was so eclectic in his choice of mentors. Nevertheless, he did make certain statements about beliefs and philosophies over his career as a whole which point in certain directions. About Christianity he once said in a letter from the front: "If I were an orthodox Christian this war would have shattered my belief in Christianity; but being a Christian to whom 'Christianity' is a merely formal symbol, the war does not affect the question for me." [12] Perhaps his most comprehensive statement on what he "believed" was made in the Preface to his *Scenes and Portraits*:

There are in reality only two religions on this little planet and they perhaps begin and end with man. They are: the religion of the humble folk, whose life is a daily communion with natural forces, and a bending to them; and the religion of men like Protagoras, Lucretius, and Montaigne, a religion of doubt, of tolerance, of

agnosticism. Between these two poles is nothing but a dreary formalism, Pharisa-
ism, "perplexed subtleties about Instants, Formalities, Quiddities, and Relations,"
all that bewildering of brains which comes from being shut up in a narrow system,
like an invalid in a poisoned and stifling room.[13]

He goes on to say that all the world's greatest men have had this quality
of double-mindedness and sets up Epicureanism as an example of that
quality: counseling a temperate pleasure and yet condemning the whole
of life as being merely the pursuit of an unattainable desire; reconciling us
to life by the prospect of death and reconciling us to death by showing us
the vain efforts and innumerable vexations of life. Epicureanism has often
been called a hedonism close to asceticism.

I do not have a single philosopher or outlook to propose as Manning's
teacher, since there is such an abundance of them, but I can suggest one
ancient outlook that was especially appealing to him. When it is remembered that most of what we know about Epicureanism comes from Lucretius (mentioned in the above quote from Manning) and that then, above
once more, Manning names Epicureanism as an example of the "double-
mindedness" he wants in thinkers, I do not think it amiss or improbable
to suggest Epicurus as a congenial philosopher for Manning. This proposition is further enhanced by the fact that when Peter Davis in 1926 issued
the Charlton [1619–1707] translation of what is called *Epicurus' Morals*, it
was Manning who wrote a complex and sympathetic introduction.

Further, there were certain basic cultural and historical similarities between Lucretius's time (94–55 B.C.) and the time of Frederic Manning,
the late nineteenth and early twentieth period in modern European history. Some of them are spelled out by Cyril Bailey in the Introduction to
his translation, *Lucretius on the Nature of Things*. Lucretius was an Epicurean of the last century B.C. living in a period of disturbances and disso-
lution, intellectually, socially, and politically. The Republican regime was
breaking down, with its system of morals and beliefs, and the old Roman
religion had lost its hold. The only thing left was a sense of insecurity:
fear of the gods and fear of death. Among the educated a severe skepticism prevailed, and the only tenable outlooks were the Stoic and the
Epicurean.[14]

Once more, as with the Shakespearean epigraphs, there is hardly time
or space to do a complete comparison between Epicureanism and the outlook of Frederic Manning. Manning himself has already provided some
reason, as stated above, for his attraction to Epicurus: he was an apostle
of doubt, tolerance, and agnosticism, and he was "double-minded." There

are a few other aspects of Epicureanism that would have appealed to
Manning. Epicurus taught that we should not enter into public life or
hold office (just as Bourne resists becoming an officer). He also held that
friendships were one of the highest felicities of human life although, at the
same time (always double-minded) one must protect one's independence.
Epicurus said: "*He hath well lived, who hath well concealed himself.*" [15] This
combination of valuing, even treasuring, friendship and yet maintaining a
firm private self is not an inaccurate description of Bourne.

Epicurus, of course, had many suggested consolations for the great
ills of human life, for pain, and above all for death, which he considered
the greatest fear inflicted on human kind. How helpful these consolations
would have been to men on the Western Front from 1914–1918 is impossible to estimate. But the rhythms of suffering in *Her Privates We* roughly
approximate what Epicurus said of pain: "*No pain is either Intolerable, or
Perpetual*; because, if it be long, it must be light; if great, short" (Charlton
trans., 81). On death he said, among many other things:

We said, that *Death* (accounted the King of Terrors, and most horrid of all Evils)
doth nothing concern us, because, while we are, Death is not, and when Death is, we
are not; so that he, who profoundly considers the matter, will soon conclude that
Death doth concern neither the Living, nor the Dead; not the living, because it
toucheth them not, not the Dead, because they are not. (Charlton trans., 76)

In his introduction to the Charlton translation of Lucretius, Manning
deals with an Epicurean view of human character and the insoluble conun-
drum of fate and free will. First, Manning says, "Character is invariable,
and action only serves to elicit its true nature" (Charlton trans., xxi). Manning then goes on to point out some of the paradoxes and ambiguities of
personal memories. In other words, each human character is a "given,"
reveals itself by its actions, and has many mysteries, of which memory is
one. So in *Her Privates We* Manning has Bourne think: "It is a little curious to reflect that while each man is a mystery to himself, he is an open
book to others; the reason being, perhaps, that he sees in himself the per-
plexities and torment of the mental processes out of which action issues,
and they see in him only the simple and indivisible act itself" (39). This
same paradox about human nature is put in another way about Bourne
himself by Captain Malet, one of the most perceptive characters in the
novel. Talking to the redoubtable Sergeant-Major Tozer, Malet says:
"[H]e's [Bourne] a queer chap. . . . You needn't make things easy for
Bourne, you know; in fact, it would be better if you put him through it a
bit. He looks at a question upside down and inside out, and then in the

long run he does just what an ordinary sensible man would do. Keep him at it" (91). Elsewhere it is said of Bourne that he was one of those men who will try to cross a bridge before he comes to it. As for fate and free will, Epicurus's universe is deterministic and atomistic, but the atoms are allowed a "swerve" that constitutes a break in the absolute determinism of the system, allowing for chance and for man's exercise of choice and freedom; we must turn the "edge of our wit" against Fate as necessity. Manning also discusses this aspect of Epicurus's thought. I shall not attempt to formulate his full elaboration of it but rather present his conclusions: "In self-consciousness we have the clear and evident proof of our existence, and the guarantee of our freedom. . . . Our freedom is in direct proportion to the degree of consciousness possessed by us" (xxxv). Applying this line of reasoning to *Her Privates We*, we find that Bourne is the most "free" of the characters since his is the highest degree of consciousness although some of the admired officers, such as Captain Malet, might well have equaled Bourne in this respect but we are never let inside their heads.

Finally, concerning Epicureanism in Manning's novel, Cyril Bailey, in his Introduction to Lucretius, argued that Lucretius somewhat obscured Epicurus's thought and did not make clear what was the true sustaining argument: "The whole system is really knit together by the single principle of the certainty of sensation" (Bailey, 21). That is to say, "sensation is true," "I know what I feel." So Manning states, when Bourne and the others are trying to sleep on their first night out of action after the Somme, their minds overwhelmed by remembered horrors, that their senses remained alert, intact, responsive: "The senses certainly have, in some measure, an independent activity of their own, and remain vigilant even in the mind's eclipse" (6).

That other religion mentioned in the Preface to *Scenes and Portraits*, that of the humble folk, in a "daily communion with natural forces, and a bending to them," also appears in *Her Privates We*. Implicitly, this is certainly the "religion" of the bulk of the foot soldiers. It is also, as Manning explicitly says, the religion of the French civilians, especially the peasants, who appear and reappear in *Her Privates We*, and to whom the war seemed "as natural and inevitable as a flood or an earthquake" (108). Even close to the line the peasants would plow, sow, and wait for their harvest, taking the chance that battle might overflow their fields and ruin their crops, just as in peacetime a wet season or a drought could do.

Thus the two "religions" of the universe of *Her Privates We* are the bending to an inexorable Fate and Necessity and an attempting to rise

above them, at least partially, by the exercise of a high and full consciousness. It is in the soldiers in action that the two "religions" converge.
Bourne floundering in the viscous mud in the attack at Ancre is described
as "at once the most abject and most exalted of God's creatures" (215).

III

The two most interesting aspects of *Her Privates We* are the running
descriptions of the psychology of men in war and the various speculations
by Bourne-Manning on the meaning of the Great War and, by extension,
on life itself, for the two—war and life—are not seen as antithetical but as
complementary.

Regarding the psychology first, I would not wish to give the impression that the horrors and terrors of the warfare on the Western front are
muted in any way in *Her Privates We*, although so far, I've not mentioned
them much. The whole last part, the moving up to the front for the attack
at Ancre, in the mud and the cold of October and November 1916, with
German shells raining down, is as harrowing as anything that has been
written on the subject, all building up to the moment of sheer terror just
before the take-off: "Bourne's fit of shakiness increased, until he set his
teeth to prevent them chattering in his head; and after a deep, gasping
breath, almost like a sob, he seemed to recover to some extent. Fear
poisoned the very blood. . . . Some men moaned; or even sobbed a little,
but unconsciously, and as though they struggled to throw off an intolerable burden of oppression" (212). This is the emotional climax of the
book—but equally interesting, from a psychological point of view, are
the running descriptions of the minds of the men in the book as a whole.
Much has already been said about the significance of "comradeship"
and the relations between officers and men. These two aspects are the
enduring psychological strains that run from first to last. But, of course,
within these enduring confines, the emotions of individual men are like
kaleidoscopes, volatile in the extreme, as befits an extreme situation.
Manning once said in a letter that being in battle was like gambling with
God (of which he did not disapprove, and he had elsewhere rejected
Pascal's "Wager"): "Well, it is good that a man should throw dice with
God once in his life."[16] The most interesting stretch of psychological
analysis comes, as might be expected, near the climax, the great variety
of moods and feelings, the contradictions, the ambiguities in the minds
of the men as they are preparing for the Ancre assault, beginning in

chapter 14 and continuing on to the moment of all-consuming fear, quoted above, just before they launch themselves into the mud. This sequence is extraordinarily complex; and one can only point out some of its salient features.

First, there is the sense of being at the disposal of an inscrutable power that used men for its own purposes and was utterly indifferent to them as individuals. This was the most "tragic" element of their situation. (Yet, as will be pointed out below, in Manning's speculations on the meaning of war, that same "inscrutable" power is not finally seen as completely alien to them either.) This same feeling of helplessness generated another sense, namely, that they are involved in a "mystery," (this perhaps the key word in the whole book) and that that mystery encompasses both themselves and that inscrutable power. In such an extreme situation all ordinary resentments against officers, against authority, meant very little and fell away from them. As they got deeper and deeper into the cold and mud of the bleak October-November weather, the men seemed to lose a great deal of their individuality—their characters, even their faces, appeared to become more uniform. They worked better, the work seeming to take some of the strain off their minds, the strain of waiting.

At the same time each man had become supremely aware of his own personality as of something very hard and sharply defined against the background of his fellows, who had now become generalized as simply "the others." They all sought, inwardly, in a terrible struggle, to maintain the coherence of their own psyches—slippery affairs at best, crumbling edifices at worst—and to affirm their own wills in the face of death, all this in an aloneness never before experienced. But one cannot do justice to Manning's presentation of this state of mind by paraphrase; so I shall quote this passage, one of the most important in the book, in full:

The mystery of his own being increased for him enormously; and he had to explore the doubtful darkness alone, finding a foothold here, a handhold there, grasping one support after another and relinquishing it when it yielded, crumbling; the sudden menace of ruin, as it slid into the unsubstantial past, calling forth another effort, to gain another precarious respite. If a man could not be certain of himself, he could be certain of nothing. The problem which confronted them all equally, though some were unable or unwilling to define it, did not concern death so much as the affirmation of their own will in the face of death; and once the nature of the problem was clearly stated, they realized its solution was continuous, and could never be final. Death set a limit to a continuance of one factor in the problem, and peace to that of another; but neither of them really affected the nature of the problem itself. (184)

Of courage, Manning says, they had enough to share with others but were very uncertain of their own. It is in this sequence that Manning juxtaposes the supreme coward, Miller, and the supreme epitome of courage, Weeper Smart. Miller has been exhibited, with his "degenerate face," and Manning switches immediately to Weeper. No one could have had a greater horror and dread of war than Weeper; it was a continuous misery to him and yet he endured it and could always be depended upon. It is said, indeed, that Weeper faced the facts of war with a directness that almost nobody else, including Bourne, could muster, for they refused to think of it except when actually involved in battle; whereas Weeper's imagination was never at rest. But that same imagination, thinks Bourne, was his very strength, for it left him with no illusions:

The unbounded pity he felt for himself did, in spite of his envious and embittered nature, extend to Others. Glazier was the kind of person who killed automatically, without either premeditation or remorse, but Weeper was a very different type. He dreaded the thought of killing, and was haunted by the memory of it; and yet there was a kind of fatalism in him now, as though he were the instrument of justice, prepared for any gruesome business confronting him. (201)

Through it all the men, rude and brutal as many were, are helpful to one another; they "comforted, encouraged, and reconciled each other to fate, with a tenderness and tact which was more moving than anything in life" (205). Then, counteracting all of this, there was a collective sense of actual relief that the inexorable hour was approaching—the very skin on their faces seemed shinier and tighter and their eyes burned with a hard brightness. But, at the same time, the feeling of aloneness of each man deepened and expanded. They could depend on nobody but themselves, and yet they remained uncertain of how much they could depend on themselves. In the last analysis, according to Manning, it all came down to an exceedingly precarious balancing act: "the strength of one's hope strove to equal the despair which oppressed it; one's determination could only be measured by the terrors and difficulties it overcame. All the mean, peddling standards of ordinary life vanished in the collision of these warring opposites. Between them one could only attempt to maintain an equilibrium which every instant disturbed and made unstable" (214). Shortly after this description, the men go on the attack.

In no other novel of war, from Scott, Stendhal, and Tolstoy on down, has there been such a complex, subtle, extensive analysis of the whirlwinds of emotions and thoughts that sweep through the minds of men faced with the prospect, almost the certainty, that death or mutilation or wounding is soon to be their lot. How and why the generation of 1914 to 1918 was able to "carry on" in the face of what they were called upon to endure will probably always remain, in the last analysis, a mystery, but Manning came as close to the heart of that mystery as anyone. Seldom has the meaning of the phrase "precarious balance" been so excruciatingly dramatized. At another place Manning makes the same point in another way, namely, that the older men in the ranks had ceased to hope for themselves but yet were undefeated, which is also what Graves had said of the English soldier in *Goodbye to All That*.

In his general outlook on the army and the war Manning-Bourne exhibits that same "double-mindedness" that Manning had praised in his favorite philosophers. On the one hand, Bourne is the "grunt," the "sweat," the virtually anonymous ranker, who bears the real burdens and who is often the victim of mistakes made by the higher-ups: ". . . there are precious few mistakes made in the army that are not ultimately laid on the shoulders of the men" (95); this point of view usually is accompanied by the usual complaints about "chateaux generals" "planning" it all. Yet in *Her Privates We* Bourne, while sharing all the gripes of the men, also defends the planners. During a gripe session in chapter 12, Bourne, who has been mostly silent, suddenly speaks up on behalf of the brass-hats: they are not "inhuman"; they have to draw up a plan, usually from scrappy information; they know very well that many things can go wrong—"The original plan is no more than a kind of map" (155).

Again, while Bourne sees officerdom as a kind of inhuman machine, at the same time he sees the functioning of the whole gigantic apparatus, from top to bottom, as always shading into a series of personality clashes: "sometimes what is only the inexorable functioning of the machine, takes on the character of a duel between opposed personalities; while the mechanical action, having attained its object, ends, the other is more lasting" (68). Much of the novel is taken up with the sheer waste of war: the mistakes that cost lives; the impossible attacks on impregnable positions; the sheer chanciness of the whole affair (most World War I memoirs are haunted by the freaks of happenstance); and looming over it all, the great question of whether there is any discernible purpose to it all. Yet Manning creates a monologue for Sergeant Tozer, which Bourne listens to sympathetically, whose burden is that the war is not "a bloody waste":

You know, to my way o' thinking some of us'ns 'ave a dam' sight more religion than some o' the parsons who preach at us. We're willing to take a chance, we are. 'Uman nature's 'uman nature, an' you may be right or you may be wrong, but if you bloody well think you're right, you may as well get on with it. What does it matter if y'are killed? You've got to die some day. (76)

In short many different voices and points of view are given a sympathetic hearing in *Her Privates We*, as contrasted to the obsessive single-mindedness of most World War I novels, that is, that "war is hell," a proposition that no one would contest or disagree with.

As for the meaning of the total experience of the Great War, Manning is, on one side of his complicated mind, expressly at one with so many of the novelists and memorialists of the Great War in averring that the war had become like some enormous, inhuman machine that nobody could either understand or control; that for the participants it has become a universe in itself that wiped out all one's previous experiences; that it would go on forever; and that the common soldier had not the slightest idea of what was really happening (in "The English Public Schools in the War" Sherriffs said that the officers in the trenches were never told anything either). Thus Bourne:

Bourne looked at his newspaper, in the hope of learning something about the war, but apart from a few colourless details from the French front there was nothing; no one knew anything about it; it was like one of the blind forces of nature; one could not control it, one could not comprehend it, and one could not predict its course from hour to hour. The spirit of the troops was excellent, the possibility of defeat was incredible; but to calculate the duration of the conflict was quite beyond the resources of the human mind. (42)

Blunden and Graves had both said in their memoirs that to the men and themselves the war appeared to be endless but that they believed when it did end it would end in an Allied victory.

But where Manning parts company with many of the other fictionalists and memorialists it is to insist from first to last on the fact that the war is an expression of, a creation of, human nature itself. In his "Prefatory Note" to *Her Privates We* Manning declared: "War is waged by men; not by beasts, or by gods. It is a peculiarly human activity. To call it a crime against mankind is to miss at least half of its significance; it is also the punishment of a crime." Again he says that there is "nothing in war which is not in human nature," but the violence and passions of men in the aggregate do finally become an impersonal force, which no one controls or understands—it can only be endured (108–9). Yet at the same time war was always, in one of its aspects, *you*: "A man might rave against war; but war, from among its myriad faces, could always turn towards him one, which was his own" (182).

It is difficult to sum up simply and concisely just what Manning did think was the meaning of the war. I have already indicated one bifurcation: war was an expression of human nature and you could always discern your own face among the myriad of faces that war showed forth. Yet, looked at from another angle, it was a great thing, an uncontrollable, incalculable force. But a third point of view maintained that war was different only in degree, not in kind, from peacetime existence, and the soldier and the saint shared the same perspective: "the soldier also, as well as the saint, might write his *tractate de contemptu mundi*, and differ from him only in the angle and spirit from which he surveyed the same bleak reality" (76).

So what does one believe when one is inclined, like Manning, to a religion of doubt, of tolerance, of agnosticism, of double-mindedness? The answer is: not in much, save in the most important thing of all, the power, resilience, and enduringness of the human spirit. Specifically, Manning believed, in a phrase (his own), that "Life was a hazard enveloped in mystery" (76), and he also believed that this same description held for war as well, which was life heightened to the *n*th degree, an opinion that was shared by many of the other participants of the Great War. The key word for Manning in these matters, and for *Her Privates We*, is the word "mystery," which resounds throughout the novel: "There was no man of them unaware of the mystery which encompassed him, for he was a part of it; he could neither separate himself entirely from it, nor identify himself with it completely" (182). The human condition constituted a supreme aloneness whose outer edges both within, in oneself (the subjective world) and without, in the universe itself (the objective world) verged into, disappeared into—mystery. Just before the attack the men's state of mind is described as follows: "And then, one by one, they realized that each must go alone, and that each of them was alone with himself, helping the others perhaps, but looking at them with strange eyes, while the world became unreal and empty, and they moved in a mystery, where no help was" (209–10). Of the loneliness of the field of battle Richard Holmes in *Acts of War* quotes S. L. Marshall: "The battlefield is cold. It is the lonesomest place which men share together."[17] Elsewhere Holmes speaks of the modern battlefield as a place of "emptiness, puzzlement and disorganization" (67).

Thus each man is somewhat of a mystery to himself and somewhat of a mystery to others: we all appear to have a "secret" of some kind, but nobody knows what it is, including ourselves.

At the very end of the novel Sergeant-Major Tozer, one of Manning's real spokesmen and the very epitome of enduringness, since he is one of the few survivors, both physically and spiritually, and because he remains undaunted, looks at the dead Bourne, whom he liked and thought would have made a good officer, and muses: "There was a bit of a mystery about him; but then, when you come to think about it, there's a bit of a mystery about all of us" (247). Then he looks at the surviving men who lift their faces and look at him "with patient, almost animal eyes." Finally, as the German shells begin to rain down in retaliation for the night raid, the men bow their heads once more (the last sentence in the book): "They sat there silently; each man keeping his own secret."

Travelling Theory Reconsidered

EDWARD W. SAID

IN AN ESSAY ("TRAVELLING THEORY") WRITTEN several years ago I discussed the ways in which theories sometimes "travel" to other times and situations, in the process of which they lose some of their original power and rebelliousness. The example I used was Georg Lukács's theory of reification, which is fully explained in the famous fourth chapter of his masterpiece, *History and Class Consciousness*. Underlying my analysis was a common enough bias that, even though I tried to guard against and mitigate its influence, remains in the essay. This bias can be put simply as follows: the first time a human experience is recorded and then given a theoretical formulation its force comes from being directly connected to and organically provoked by real historical circumstances. Later versions of the theory cannot replicate its original power; because the situation has quieted down and changed, the theory is degraded and subdued, made into a relatively tame academic substitute for the real thing, whose purpose in the work I analyzed was political change.

As a revolutionary in early twentieth-century Hungary, Lukács was a participant in the dramatic social upheavals that in his work he linked to the whole social deformation of alienation, the radical separation of object and subject, the atomization of human life under bourgeois capitalism. To resolve the crisis represented by these things Lukács spoke about "the viewpoint of the proletariat," a dynamic theoretical reconciliation of subject with object that was enabled by getting beyond fragmentation and imagining a revolutionary vision of "totality." *History and Class Consciousness* is full of the agony of life in a brutally capitalist society: the way in which every human relationship and impulse is compelled into "alienated" labor, the bewildering rule of facts and figures with no bonds between

people except those of the cash nexus, the loss of perspective, the fragmentation of every experience into saleable commodities, the absence of any
image of community or wholeness. When he comes to the remedy for such
diminishments and deprivations Lukács presses into service a Marxism
that is principally the result of an alteration of consciousness. To be conscious of how widespread is reification—how everything is turned into a
"thing"—is for the first time to be aware of the *general* problem of life
under capitalism, and for the first time to be conscious of the class of
individuals, the proletariat, who are capitalism's most numerous victims.
Only in this way can subjectivity understand its objective situation, and
this in turn makes possible an understanding of what kept subject and
object apart, and how they can be rejoined.

   The point I made about all this was that when they were picked up by
late European students and readers of Lukács (Lucien Goldmann in Paris,
Raymond Williams in Cambridge) the ideas of this theory had shed their
insurrectionary force, had been tamed and domesticated somewhat, and
became considerably less dramatic in their application and gist. What
seemed almost inevitable was that when theories travelled and were used
elsewhere they ironically acquired the prestige and authority of age, perhaps even becoming a kind of dogmatic orthodoxy. In the setting provided by revolutionary Budapest, Lukács's theory of the subject-object
split and of reification was actually an inducement to insurrectionary action, with the hope that a proletarian perspective in his highly eccentric
view of it would see "reality" as eminently changeable because largely a
matter of perspective. His later readers regarded the theory as essentially
an interpretive device, which is not to take away from their work some
considerable and even very brilliant achievements.

   What now seems to me incomplete and inadequate in such an account
of Lukács's theory and its subsequent travels is that I stressed the reconciliatory and resolvable aspects of his diagnosis. Those who borrowed from
Lukács—and for that matter Lukács himself—saw in the reifications imposed epistemologically on the split between subject and object something
that could be remedied. For such a view Lukács of course was indebted to
Marx and Hegel before him, in whose theories the dialectic between opposed factors was routinely to result in synthesis, resolution, transcendence, or *Aufhebung*. Lukács's particular elaboration (some would say im-
provement) on the Hegelian and Marxian dialectic was to stress both the
extraordinarily widespread infection of all of human life by reification—
from the family to professional pursuits, psychology, and moral concerns—

as well as the almost aesthetic character of the reconciliation or healing process by which what was split asunder could be rejoined.

In this perhaps more comforting phase of the theory the work of several recent Lukács scholars, chief among them Michael Löwy,[1] is useful. They have shown the powerful influence on the young Lukács, the romantic anticapitalist, of Dostoevsky and Kierkegaard, whose explorations of modern angst found so devastatingly thorough and analytic a realization not only in *History and Class Consciousness* but also in his earlier treatises, *Soul and Form* and *Theory of the Novel*. But, it can be argued, so too can the Kierkegaardian and Dostoevskian influences be found in Lukács's specifically Marxist resolution, or even redemption. As contained in subject-object reconciliation within the largely unreal, projected, or "putative" category of "totality," Lukács's leap from present misery to future healing recapitulates (if it does not actually repeat) the great nineteenth-century irrationalists' leaps of faith.

But what if some of Lukács's readers, totally influenced by his description of reification and the subject-object impasse, did not accept the reconciliatory denouement of his theory, and indeed deliberately, programmatically, intransigently refused it? Would this not be an alternative mode of travelling theory, one that actually developed *away* from its original formulation, but instead of becoming domesticated in the terms enabled by Lukács's desire for respite and resolution, flames out, so to speak, restates and reaffirms its own inherent tensions by moving to another site? Is this different kind of dislocation so powerful as retrospectively to undermine Lukács's reconciliatory gesture when he settles the subject-object tensions into what he calls "the standpoint of the proletariat?" Might we then not call this surprising later development an instance of "transgressive theory," in the sense that it crosses over from and challenges the notion of a theory that begins with fierce contradiction and ends up promising a form of redemption?

I

Let us return briefly to the early Lukács. In the principally aesthetic works that anticipate *History and Class Consciousness* (1923) he brilliantly examines the relationship between different aesthetic forms on the one hand, and the concrete historical or existential experience from which they derive and to which they are a response. The most famous of these early works is *Theory of the Novel* (1920), premised on the notion that in a world abandoned by God the novel embodies the trajectory of an epic whose hero is either demonic or mad, whose constitutive element is a temporality basically disappointing and demystifying, and whose representative status as the art form of modernity is based on its tremendous constitutive ironies, the irony of "errant souls [adventuring] in an inessential, empty reality," or that of speaking "of past gods and gods . . . to come" but never of what is present, or "the irony [which] has to seek the only world that is adequate to it along the *via dolorosa* of interiority but is doomed never to find it there."[2]

Before he becomes a Marxist, therefore, Lukács's overpowering sense of the disjunctions of modernity (which in his *Logos* essay of 1917 he abstracted into "the subject-object relationship") led him to regard the aesthetic as a site where their contradictions are manageable, and even pleasurable. For this view he is indebted to both Kant and Schiller, although his inflection of the thesis is largely original. Each art form, he says, is itself in a sense the incarnation of a particular phase in the subject-object relationship. The essay, for example, is about heralding a resolution but never giving it; the tragedy is the fatal clash between subjects, and so forth. That the novel has a special privilege in modernity is underscored by its scope, its hero, and (although Lukács never actually says this) by the fact that theoretical discourse (such as his) can express and by its sheer complexity represent the form's quintessential ironies. The transformation in Lukács's politics that occurs after *Theory of the Novel* and in *History and Class Consciousness* is that Marxism, as borne and reflected in "the class consciousness of the proletariat," is explicitly revealed to be the theoretical discourse resolving the subject-object relationship.

Nevertheless Lukács actually says that that resolution is almost by nature postponed and thus hasn't happened yet. There is an unwonted certainty in his accents that, it must be said immediately, supplies his later work with its gruffly dogmatic authority and assertiveness. Clearly, however, not every reader of Lukács went as far in *that* direction, as the dogged stubbornness of Adorno quite plainly shows. Adorno, I believe, is virtually unthinkable without the majestic philosophical beacon provided by *History and Class Consciousness*, but he is also unthinkable without his own great resistance to its triumphalism and implied transcendence. If for Lukács the subject-object relationship, the fragmentation and lostness, the ironic perspectivism of modernity were supremely discerned, embodied, and consummated in *narrative* forms (the rewritten epics both of the novel and the proletariat's class consciousness), for Adorno that particular choice was, he said in a famous anti-Lukács essay, a kind of false reconciliation under duress. Much more typical, more in keeping with the irremediably "fallen" character of modernity was "new" music, which, for Adorno, was Schoenberg, Berg, and Webern, *not* Stravinsky and Bartók.

II

Philosophie der neuen Musik (1948) is a quite spectacular instance of a travelling theory gone tougher, harder, more recalcitrant. In the first place its language is a good deal more difficult to decode even than Lukács's, which in the reification essay of *History and Class Consciousness* had already had a programmatically unattractive density and philosophical obscurity to it. Lukács's choice of the history of classical philosophy—here too the *narrative* of increasing desperation and abstraction was an illustration of subject-object tension unrelieved by reconciliation—was meant to show how deeply alienation had penetrated, and therefore where, in its most abtruse version, it could be analyzed as a pure symptom of the overall *anomie* of modern life. Adorno goes a step further. Modern music, he says, is so marginal, so rarefied, so special an expression as to represent a total rejection of society and any of its palliatives. This is why Schoenberg is such a heroic figure to Adorno. No longer is the composer a figure like Beethoven, who stands for the newly triumphant bourgeoisie, or like Wagner, whose sorcererlike art camouflages the irreconcilability between the aesthetic and the commercial. The twentieth-century composer stands outside tonality itself, proclaiming an art of so totally, irrecusably rebarbative a mode as to reject listeners altogether. Why? Because according to Schoenberg as described by Adorno "the middle road . . . is the only one which does not lead to Rome."[3]

For indeed the subject-object compromise enacted by Lukács does resemble a middle-of-the-road synthesis; whereas Schoenberg's twelve-tone theory was based upon and, more definitively than any other language, reasserted the impossibility of synthesis. Its premise was dissonance, the subject-object impasse raised to the level of an uncompromisable principle, "forced into complete isolation during the final stage of industrialism" (6). Standing apart from society with a uniquely brooding severity and a remorseless self-control, the new music's loneliness pitilessly showed how all other art had become kitsch, other music ruled by "the omni-present hit tune," "false interpretations and stereotyped audience reaction patterns." These, Adorno said sternly, needed to "be destroyed."

Any illusions that the tonality rejected by Schoenberg was somehow natural are rejected: according to Adorno, tonality corresponds to "the closed and exclusive system [of] mercantile society," music submitting to the demands of trade, consumerism, administration. Not for nothing then in a later essay did Adorno attack Toscanini as the *maestro* of conventional music, with its limitless reproducibility, inauthentic perfection, and heartless rhythms contained in the conductor's ironlike dominance and precision.

For Lukács the atomized individual consciousness in surveying its alienation from the product of its own labor desired a kind of healing unity; this was afforded it by "class consciousness," made tenuous, it is true, because, in Lukács's rather circumspect description, consciousness was not empirical or actually and immediately experienceable but "imputable" (*zugerechnetes*). Such a deferral of the clubby gregariousness normally associated with class feeling undercuts the "vulgar Marxism" that Lukács was so polemically energetic in trying to discredit. But it also allowed him to reharness the aesthetic powers of imagination and projection that had been central to his work before he became a Marxist. "Imputable consciousness" was a daring composite made up not only of what was later to be called Marxist humanism, but in addition borrowing from Schiller's play instinct, Kant's aesthetic realm and Hans Vaihinger's *als ob*. In all, then, it held a good deal of optimism and even enthusiasm for the promised reconnection of the subject with itself, other subjects, and objects.

None of this is permitted by Adorno in his stirringly bleak account of Schoenberg's emergence and rather repellent triumph. Instead of social relevance Schoenberg's aesthetic chooses irrelevance; instead of amiability the choice is intransigence; instead of antinomian problematics being overcome (a central notion in Lukács's history of classical philosophy) they are vindicated; instead of class consciousness there is the monad; instead of positive thinking there is "definitive negation"

In the process of pursuing its own inner logic, music is transformed more and more from something significant into something obscure—even to itself. No music today, for example, could possibly speak in the accents of "reward." Not only has the mere idea of humanity, or of a better world no longer any sway over mankind—though it is precisely this which lies at the heart of Beethoven's opera [*Fidelio*]. Rather the strictness of musical structure, wherein alone music can assert itself against the ubiquity of commercialism, has hardened music to the point that it is no longer affected by those external factors which caused absolute music to become what it is. . . . Advanced music has no recourse but to insist upon its own ossification without concession to that would-be humanitarianism which it sees through, in all its attractive and alluring guises, as the mask of inhumanity. (19–20)

Music thus insistently becomes what Lukács's reconciled conscious-ness has given up—the very sign of alienation which, says Adorno, "pre-serves its social truth through the isolation resulting from its antithesis to society." Not that this isolation is something to be enjoyed as, say, an 1890's aesthete might have enjoyed the status of arty eccentric. No; in the awareness of an advanced composer that his work derives from such ap-palling "social roots" as this, there is consequently a recoil from them. So between that awareness and an attitude that "despises [the] . . . illusion of reconciliation" stands new music. Precisely because its constitutive prin-ciple is the disjunctive twelve-note series, its harmony a mass of disso-nances, its inspiration the remorseless "control" of the composer who is bound by the system's unbreakable laws, music aspires to the condition of theoretical knowledge. Of what? The contradiction.

With this clearly stated, Adorno proceeds resolutely to an account of Schoenberg's career or "progress" (the word is fairly loaded down with irony) from the early expressionist works to the late dodecaphonic master-pieces. As if affectionately recalling, and then angrily refuting Lukács, Adorno describes the twelve-tone method in terms taken almost verbatim from the subject-object drama, but each time there is an opportunity for synthesis Adorno has Schoenberg turn it down.

The further irony is that very far from liberating him, Schoenberg's mastery of the atonal technique he invented for escaping "the blind domi-nation of tonal material" ends up by dominating him. The severity, objec-tivity, and regulatory power of a technique that supplies itself with an alternative harmony, inflection, tonal color, rhythm—in short a new logic for music, the object of the subject's compositional skill—become "a second blind nature," and this "virtually extinguishes the subject" (68–69). In Adorno's descriptions here there is a breathtakingly regressive se-quence, a sort of endgame procedure by which he threads his way back along the route taken by Lukács; all the laboriously constructed solutions devised by Lukács for pulling himself out of the slough of bourgeois de-spair—the various satisfactory totalities given by art, philosophy, Marx-ism—are just as laboriously dismantled and rendered useless. Fixated on music's absolute rejection of the commercial sphere, Adorno's words cut out the social ground from underneath art. For in fighting ornament, illusion, reconciliation, communication, humanism, and success, art be-comes untenable:

258 EDWARD W. SAID

Everything having no function in the work of art—and therefore everything transcending the law of mere existence—is withdrawn. The function of the work of art lies precisely in its transcendence beyond mere existence. Thus the height of justice becomes the height of injustice: the consummately functional work of art becomes consummately functionless. Since the work, after all, cannot be reality, the elimination of all illusory features accentuates all the more glaringly the illusory character of its existence. This process is inescapable. (70)

An even more drastic statement comes later, when Adorno avers as how the fate of new music in its illusionless self-denial and ossified self-sacrifice is to remain unheard: "music which has not been heard falls into empty time like an impotent bullet" (133). Thus the subject-object antithesis simply disappears, because Adorno has Schoenberg rejecting even the ghost of achievement and experience. I say it this way to underscore Adorno's manipulation of Schoenberg, and also to contrast it with Mann's *Doctor Faustus* (based on Adorno's book), a tamer version of Adorno's Schoenberg. Mann's hero is an Adornian emanation, but the novel's technique, especially the presence of Serenus Zeitblom, the humanist narrator, recuperates and to a degree saves or domesticates Adrian by giving him the aura of a figure representative of modern Germany, now chastened and perhaps redeemed for postwar elegiac reflection.

III

But Lukács's theory has voyaged elsewhere too. Recall that between Lukács and Adorno there is first of all a common European culture and more particularly the affinity stemming from the Hegelian tradition to which they both belong. It is therefore quite startling to discover the subject-object dialectic deployed with devastating intellectual and political force in Frantz Fanon's last work, *The Wretched of the Earth*, written in 1961, the very year of its author's death. All of Fanon's books on colonialism show evidence of his indebtedness to Marx and Engels, as well as to Freud and Hegel. Yet the striking power that differentiates his last work from, say, the largely Caribbean setting of *Black Skins, White Masks* (1952) is evident from the unflagging mobilizing energy with which in the Algerian setting Fanon analyzes and situates the antinomy of the settler versus the native. There is a philosophical logic to the tension that is scarcely visible in his previous work, in which psychology, impressions, astute observation, and an almost novelistic technique of insight and vignette give Fanon's writing its ingratiatingly eloquent inflections.

Two things seem to have happened between *L'An V de la revolution algérienne* (1959), his first collection of essays after he changed his focus from the Caribbean to North Africa, and *The Wretched of the Earth*. One of them, obviously, is that the progress of the Algerian revolution had deepened and widened the gulf between France and its colony. There was a greater drive toward separation between them, the war had become uglier and more extensive, sides were being taken both in Algeria and in the metropolis, with rifts and internecine conflicts in both of the two great hostile encampments. Second—and here I speculate—Fanon seems to have read Lukács's book and taken from its reification chapter an under-standing of how even in the most confusing and heterogenous of situa-tions, a rigorous analysis of one central problematic could be relied on to yield the most extensive understanding of the whole. The evidence I have is, to repeat, not firm, but it is worth noting: a French version of Lukács's central work, *Histoire et conscience de classe*, appeared in 1961, in an excellent translation by Kostas Axelos and Jacqueline Bois, published by Editions de Minuit. Some of the chapters had already appeared in *Argu-ments* a few years earlier, but 1961 was the first time the entire book had made its appearance anywhere at all, ever since Lukács had recanted the book's most radical tenets a generation earlier. In his preface Axelos com-pared Lukács to Brecht's Galileo, associating him also with those other martyrs to truth, Socrates, Christ, and Giordano Bruno; according to Axelos, the main point for twentieth-century thought, however, was that Lukács's great treatise was expunged both from history and class con-sciousness, with no visible effects on those working people the book was designed to assist.

How strongly the subject-object dialectic resonated *outside* Europe, and for an audience made up of colonial subjects, is immediately apparent from the opening pages of *The Wretched of the Earth*. The Manicheanism Fanon describes as separating the clean well-lighted colonial city and the vile disease-ridden darkness of the *casbah* recalls the alienation of Lukács's reified world. And Fanon's whole project is first to illuminate and then to animate the separation between colonizer and colonized (subject and ob-ject) in order that what is false, brutalizing, and historically determined about the relationship might become clear, stimulate action, and lead to the overthrow of colonialism itself. As Lukács put it in his supremely He-gelian 1922 Preface to *History and Class Consciousness*: "It is of the essence of dialectical method that concepts which are false in their abstract one-sidedness are later transcended."[4] To this Fanon will answer that there is nothing abstract or conceptual about colonialism, which, as Conrad once said, "mostly means the taking it [land] away from those who have a different complexion or slightly flatter noses than ourselves." Thus, according to Fanon,

for a colonized people the most essential value, because the most concrete, is first and foremost the land: the land which will bring them bread and, above all, dignity. But this dignity has nothing to do with the dignity of the human individual: for that human individual has never heard tell of it. All that the native has seen in his country is that they can freely arrest him, beat him, starve him: and no professor of ethics, no priest has ever come to be beaten in his place, nor to share their bread with him. As far as the native is concerned: morality is very concrete; it is to silence the settler's defiance, to break his flaunting violence—in a word, to put him out of the picture.[5]

Lukács's dialectic is grounded in *The Wretched of the Earth*, actualized, given a kind of harsh presence nowhere to be found in his agonized rethinking of the classical philosophical antinomies. The issue for Lukács was the primacy of consciousness in history; for Fanon it is the primacy of geography in history, and then the primacy of history over consciousness and subjectivity. That there is subjectivity at all is because of colonialism—instituted by Europeans who like Odysseus came to the peripheries to exploit the land and its people, and thereafter to constitute a new aggressive selfhood—and once colonialism disappears the settler "has no longer any interest in remaining or in co-existing" (45). The subjective colonizer has turned the native into a dehumanized creature for whom zoological terms are the most apt; for the settler the terms used to falsify and palliate his or her repressive presence are borrowed from "Western culture," which whenever it is mentioned "produces in the native a sort of stiffening or muscular lockjaw" (43).

At the same time that Fanon uses the subject-object dialectic most energetically he is quite deliberate about its limitations. Thus, to return to the relationship between the colonial enclave and the native quarter: these "two zones are opposed," says Fanon, "but not in the service of a higher unity. . . . They both follow the principle of reciprocal exclusivity. No conciliation is possible, for of the two terms one is superfluous" (38–39). At the same time that he uses what is a patently Marxist analysis Fanon realizes explicitly that such "analysis should always be slightly stretched" in the colonial situation. For neither the colonist nor the colonized behaves as if subject and object might some day be reconciled. The former plunders and pillages; the latter dreams of revenge. When the natives rise in violent insurrection, it "is not a rational confrontation of points of view. It is not a treatise on the universal, but the untidy affirmation of an original idea propounded as an absolute" (41).

No one needs to be reminded that Fanon's recommended antidote for the cruelties of colonialism is violence: "the violence of the colonial regime and the counter-violence of the native balance each other and respond to each other in an extraordinary reciprocal homogeneity" (88). The logic of colonialism is opposed by the native's equally strict and implacable counterlogic. What operates throughout the war of national liberation is therefore a combative subject-object dialectic whose central term is violence which at brief moments appears to play a reconciling, transfiguring role. True, Fanon says there is no liberation without violence and certainly he admits that there is no "truthful behavior" in a colonial setting: "good is quite simply that which is evil for 'them' " (50). But does Fanon, like Lukács, suggest that the subject-object dialectic can be consummated, transcended, synthesized, and that violence in and of itself is that fulfillment, the dialectical tension resolved by violent upheaval into peace and harmony?

The by now conventional notion about Fanonist violence is exactly that, a received idea, and is a caricatural reduction more suited to the Cold War (Sidney Hook's attack on Fanon being a case in point) than to what Fanon actually says and to how he says it. In other words, Fanon can too easily be read as if what he was doing in *The Wretched of the Earth* was little more than a replication of Lukács, with the subject-object relationship replaced exactly by the colonizer-colonized relationship, the "new class-consciousness of the proletariat," Lukács's synthesizing term, replaced by revolutionary violence in Fanon's text. But that would be to miss Fanon's crucial reworking and critique of Lukács, in which the *national* element missing in *History and Class Consciousness*—the setting of that work, like Marx's, is entirely European—is given an absolute prominence by Fanon. For him, subject and object are European and non-European respectively; colonialism does not just *oppose* the terms and the people to each other. It obliterates and suppresses their presence, substituting instead the lifeless dehumanizing abstractions of two "masses" in absolute uncommunicating hostility with each other. Whereas Lukács saw the subject-object antinomy as integral to European culture, and as in fact its partial symbol, Fanon sees the antinomy as imported from Europe, a foreign intrusion that has completely distorted the native presence. "Thus the history which he [the colonist] writes is not the history of the country which he plunders but the history of his own nation in regard to all that she skims off, all that she violates and starves" (51).

Fanon had made earlier use of the subject-object dialectic in an expressly Hegelian manner; this is most notably evident in *Black Skins*, where he uses the master-slave dialectic to show how the Negro had been turned by racism into an "existential deviation." Yet even there Fanon distinguished the dialectic as Hegel envisioned it for white Europe, and how it might be used by whites against Negroes: "here [in the colonial relationship between races] the master differs basically from the master described by Hegel. For Hegel there is reciprocity; here the master laughs at the consciousness of the slave. What he wants from the slave is not recognition but work."[6] In *The Wretched of the Earth* existential racial relationships have been superseded, in a sense: they are now located and resituated geographically in the colonial setting. And from this derives that "world divided into compartments, a motionless Manicheistic world, a world of statues" (51).

In short, the colonial antinomy can now be reinterpreted as an antagonism between nations, one dominating the other, and in the process actually preventing the other from coming into being. The new complication therefore is nationalism, which Fanon introduces as follows:

The immobility to which the native is condemned can only be called in question if the native decides to put an end to the history of colonization—the history of pillage—and to bring into existence the history of the nation—the history of decolonization. (51)

The unresolvable antinomy is the opposition between two nations which in the colonies cannot be brought to coexist. Fanon matches two sets of terms: pillage and colonization versus the nation and decolonization, and they emerge in the anticolonial struggle itself as absolutely opposed as they were before it began, before the liberation movement was born, before it started to fight, before it challenged the colonizer. The violence of decolonization is no more than an explicit fulfillment of the violence that lurks within colonialism, and instead of the natives being the object of colonial force, they wield it back *against* colonialism, as subjects reacting with pent-up violence to their own former passivity.

Were liberation therefore only to consist in the violence of nationalism, the process of decolonization might be seen as leading inevitably to it, one step along the way. But Fanon's essential point—and here he also rejects Lukács's own resolution—is that nationalism is a necessary but far from sufficient condition for liberation, perhaps even a sort of temporary illness that must be gone through. By the approximate terms of the subject-object antinomy, the natives who reject their reified status as negation and evil take on violence as a way of providing themselves with "a royal pardon" (86): since they stand outside the European class system about which Lukács wrote, colonized natives need an extra measure of rebelliousness to afford them the dubious position of antagonists (their dreams, Fanon remarks, are full of jumping, swimming, running, climbing, as if trying to imagine what it would be like *not* to stay in place). Once antagonists of the colonizers, however, they are only the *opposite* of colonialism: this is why Fanon says that only at an initial stage can violence be used to organize a party. Colonial war is of the colonial dialectic, the replication of some of its mutually exclusive and antagonistic terms on a national level. The opposites reflect each other. For the Europeans this will lead to expulsion; for the native this will mean that national independence will be achieved. Yet both expulsion and independence belong essentially to the unforgiving dialectic of colonialism, enfolded within its unpromising script.

Thereafter Fanon is at pains to show that the tensions between colonizer and colonized will not end, since in effect the new nation will produce a new set of policemen, bureaucrats, merchants to replace the departed Europeans. And indeed after his opening chapter on violence Fanon proceeds to show how nationalism is too heavily imprinted with the *unresolved* (and unresolvable) dialectic of colonialism for it to lead very far beyond it. The complexity of independence, which is so naturally desireable a goal for all colonized people, is that simultaneously it dramatized the discrepancy between colonizer and colonized so basic to colonialism, and also a discrepancy (*décalage*) between the people and their leaders, leaders who perforce are shaped by colonialism. Thus after the opening chapter on violence, Fanon proceeds to develop the new difficulties of nationalism as it continues the war against colonialism decreed by the subject-object antinomy, while at the same time an entirely new consciousness—that of liberation—is struggling to be born.

It is not until the chapter on "The Pitfalls of National Consciousness" that Fanon makes clear what he has been intending all along: national consciousness is undoubtedly going to be captured by the colonial bourgeois elite, the nationalistic leaders, and far from guaranteeing real independence this will perpetuate colonialism in a new form, a "sterile formalism." Thus, he says, if nationalism "is not enriched and deepened by a very rapid transformation into a consciousness of social and political needs, in other words, into humanism, it leads up a blind alley" (204). Borrowing from Aimé Césaire, Fanon suggests that the necessity is to "invent souls," not to reproduce the solutions and formulas either of colonialism or the tribal past. "The living expression of the nation is the moving consciousness of the whole of the people; it is the coherent, enlightened action of men and women" (204). A few sentences later he states that a national government (the only government ever known!) ought to cede its power back to the people, dissolve itself.

Fanon's radicalism, I think, is and has been since his death too strenuous for the new postcolonial states, Algeria included. The gist of his last work plainly indicts them for this insufficiently visionary response to the colonialist dialectic, from which they have never fully liberated themselves, satisfied as they have been with the imitations and simulacra of sovereignty that they have simply have taken over from European masters. But even in this extraordinary turn Fanon relies to some degree on Lukács, although it is a Lukács that had been either rejected or toned down by Lukács himself. So that even for a colonial setting, as he criticized the subject-object reconciliation advocated by *History and Class Consciousness* as the "class consciousness of the proletariat," Fanon takes from Lukács the real dissatisfaction with that resolution that surfaces briefly near the end of the essay on "Class Consciousness," the short essay that precedes the reification chapter. "The proletariat," says Lukács, "only perfects itself by annihilating and transcending itself . . . it is equally [therefore] the struggle of the proletariat against itself" (80).

There is concurrence here between Fanon and this more (and perhaps only momentarily) radical Lukács on the one hand, and between Lukács and Adorno on the other. The work of theory, criticism, demystification, deconsecration, and decentralization they imply is never finished. The point of theory therefore is to travel, always to move beyond its confinements, to emigrate, to remain in a sense in exile. Adorno and Fanon exemplify this profound restlessness in the way they refuse the emoluments offered by the Hegelian dialectic as stabilized into resolution by Lukács—or the Lukács who appeared to speak for class consciousness as something to be gained, possessed, held onto. There was of course the other Lukács which both his brilliant rereaders preferred, the theorist of permanent dissonance as understood by Adorno, the critic of reactive nationalism as partially adopted by Fanon in colonial Algeria.

IV

In all this we get a sense, I think, of the geographical dispersion of which the theoretical motor is capable. I mean that when Adorno uses Lukács to understand Schoenberg's place in the history of music, or when Fanon dramatized the colonial struggle in the language of the manifestly European subject-object dialectic, we don't think of them simply coming after Lukács, using him at a belated second degree, so to speak, but rather as pulling him from one sphere or region into another. This movement suggests the possibility of actively different locales, sites, situations for theory, without facile universalism or over-general totalizing. One would not, could not, want to assimilate Viennese twelve-tone music to the Algerian resistance to French colonialism: the disparities are too grotesque even to articulate. But in both situations, each so profoundly and concretely felt by Adorno and Fanon respectively, is the fascinating Lukácsian figure, present both as travelling theory and as intransigent practice. To speak here only of borrowing and adaptation is not adequate. There is in particular an intellectual, and perhaps moral, community of a remarkable kind, *affiliation* in the deepest and most interesting sense of the word. As a way of getting seriously past the weightlessness of one theory after another, the remorseless indignations of orthodoxy, and the expressions of tired advocacy to which we are often submitted, the exercise involved in figuring out where the theory went and how in getting there its fiery core was reignited is invigorating—and is also another voyage, one that is central to intellectual life in the late twentieth century.

REFERENCE MATTER

Notes

TODOROV: *Fictions and Truths*

1. Paul Valéry, *Regard sur le monde actuel* (Paris: Gallimard, 1962), pp. 11–12, trans. Jennifer Curtiss Gage (hereafter abbreviated as J. C. G.).

2. Marc Augé, *La Traversée du Luxembourg* (Paris: Hachette, 1985), pp. 18–19, trans. J. C. G.

3. Ibid., p. 26.

4. Stendhal, *Oeuvres intime* (Paris: Gallimard, 1982), vol. 2, p. 198, trans. J. C. G.

5. Jean-Jacques Rousseau, *Oeuvres complètes* (Paris: Gallimard, 1980), p. 777, trans. J. C. G.

6. Much of the information on Psalmanazar has been taken from the work of Frederic J. Foley, *The Great Formosan Impostor* (St. Louis, Mo.: Jesuit Historical Institute, 1968).

7. George Psalmanazar, *Description de l'île Formosa en Asie* (Amsterdam: 1704 [Actual date, 1705]), pp. 66–67, trans. J. C. G.

8. *Histoire des Ouvrages des Savans* (Paris, 1687–1709), November 1704, p. 518.

9. George Psalmanazar, *Memoirs* (London: 1764).

10. Francis Jennings, *The Invasion of America* (New York: Norton, 1976).

11. Martin Waldseemüller, *Cosmographiae Introductio*, English translation by Joseph Fischer and Franz von Wieser (Ann Arbor, Mich.: University Microfilms, 1966).

12. Edmundo O'Gorman, *La Idea del descubrimiento de America* (Mexico: Centro de Estudios Filosoficos, 1951); in English, *The Invention of America* (Bloomington: Indiana University Press, 1961).

13. Amerigo Vespucio, *El Nuevo Mundo: Cartas relativas a sus viajes y descubrimientos, textos en Italiano, Español e Ingles, estudio preliminar de Roberto Levillier* (Buenos Aires: Nova, 1951), "the Levillier edition." The English translation of Amerigo Vespucci is taken from this edition. All subsequent quotations from Ves-

pucci, unless otherwise indicated, are from this edition and are cited in parentheses in the text.

14. Vespucio, *El Nuevo Mundo*.

15. Peter Martyr, *De orbe novo. Les huit décades* (Paris: 1907), p. 16, trans. J. C. G. In English, *De Orbe Novo*, 3 vols. (New York: Putnam, 1912).

16. Christopher Columbus, *Oeuvres* (Paris: Gallimard, 1961), p. 237, trans. J. C. G. Subsequent quotations from Columbus are from this edition. In English, Columbus, *Journals and Other Documents* (New York: Heritage, 1963).

17. Charton, Eduard Thomas, ed., *Voyageurs anciens et modernes* (Paris: 1863), vol. 3, p. 201, trans. J. C. G.

18. Vespucio, *El Nuevo Mundo*.

19. Alberto Magnaghi, *Amerigo Vespucci: Studio critico* (Rome: Treves, 1926).

20. Vespucio, *El Nuevo Mundo*, p. 13.

21. Bartholomé de Las Casas, *Historia de las Indias* (Madrid: M. Aguilar, [pref. 1927]).

22. Antonio de Herrera, *Historia General de los Castellanos* (Madrid: 1625); M. Fernandez de Navarette, *Viajes de Americo Vespucia* (Madrid: Calpe, 1935); Clement Robert Markham, *The Life of Christopher Columbus* (London: G. Philip & Son, Ltd., 1902); Washington Irving, *History of the Life and Voyages of Christopher Columbus* (London: John Murray, 1828).

23. Ralph Waldo Emerson, *English Traits* (Boston: Phillips, Sampson, 1856), pp. 154—55.

24. Alexander von Humboldt, *Travels and Researches* (Edinburgh: 1836); Francisco Adolpho de Varnhagen, *Amerigo Vespucci* (Lima: 1865); Henri Vignaud, *Americ Vespuce* (Paris: Leroux, 1917); Henry Harrisse, *Americus Vespuccius* (London: B. F. Stevens, 1895); Roberto Levillier, *America la bien llamada* (Buenos Aires: Kraft, 1948); and O'Gorman, *La Idea*.

LEVENSON: *Private Life of a Public Form*

1. Ian Watt, *The Rise of the Novel* (Berkeley: University of California Press, 1971), p. 190.

2. Ibid., p. 195.

3. Sigmund Freud, *Civilization and Its Discontents*, in vol. 21 of *The Standard Edition of the Complete Psychological Works of Sigmund Freud*, ed. and trans. James Strachey, 24 vols. (London: Hogarth, 1961); hereafter, this edition will be cited as SE.

4. Freud, "The Uncanny," in *SE*, 17: 270.

5. Ibid., p. 247.

6. Charles Dickens quoted in John Forster, *The Life of Charles Dickens* (New York: Charles Scribner's Sons, 1907), p. 29.

7. Ibid., p. 27.

8. Roger Scruton, "Fantasy, Imagination and the Screen," in *The Aesthetic Understanding* (Manchester, Eng.: Carcanet Press, 1983), p. 127.

9. Freud, *Introductory Lectures on Psycho-Analysis*, in *SE*, 16: 372.

10. Scruton, "Fantasy," p. 130.

11. Ibid., p. 131.

12. Ibid., p. 132.

13. Samuel Taylor Coleridge, quoted in Watt, *Rise*, p. 200.

14. Watt, *Rise*, p. 200.

15. Ibid., p. 202.

16. Charles Dickens, *The Personal History of David Copperfield* (London: Oxford University Press, 1966), ch. 48. All subsequent references to this work will be in the text, parenthetically by chapter number.

17. Watt, *Rise*, p. 32.

18. Sigmund Freud, "'A Child Is Being Beaten': A Contribution to the Study of the Origin of Sexual Perversions," in *SE*, 17: 186.

19. Freud, "Child," p. 187.

20. Ibid., p. 189.

21. Ibid., p. 185.

22. Ibid., p. 186.

23. Ibid., p. 190.

24. Ibid., p. 180.

25. Ibid., p. 190.

26. Ibid., p. 191.

27. Freud, *Introductory Lectures*, in *SE*, 16: 98.

28. Freud, "Screen Memories," in *SE*, 3: 321.

29. Freud, "Creative Writers and Day-Dreams," in *SE*, 9: 153.

30. Richard Wollheim, *The Thread of Life* (Cambridge, Mass.: Harvard University Press, 1984), p. 73.

31. Ibid., p. 74.

32. Dickens, Preface to the Charles Dickens edition, *David Copperfield*.

33. Freud, *Introductory Lectures*, in *SE*, 16: 372.

34. William Makepeace Thackeray, *The History of Henry Esmond* (Harmondsworth: Penguin, 1980), p. 438.

35. Watt, *Rise*, p. 204.

36. Ibid.

POLHEMUS: *Faith in the Child*

1. See Robert M. Polhemus, *Erotic Faith: Being in Love from Jane Austen to D. H. Lawrence* (Chicago: University of Chicago Press, 1990), p. 4, for a similar discussion of art and faith.

2. See Robert M. Polhemus, *Comic Faith: The Great Tradition from Austen to Joyce* (Chicago: University of Chicago Press, 1980), pp. 3–23 (especially pp. 19–20), for a full definition and discussion of comic faith.

3. See Polhemus, *Erotic Faith*, pp. 1–27.

4. Charles Dickens, *The Old Curiosity Shop* (Harmondsworth: Penguin, 1972), ed. Angus Easson, ch. 1, p. 56. All subsequent citations, given in text by chapter and page, are to this edition. For a thorough, informative, and indispensable record and history of the bibliography, reviews, criticism, and scholarly discussions of *The Old Curiosity Shop*, see Priscilla Schlicke and Paul Schlicke, *The Old Curiosity Shop: an Annotated Bibliography* (New York: Garland, 1988).

5. John Ruskin, *The Stones of Venice*, 3 vols., (London, 1851–53), vol. 2, ch. 4.

6. Matthew Lewis, *The Monk* (Oxford and New York: Oxford University Press, 1980), I, 1: 7. Subsequent citations in text, given by volume, chapter, and page, are to this edition.

7. See Polhemus, *Erotic Faith*, pp. 20–25, for a more detailed discussion of *The Monk*.

8. *The Confessions of Jean-Jacques Rousseau* (Harmondsworth: Penguin, 1953), trans. J. M. Cohen, pp. 302–3.

9. See George Ford, *Dickens and His Readers* (New York: Norton, 1965), pp. 55–71, for an illuminating discussion of the reception of *The Old Curiosity Shop*.

10. James Joyce, *Finnegans Wake* (New York: Viking, 1958), pp. 429–457.24. Subsequent citations to this book are given in parentheses in text by page and line.

11. Sigmund Freud, "On the Universal Tendency to Debasement," in "Contributions to the Psychology of Love" II, in *The Standard Edition of the Complete Psychological Works*, ed. and trans. James Strachey (London: Hogarth, 1953–66), II: 179–90.

12. See Polhemus, *Erotic Faith*, pp. 151–53 for a discussion and comparison of Freud's "Universal Tendency" and Dickens's *Great Expectations*.

13. Freud, "Universal Tendency," p. 183.

14. Ibid., p. 184.

15. Ibid., p. 186.

16. Ibid., p. 190.

17. Mark Spilka, "On the Enrichment of Poor Monkeys by Myth and Dream; or, How Dickens Rousseauisticized and Pre-Freudianized Victorian Views of Childhood," in *Sexuality and Victorian Literature*, ed. Don Richard Cox (Knoxville: University of Tennessee Press, 1984), p. 168.

18. See Polhemus, *Erotic Faith*, for extended discussion of the relationship between Victorian fiction, Victorian idealism of the family, and incestuous desire.

19. *The Works of Charles Dickens in Thirty-four Volumes, with Introductions, General Essay, and Notes by Andrew Lang* (London: Chapman and Hall; New York: Scribner's, n.d.; "Gadshill Edition"), vol. 10, *The Old Curiosity Shop*; vol. 1, Introduction, p. x.

HENKLE: *Representation in 'Dombey and Son'*

1. For a discussion of this phase of Dickens's career, see chapter 7 of Steven Marcus, *Dickens from Pickwick to Dombey* (New York, 1965).

2. Charles Dickens, *Dombey and Son*, ed. Alan Horsman (Oxford: Clarendon Press, 1974), p. 225. Subsequent page references to this edition appear in the text.

3. Dickens's original plan to have Dombey cuckolded later in the novel underscores the motif of male anxiety. See Horsman, "Introduction" to *Dombey and Son*, p. xxxv.

4. We can speculate that Dickens was conscious of the reduction of sentimentality to an easily reproduced formula by the 1840's. Anyone as conscious as he of its rhetorical powers may well have become aware of its "commodification" in the

literary marketplace. For a discussion of a related phenomenon, see Roger Henkle, "Comedy as Commodity: Thomas Hood's Poetry of Class Desire," *Victorian Poetry* 26 (Autumn 1988), pp. 301–18.

5. An excellent treatment of these effects of the railroad is Wolfgang Schivelbusch, *The Railway Journey: The Industrialization of Time and Space in the Nineteenth Century* (Berkeley: University of California Press, 1977).

6. Ian Watt, "*Robinson Crusoe*, Individualism and the Novel," in *The Rise of the Novel: Studies in Defoe, Richardson and Fielding* (Berkeley: University of California Press, 1962).

7. Norman Russell, *The Novelist and Mammon: Literary Responses to the World of Commerce in the Nineteenth Century* (Oxford: Oxford University Press, 1986), chs. 5, 6, and 7.

8. I am indebted to Christine Alfano for this observation.

9. Raymond Williams, *The Country and the City* (Oxford: Oxford University Press, 1973), ch. 15.

10. See N. N. Feltes, *Modes of Production of Victorian Novels* (Chicago: University of Chicago Press, 1986).

11. Thomas DeQuincey, *The Collected Writings*, ed. David Masson (Edinburgh: Adam and Charles Black, 1890), vol. 13, p. 284.

BENDER: *Impersonal Violence in 'Caleb Williams'*

1. Jonathan Swift, *A Tale of a Tub*, ed. A. C. Guthkelch and D. Nichol Smith, 2d ed. (Oxford: Clarendon Press, 1958), pp. 173–74.

2. See Don Locke, *A Fantasy of Reason: The Life and Thought of William Godwin* (London: Routledge & Kegan Paul, 1980), p. 8; and Peter Marshall, *William Godwin* (New Haven: Yale University Press, 1984), p. 48. Both Blake and Godwin in their different ways anticipate Max Horkheimer and Theodor Adorno's attack on the instrumental perversion of reason in their *Dialectic of Enlightenment*, trans. John Cumming (New York: Herder and Herder, 1972).

3. Jacques Derrida, *Writing and Difference*, trans. Alan Bass (Chicago: University of Chicago Press, 1978), pp. 91–92. Other quotations from this essay might be added: "Heidegger still would have questioned and reduced theoretism from within, and in the name of, a Greco-Platonic tradition under the surveillance of the agency of the glance and the metaphor of light. That is, by the spatial pair inside-outside . . . which gives life to the opposition of subject and object" (88); or again, "After having spoken of taste, touch, and smell, Hegel . . . writes in the *Aesthetics*: '*Sight*, on the other hand, possesses a purely ideal relation to objects by means of light, a material which is at the same time immaterial, and which suffers on its part the objects to continue in their free self-subsistence.' . . . This neutralization of desire is what makes sight excellent for Hegel. But for Lévinas, this neutralization is also . . . the first violence. . . . Violence, then, would be the solitude of a mute glance, of a face without speech, *the abstraction* of seeing. According to Lévinas the glance *by itself*, contrary to what one may be led to believe, does not *respect* the other" (99).

4. William Godwin, *Caleb Williams*, ed. David McCracken (London: Oxford University Press, 1970), p. 339. All subsequent citations are to this edition and appear parenthetically in the text. Godwin's retrospective description of the composition of *Caleb Williams* appears in his preface to the "Standard Novels" edition (1832) of his novel *Fleetwood*.

5. Ronald Paulson, *Hogarth's Graphic Works*, 3d rev. ed. (London: The Print Room, 1989), plates 190, 190a and, for commentary, pp. 148–52. The corpse is not visibly castrated but in neither the preparatory drawing nor the final plate does the corpse appear with genitals. Sean Shesgreen refers to "intimations of cannibalism" in the drawing. See Sean Shesgreen, ed., *Engravings by Hogarth* (New York: Dover Publications, 1973), plate 80.

6. See Dorrit Cohn, *Transparent Minds: Narrative Modes for Presenting Consciousness in Fiction* (Princeton: Princeton University Press, 1978); Käte Hamburger, *The Logic of Literature*, trans. Marilynn J. Rose (Bloomington: Indiana University Press, 1973); Roy Pascal, *The Dual Voice* (Manchester, Eng.: Manchester University Press, 1977); and Ann Banfield, *Unspeakable Sentences: Narration and Representation in the Language of Fiction* (Boston: Routledge & Kegan Paul, 1982). The quotation from Flaubert comes from *The Letters of Gustave Flaubert, 1830–1857*, ed. and trans. Francis Steegmuller, 2 vols. (Cambridge, Mass.: Harvard University Press, 1980–82), I. 230. Bakhtin/Voloshinov says of this technical narrative device: "Some . . . shift had to have occurred within socio-verbal intercourse . . . for that essentially new manner of perceiving another person's words, which found expression in [free indirect discourse], to have been established. . . . The inner subjective personality with its own self-awareness does not exist as a material fact . . . but it exists as an ideologeme. . . . *A word is not an expression of inner personality; rather, inner personality is an expressed or inwardly impelled word.*" Compressed from Mikhail M. Bakhtin and Valentin N. Voloshinov, *Marxism and the Philosophy of Language*, trans. Ladislav Matejka and I. R. Titunik (New York: Seminar Press, 1973), pp. 143 and 152–53.

7. On Bentham and the correlation with free indirect discourse, see John Bender, *Imagining the Penitentiary: Fiction and the Architecture of Mind in Eighteenth-Century England* (Chicago: University of Chicago Press, 1987), ch. 7.

8. On Smith and free indirect discourse, see ibid.

9. See John Bender, "Prison Reform and the Sentence of Narration in *The Vicar of Wakefield*," pp. 168–88 in Felicity Nussbaum and Laura Brown, eds., *The New Eighteenth Century: Theory, Politics, English Literature* (New York and London: Methuen, 1987); on the reinscription of certain kinds of first-person narration as quasi free indirect discourse, see especially pp. 184–85.

10. See Laura Mulvey, "Visual Pleasure and Narrative Cinema" and "Afterthoughts on 'Visual Pleasure and Narrative Cinema,'" in Constance Penley, ed., *Feminism and Film Theory* (New York: Routledge, 1988), pp. 57–68 and 69–79. For a convenient summary of theories of the "gaze" in feminist film theory, see Tania Modleski, *The Women Who Knew Too Much: Hitchcock and Feminist Theory* (New York: Methuen, 1988), pp. 1–15. See also Constance Penley, *The Future of an*

Illusion: Film, Feminism, and Psychoanalysis (Minneapolis: University of Minnesota Press, 1989), pp. 41–54, and Mary Ann Doane, *The Desire to Desire: The Woman's Film of the 1940's* (Bloomington: Indiana University Press, 1987), pp. 38–69. The main text by Michel Foucault is *The Birth of the Clinic: An Archaeology of Medical Perception*, trans. A. M. Sheridan Smith (New York: Vintage Books, 1975), especially chapters 7 and 8.

Although rarely mentioned in recent discussions, the chapter on "the gaze" (*le regard*) in Sartre's *Being and Nothingness* (part 3, ch. 1, section 4) marked out much of the philosophical terrain. Jacques Lacan has been very influential, especially in film theory; see, for example, *The Four Fundamental Concepts of Psycho-Analysis*, ed. Jacques-Alain Miller and trans. Alan Sheridan (New York: W. W. Norton, 1973), pp. 67–105. For a current development of the Lacanian theory of the gaze, see Slavoj Zizek, "Pornography, Nostalgia, Montage: A Triad of the Gaze," in *Looking Awry: an Introduction to Jacques Lacan Through Popular Culture* (Cambridge, Mass.: MIT Press, 1991), pp. 107–22.

11. See Foucault, *The Birth of the Clinic*, chs. 7 and 8, and Norman Bryson, *Vision and Painting: The Logic of the Gaze* (New Haven: Yale University Press, 1983). Svetlana Alpers, in *The Art of Describing* (Chicago: University of Chicago Press, 1983), treats this opposition as a contrast between southern and northern European ways of seeing. For a discussion of the possibility of alternate gazes that do not participate in the violence and domination, see Edward Snow, "Theorizing the Male Gaze: Some Problems," *Representations* 25 (1989): 30–41.

A point often submerged in discussions of the gaze is that its analytic and sequential character (in contrast to the "glance" or the "*coup d'oeil*") makes it a narrative mode. Indeed, one of Foucault's central points is that the clinical gaze organizes its findings through linguistic description.

12. Leo Bersani and Ulysse Dutoit, *The Forms of Violence: Narrative in Assyrian Art and Modern Culture* (New York: Schocken, 1985), pp. 38, 40–56. See also, by the same authors, "Merde Alors," in Beverly Allen, ed., *Pier Paolo Pasolini: The Poetics of Heresy* (Saratoga, Calif.: Anma Libri, 1982), pp. 82–95. I read David Marshall's *The Surprising Effects of Sympathy* (Chicago: University of Chicago Press, 1988) after this essay was written, but his argument linking violence and sympathy anticipates mine.

13. Every critic I have encountered on the novel attempts a unified reading, even those who, like Mitzi Myers in a marvelous essay, "Godwin's Changing Conception of *Caleb Williams*," *SER* 12 (1972): 591–628, and Mark Philp in his book on *Political Justice* (London: Duckworth, 1986), lay stress on the rapid shifts that occurred in Godwin's thought between 1793 and 1798—five years that include the original publication of both treatise and novel as well as considerable revision. Kenneth W. Graham takes up questions about the novel's unity and about the influence of *Caleb Williams* on the revision of *Political Justice* in *The Politics of Narrative: Ideology and Social Change in William Godwin's 'Caleb Williams'* (New York: AMS Press, 1990), a book that appeared after this essay was written.

14. In what follows, for the sake of economy, I interweave manifest facts and

accepted interpretations of Godwin's views with my own inferences. Limits of space cause me to focus upon my main assertions rather than upon the textual evidence that underlies my understanding of the novel.

15. On Godwin's attitude toward contract-governed society see Ian Balfour, "Promises, Promises: Social and Other Contracts in the English Jacobins (Godwin/Inchbald)," in David Clark and Donald Goellnicht, eds., *New Romanticisms* (Toronto: University of Toronto Press, forthcoming). See also Leo Damrosch, *Fictions of Reality in the Age of Hume and Johnson* (Madison: University of Wisconsin Press, 1989), ch. 7. The contrast between shame and guilt as cultural orientations and modes of social control is compactly developed by Alvin W. Gouldner in *Enter Plato: Classical Greece and the Origins of Social Theory* (New York: Basic Books, 1965), pp. 81–87. See also Bender, *Imagining the Penitentiary*, p. 221.

16. Godwin, *Political Justice* (1793), book I, ch. 4. See William Godwin, *Enquiry Concerning Political Justice and Its Influence on Morals and Happiness*, 3 vols., ed. F. E. L. Priestley (Toronto: University of Toronto Press, 1946), 3: 247. This edition is cited hereafter as "Priestley."

17. Godwin, *Political Justice* (1793), book I, ch. 2 and book I, ch. 4. See Priestley, 1: 126 and 2: 239.

18. Philp, *Godwin's Political Justice*, p. 47.

19. Banfield, *Unspeakable Sentences*, especially pp. 180, 227, and 257. For examples of "encoded" free indirect discourse, see the analysis below as well as Bender, "Prison Reform and the Sentence of Narration in *The Vicar of Wakefield*," pp. 183–85.

20. Bersani and Dutoit, *The Forms of Violence*, pp. 52 and 38. See also p. 41 on the idea that capacity to stir "imaginative sympathy," often described (e.g., by E. H. Gombrich) as an innovation of Greek narrative art and associated with realism, aimed to excite audiences "out of themselves and into new identities as a result of high narrative skills."

21. *Caleb Williams* reveals this truth in numerous episodes that I cannot discuss here, but an elaborate paragraph about the standing as testimony in court of Caleb's version of the Collins narration makes it clear that such issues are alive in the text (106).

22. Roland Barthes proposes a similar test during a discussion of personal and apersonal narration as systems or codes independent of superficial linguistic markers: "there are narratives or at least narrative episodes . . . which though written in the third person nevertheless have as their true instance the first person." He then proceeds to rewrite the third-person pronouns of such a text in the first person. Run in reverse, his test reveals how first-person narration can venture obliquely upon the representation of consciousness from the impersonal, all-penetrating perspective that free indirect discourse makes possible. Roland Barthes, "Introduction to the Structural Analysis of Narratives," in *Image-Music-Text*, ed. and trans. Stephen Heath (New York: Hill and Wang, 1977), pp. 112–13; reprinted in *A Barthes Reader*, ed. Susan Sontag (New York: Hill and Wang, 1982), pp. 283–84.

23. Quoted in Thomas N. Haviland and Lawrence Charles Parish, "A Brief Ac-

count of the Use of Wax Models in the Study of Medicine," *Journal of the History of Medicine* 25 (1970), p. 62.

The present essay is part of a work in progress that parallels the technical practices of the later eighteenth-century novel with anatomical science, medical electricity, and other invasions of the body and nervous system during the period. Central to this study are the amazing wax anatomical models that survive in Florence, Vienna, London, and other sites. This kind of model appears to have been devised more or less simultaneously by several eighteenth-century makers. Not only are they realistic, they are narrative figurations of the body, since their organs may be progressively displayed by the removal of layers that reveal a succession of tableaus that mimic dissection. A number of these models display a seductive sexuality that is new to anatomic figures and that may be considered a symptom of the early modern gendering of the gaze as a tool of scientific inquiry. More terrifying, even, than Chovet's machine would have been are the "models" constructed from dissected corpses between 1766 and 1771 by Honoré Fragonard at the Ecole Vétérinaire in Alfort. On the Italian models, see Ludmilla Jordanova, "Gender, Generation and Science: William Hunter's Obstetrical Atlas," in W. F. Bynum and Roy Porter, eds., *William Hunter and the Eighteenth-Century Medical World* (Cambridge, Eng.: Cambridge University Press, 1985), pp. 385–412; and "Natural Facts: A Historical Perspective on Science and Sexuality" in Carol P. MacCormack and Marilyn Strathern, eds., *Nature, Culture, and Gender* (Cambridge, Eng.: Cambridge University Press, 1980) pp. 42–69; also Barbara Maria Stafford, *Body Criticism: Imaging the Unseen in Enlightenment Art and Medicine* (Cambridge, Mass.: MIT Press, 1991), p. 21. On Fragonard, see Annie Le Brun, *Petits et Grands Théâtres du Marquis de Sade* (Paris: Paris Art Center, 1989), pp. 69, 77, and 79.

DEKKER: *James and Stevenson: The Mixed Current*

1. For convenience and brevity of documentation, I draw as many quotations as possible from Janet Adam Smith's compilation of James's and Stevenson's writings to and about each other, *Henry James and Robert Louis Stevenson: A Record of Friendship and Criticism* (London: Rupert Hart-Davis, 1948), cited hereafter in these notes as Smith. Page references for quotations from Smith are given parenthetically in the text. When immediately succeeding quotations come from the same or adjacent pages in Smith, no page references are given.

2. For a recent concise account of the origins and progress of the novel-versus-romance controversy, see George Dekker, *The American Historical Romance* (Cambridge, Eng., and New York: Cambridge University Press, 1987), pp. 14–28. The most influential modern reemployments of the novel/romance polarity are Richard Chase, *The American Novel and Its Tradition* (Garden City, N.Y.: Doubleday, 1957), and Northrop Frye, *Anatomy of Criticism: Four Essays* (Princeton: Princeton University Press, 1957). Chase's contention that the romance form of the novel dominates the American novel tradition has spawned a voluminous critical literature, a current summary of which is given in the end notes to Emily Miller Budick, "Sacvan Bercovitch, Stanley Cavell, and the Romance Theory of American Fic-

tion," *PMLA* 107 (1992): 78–91. A good account of James's relation to the romance tradition is Elsa Nettles, *James and Conrad* (Athens: University of Georgia Press, 1977), pp. 80–109.

3. All of James's and Stevenson's biographers pay some attention to what was, after all, a very famous literary friendship. The fullest and most thoughtful account of their literary relations is in Smith, pp. 9–47. Especially pertinent to the issue of the James/Stevenson debate about realism and romance is Sarah B. Daugherty, *The Literary Criticism of Henry James* (Athens: Ohio University Press, 1981), pp. 121–22, 162–64.

4. Leo Bersani, *A Future for Astyanax* (Boston: Little, Brown, 1976), p. 132: "the recurrent Jamesian subject . . . is freedom."

5. Letter to William Dean Howells, dated March 30, 1877, *Henry James Letters*. Vol. 2: *1875–1883*, ed. Leon Edel (Cambridge, Mass.: Belknap Press of Harvard University Press, 1975), p. 105.

6. Ian Watt, *The Rise of the Novel: Studies in Defoe, Richardson, and Fielding* (1957; rpt., Harmondsworth: Penguin, 1963), p. 313.

7. Walter Besant, *The Art of Fiction: A Lecture Delivered at the Royal Institution* (London: Chatto and Windus, 1884), p. 38.

8. Watt, *Rise*, p. 13.

9. Edmond de Goncourt, *Préfaces et manifestes littéraires* (Paris: G. Charpentier, 1888), p. 59.

10. Ibid., p. 67.

11. Ibid., p. 66.

12. Robert Louis Stevenson, "A Gossip on Romance," *Memories and Portraits* (New York: Charles Scribner's Sons, 1887), p. 255.

13. Ibid., pp. 255–56.

14. William Wordsworth, *The Prelude* (1850), XII: 88–207.

15. When Stevenson revised "A Humble Remonstrance" for inclusion in *Memories and Portraits*, he changed "a pirate is a beard in wide trousers and literally bristling with pistols" to "a pirate is a beard, a pair of wide trousers and a liberal complement of pistols" (p. 289). The cleaned-up version is less vivid and suggestive, and also less open to objection.

16. For Stevenson's oddest judgments on James's fiction, see Smith, pp. 108, 165–66, and 207–8.

17. Stevenson, "A Humble Remonstrance," pp. 298–99.

18. "Henry James, Jr.," rpt. in *Discovery of a Genius: William Dean Howells and Henry James*, ed. Albert Mordell (New York: Twayne, 1961), pp. 117–18.

19. *The Complete Notebooks of Henry James*, ed. Leon Edel and Lyall H. Powers (New York: Oxford University Press, 1987), p. 584.

20. Letter to Sir John Clark dated December 13, 1891, *Henry James Letters*, Vol. 3: *1883–1895*, ed. Leon Edel (Cambridge, Mass.: Belknap Press of Harvard University Press, 1980), p. 367.

21. Letter to Edmund Gosse, December 17, 1894, *Henry James Letters*, vol. 3, p. 495.

22. Johann Huizinga, *Homo Ludens: A Study of the Play-Element in Culture* (Bos-

ton: Beacon Press, 1955 [1938]), pp. 7, 10. More recent theorists of play, such as Roger Caillois and Herbert Marcuse, offer insights pertinent to the argument of the present essay, but Huizinga's cultural perspective and vocabulary are closer to those of James and Stevenson.

23. Stevenson, "A Gossip on Romance," p. 264.

24. When he revised "Robert Louis Stevenson" for publication in *Partial Portraits* (1888), James changed "imaginary" to "imaginative." See *Henry James: Literary Criticism*, ed. Leon Edel (The Library of America; Cambridge, Eng.: Cambridge University Press, 1989), p. 1249.

25. Preface to *The American* (1907), rpt. in *French Writers, Other European Writers, The Prefaces to the New York Edition*, ed. Leon Edel (The Library of America; Cambridge, Eng.: Cambridge University Press, 1984), p. 1057. Subsequent page references to this edition of the preface are given parenthetically in the text; they may be readily differentiated from Smith references because they have four digits. Wordsworth appended a note to "Tintern Abbey" explaining that, contrary to appearances, it had many of the leading features of an ode (e.g., rapid transitions and impassioned versification) and suggesting that a flexible approach to questions of generic identity might serve readers well by highlighting such features where they might not be expected.

26. Daniel Mark Fogel, *Henry James and the Structure of the Romantic Imagination* (Baton Rouge: Louisiana State University Press, 1981), p. 5.

27. *Vailima Letters: Correspondence Addressed to Sidney Colvin, November 1890 to October 1894*, in *Letters and Miscellanies of Robert Louis Stevenson*, vol. 17 (New York: Charles Scribner's Sons, 1896), p. 96.

28. Michael Davitt Bell, *The Development of American Romance: The Sacrifice of Relation* (Chicago: University of Chicago Press, 1980), p. 8.

29. Stevenson, "Æs Triplex," *Virginibus Puerisque*, in *The Travels and Essays of Robert Louis Stevenson*, vol. 13 (New York: Charles Scribner's Sons, 1898), p. 104.

30. Huizinga, *Homo Ludens*, p. 3.

31. For James on the subject of social determinism in Zola and Balzac, see "Honore de Balzac" (1913), *French Writers*, p. 151.

32. Peter Brooks, "The Turn of *The American*," in Martha Banta, ed., *New Essays on The American* (Cambridge, Eng.: Cambridge University Press, 1987), pp. 43–67. Besides offering a brilliant reading of the novel, Brooks provides an excellent brief account of its relation to the French realist tradition.

33. I am not alone in arguing for the positive "liberating" connotations of romance in James's fictional theory. Cf. Mark Seltzer, *Henry James and the Art of Power* (Ithaca, N.Y.: Cornell University Press, 1984), p. 138: "Nor does the recourse to romance indicate merely a desire to escape the real. . . . His art, James declares, is an attempt to project the ideal alternative and 'antidote' to a limited and limiting social scene." Martha Banta, *Henry James and the Occult: The Great Extension* (Bloomington: Indiana University Press, 1972), pp. 54–61, explains how romance is the necessary vehicle for treating the "more things in heaven and earth than are dreamt of in the philosophy" of positivistic science and realistic fiction.

34. Stevenson, "AEs Triplex," p. 103. James quotes this passage in his 1888 essay on Stevenson (Smith, p. 143).

CHACE: *Joycean Realism*

1. James Joyce, *Ulysses* [The Corrected Text] (New York: Random House, 1986), pp. 175–76, ll. 1067, 1078. All further references to *Ulysses* will be to this edition, and both page and line references will be given in parentheses in the text.

2. If we agree that "greater love hath no man than hearing his friend out patiently," we can see that Stephen is here listening, with some loving fascination, to the several sides of his own self.

3. James Joyce, *A Portrait of the Artist as a Young Man*, ed. Chester G. Anderson (New York: Viking, 1968), p. 215.

4. As quoted in Don Gifford and Robert J. Seidman, eds., *Notes for Joyce: An Annotation of James Joyce's Ulysses* (New York: Dutton, 1974), p. 165.

5. James Joyce, *Letters*, vol. 1, ed. Stuart Gilbert (New York: Viking, 1966), p. 297. The letter was written Jan. 3, 1931.

6. Joyce, letter of May 5, 1906, to Grant Richards, *Letters of James Joyce*, vol. 2, ed. Richard Ellmann (New York: Viking, 1966), p. 134.

7. Frank Budgen, *James Joyce and the Making of Ulysses* (New York: Oxford University Press, 1972), p. 69.

8. Richard Brinkmann, "Afterthoughts on Realism," in Nicholas Boyle and Martin Swales, eds., *Realism in European Literature: Essays in Honour of J. P. Stern* (New York: Cambridge University Press, 1986), p. 197.

9. Robert Martin Adams, *Surface and Symbol: The Consistency of James Joyce's Ulysses* (New York: Oxford University Press, 1967), p. 97.

10. J. P. Stern, *On Realism* (London and Boston: Routledge & Kegan Paul, 1973), p. 52.

11. Ibid., pp. 28, 171.

12. Ian Watt, *The Rise of the Novel* (Berkeley: University of California Press, 1957), p. 288. See also his "Second Thoughts on *The Rise of the Novel*," *Novel* 1, 3 (1968): 213–14.

13. Stern, *Realism*, p. 75.

14. Ibid., p. 121.

15. Stephen Heath, "Realism, Modernism, and 'Language-Consciousness,'" in Boyle and Swales, *Realism in European Literature*, p. 120.

16. Ibid., pp. 111, 110.

17. Ian Watt, "The First Paragraph of *The Ambassadors:* An Explication," *Essays in Criticism* 10, 3 (July 1960): 261.

18. For a fuller development of this line of analysis, see C. H. Peake, *James Joyce: The Citizen and the Artist* (Stanford: Stanford University Press, 1977), pp. 264ff.

19. Watt, *Rise*, p. 29.

20. Ibid., p. 27.

21. Joyce, *Letters* (Gilbert, ed.), vol. 1, pp. 159–60. The letter was written in Feb. 1921.

22. As "Ithaca" ends, what curiously look like the discarded elements of other verbal forays on Joyce's part come strangely to the surface: "Going to dark bed there was a square round Sinbad the Sailor's roc's auk's egg in the night of the bed of all the auks of the rocs of Darkinbad the Brightdayler" (606: 2328–30). The notion of introduced error as human signature was first mentioned by Clive Hart, *James Joyce's Ulysses* (Sydney: Sydney University Press, 1968), p. 74.

23. As quoted in Joyce, *Letters* (Gilbert, ed.), vol. i, pp. 176, 172. The letters were written Nov. 6 and Oct. 7, 1921, respectively.

24. Hugh Kenner, *Joyce's Voices* (Berkeley and Los Angeles: University of California Press, 1978), p. 17.

25. Watt, "The First Paragraph of *The Ambassadors*," p. 261.

26. Peake, *James Joyce*, pp. 320–21.

27. Joyce, *Letters* (Gilbert, ed.), vol. i, p. 170. The letter was written Aug. 16, 1921.

28. Henry James, Preface to *The Ambassadors* (New York: Charles Scribner's Sons, 1909), p. xxiii.

FRANK: *The Making of 'Crime and Punishment'*

1. The relevant passages of this letter can be found in Feodor Dostoevsky, *Crime and Punishment*, trans. Jessie Coulson, ed. George Gibian (New York: Norton, 1975), pp. 476–77.

2. Ibid., p. 478.

3. See Gary Rosenshield's excellent and too-little-appreciated study, *Crime and Punishment: The Techniques of the Omniscient Narrator* (Lisse: Peter de Ridder Press, 1978), p. 15. "The chapter which included the preparations for the murder and the murder itself is lost," Rosenshield writes of the Wiesbaden version. But this simply assumes that such a chapter included a depiction of the murder itself—which in my opinion is open to serious question.

4. Fyodor Dostoevsky, *The Notebooks for Crime and Punishment*, ed. and trans. Edward Wasiolek (Chicago: University of Chicago Press, 1967), p. 118. Subsequent references to this work will be indicated by page numbers in the text in parentheses. Within quotes the material in parentheses represents Dostoevsky's own additions and alterations of his notes; the material in brackets was crossed out by Dostoevsky but is retained as part of the original. There are some differences in wording between this translation and my citations. My glosses and comments are identified with my initials.

5. D. I. Pisarev, *Sochineniya*, 4 vols., (Moscow: Gos. Izdat. Khudozh. Lit., 1955), 2: 10–11.

6. Ibid., pp. 11, 10.

7. Ibid., p. 15.

8. E. M. de Vogüé, *Le Roman Russe* (Paris: Librairie Plon, 1910), p. 253.

9. See F. M. Dostoevsky, *Polnoe Sobranie Sochinenii*, ed. and annotated by G. M. Fridlender, et al., 30 vols. (Leningrad: Izdatelsto Navka, 1972–90), 7: 325. The letter is cited in the extensive commentary to this volume.

10. Ibid., p. 326.

MOSER: *Faulkner's Muse*

1. Quoted in William Faulkner, *The Sound and the Fury*, Norton Critical Edition, ed. David Minter (New York: Norton, 1987), pp. 222–23, 243.

2. My initial sense of Estelle Oldham's inspiring effect upon Faulkner came from reading, in the 1960's, his brothers' memoirs; it was strengthened in the 1970's by reading Joseph Blotner's *Faulkner: A Biography*, 2 vols. (New York: Random House, 1974). Valuable insights appeared in an interview with Estelle's granddaughter: "The Faulkners, the Franklins, and the Fieldens: A Conversation with Victoria Fielden Johnson," conducted by Louis Daniel Brodsky, *The Southern Review* 25 (1989): 95–131.

In a perceptive article, Carl E. Rollyson, Jr., argued for Estelle as Faulkner's inspiration throughout their life together but did not deal with the works or with the 1920's: "'Counterpull': Estelle and William Faulkner," *South Atlantic Quarterly* 85 (1985): 215–27. An interesting volume of early letters from Faulkner to his parents appeared too late for consideration here: *Thinking of Home: William Faulkner's Letters to His Mother and Father, 1918–1925*, ed. James G. Watson (New York: Norton, 1992). Although many scholars have, in passing, yoked Estelle with Caddy, only two, Judith L. Sensibar and Frederick R. Karl, have developed the notion in detail or insisted upon the importance of Estelle to Faulkner's creative imagination. Karl's book, *William Faulkner: American Writer* (New York: Weidenfeld and Nicolson, 1989), appeared after my essay was essentially finished. Karl so contradicts himself about the role of Estelle in Faulkner's life and writings that I simply do not know how to deal with his book.

On the other hand, I have benefited much from reading Sensibar's account of Estelle's impact upon Faulkner's poetry-writing in her critical book *The Origins of Faulkner's Art* (Austin: University of Texas Press, 1984), and in her edition of Faulkner's poem-sequence *Vision of Spring*. I am deeply indebted to Sensibar for continuing to share with me the results of her current research for a group biography of Faulkner's mother, his black nanny, and his wife. (Sensibar's work in progress is foreshadowed in her two recent essays: "'Drowsing Maidenhead Symbol's Self': Faulkner and the Fictions of Love," in Doreen Fowler and Ann J. Abadie, eds., *Faulkner and the Craft of Fiction* [Jackson: University Press of Mississippi, 1989], pp. 124–47; "Faulkner's Fictional Photographs: Playing with Difference," in Laura Claridge and Elizabeth Langland, eds., *Out of Bounds: Male Writers and Gender(ed) Criticism* [Amherst: University of Massachusetts Press, 1990], pp. 290–315.) Unless otherwise indicated, all biographical information comes either from Blotner's 1974 work (hereafter referred to in the notes as Blotner 1) or from his revised and updated one-volume version (New York: Random House, 1984; hereafter referred to as Blotner 2). In addition, Sensibar has checked and corrected Estelle's chronology.

I am personally indebted to Joseph Blotner for his generosity over the years; to my Faulknerian friends Maclin Bocock, Albert J. Gelpi, Albert J. Guerard, David Levin, and Judith Sensibar for reading this essay in manuscript; and to Barbara Charlesworth Gelpi, Robert M. Polhemus, and especially to my wife Joyce Penn

Moser for much and varied assistance. Research for this essay began during a Guggenheim Fellowship year.

3. Blotner 2, p. 16.

4. Ibid., p. 679.

5. Jay Martin, "'The Whole Burden of Man's History of His Impossible Heart's Desire': The Early Life of William Faulkner," *American Literature* 53 (Jan. 1982): 611–12. Judith Bryant Wittenberg, *Faulkner: The Transfiguration of Biography* (Lincoln: University of Nebraska Press, 1979), pp. 24–25. Wittenberg calls young Estelle Billy's "twin sister" and their early relationship that of "fraternal childhood playmates," p. 23.

6. Blotner 2, p. 59.

7. John Faulkner, *My Brother Bill* (New York: Trident Press, 1963), p. 133.

8. See "The Autograph MSS of Faulkner's 'The Lilacs,'" by Louis Daniel Brodsky, *Studies in Bibliography*, ed. Fredson Bowers, vol. 36 (Charlottesville: University of Virginia Press, 1983), pp. 240–52; and William Faulkner, *A Green Bough* (New York: Smith and Haas, 1933), pp. 7–11. For detailed psychological, historical, and critical discussions not only of "The Lilacs" but also of *The Marionettes* and *Vision in Spring*, see Sensibar, *Origins*.

9. Sensibar, *Origins*, pp. 41, 43, 50. For the relation between imagined war wounds and actual disappointment in love, see also Jay Martin, "William Faulkner: Construction and Reconstruction in Biography and Psychoanalysis," *Psychoanalytic Inquiry* 3 (1983): 320–21.

10. William Faulkner, *The Marble Faun and A Green Bough* (New York: Random House, 1965), p. 15. Subsequent quotations come from this edition.

11. William Faulkner, *Mississippi Poems*, introduction by Joseph Blotner (Oxford, Miss.: Yoknapatawpha Press, 1979), p. 39.

12. John B. Cullen, *Old Times in the Faulkner Country* (Chapel Hill: University of North Carolina Press, 1961), p. 9.

13. Blotner 2, p. 73.

14. William Faulkner, *The Marionettes*, ed. Noel Polk (Charlottesville: University Press of Virginia, 1977), p. 89. Subsequent quotations come from this edition.

15. Ben Wasson, *Count No 'Count: Flashbacks to Faulkner* (Jackson: University Press of Mississippi, 1983), pp. 52–53.

16. William Faulkner, *Vision in Spring*, ed. with an introduction by Judith L. Sensibar (Austin: University of Texas Press, 1984), p. 63. Subsequent quotations come from this edition.

17. Blotner 2, p. 114.

18. William Faulkner, *Helen: A Courtship*, with an introduction by Carvel Collins (New Orleans: Tulane University Press, 1981), p. 28.

19. Ibid., p. 75. My emphasis.

20. *Mississippi Poems*, p. 33. Subsequent quotations come from this edition.

21. Faulkner, *A Green Bough*, p. 60; Blotner 1, p. 377.

22. Blotner 1, p. 376.

23. William Faulkner, *Uncollected Stories*, ed. Joseph Blotner (New York: Random House, 1979), p. 471.

24. Quoted by Sensibar, *Origins*, p. 209. William Faulkner, *Soldiers' Pay* (New York: Boni and Liveright, 1926), p. 41. Subsequent quotations are cited parenthetically in the text.

25. *William Faulkner: A Life on Paper*, script by A. I. Bezzerides (Jackson: University Press of Mississippi, 1980), p. 67.

26. William Faulkner, *Elmer*, ed. Dianne L. Cox, *Mississippi Quarterly* 36 (1983): 444, 447. Sensibar discusses *Elmer* in *Origins*, pp. 213–15.

27. William Faulkner, *Mosquitoes* (New York: Boni and Liveright, 1927), pp. 27, 82. Subsequent quotations are cited parenthetically in the text.

28. Blotner 1, p. 506.

29. Blotner 2, p. 190.

30. William Faulkner, *The Wishing Tree* (New York: Random House, 1964), pp. 5–6. Subsequent quotations are cited parenthetically in the text.

31. Quoted in the Norton edition of *The Sound and the Fury*, p. 222.

32. William Faulkner, *Flags in the Dust*, ed. Douglas Day (New York: Random House, 1973), p. 171. Subsequent quotations are cited parenthetically in the text.

33. William Faulkner, *Father Abraham*, ed. James B. Meriwether (New York: Random House, 1983), p. 7. Subsequent quotations are cited parenthetically in the text.

34. Wasson, *Count No 'Count*, pp. 76–77.

35. The motives for marriage are unclear. Faulkner told his publisher Harrison Smith that he was doing it to save Estelle's sanity. His brothers believed that he had never stopped loving her. Estelle's granddaughter Victoria Fielden Johnson believes he finally won Estelle by the affection he showed to her daughter Cho-Cho. As to whether they were physical lovers before marriage, that, too, is unclear. They apparently *looked* to Oxonians as if they were having an affair.

MCMASTER: *Emma Watson*

1. Since I argue that Jane Austen's reason for permanently discontinuing *The Watsons* was not its artistic inferiority, I have of course my own speculation on what *was* her reason, though I would not want my case for the intended shape of the completed novel to rest on the acceptance of my speculation. I have outlined my own guess at her reason elsewhere, in "'God gave us our relations': The Watson Family," *Persuasions* 8 (1986), 71–72. In brief, I believe that Austen abandoned *The Watsons* for personal *and* artistic reasons, because of a painful coincidence in the events of her life with those in her fiction. We know that Mr. Watson was soon to die; and we also know that in her completed novels, by and large, Austen avoided the dramatization of death. (Among the few characters to die in her novels is Mrs. Churchill in *Emma*, a character we never meet; and even she dies offstage.) Mr. Watson was to be the exception. He is a prominent character in the novel, the sensible but selfish father of the heroine. Presumably his death was to be dramatized; certainly it was to change the heroine's life profoundly. As Austen was warming herself up to eliminating this erring father, her own father died, suddenly and unexpectedly. It must have seemed as though the planned episode of *The*

Watsons had nightmarishly slipped from her fiction to her life. An understandable pang of guilt, strong though irrational, could well have been enough to make her close those pages for good.

2. B. C. Southam, *Jane Austen's Literary Manuscripts* (Oxford: Clarendon Press, 1964), pp. 64–65.

3. John Halperin, *The Life of Jane Austen* (Baltimore: Johns Hopkins University Press, 1984), p. 145.

4. Q. D. Leavis, "A Critical Theory of Jane Austen's Writings (I)," *Scrutiny* 1941; reprinted in *A Selection from Scrutiny*, 2 vols. (Cambridge, Eng.: Cambridge University Press, 1968), 2: 3, 14–19.

5. Joseph Wiesenfarth, "*The Watsons* as Pretext," *Persuasions* 8 (1986): 105ff.

6. Margaret Drabble, Introduction to *Lady Susan / The Watsons / Sanditon* (Harmondsworth: Penguin, 1974), p. 19.

7. *The Watsons*, in J. David Grey, A. Walton Litz, and Brian Southam, eds., *The Jane Austen Companion* (New York: Macmillan, 1986), p. 398.

8. Marvin Mudrick, *Jane Austen: Irony as Defense and Discovery* (Princeton: Princeton University Press, 1952), pp. 150–51.

9. A. Walton Litz, *Jane Austen: A Study of Her Artistic Development* (London: Chatto and Windus, 1965), p. 89.

10. Southam, *Austen's Literary Manuscripts*, p. 68.

11. Ibid.

12. Litz, *Jane Austen*, p. 86.

13. Quotations from Jane Austen are from the third edition of R. W. Chapman's *The Works of Jane Austen* (London: Oxford University Press, 1932–33). In citing the major novels, I use the usual abbreviations: *E* for *Emma*, *MP* for *Mansfield Park*, *NA* for *Northanger Abbey*, and *P&P* for *Pride and Prejudice*. *The Watsons* appears in Chapman's volume 6, *Minor Works*, 1954 (rev. 1963). Chapman's text and my quotations preserve the occasional errors in spelling and punctuation of Austen's unrevised draft.

14. Southam, *Austen's Literary Manuscripts*, pp. 68–69.

15. Drabble, Introduction, p. 22.

16. I have discussed the "rescues" in Jane Austen's fiction in *Jane Austen on Love* (University of Victoria: English Literary Studies Monograph Series, 1978), pp. 73–75.

17. Ian Watt, "On *Sense and Sensibility*," in Watt, ed., *Jane Austen: A Collection of Critical Essays* (Englewood Cliffs, N.J.: Prentice-Hall, 1963), p. 47.

18. William Makepeace Thackeray, *The Book of Snobs* (1846–47), in *The Oxford Thackeray*, ed. George Saintsbury, 17 vols. (London: Oxford University Press, 1917), 9: 383.

19. James Edward Austen-Leigh, *A Memoir of Jane Austen*, 3d ed. (London: Richard Bentley, 1872), p. 364.

20. Lionel Trilling, "Manners, Morals and the Novel," in *The Liberal Imagination* (Garden City, N.Y.: Doubleday, 1953), p. 203.

21. Thackeray, *Book of Snobs*, p. 273.

22. On more than one occasion adults are examined and judged on the basis of their dealings with children. We know that Miss Osborne is callous and untrustworthy because she breaks her promise to ten-year-old Charles Blake and that Emma is good and charming because she saves him from disappointment. Mrs. Robert Watson adds to her many other failings the severe one of bad faith in her dealings with her little daughter: "I assure you it went very hard with Augusta to have us come away without her. I was forced to say we were only going to Church & promise to come back for her directly" (350). Needless to say she does not come back.

23. Tony Tanner, *Jane Austen* (Cambridge, Mass.: Harvard University Press, 1986), pp. 75ff.

RALEIGH: *Manning's 'Her Privates We'*

1. Frederic Manning (1882–1935) was born in Sydney, Australia, of a family distinguished in public service. He suffered from asthma most of his life, attended school only briefly, and was educated by tutors. At the age of fourteen he went to London with Arthur Galton, former private secretary to Sir Robert Duff, governor of New South Wales, and lived with him for some years. From 1909 to 1914 Manning was principal reviewer for the *Spectator*, and gained his first literary fame through his *Scenes and Portraits* (1909), a series of dialogues between real and imaginary historical personages—Euripides, Machiavelli, and Thomas Cromwell, among others, appear therein. Manning also wrote poetry: *The Vigil of Brunhild* (1907) and *Eidola* (1917), a collection of war poems. In October 1915 he enlisted in the King's Shropshire Light Infantry as a private and participated in the Somme and Ancre campaigns.

When his outfit was not in action, Manning was several times in serious trouble with authorities because of his heavy drinking—once, for example, he was dismissed from an officer's training camp. Manning's alcoholism was not generally known until 1988 with the publication of Jonathan Marwil's excellent biography, *Frederic Manning: An Unfinished Life* (Durham, N.C.: Duke University Press, 1988). After 28 months of his often troubled Army career he was allowed to resign in February, 1918.

In the later 1920's, prodded by his publisher, Peter Davies, he wrote his war novel in only six months. Marwil says the holograph has very few corrections or interlineations. It was first published anonymously in 1929 as *The Middle Parts of Fortune*. In 1930, in an expurgated form, minus certain four-letter words, it was issued as *Her Privates We* under Manning's name. Since then it has been regularly republished in its unexpurgated form. The present essay cites the Hogarth Press edition of 1986.

The rest of Manning's rather short life—he died at age 53—was anti-climactic. Even before the War he had been very much admired as a writer by his creative peers in England and especially by those two great entrepreneurs of early-twentieth-century literary movements and creative talents, T. S. Eliot and Ezra Pound. Pound encouraged him and promoted him with all the zeal he gave to

Eliot, Joyce, and others. Eliot, who wrote his obituary and attended his funeral, had also encouraged him, inviting him to write for *Criterion* and Faber and Faber. But Manning's writing career dwindled, for reasons of health or habits of whatever, leaving only one small start, the first part of a proposed historical novel, "The Guilded Coach," set in seventeenth-century France. This 100-page MS now resides in the Mitchell Library in Sydney.

There are biographical accounts of Manning in L. T. Hergenham, "Frederic Manning," *Quadrant* 6 (Spring 1962); L. T. Hergenham, "Novelist at War: Fredric Manning's *Her Privates We*" (which contains generous selections from Manning's correspondence), *Quadrant* 14 (July–Aug. 1970); and C. N. Smith, "The Very Plain Song of It: Frederic Manning, *Her Privates We*," in Holger Klein, ed., *The First World War in Fiction* (London: Macmillan, 1976), pp. 174–82. These essays also contain critical discussions of *Her Privates We*.

More purely critical treatments of *Her Privates We* are contained in Eric Partridge, "The War Continues," *Window* 1 (Apr. 1, 1930): 62–85—"uncontradictably the best English war novel" (p. 77); H. M. Klein, "The Structure of Frederic Manning's War Novel *Her Privates We*," *Australian Literary Studies* 6 (Oct., 1974): 404–17; H. M. Klein, "In the Midst of Beastliness: Concepts and Ideals in Manning's *Her Privates We*," *Journal of Commonwealth Literature* 12 (Dec. 1977): 136–52.

2. Ernest Hemingway, ed., *Men at War* (New York: Crown Publishing, 1942), p. xvi.

3. Michael S. Reynolds says that when Hemingway moved to Cuba in 1940, he crated his books, 24 boxes in all, but left behind *Her Privates We* (along with *Huckleberry Finn*). So two years later, in 1942, the date of the Introduction to *Men at War*, he could not have reread it unless he obtained another copy. Reynolds says, however, that at this point Manning's novel was out of print. *Hemingway's Reading, 1916–1940* (Princeton: Princeton University Press, 1981), p. 30.

4. Cyril Falls, *War Books* (London: Peter Davies, 1930), p. 292

5. Charles Edmunds (Carrington's pseudonym), *A Subaltern's War* (London: Peter Davis, 1929), pp. 120–21.

6. Frederic Manning, *Her Privates We* (London: Hogarth, 1986), p. 241. All subsequent page references will be given in parentheses in the text.

7. Quoted by Andrew Rutherford, *The Literature of War* (London: Macmillan, 1978), p. 71. Rutherford provides an extensive and intelligent analysis of *Her Privates We*, pp. 99–112.

8. R. C. Sherriffs, "The English Public Schools in the War," in George Panichas, ed., *Promise of Greatness* (London: Cassell, 1968), p. 152.

9. Hergenham, "Novelist at War," p. 20.

10. Paul Fussell, *The Great War and Modern Memory* (New York: Oxford University Press, 1975), p. 156.

11. Eric Larrabee, *Commander in Chief* (New York: 1987), p. 440.

12. Quoted by Hergenham in "Novelist at War," p. 26.

13. Frederic Manning, *Scenes and Portraits* (New York: Putnam's, 1909), p. ix.

14. Cyril Bailey, trans., *Lucretius on the Nature of Things* (Oxford: Clarendon Press, 1916), p. 6.

15. Walter Charlton, trans., *Epicurus' Morals* (London: Peter Davies, 1926), with an introduction by Frederic Manning, p. 59.

16. Hergenham, "Novelist at War," p. 27.

17. Richard Holmes, *Acts of War* (New York: Free Press, 1985), p. 149.

SAID: *Travelling Theory Reconsidered*

1. Michael Löwy, *Georg Lukács: From Romanticism to Bolshevism*, trans. Patrick Camiller (London: NLB, 1979).

2. Georg Lukács, *Theory of the Novel*, trans. Anna Bostock (London: Merlin Press, 1971), p. 92.

3. Theodor Adorno, *Philosophy of Modern Music*, trans. Anne G. Mitchell and Wesley V. Blomster (New York: Seabury Press, 1973), pp. 40 ff. Quotations will hereafter be cited in parentheses in the text.

4. Georg Lukács, *History and Class Consciousness: Studies in Marxist Dialectics*, trans. Rodney Livingstone (London: Merlin Press, 1971), p. xlvi.

5. Frantz Fanon, *The Wretched of the Earth*, trans. Constance Farrington (New York, Grove Press, 1963), p. 44.

6. Frantz Fanon, *Black Skins, White Masks*, trans. Charles S. Markmann (New York: Grove, 1967), p. 220.

Index

In this index "f" after a number indicates a separate reference on the next page, and "ff" indicates separate references on the next two pages. A continuous discussion over two or more pages is indicated by a span of numbers. *Passim* is used for a cluster of references in close but not consecutive sequence.

Adams, Henry, 138, 148
Adams, Robert Martin, 156, 164
Adorno, Theodor, 273n2; *Philosophy of Modern Music*, 18, 255; and Georg Lukács, 254–58, 264f
Alexander of Rhodes, 32f
America, "discovery" of, 9, 33; representation of, 42–45. *See also* Cabot, John; Columbus, Christopher; Peter Martyr; Vespucci, Amerigo
Amerigo, *see* Vespucci, Amerigo
Ancre, Battle of the, 232f, 244, 286n1
Anderson, Sherwood, 191
Antheil, George, 153
Aristotle, 23
Armstid, Henry, 210
Atlantic Monthly, 129
Audience, *see* Readers
Auerbach, Eric, 4
Augé, Marc, 22–23
Auschwitz, 24, 30
Austen, Jane, 15, 130, 184; *The Watsons*, 8, 16, 212–30, 284n1, 286n22; *Emma*, 212–16 *passim*, 220–27 *passim*, 284n1;

Lady Susan, 212; *Mansfield Park*, 212–18 *passim*; *Northanger Abbey*, 212, 214, 219; *Persuasion*, 212–20 *passim*, 227f; *Pride and Prejudice*, 212–27 *passim*; *Sanditon*, 212; *Sense and Sensibility*, 212, 214, 222, 229
Autobiography, and fiction, 10, 54–55, 67, 90
Axelos, Kostas, 259

Bailey, Cyril, 241, 243
Baird, Helen, 188, 191, 197–208 *passim*
Bakhtin, Mikhail, 184, 274n6
Balzac, Honoré de, 22, 24, 131, 135f, 143, 148f
Banfield, Ann, 120
Banta, Martha, 279n33
Barbusse, Henri, 238
Barthes, Roland, 276n22
Bartók, Belá, 255
Baudelaire, Charles, 24
Beardsley, Aubrey, 195
Beckett, Samuel, 158
Beethoven, Ludwig von, 255f

Library of Congress Cataloging-in-Publication Data

Critical reconstructions : the relationship of fiction and life /
edited by Robert M. Polhemus and Roger B. Henkle.

p.   cm.

Includes index.

ISBN 0-8047-2243-9 (acid-free paper) :

1. Fiction—Technique.   2. Reality in literature.   3. Truth in
literature.   4. Realism in literature.   5. Narration (Rhetoric)
I. Polhemus, Robert M.   II. Henkle, Roger B.

PN3335.C75   1994

809.3—dc20

93-24129

CIP

♾ This book is printed on acid-free paper